English G Neue Ausgabe

W0313078

Band A5

für das 9. Schuljahr
an Gymnasien

Cornelsen

English G · Neue Ausgabe
Band A 5

Im Auftrage des Verlages herausgegeben und erarbeitet von
Prof. Hellmut Schwarz, Mannheim · Carl Taylor M.A., Maidencombe, Devon · Prof. Franz Vettel, Heppenheim

unter Mitarbeit von
StD Udo J. Hennig, Neuwied

in Zusammenarbeit mit der Fremdsprachenredaktion
Michael R. Ferguson M.A. (Projektleitung), Cedric J. Sherratt, Susanne Döpper, Margaret Kersten, Uwe Tröger M.A., Hartmut Tschepe · *Redaktionsassistenz:* Kirsten Bleck, Nicola Brown *sowie* Victor Dewsbery

Weitere Mitarbeit
StRin Helga Haubrichs, Bobenheim · Prof. Dr. Liesel Hermes, Karlsruhe · Prof. Dr. Günter Nold, Frankfurt am Main/PH Ludwigsburg · StR Mervyn Whittaker M.A., Bad Dürkheim

Beratende Mitwirkung
John Eastwood M.A., Street, Somerset · StD Erich Fleischhack, Ebern/Unterfranken · StD Dr. Jens-Peter Green, Madison, Wisc. · StDin Hildegard Krechting, Tecklenburg · OStD Hans-Günter Kruppa, Osnabrück · StD Bernd Dieter Laser, Seevetal · StD Adolf Menzel, München · MR Burkhart Nather, Mülheim (Ruhr) · StD Dr. Peter Potansky, Holzkirchen · Prof. Dieter Vater, Weinheim · StD Dieter Weis, Hochspeyer

Grafik
Robert Broomfield, Tunbridge Wells · Gabriele Heinisch, Berlin · Hewett Street Studios, London: David Graham, Graham Humphreys, Mike Mosedale

Layout
Bernd Lenzner

Bild-, Text- und Liedquellen
s. Verzeichnis auf S. xx

Zusatzmaterialien zum vorliegenden Schülerbuch:

Workbook (Best.-Nr. 51315)
1 Cassette zum Schülerbuch (Kurzfassung für Schüler 51366) · 2 Cassetten (Vollfassung für Lehrer 53180)

Auf weitere Bestandteile des Lehrwerks *English G · Neue Ausgabe* wird im Lehrerhandbuch (Best.-Nr. 51331) verwiesen.

1. Auflage – 5. Druck 1993

Alle Drucke dieser Auflage können, weil untereinander unverändert, im Unterricht nebeneinander verwendet werden.

© 1989 Cornelsen Verlag, Berlin

Das Werk und seine Teile sind urheberrechtlich geschützt. Jede Verwertung in anderen als den gesetzlich zugelassenen Fällen bedarf deshalb der vorherigen schriftlichen Einwilligung des Verlages.

Satz DSD · Demmer Satz + Daten GmbH, Berlin
Reproduktion O.R.T. OffsetReproTechnik, Berlin
Druck Cornelsen Druck, Berlin
Bindearbeiten Fritzsche-Ludwig, Berlin

ISBN 3-464-05130-7 – broschiert
3-464-05080-7 – gebunden

Bestellnummer 51307 – broschiert
50807 – gebunden

Um die Wiederverwendbarkeit zu gewährleisten, darf in dieses Buch nicht hineingeschrieben werden.

Contents

Pflichtbereich: Units

○ = wahlfrei

Wahlbereich: Options

Obwohl die *Options* einzelnen Units thematisch zugeordnet sind, können sie beliebig im Laufe des Unterrichtsjahres eingesetzt werden. (Die Durchnahme der *Options* 1, 4, 7 und 8 ist jedoch in Baden-Württemberg obligatorisch.)

Die Options 2, 3, 5, 6, 9, 11, 14 und 22 sind auf der Lehrercassette (53180).

Units and Options at a glance

	"Text" Options	"Skills" Options	Revision Options
Unit 1	1, 2	15	21
Unit 2	3	15, 16	22, 23
Unit 3	4, 5, 6	15, 17	24
Unit 4	7, 8, 9	15, 18	25
Unit 5	10, 11, 12	15, 19	26
Unit 6	13, 14	20	–

Unit 1: Introduction and Revision

THE UNITED KINGDOM

Do you have any plans to visit Britain this year?
For a number of German schools the 9th form is the year when pupils go on exchanges or class trips to the United Kingdom.
Would *you* like to visit Britain? How would you like to go: with your school, your parents or with an organized group?
Why? What would you like to do and see there?

During the past years you have learnt quite a lot about Britain. Look at the photos on these pages. Try to describe what they show. Say what you think attracts thousands of visitors of all ages to the UK each year.

Use these notes to write a short text or give a short talk on one of the following. You can prepare this in group work first if you like. If you know or can remember any further information which is not mentioned here, then please add it.

Guards at Buckingham Palace

The British Isles:
(Great) Britain – Ireland – number of smaller islands

The United Kingdom:
Britain and Northern Ireland; nationality – all citizens – British; capital – London

Great Britain:
England, Scotland, Wales

London:
capital – largest city; famous historical buildings: St Paul's – Tower – . . .; West End – theatres – famous stores; the City – . . . *Go on.*

England:
lots of tourist attractions – attractive villages and towns; Cornwall – ruins of Celtic past; St Albans – Britain's Roman past; the North – industrial area – coal mines – factories – Industrial Revolution – 19th century; north-west England – Lake District – holiday area – mountains – lakes; . . . *Go on.*

Wales:
smallest country – Britain; bit smaller – state of Hessen; three National Parks; Snowdon – highest mountain; own language – still widely spoken; . . . *Go on.*

Scotland:
centre – British oil industry; northern parts – huge empty areas – Highlands; climate – generally colder – rest of Britain – skiing – winter; west coast – Isle of Skye – Bonnie Prince Charlie – hide – after – defeat – English army; . . . *Go on.*

Polperro, Cornwall

Stonehenge

Snowdon Mountain Railway

York Minster

Eilean Donan Castle, Highlands

The following three pages show four more aspects of the UK. Read and talk about each of the texts separately. Then do the tasks on page 11. They will help you to see what the texts have in common.

1 Peace in danger?

It was already dark when they reached the border. The Stewarts were surprised that there was quite a long queue of cars in front of them. "What's wrong now?" said Mrs Stewart. "We normally drive straight through." Mr Stewart sighed and looked impatiently at his watch. "I hope we won't be here too long." Mrs Stewart switched on the radio and looked for a programme with music. "It's probably a security check. Two policemen were killed at the weekend. Or have you forgotten already?"

"What time is it?" asked their daughter Linda from the back seat.

"Half past six," said her father. "Another fifty miles," said Mrs Stewart, "and we'll be home."

Above them, not very high in the air, they could hear a helicopter. Mr Stewart drove slowly forward until Linda could see the policemen at the side of the road.

When it was their turn, Mr Stewart opened his window and Linda saw the face of the policeman as he looked into the car. Quickly his eyes went from person to person. "Good evening," he said. "How long have you been in the Republic?"

"Just since Friday."

"Why did you go there?"

"A weekend trip with the family."

"Where are you going now?"

"To Helen's Bay."

"Do you live there?"

"That's right."

"Can I see your driving licence, please, sir?"

The policeman stood back and looked carefully at the car. The three people inside waited patiently. Linda looked out of the window into the dark night. The noise of the helicopter had got louder; it was obviously going to land somewhere near the border. Just then a large army vehicle started and drove away along the road they would soon take. As her eyes followed the lorry, Linda saw several small red dots in the air, like little lamps. She watched them as they sometimes got redder and sometimes moved in the darkness. Funny, she thought, like large glow worms.

The policeman had now walked round the car. He carefully looked under the car and finally asked Mr Stewart to open the boot. When he was satisfied, he gave Mr Stewart his licence back. Mr Stewart started the engine. As he drove away, his lights fell on one of the red dots and Linda saw a group of soldiers in army uniforms, their machine guns held ready; they were pointed in the direction of their car. The red dots Linda had seen were the cigarettes the soldiers were smoking. For a second the sight came to her as a shock, but as the car went faster they passed more soldiers and she saw more army vehicles along the road. Over the sound of the car engine she heard the helicopter once again as it rose into the air and flew over them.

"If the roads are clear," her father said, "we should be home by eight."

1. Where do you think this event takes place? Find evidence in the text and picture.
2. Why do you think Linda is shocked only "for a second" when she first sees the soldiers?
3. How do Mr and Mrs Stewart react to the security check? – How would you feel in such a situation?

2 A new start "down under"

Dear Sarah,

Great news! I've been accepted. My visa arrived this morning. As soon as I got to work, I told Dr Matthews that I was leaving. She was shocked – and disappointed. You know, the old story, how much the hospitals need nurses. So I told her. I couldn't keep it back, I can tell you. I said, with the hours we work, a lot of people wouldn't even get out of bed for the money we earn. I can hardly afford to live, especially as Olivia is now 14. She wants clothes, records and magazines, and we only have my salary. I said I'm quite happy with my work. I'm not happy with the money.

I'll be sad to leave. But what's the alternative? Even if I should leave the profession and move to the south, where there are more jobs and higher salaries than here in the north, I could never afford to buy a house there. Dr Matthews sighed and said she understood.

The others were so jealous. How had I done it? Easy, I said. I have a profession that they need. I've only got Olivia. And I've got a sister living there who can help me.

The hospital has also written that I can start in January. That's a good time for Olivia, as the school year starts in January, too. I've now decided to fly across in October and spend a few weeks with you and Lyle before going on to Brisbane. Will it really be spring when we arrive? Do you really spend Christmas on the beach? Every time I see a programme on TV about life "down under", I smile and think only a few more months and we'll be there.

Mum is obviously sad. One daughter has already gone and now another. She sends her love and asks if we'll come back together to see her. I can't wait to see you again!

Love,
Helen

1. What country is Helen planning to move to, do you think? How do you know? What clues are given in the letter?
2. What do you learn about Helen – directly and indirectly – from the letter?
   – Go through the letter and make notes about her personal situation, her home, her job, her plans and the reasons for her plans.
   – Arrange your notes and then present the information to the class orally or in a written text.
3. Who must Sarah and Lyle be? Find evidence from the letter.

3 Different cultures

Rita went straight to her room and threw her school bag onto her bed. She took off her uniform and put on her jeans and pullover. She sat on the edge of her bed and opened the magazine she bought every Wednesday: this week it had a poster of her favourite pop singer. She wondered if she should put it on the wall somewhere. Just then her younger brother Sumit came in.
"Don't you ever knock?" she said.
"Rita," he asked, "have I got a passport?"
"Of course you have. Dad keeps it."
"Am I a British citizen?"
"We all are. Why?"
"Some kids at school said I wasn't."
"They're silly. You were born here just like me."
Rita went downstairs into the kitchen. Her mother was wearing traditional clothes, as she usually did. Rita especially liked the long saris, though she couldn't imagine wearing one herself. She also loved the rich smell of the food. Together with the Asian music from the cassette-recorder – her mother listened to it all the time – it gave her the feeling of being in another world.

1. Where do you think this family lives?
2. How do you explain Rita's feeling of "being in another world" when she is in the kitchen with her mother? Find evidence in the text to support your opinion.

4 Two schools – two different worlds

"When the coach drove through the school gates and we saw the green playing fields and the old buildings, I couldn't believe we were in England. Or even in the twentieth century. It was like a scene from a wonderful time in the past. Rugby School, one of England's most famous and expensive public schools, lay before us. Everything was so peaceful, with flowers and trees everywhere. Pupils were playing cricket, or lying on the grass.
"We had come from Liverpool, a group of ten comprehensive pupils, to spend a week at Rugby School. Afterwards we would take ten Rugby pupils back to our homes and our school. But what would be waiting for them? A modern town centre that could be anywhere in England, uninteresting buildings, long rows of streets all looking the same, houses with small rooms, ordinary people doing ordinary things. Here was space, room to breathe. Here was an exclusive way of life for a small group of privileged people. I knew it existed, but I had never seen it before."

1. Who is speaking in this text?
2. What do you think the pupil really means by "a scene from a wonderful time in the past"?
3 Compare Rugby School with the pupil's home town.

As long as one doesn't know a country and its people well, it is easy to talk about "the Germans", "the Americans" or "the British", as if everybody in that country was the same or had the same opinions. However, the better you get to know a country, the more you will realize how many different aspects it has, and how many contrasts there are within it. In this respect the United Kingdom is just like any other country in the world. People have their different ways of life, their different opinions and habits; and they have their conflicts.

1. The four texts you have read illustrate some of the contrasts within the United Kingdom. The following words and expressions will help you to say what they are:

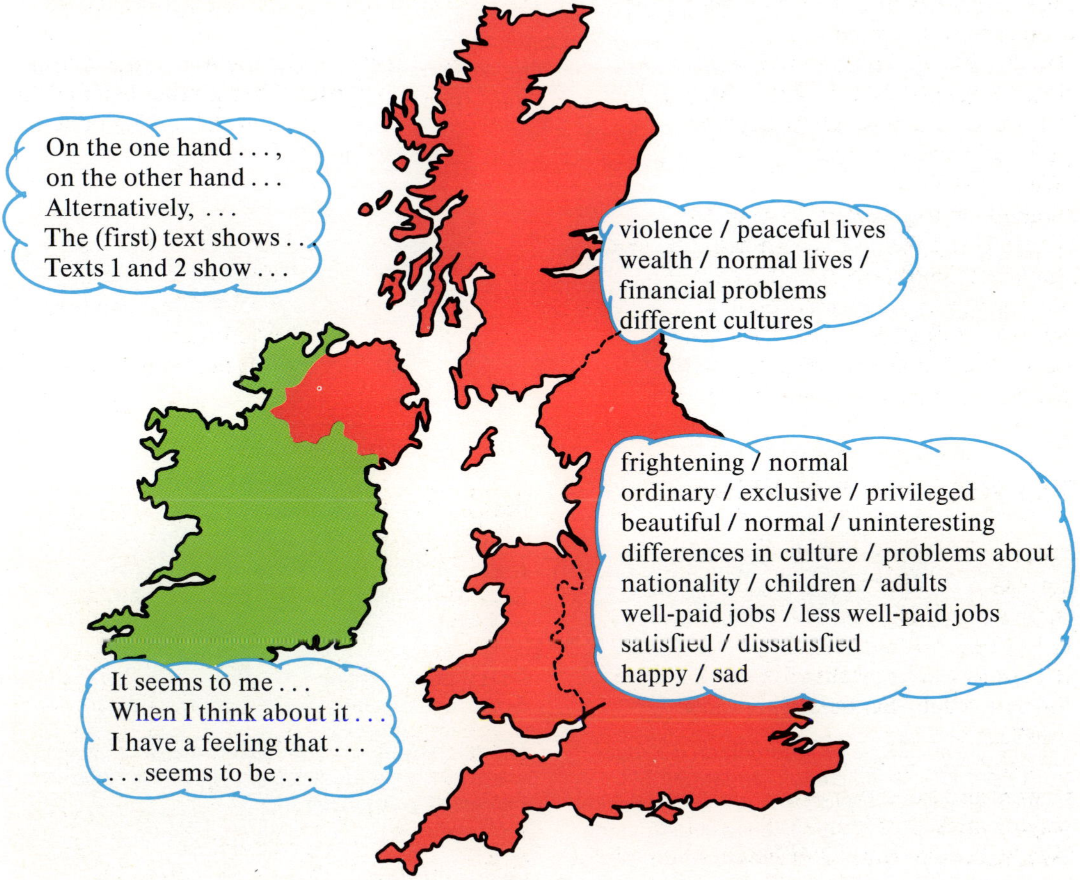

Examples:
All four texts show different aspects of the UK. On the one hand, text 1 shows that violence seems to be a problem in some areas of the UK. On the other hand, . . . I can see that in text 1 because . . . It seems to me that text 2 illustrates very well that . . . On the one hand, some people in Britain seem to lead privileged lives . . . *Go on.*

2. Have you heard about or seen any other contrasts in the UK?
3. In some respects Germany and the UK are very similar. Can you think of any contrasts in Germany, for example, that foreigners or strangers might notice?

→ Option 1: The UK — facts and figures → Option 2: British humour

Revision: Conditional sentences III[1] (Ex 1-3)

a In many respects Britain is different from its European neighbours. Take driving on the left, for example, or playing cricket. One reason for this may be that Britain is an island and has not been invaded since 1066, the year when the Normans arrived from France. That does not mean that nobody has tried since then. In 1588 the Spanish Armada, a fleet sent by King Philip II of Spain, around 1810 Napoleon and in 1940 Hitler: they all tried to invade Britain – but without success. Many people remember these dates proudly, especially 1588. And in connection with this date they think of Sir Francis Drake as the hero who defeated the Armada. – However, historically this is not the whole story. There were other reasons why the Spanish were defeated:

- The Spanish ships were big and slow. The smaller English ships were able to attack and get away quickly before the Spanish ships could catch them.
- A strong north-west wind helped the English. The Armada couldn't get out to the open sea.
- The Spanish ships couldn't sail south, back to Spain. The English ships were in their way.
- Heavy storms later sank many of the Spanish ships that escaped round the north of Scotland.

Looking back one can say: **If** the Spanish ships **had been** smaller, they **would have been** faster, too. And **if** they **hadn't been** so slow, they **could have caught** the English ships. **If** . . .

b

If-Satz (*if*-clause)	Hauptsatz (main clause)
If the Spanish ships **had been** smaller, Wenn die spanischen Schiffe kleiner gewesen wären,	they **would have been** faster, too. wären sie auch schneller gewesen.
If they **hadn't been** so slow, Wenn sie nicht so langsam gewesen wären,	they **could have caught** the English ships. hätten sie die englischen Schiffe einholen können.
If weather conditions **hadn't helped** the English, Wenn die Wetterverhältnisse den Engländern nicht geholfen hätten,	the Armada **might have had** a better chance. hätte die Armada vielleicht eine bessere Chance gehabt.

Im *if*-Satz steht das Verb im *past perfect (= had + past participle).*

Im Hauptsatz stehen *would/could/might + have + past participle.*

Die mit diesem *if*-Satz ausgedrückten Bedingungen beziehen sich auf die Vergangenheit. Mit ihnen stellen wir uns etwas vor, das in Wirklichkeit nicht so war oder nicht geschehen ist. Man nennt diese Bedingungen daher irreal *(unreal)*.

Mit dem Hauptsatz drücken wir aus, was gewesen wäre, falls diese Bedingungen in der Vergangenheit erfüllt worden wären. („Was wäre gewesen, wenn . . . ?")

Vergleiche:

The Spanish ships **were** slow. (So war es in Wirklichkeit.)

If they **hadn't been** slow, . . . (Das stellen wir uns nur vor.)

⚠ *'d* kann Kurzform von *had* oder *would* sein:

If they**'d** (= they **had**) been smaller, they**'d** (= they **would**) have been faster, too.

→ Vocabulary p. 142 (German „hätte/wäre")

c If the Spanish had conquered Britain, the British **would/might speak** Spanish today.
Wenn die Spanier Großbritannien erobert hätten, würden die Briten heute (vielleicht) Spanisch sprechen.

Im Hauptsatz mit *would/might/could* + Infinitiv drücken wir aus, was in der Gegenwart oder Zukunft wäre, falls die Bedingung im *if*-Satz erfüllt worden wäre.

→ Option 21: Conditional sentences

[1] Für Bundesländer, in denen *conditional sentences III* in Klassenstufe 8 nicht verpflichtend waren, sind die Seiten 12 und 13 keine *"Revision"*.

1 Sir Francis Drake, pirate and Admiral of the English Crown

Complete these conditional sentences III with the correct form of the verbs.

1. Perhaps people would have forgotten Drake long ago if he (be) less successful as a pirate in his younger years.
2. And if British teachers hadn't told their pupils so much about Drake's adventures, he (could/never/become) such a popular hero.
3. Some people say that the Armada might have landed successfully in England if King Philip (give) his admirals different orders.
4. If he (not send) the Armada to the Netherlands first, it (might/not have) so many problems.
5. Some people believe that the Spanish (defeat) the English if Drake (not be) so calm when the Armada sailed along the English coast.

2 The problems of DIY (Do-It-Yourself)

a *Look at the picture and say what problems John Nutter had when he put up some bookshelves.*

b *Complete these conditional sentences III. Use "would", "could" or "might" in the main clause.*

1. If John (plan) his job properly, he (not have) all these problems.
2. If he (compare) the price of wood in different shops, he (save) a lot of money.
3. He (cut) the wood more easily if he (have) a better saw.
4. He (finish) putting up his shelves at the weekend if he (buy) enough wood.
5. If he (use) screws instead of nails, his first shelf (not fall) off the wall.
6. And if he (know) it was so much trouble, he (ask) his wife to put up the shelves.

3 It's not always easy to make the right decisions

a *Say in just one sentence whether you would have done the same as these people.*

1. Alan won a trip round the world for two people. He gave the tickets to his grandparents.
2. Mr Corfield kicked the dog that jumped at him and made his trousers dirty.
3. When a homeless man asked Jennifer for £5, she just gave it to him and walked on.
4. When Mrs Rush saw that two young people were trying to get into Mrs Buxton's house through the back door, she called the police.

b *Choose one of these situations and write down what you would have done. Explain why you would have behaved in this way.*

4 Revision: Adjectives and adverbs

a What happens in "England"? *Find one or two adjectives for each letter in "England". Form adverbs from the adjectives and then use them in sentences. Try to make some funny sentences, too.*

E – easy ▷ My favourite football team usually wins its matches easily.
– excellent ▷ Last weekend my team played excellently.
N – nervous ▷ Some pupils were waiting nervously for the results of their exams.
– noisy ▷ ...
G – good ▷ I was standing in a good place during the concert so I could see Bruce well.
– ... ▷ ...
L – ... ▷ ...

b **"Home, sweet home"**

Adjective or adverb?

Holidays in a southern country are what we British think about (endless) all year. We dream of weeks of (brilliant) sunshine and imagine feeling (comfortable) in a nice hotel. But then, after a week in the (hot) sun, we begin to think (sad) of the (light) English rain. In our imagination it falls (peaceful) on the fields in the country-side and the pavement in towns. The air smells (fresh) although we know it is (heavy) polluted in most places. From that moment on we wait (impatient) for the last day of our holiday in the sun. Happiness only returns when our plane has landed (safe) at a crowded British airport ...

(Based on an article by W. G. Hoskins in *The English Difference*)

Do you think this is really typically British, or does anything similar happen to other people, too?

Revision: Active or passive? (Ex 5, 6)

5 These sentences are all from different British newspapers and must not be taken seriously. *Complete them with the correct active or passive forms (simple past, will-future) and then say what is strange about them.*

1. "The situation of families with more than 500,000 children (improve) a lot next year," Mrs Thatcher (say) when she (ask). "They (give) £3 more a week by the government."

2. 

Just before 10 pm yesterday, a ghost (see) near the church. The police (go) there and (bring) it back to the police station.

3. ... A goldfish (save) from drowning last week by Pete Hunt, aged 75. A report (send) to the RSPCA* before the end of this month.
* Britischer Tierschutzverein

4. ... Yesterday two hearts (successfully/transplant) at Queen Anne's hospital, but unfortunately both people (die).

5. Mr James Price – he (die) not long ago – (interview) on life after death on tomorrow's programme.

6 An attractive partner? (Adapted from *Boothroyd at Bay,* radio talks by Basil Boothroyd)

Use the correct tense in the active or passive to complete the sentences.

"A lot of people in this country aren't able to recognize an intelligent idea when it (put) in front of them, especially when it (come) from the USA.

"I (talk), of course, about the new plastic people, or perhaps they (make) of rubber, who (buy) by Americans so that they (not have to) travel alone in their cars on lonely journeys. The reason: More and more Americans travelling on their own (attack) or (rob) over the past few years.

"Now it's not just on lonely journeys that you (can/attack) by all kinds of strange people. If I took *Plastic Peter* to a party, for example, and (pretend) to talk to him in a corner, not so many boring people (attack) me. And if you (take) him to the beach, he (look after) your clothes, money and watch while you are swimming in the sea. On the other hand, a lot (write) about 'man-made people' over the past centuries, and these stories (never come) to a good end. Just think of Frankenstein's monster!

"One never knows: One day my role (might/play) by *Plastic Peter* and people (might/look at) me as *his* plastic friend. – I think I'll continue 'travelling' on my own."

7 Tricky sentences

Complete the sentences. In some of them you will have to find the right tense, in others you will have to add a word or two, and/or you will have to find the right word order.

1. Do your parents still smoke? – No, they (give up/smoke) a long time ago.
2. I reached a speed of 40 (miles/hour) on my moped yesterday when I (go down) a hill.
3. You can play the piano very well. How long (you/play)?
4. Susan told me she (buy) a present for Tom tomorrow.
5. (me/you/explain/can) how you start this program on your computer?
6. Some people have only just begun to realize that we must stop (destroy/nature).
7. We save quite a lot of water by (collect/rainwater).
8. What did Alan ask you? – Oh, he wanted (write/an essay/for him).
9. (you/enjoy/clean/your car/yesterday)? – No, I only (do) it because (me/my mother/do/it/make).
10. I asked Pam who (make) those fantastic sandwiches for her last party.

→ Option 15: Translation practice, p. 109

Just for fun

Please help the police – with punctuation[1]

Jones, Smith and Brown were policemen, and Brown sent this note to the Inspector one day. "Jones where Smith had had had had had had had had had had had the Inspector's approval[2]."

What does it mean, if anything?

Answer: Jones, where Smith had had "had", had had "had had". Had "had had" had the Inspector's approval?

[1] punctuation [ˌpʌŋktʃʊˈeɪʃn] *Zeichensetzung* [2] approval [əˈpruːvl] *Zustimmung*

Unit 2

Schools in Britain

Focus on WORDS: Talking about school

1 This is what some British teenagers think about school:

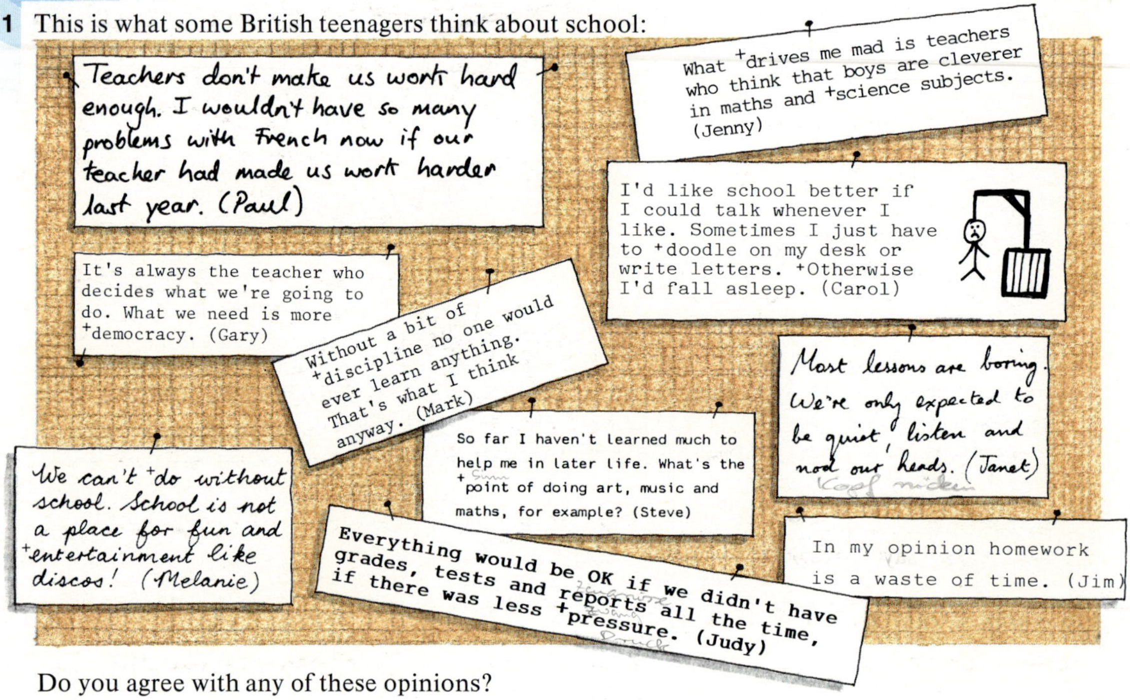

Do you agree with any of these opinions?
Say what *you* think about school.

+ = new word

2 Use "school" as the main key word and other key words like "teachers", "subjects", "classmates", etc. and develop two networks with "school words" in your exercise book, one showing what you like about school, the other showing what you don't like. You could start like this:

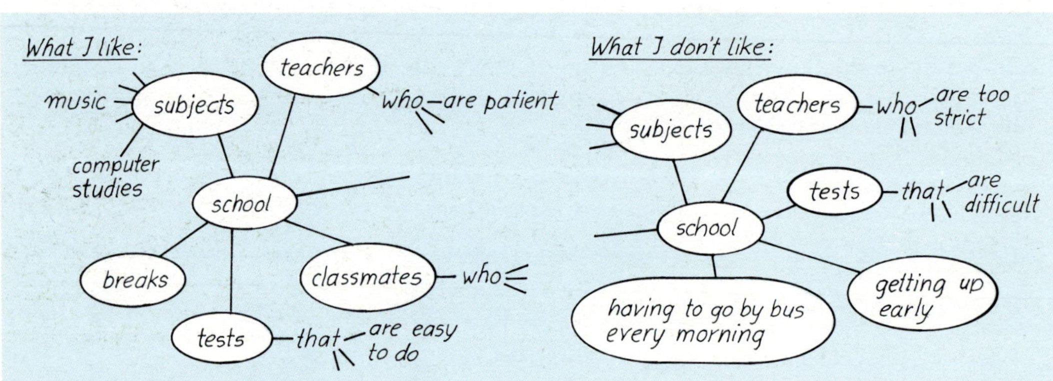

3 Write two short texts:

a What I like/don't like about school.

b What the school of my dreams would be like.

→ Ex 1

Gary King:
A profile of a young Liverpudlian

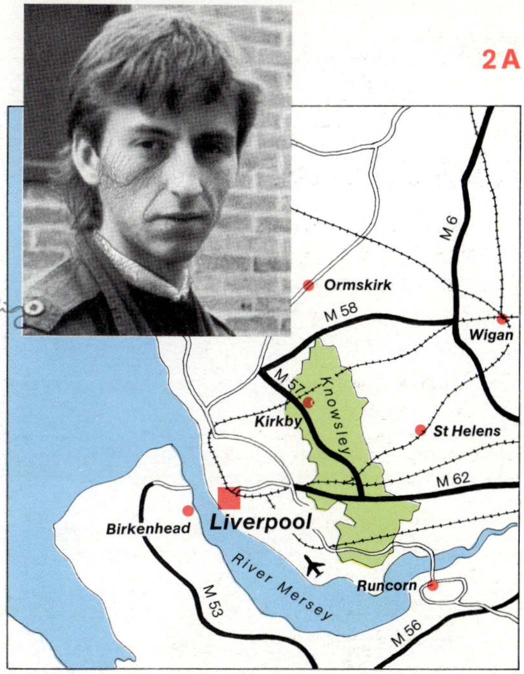

1 Gary King lives in Kirkby[1] on the edge of Liverpool. Look at these notes and write a short text about Gary, his family and his interests.

Gary – 17; one brother – 15; father – self-employed – small engineering firm; mother – work – firm; pupil – Ruffwood Comprehensive School – home – ten minutes from school – usually walk; large school – 1700 pupils – 150 – sixth form; Gary – sixth form – subjects – biology – art – design; take – A-levels – next year; would like – go – university – if – pass – A-levels; after that – work – designer – theatre – television; Gary – mainly interested – theatre – music (jazz); go – concerts – plays – whenever possible

2 Unlike German teenagers, British teenagers don't have a lot of free time during the week. Read what Gary says and compare his life with yours.

"School dominates my life during the week. By the time I get home in the afternoon it can be almost five o'clock. Then I have tea, so it can be six, sometimes seven o'clock, before I start my homework, and that can take a couple of hours. So when I've finally done everything, it's usually too late to go out. I sometimes watch a bit of TV and then go to bed.

"Of course I don't stay at home every evening. Sometimes a friend at school might say there's a jazz concert at the university or a rock group is playing in a pub in Liverpool. So a few of us might decide to go that evening. It doesn't take long to get from Kirkby to the city centre.

"There's a sports centre in Kirkby where you can swim or play squash. I used to do a lot of sport when I was younger, but not now. Still, if some of my friends decide to go, I usually go along too. At the weekends I sometimes go into Liverpool with my girlfriend Janet, or we go to a party at somebody's house. If the weather is nice, a group of us sometimes go camping to the Lake District or North Wales. Our biggest problem is money. We get pocket-money from our parents, but it's never enough. So we have to earn our own, and that's why most of us have weekend jobs."

Gary and friends camping in the Lake District

Now try to write a profile of yourself or a partner. (Interview your partner to get the information you need to write a profile of him or her.)

[1] Kirkby ['kɜ:bɪ]

Focus on GRAMMAR: *Simple form* und *progressive form* (Differences in aspect)

a Gary has a part-time job. Every Saturday he works in a fish-and-chip shop in the Kirkby shopping precinct. He begins at ten o'clock and finishes at six o'clock in the evening. He started the job a year ago to get some extra pocket-money. He thinks the job is OK, but of course it is not what Gary will do when he leaves school. He has applied to go to university. Imagine you have walked into the chip shop. It is 12.30 pm, the busiest time of the day. Lots of people are standing in a queue. A radio is playing on a shelf. Gary and Janet – both in white jackets – have been serving the customers for over an hour. But the queue is getting longer and longer. At eleven o'clock they were sitting comfortably at a table. They were talking about their plans for the future and having a cup of tea together. Then the lunchtime rush began. In an hour the rush will be over. At 6.30 pm Gary will be sitting on the bus home and looking forward to a nice hot bath.

Rev. b

Simple forms	Progressive forms
1. Every Saturday Gary **works** in a fish-and-chip shop. He **lives** only a short bus ride from the shop. Wir verwenden das *simple present*, um auszudrücken, daß eine Handlung immer wieder oder nie stattfindet. Es wird auch verwendet, um einen Dauerzustand zu beschreiben. Häufige Zeitbestimmungen: *every day, always, usually, sometimes, never* usw.	Gary is busy at the moment. He**'s serving** some customers. He hasn't got much time this week because he**'s working** on a school project. Wir verwenden das *present progressive*, um auszudrücken, daß eine Handlung zum Zeitpunkt des Sprechens im Verlauf ist. Es wird auch verwendet, wenn die Handlung im Moment des Sprechens vorübergehend unterbrochen ist. Häufige Zeitbestimmungen: *now, at the moment, this week* usw.
2. Last year Gary **decided** to earn his own money. Wir verwenden das *simple past*, um auszudrükken, daß eine Handlung in der Vergangenheit stattgefunden hat. Es kann nur verwendet werden, wenn der Zeitpunkt bekannt ist oder nach dem Zeitpunkt gefragt wird.	An hour ago Gary and Janet **were having** a cup of tea, when suddenly a lot of customers came in. Wir verwenden das *past progressive*, um auszudrücken, daß eine Handlung zu einem bestimmten Zeitpunkt in der Vergangenheit im Verlauf war. Jemand war mit etwas beschäftigt.
Häufige Zeitbestimmungen: *last year, an hour ago, yesterday, in 1985, during the holidays* usw.	
3. Gary **has applied** to go to university. Wir verwenden das *simple present perfect*, um auszudrücken, daß eine Handlung irgendwann stattgefunden hat. Der genaue Zeitpunkt ist unbekannt oder unwichtig. Häufige Zeitbestimmungen: *already, before (now), ever, just, never, often, (not) yet, so far*	Gary **has been working** in the shop for a year. Wir verwenden das *present perfect progressive*, um auszudrücken, daß eine Handlung in der Vergangenheit begonnen hat und bis (oder fast bis) in die Gegenwart andauert. Häufige Zeitbestimmungen: *for three hours, since ten o'clock*
4. Gary **will** probably **go** to university next year. Wir verwenden das *will-future*, um vorherzusagen, was jemand unserer Meinung nach in der Zukunft tun wird oder was sein wird.	At about 7 tonight Gary **will be enjoying** a hot bath. Wir verwenden das *will-future progressive*, um vorherzusagen, womit jemand zu einem Zeitpunkt in der Zukunft beschäftigt sein wird.

Die *simple form* wird verwendet	Die *progressive form* wird verwendet für eine Handlung, die zu einem bestimmten Zeitpunkt im Verlauf war, ist oder sein wird. Die Handlung ist noch nicht abgeschlossen. Anfang und Ende sind unwichtig.
– für eine Handlung, die immer wieder, oft auch gewohnheitsmäßig, oder nie stattfindet. – für eine Handlung, die eindeutig abgeschlossen ist oder sein wird.	

c Die Verwendung der *simple form* und der *progressive form* bei verschiedenen Verbgruppen
(The use of the simple and progressive forms with different kinds of verbs)

1. **Activity verbs**[1] (Tätigkeits- und Vorgangsverben)

Gary often **goes** to discos in Liverpool. – Where **are** you **going**, Gary? To the disco?
It usually **snows** a lot here. – It **has been snowing** heavily since early this morning.

Verben, die Tätigkeiten ausdrücken, z. B. *go, work, leave, wait,* und Verben, die Vorgänge ausdrücken, z. B. *snow, rain, grow* (= wachsen), *become* (= werden), bezeichnet man als *activity verbs.* Sie bilden die weitaus größte Gruppe der Verben und können sowohl in der *simple form* als auch in der *progressive form* verwendet werden.

2. **State verbs**[2] (Zustandsverben)

"A portion of fish and chips hardly looks like a good meal. But, believe me, it tastes delicious and doesn't cost a lot. I love fish and chips. – The shop belongs to my mother's friends. They're nice, friendly people. The only problem is, fish-and-chip shops smell. And I smell too when I get home. So I need a good bath before I go out to meet my friends. I know it's not the best job in the world. But I think I'll keep it until I leave school."

fish and chips

Verben wie *look* (= aussehen), *taste* (= schmecken), *smell* (= riechen, stinken), *cost, belong to, need* und *have* (= besitzen) sind sogenannte *state verbs.* Sie drücken nicht aus, was jemand tut oder was geschieht. In der Regel werden sie nur in der *simple form* verwendet. Zu den *state verbs* gehören auch:
– Verben des Meinens und Wissens: *think* (= meinen, glauben), *suppose, know* usw.
– Verben des Mögens/Nichtmögens und Wollens: *like, love, hate, prefer, want* usw.
– Verben der Wahrnehmung: *see, hear*

Tip: Mit Hilfe einer „Imperativprobe" kannst du fast immer feststellen, ob ein bestimmtes Verb ein *state verb* ist. Von einem *state verb* wie *belong* kann man keinen sinnvollen Imperativ bilden. Eine Aufforderung wie *Belong to Mrs Miller* ergibt keinen Sinn. → Vocabulary p. 144 (Verbs not normally used in the progressive form)

3. **Verbs used as activity or state verbs**

State verbs wie *know* oder *belong* stehen immer in der *simple form*, da sie keine Handlung im Verlauf beschreiben können. Einige Verben wie *look, think, have, see* haben jedoch mehrere Bedeutungen. Je nach ihrer Bedeutung sind sie *activity verb* oder *state verb*:

Activity verbs → progressive oder simple form	**State verbs → nur simple form**
Gary **is looking** for his keys. He **looks** for them every day. Gary sucht seine Schlüssel. Er sucht sie jeden Tag.	The dessert **looks** delicious. Der Nachtisch sieht lecker aus.
What **are** you **thinking** about? Worüber denkst du nach?	What **do** you **think** of your new job? Was hältst du von deiner neuen Arbeit?
Janet **is having** a bath/lunch/a party/a good time/. . . Janet badet/ißt zu Mittag/gibt eine Party/. . .	Janet **has** (got) a new moped/time/. . . Janet hat ein neues Moped/Zeit/. . .
Gary **is seeing** his grandfather tonight. Gary besucht heute abend seinen Großvater.	**Do**/Can you **see** that sign over there? Siehst du das Schild da drüben?

→ Ex 2-5

→ Option 16: Explaining grammar in English → Option 23: Past tense and present perfect

[1] *Activity verbs* werden auch *dynamic verbs* [daɪˈnæmɪk] genannt.
[2] *State verbs* werden auch *stative verbs* [ˈsteɪtɪv] genannt.

One kind of exchange: Twin towns

Many British towns are "twinned" with towns in other countries in Europe. Kirkby, for example, is part of the borough of Knowsley, and Knowsley is twinned with Moers in North Rhine-Westphalia.

Every year groups of young people from both towns – youth orchestras, choirs, sports teams, etc. – visit each other for a week or two and stay in each other's homes. Compare Knowsley and Moers and say why you think they are twinned with each other.

Knowsley	*Moers*
– population 160,000	*– population 110,000*
– edge of Liverpool	*– near Duisburg*
– part of industrial north	*– belongs to Ruhrgebiet (the Ruhr)*
– Liverpool, large port	*– Duisburg largest inland port in Europe*

Ruffwood Comprehensive has taken part in several exchanges with schools in Moers. The German pupils usually visit Kirkby in the summer, and the Kirkby pupils go on a return visit in the autumn. Here is part of the programme for the German pupils one year:

Ruffwood Comprehensive/Gymnasium Rheinkamp
Programme of events

MONDAY, 6 JULY	Visit to Alton Towers Pleasure Park; 7.30 pm disco at Ruffwood.
TUESDAY, 7 JULY	Visit to school; 2 pm sports competition in Kirkby Sports Centre.
WEDNESDAY, 8 JULY	Visit to York. Depart Ruffwood 8.00 am. Return 7.00 pm. Evening free.
THURSDAY, 9 JULY	Visit to North Wales (Conwy and Rhyl). Depart Ruffwood 9.00 am. Return 6.00 pm. NB: Bring swimming costumes and towels for Rhyl Sun Centre.
FRIDAY, 10 JULY	Coach trip to Lake District. Depart Ruffwood 8.00 am. Return 6.00 pm. Evening – Farewell disco (with parents) at Ruffwood Comprehensive 7-11 pm.
11/12 JULY	The weekend is free with families.

On Monday the pupils went .... In the evening there was a .... *Go on.*

- Is your town twinned with a town in Britain or any other country? If you don't know, try to find out.
- Have you ever been on an exchange? Do you know anybody who has been on one? Where did you/they go? Did you/they enjoy it? What did you/they do? What impressions did you/they have of the town/country/people?
- Would you like to take part in an exchange? Give reasons.
- Do you think twinning can improve the relations between different countries?

→ Ex °6 → Option 22: Preparing for a trip to Britain

A different kind of exchange

While Gary was in the sixth form, he unexpectedly had the chance to take part in a different kind of exchange. It was organized by BBC television and was called "Changing Places". He and nine other Ruffwood pupils were asked to spend a week at Rugby School, a very famous and expensive public school in the Midlands (near Coventry). Then ten Rugby pupils returned with them to Kirkby and went to Ruffwood Comprehensive for a week.

"When we organized 'Changing Places', we wanted to find out what young people from different social backgrounds – well-off families, average families and not so well-off families – thought of each other. We expected the programme to show that there is really not much difference between young people anywhere in Britain today. Of course people have their different opinions and prejudices about each other. One Ruffwood girl said about Rugby pupils before the exchange, 'They'll probably think we're northern rabble, while we think they have their noses in the air and silver spoons in their mouths.' However, both groups believed they would soon discover that their opinions about each other were no more than ignorant prejudice. How wrong they, and we, were".

(Chris Curling, producer of "Changing Places")

Gary, Paul (Ruffwood) Mark, Jolyon (Rugby)

Go through the text carefully, make notes and then say what Chris Curling means by the last sentence.

Rugby – a public school

In Britain there are 2,460 independent schools with about 580,000 pupils. These schools are for pupils whose parents do not want to send them to a state school. However, the parents must pay fees. Many parents are prepared to spend a large amount of the money they earn on school fees, as they believe their children will get a better education and have a better chance of going to university or getting a good job. Some of these schools, such as Eton, Winchester, Rugby or Roedean, are also known as public schools. Traditionally, children from rich families go to these schools. However, all the schools offer scholarships to especially talented children from less well-off families. Many independent schools are boarding schools, although they all take day pupils too.

Rugby School, Rugby, Warwickshire;
founded 1567; high academic standard; fees for 1989/90: day £4,425, boarding £7,575; entrance exam; 800 pupils aged 13 to 18; 354 in sixth form (70 girls); lower forms boys only; 50% of pupils live in the school, in ten boarding houses; A-levels offered in all subjects; most sixth formers go on to university; large choice of sports, clubs and activities.

Why do you think the two schools were chosen by the BBC for the exchange? Use the information in the text in Unit 1 as well as the information given on pages 17-20.

Pupils in
independent schools: 7%
state schools: 93%

1 Revision: The school system in Britain

a **Do you still remember what you learnt in Book 3?** *Find the right ending for each sentence.*

In Britain children are at primary school from the age of five to eleven. After primary school about 90% of the pupils . . . Only a small number . . . However, all pupils stay at school . . . In the fifth form they can take . . . The GCSE is similar to . . . Pupils who don't leave at the age of 16 . . . The sixth form consists of . . . In the sixth form pupils usually concentrate . . . After two years in the sixth form, pupils . . . A-level grades and an interview decide . . .

a) . . . until they are 16. b) . . . take the A-level exam in their three subjects. c) . . . go to comprehensive schools. d) . . . the German "Mittlere Reife". e) . . . from the age of five to eleven. f) . . . if they can go to a university or college. g) . . . go to secondary modern, grammar or independent schools. h) . . . then go into the sixth form. i) . . . on three subjects only. j) . . . the GCSE exam in a number of subjects. k) . . . the lower and the upper sixth.

b *Ask each other questions about school in Britain and in Germany, and about your school.*
Examples: When do British children take the GCSE exam? How many classes are there in the fifth form of our school? What's the English word for our kind of school? . . .

2 Gary about himself *Simple present or present progressive?*

1. Our art teacher (often give) us a project to do at home. That means everyone in the class (do) some art work in their free time. At the moment I (work) with three other pupils on a model of a perfect classroom.
2. I (not normally work) at the chip shop more than one day a week. But in the holidays I (sometimes work) two or three days a week.
3. At the moment I (save) as much as I can. My friend Paul and I (plan) to go camping during the holidays.

3 Janet and Gary *Write a dialogue. Pay attention to the tenses and to the aspect.*

jazz concert – university – tomorrow / what – plan to do – tomorrow evening? / like – come?

have to stay at home / spend all my money – last weekend / if – lend me some, – give back – next week

hear that before, Gary, – still wait – money – lend you – some time ago / why – not ask – father – mother?

sorry – not give back – yet / I promise – give back – soon / anyway, who – play?

"The Wakefield Five"; – you – always want – hear them

suppose – ask – parents, then / not want – miss them

4 Which of these questions and answers go together?

Is Janet . . .

1. at home?
2. new at the chip shop?
3. still at the shop?
4. very tired this morning?
5. busy at the moment?
6. at home on Saturdays?
7. new to this kind of job?

a) No, she has been working there for over a year.
b) No, she works in the chip shop.
c) Yes, she'll be there for another hour.
d) No, she has worked in another chip shop before.
e) Well, she was serving customers half an hour ago, but I don't know if she has anything to do now.
f) No, she's working in the chip shop.
g) Yes, she came home late last night.

5 Activity verb or state verb?

Before you decide which of these verbs is an activity or a state verb or both, try to imagine if it is possible to "see an activity in progress" with that verb or not.

need rain think read have
believe consist of see look (for)
know understand wonder run
ask belong

Examples:

Read is an activity verb. Here are two sentences: Tom doesn't want to watch TV, he's reading at the moment. He often reads adventure stories.
Believe is a state verb. You can say, "Tom doesn't believe that there are monsters."
Look is a difficult one. It can be an activity verb and a state verb. . . .

○ 6 In English, please: What some of the German pupils from Moers told their parents on the phone while they were in Kirkby on the exchange

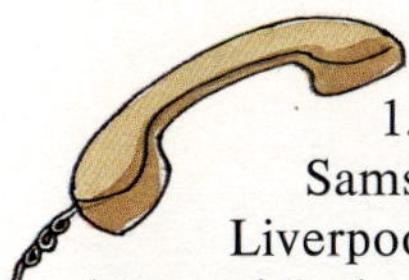

1. Meine Familie hat mich am Samstag mit zu einem Spiel des FC Liverpool genommen. – Eine tolle Atmosphäre! . . . Ich habe während des ganzen Spiels versucht, Rowdies zu sehen, weil die Zeitungen oft über englische Fußballrowdies schreiben. Aber alle Fans waren friedlich.

2. Ich warte gerade auf Gary. Wir wollen heute abend in eine Disco gehen. . . . Ich freue mich schon auf unsere Busfahrt in den Lake District. Die Fahrt nach Nord-Wales war spitze. Wir haben während der ganzen Fahrt gesungen und uns gegenseitig Witze erzählt.

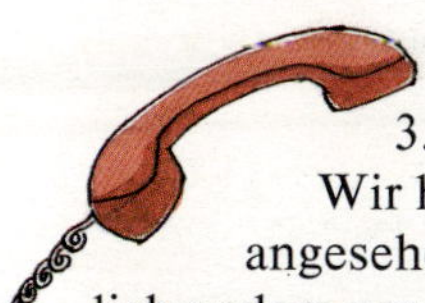

3. Ich rufe euch aus Wigan an. Wir haben uns die Stadt ein bißchen angesehen. Die Städte sehen hier wirklich anders aus als zu Hause.
. . . Wir sind schon seit heute morgen 8 Uhr mit Rädern unterwegs *(cycle)*. Aber wir radeln jetzt gleich wieder nach Kirkby zurück.

Just for fun

What belongs to you, but is used more often by others? – Your name.

If I had ten flies *(Fliegen)* on my desk and killed one, how many would there be left? – None, the others would fly away.

7 Can you get out of this?

a *Imagine you are in England. You have parked your moped on the pavement outside a shop. When you get back, you see that you have been given a ticket: the fine is £12. Write a letter to the local police to find out why you were given a ticket. Try to convince them that you* <u>*had*</u> *to park there and tell them that you don't see why you should pay the £12.*

Just for fun

Policeman: You can't park here.
Driver: Why not?
Policeman: Read that sign.
Driver: I did. It says "Fine for parking," so I parked.

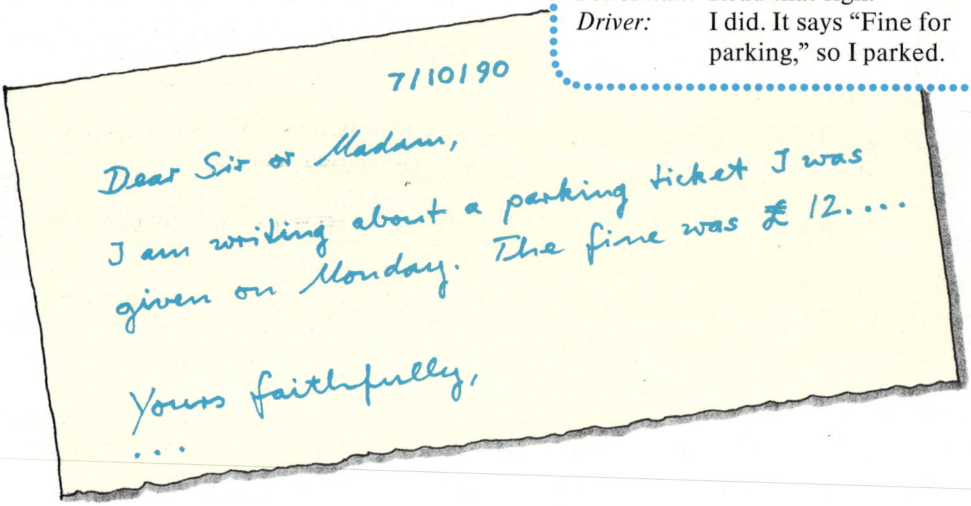
7/10/90

Dear Sir or Madam,

I am writing about a parking ticket I was given on Monday. The fine was £ 12....

Yours faithfully,

...

b *Exchange your letter with somebody else in class and decide if the letter you have received is convincing enough. Then answer the letter and explain why she/he must pay or not.*

8 Revision: Relative clauses

What is/are . . . ? *Explain the underlined words. Use relative clauses.*

1. Alan's parents are very <u>generous</u>. 2. I've got to buy a new <u>fruit bowl</u>. 3. Do you know a good <u>lawyer</u> in town? 4. Some people think cars are a <u>necessity</u> in life. 5. Susan works in a home for <u>orphans</u>. 6. I hate <u>permanent</u> noise. 7. Are you <u>superstitious</u>? 8. Old Mr Miller is a <u>widower</u>.

The following words may help you:
people somebody
container children
something person
a kind of

Example:
1. Alan's parents are people <u>who</u> like to help others and give things to them./. . . are people you can expect to help whenever they can. Even when Alan brings home a lot of friends, for example, they don't mind making a big meal for all of them.

9 WORDS WORDS WORDS

a Nouns and verbs that go together (collocations)

advice	dress	gravy	plane	sugar	train
concert	exam	meeting	pullover	test	tram
cream	exchange	money	shoes	time	trip

Each noun goes with one of the following word groups. *Example:* Advice goes with group 4. You can take/follow/refuse/ask for somebody's advice or give/offer somebody advice. *Go on.*

1. TAKE – pass – fail – work hard for – be afraid of – be worried about
2. TAKE – miss – catch – travel by – go by – wait for – get on/off
3. TAKE – spend – save – waste – forget – have – kill
4. TAKE – follow – give – offer – refuse – ask for
5. TAKE – add – pass – reach for
6. TAKE – put on – take off – buy – sell – wear – try on
7. TAKE – accept – lose – find – change – have – win – save – hide – earn
8. TAKE PART IN – enjoy – remember – be invited to – look forward to

Choose two or more verbs from each group and use them in sentences. *Example:* Jane has been working hard for the exam for months. She needn't be worried about it.

b Trouble spot: hear/listen (to) – see/look (at)/watch

Fill in the correct verb form to complete the following sentences. Add "to" or "at" if necessary.

1. ... where you're going. 2. I could ... the monkeys for hours. 3. Are you ... the radio, or shall I switch it off? 4. Tommy never ... what you tell him. 5. The thief became nervous because he felt he was being ... . 6. I'm sure the accident was the driver's fault. He should have ... more carefully. 7. Steve, ... the board, please. 8. Although we ... carefully, we couldn't ... a word of what they were saying. 9. ... ! Somebody is knocking at the door, I think. 10. When we went to the cinema we ... Helen on the other side of the street. She was ... us and shouting something we couldn't ... very well. 11. We look forward to ... from you.

c WORD BUILDER'S CORNER

Revision: Words with prefixes and suffixes

Prefixes

dis-	inter-
im-	mis-
in-	un-

Stems

agree	employ	invite	possible
arrive	fertile	like	read
begin	friend	nation	sun
electric	hope	polite	understand

Suffixes

-able	-er	-ly
-al	-ful	-ment
-ation	-ity	-ness
-ee	-less	-y

1. How many words can you make by adding a prefix or a suffix (or both) to the stems? You should only make words you have read or heard. If you are not sure, use a dictionary.
   Example: **nation** – nation**al** – national**ity**
   nation**al** – **inter**national
   Remember to make the necessary spelling changes with words such as *arrive* or *begin*.
2. If you add a suffix to a stem to make a new word, the new word belongs to a different word class: if you add *-ity* to the adjective *national*, you get the noun *nationality*. That is why syllables like *-ity* are called noun suffixes. Now look at the words you have made and put the suffixes into groups of noun suffixes, adjective suffixes and adverb suffixes.

→ Option 15: Translation practice, p. 109-110

Changing places

"Welcome to Rugby!"

Gary and the nine other Ruffwood pupils smiled nervously as they got off the coach and joined their Rugby partners waiting outside the school gates. "Just be yourselves," the producer had said. "Act normally."

Act normally – with TV cameras next to you. Was this real, Gary thought. Or was it just TV entertainment for millions of people throughout the country?

They tried not to look at the cameras as they walked towards the different buildings where they would live for the coming week.

As Gary unpacked, he looked at the room he would share with four other Ruffwood pupils. It was light and comfortable with lots of wooden cupboards and shelves. He liked the atmosphere.

Later when Gary left his room for his first meeting with the Rugby pupils and teachers, he noticed an open door. Inside he saw a huge room with a long line of beds. At the foot of each bed there was a small cupboard. Who slept there, he wondered. "You've been given the best rooms," said Mark, Gary's Rugby partner, and smiled. "Especially for the programme."

The Ruffwood pupils were introduced to the teachers and pupils who would be with them that week and some of the rules were explained to them. The boys were told that they had to be in bed by 11 o'clock and if they wanted to stay up longer they had to ask for permission. For the girls it seemed to be even stricter.

"After tea," said Mr Pattinson, the Rugby teacher who looked after the house where the girls would live, "there is only one way in and out of the house. That's through our front door. If you're going out, you'll have to sign out in a book on a table in the hall and say where you are going and what time you are going out. And then you have to sign again when you come back and put down what time you're back."

"So what are your first impressions?" the producer asked as they relaxed with tea and sandwiches.

"A feeling of confinement," said Gary. "At home we come and go as we want, but here we'll be locked in little rooms. I thought boarding school meant freedom, you know, away from home and parents, but every minute of the day seems to be organized. And there are keys everywhere."

A bell rang loudly at 7.15 in the morning. It was the loudest sound Gary had heard for a long time, and in the darkness of the boys' house a voice shouted, "Fifteen minutes". Gary pulled the blankets over his head to keep out the bell, but it went on and on. Then the voice shouted again, "Ten minutes." Slowly the boys got out of their beds and started to dress. They moved sleepily into the washrooms and toilets, washed themselves and cleaned their teeth as the bell rang again and the voice shouted loudly, "Five, four, three, two, one. Everybody out."

Everybody out – for breakfast, assembly, and then lessons. No parents who said good morning to you. No brothers or sisters.

"Why are you here?" Gary asked his partner Mark as they walked towards their first lesson.

"My parents have a large business in London. They travel abroad a lot, so this is my home."

Mark smiled. "Don't worry. You soon get used to it."

"Don't you miss your parents?" asked Gary.

"I see them during the holidays." Mark laughed. "We probably appreciate them more simply because we don't see them every day."

Gary thought for a second. "I suppose you're right," he said. Then he asked, "What do you do if you want to stay out late in town?"

"What do you think? We climb in through a window."

After a short time the cameras became welcome friends. In a situation that was both new and strange, the interviews were the only chance the Ruffwood pupils had to say how they felt. "So what are your impressions now?" asked the producer after they had been at the school for three days.

"The pupils here live in a vacuum," said Gillian. "They're protected from the world outside. They never really know how other people live or what's happening in the country. The fees are unbelievably high. It costs £6,750[1] a year to come to Rugby. Parents pay more money for their kids' education than some families in Liverpool have to live on for a whole year. And that's just the fees. Books, clothes, travel are all extra."

"When I first walked through the school gates," said Gary, "I thought we were leaving the real world. This isn't real, I thought. But I now realize that Rugby people think they belong to the real world. They have no experience of other people or the way other people live. I asked one of the teachers' wives where she came from, and she said New Zealand. Then she said, "Do you know where that is?" It's amazing. We come from Liverpool, so they think we don't know anything. Here in Rugby Mummy and Daddy pay for everything. The pupils here don't need to go out and get a job. But if you come from Liverpool and both your parents are unemployed, it's difficult to stay on and do A-levels. You've got to go to work or you won't survive. It makes me realize how much more difficult it is for us."

In most public schools it is a tradition that older pupils give jobs to younger pupils. Gary noticed how after lunch one day a sixth former ordered three younger boys to clean the path outside the house. It was meant as a form of punishment for something the boys had done. The sixth former stood by the path and watched the boys with the strictness of a teacher. He wouldn't let them go until the job had been done properly.

"It's a vicious circle," said Gary. "The sixth formers bully the first formers, and when the first formers get up here in the sixth form, they bully the first formers again. When they have children themselves, they just send their kids back here because they don't know what a family life is."

During that week the school had its May Ball. It was a beautiful day. Pupils and guests were walking across the green lawns in their finest clothes. Music came from a large tent where people were dancing. One of the guests was a politician who had once been a minister in the Conservative government. People were standing in different groups, with glasses in their hands. Gillian suddenly found she was in a group with the politician.

"Where in Liverpool are you from?" he asked.

"Kirkby," said Gillian.

"It's a pretty ugly area, isn't it?"

"Some of the houses are, yes."

"When you look out here," he said. "Do you feel jealous of the people who come here? Does it annoy you that some people have a much better chance than others? You come down here and you look out on the most beautiful cricket fields, you know, and everybody is wealthy . . . Does that hit hard?"

"It shows you that there's wealth," said Gillian. "It's just that *we* haven't got it."

After the first week, the Rugby pupils packed their cases to go back to Kirkby. "What do you think it will be like for them in Kirkby?" asked the producer.

"They'll survive," said Gary. "Better than we did here."

(Based on "Changing Places", a 40-minute documentary shown on BBC2 on 11. 2. 88)

[1] (school year 1987/88)

Working with the text

a **First impressions**

1. Talk in class about Rugby and collect – from memory – the information you find interesting.
2. Now write the information in the right order, go through the text again and add to your list all the things you find important. Use your notes to tell the class what happened at Rugby.

You can arrange your notes like this:

- on the day of the arrival: Ruffwood pupils – nervous – cameras – room – nice atmosphere ...
- on the first morning: bell – 7.15 ...
- on the third day: ...
- at the May Ball:

And here's some help for your text:

When the Ruffwood pupils arrived, they were . . . .
First of all . . . . Gary liked . . . . Later on . . . .
After they had been introduced . . . .

At 7.15 on their first morning, a bell . . .

On the third day . . .

. . .

b **Looking at the text in more detail**

Make sure you have understood some important details correctly. Pay attention to the context and try to explain how the following sentences must be understood.

1. Act normally – with TV cameras next to you. (p. 26, l. 7) 2. "You've been given the best rooms," said Mark, . . . (p. 26, l. 24) 3. For the girls it seemed to be even stricter. (p. 26, l. 34) 4. No parents who said good morning to you. (p. 26, l. 70) 5. Don't worry. You soon get used to it. (p. 27, l. 5) 6. . . . interviews were the only chance the Ruffwood pupils had to say how they felt. (p. 27, l. 18) 7. This isn't real, I thought. (p. 27, l. 35) 8. "They'll survive," . . . . "Better than we did." (p. 27, l. 95)

Example: The producer has just told the Ruffwood pupils to act normally. The sentence "Act normally . . ." shows what Gary thinks. For him it seems impossible to "act normally". He knows that the TV cameras will make everybody behave differently to how they normally behave.

c Gary phoned home on the first night and again after the May Ball.

1. Report what you imagine he said to his parents. You can start like this: Gary told his parents that he'd been given a nice room, but . . .
2. Work with a partner and make up the conversations he had on the telephone with a parent, a brother or a sister. Act out your conversations in class.

d
1. Read again what Chris Curling, the producer of the programme, expected to find out (p. 21). What did he actually find out from the first part of the exchange?
2. Here are two statements made by Ruffwood pupils after the exchange. Choose one and then write a letter to a Ruffwood pupil. Say what you think of the statement and explain why you would/wouldn't like to go to a public school like Rugby.

We said to one girl, "Your parents can't like you very much or they wouldn't have sent you here."
If I believed they'd get a better education there, yes, I'd send my children there.

e **Listening comprehension: A Rugby opinion**

Listen to what a Rugby pupil had to say about the exchange as she saw it.

→ Option 3: Class Four-D's trip to the British Museum

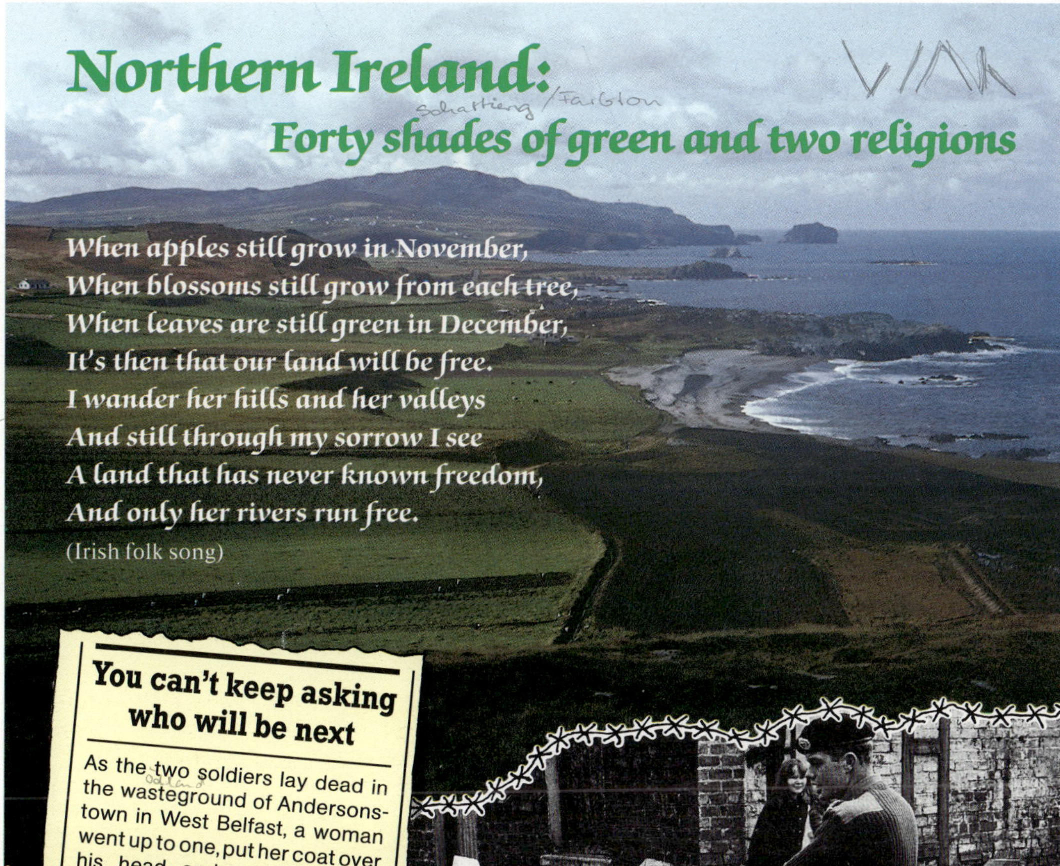

Northern Ireland:
Forty shades of green and two religions

When apples still grow in November,
When blossoms still grow from each tree,
When leaves are still green in December,
It's then that our land will be free.
I wander her hills and her valleys
And still through my sorrow I see
A land that has never known freedom,
And only her rivers run free.

(Irish folk song)

You can't keep asking who will be next

As the two soldiers lay dead in the wasteground of Andersonstown in West Belfast, a woman went up to one, put her coat over his head and said: "He was somebody's son. Lord have mercy on his soul."

She was watched by Father Alec Reid, a Catholic priest. He said, "These killings are achieving nothing. Lives are being destroyed on both sides. Whether it is Irish people, IRA men, British soldiers or Loyalists, the killing must stop. You can't keep asking who will be next."

(From *The Independent*, 21 March 1988)

- What words come to your mind when you look at the photos?
- What feelings are expressed in the song?
- How do the two people in the newspaper article feel about what happened?
- What do you know about Northern Ireland from the news and newspapers?

One island – two countries

The province of Northern Ireland is quite small, only 85 miles from top to bottom, 110 miles wide. It consists of six of the 32 counties of Ireland. On one side is the sea, on the other side the border – a border which divides the island into two countries.
Its people are divided, too, but not by the colour of their skin or by their race. They are divided by their religion.

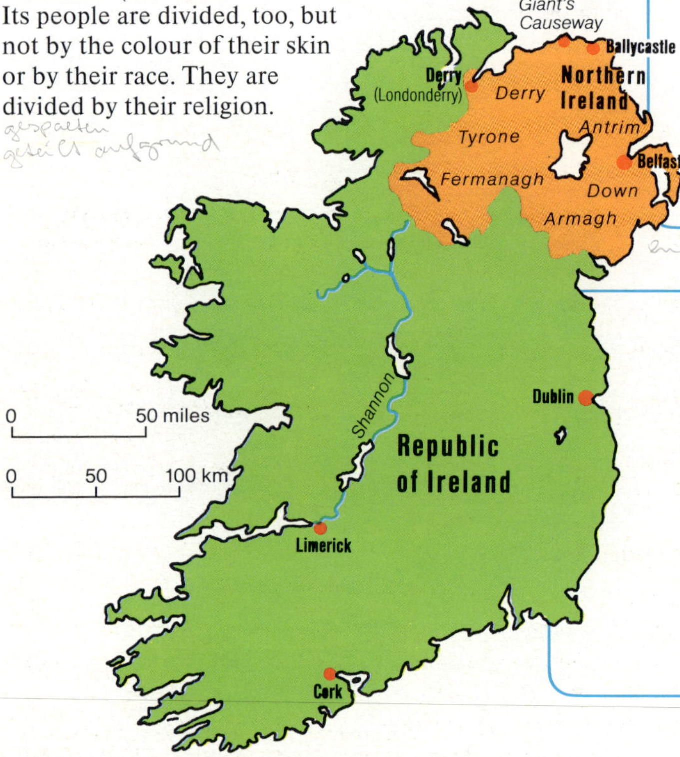

Northern Ireland
(also known as "Ulster")

Size:	*14,121 sq. km*
Population:	*1,575,200*
Catholics:	*28%*
Protestants and others:	*72%*
Capital:	*Belfast*
Currency:	*British pound*

Government: London, the British parliament, with a Secretary of State for Northern Ireland

The Republic of Ireland
(also known as "Eire")

Size:	*70,283 sq. km*
Population:	*3,540,000*
Catholics:	*94%*
Protestants and others:	*6%*
Capital:	*Dublin*
Currency:	*Irish punt*
Government:	*Independent state with own parliament in Dublin*

- Describe where Northern Ireland is. Explain from the map where Belfast is. What other information does the map give you about Northern Ireland?
- Compare Northern Ireland with the Republic. What do you notice about the figures?

A family from Northern Ireland

The Stewarts are a Protestant family and live in Helen's Bay, a village on the coast, just six miles east of Belfast. Mr Stewart works in Belfast for an American computer firm. Mrs Stewart is the manager of a fashion store in the city centre. Their daughter Linda goes to a large comprehensive school there. The Stewarts live a quite normal life. Sometimes, however, this normality can be disturbed.

Focus on GRAMMAR: Bestimmende und nicht-bestimmende Relativsätze (Defining and non-defining relative clauses)

a The Stewarts drive into Belfast every day – just like a number of other **people who** live outside the city. The road which takes them into Belfast is quite fast and there aren't often traffic jams. So the time they need for the journey isn't very long. Sometimes, however, they are stopped by soldiers and policemen who check their car for bombs and weapons. After so many years of violence, **Mrs Stewart, who** works in the city centre, no longer notices the security checks in front of her store. She thinks it is normal to walk past soldiers as she and her husband, whom she often meets in her lunch hour, go shopping in the centre of Belfast. When Linda goes to her mother's shop, which is only a short bus ride from her school, she never pays attention to the army vehicles either.

ev. b **Bestimmende Relativsätze** (Defining relative clauses)

1. A number of people drive into Belfast every day. The road is quite fast.

Aus diesen Sätzen geht nicht hervor, welche Menschen oder welche Straße gemeint sind. Um klar zu bestimmen, wer oder was gemeint ist, fügen wir bestimmende Relativsätze *(defining relative clauses)* hinzu. Sie werden im Englischen nicht durch Kommas abgetrennt:

A number of people **who live outside the city** . . . The road **which takes them into Belfast** . . .

2. The soldier **(who/whom) Mrs Stewart talked to outside her store** was still very young.

In bestimmenden Relativsätzen kann das Relativpronomen weggelassen werden, wenn es als Objekt steht *(contact clauses)*. Präpositionen stehen in der Regel hinter dem Verb (oder seinem Objekt). Im formellen – meist geschriebenen – Englisch verwendet man für Personen die Objektform *whom*. In Relativsätzen mit *which* oder *whom* kann die Präposition auch vor dem Relativpronomen stehen:
The soldier **to whom Mrs Stewart talked** . . .

→ Ex 2

c **Nicht-bestimmende Relativsätze** (Non-defining relative clauses)

1. Every day Linda drives into Belfast with her father, **who works for a computer firm.**
Linda goes to her mother's shop, **which is only a short bus ride from her school.**
Mrs Stewart and her husband, **whom she meets in her lunch hour**, often go shopping together.
Mrs Stewart, **whose store is in the city centre**, no longer notices the security checks.

In diesen Sätzen ist auch ohne einen Relativsatz klar, welche Person oder welches Geschäft usw. gemeint ist. Die hinzugefügten nicht-bestimmenden Relativsätze *(non-defining relative clauses)* geben uns lediglich Zusatzinformationen zu den Personen oder Dingen, auf die sie sich beziehen. Nicht-bestimmende Relativsätze werden vor allem im formellen Englisch verwendet. Sie werden durch Kommas und beim Sprechen durch kurze Pausen vom Hauptsatz abgetrennt.

2. Mrs Stewart's store, **in front of which there are often security checks**, is in the city centre.

Präpositionen stehen gewöhnlich vor dem Relativpronomen *whom, which* oder *whose.*

3. Mrs Stewart doesn't notice the security checks any more, **which shows that they have become quite normal.** . . . , was zeigt, . . .

Das Relativpronomen *which* (= was) kann sich auf einen ganzen Satz beziehen.

d **Relativpronomen** (Relative pronouns)

	Subjekt		Objekt		„dessen/deren"
	bestimmend	nicht-best.	bestimmend	nicht-best.	best. + nicht-best.
Personen	**who** oder **that**	nur **who**	**[who(m)** oder **that]**	nur **who(m)**	**whose**
Dinge	**which** oder **that**	nur **which**	**[which** oder **that]**	nur **which**	**whose**

[ ] = Das Relativpronomen kann weggelassen werden.

→ Ex 3-5

→ Option 24: Questions

The Troubles

In Northern Ireland children quickly learn that they belong to one of the two religious groups, Catholic or Protestant. They even learn to recognize people's religion from their names (Stewart, for example, is a Protestant name), the areas where they live or the schools they go to. The violence is worst in cities like Belfast or Derry (Londonderry), or in the border areas of County Armagh or Fermanagh. In Belfast, as in other towns, Catholics and Protestants live mostly in different areas and most children go to separate schools. The roots of Northern Ireland's problems go far back in history, when the difference between Protestant and Catholic was the difference between those who had land and wealth and ruled, and those who had nothing and so *were* ruled. Today the violence is mainly a result of radical groups fighting each other. Innocent people on both sides are often the victims.

Who is fighting whom?

The IRA (Irish Republican Army):
anti-British, illegal, wants a united independent Ireland; wants British army to leave; uses violence to achieve aims; members: Catholics.

Ulster Loyalists:
Protestants; pro-British, want to stay a part of the United Kingdom and remain British citizens; radical groups, e.g. the Ulster Defence Association (UDA) attack and kill IRA members and supporters.

The British Army:
sent in 1969 to keep the peace; now in a long battle with the IRA and its supporters, as well as Protestant extremists.

Total number of deaths from 1969 to 1989: 2,756

Read through the text on page 8 again. With the knowledge you now have, try to explain the situation at the border and also the Stewarts' behaviour.

Belfast: Who lives where?

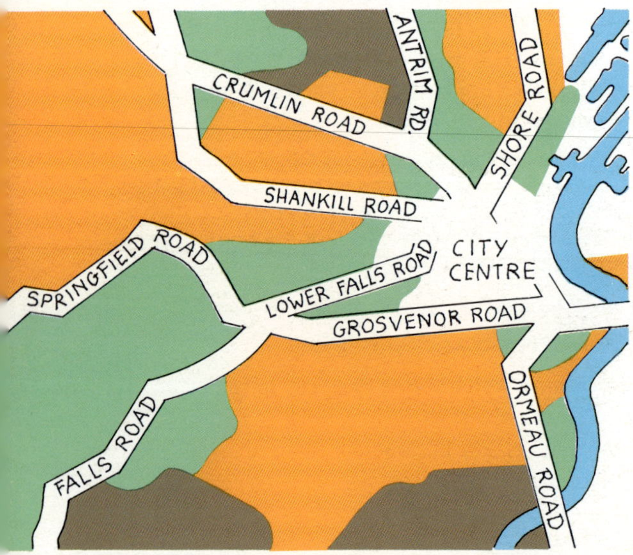

Protestants

Catholics

Mixed areas

A survey of young people's opinions in the whole of Northern Ireland [1]

		Agree %	Unsure %	Disagree %
"I would not like a brother or a sister or other close relative to marry a member of the other religion."	Cath.	20	23	57
	Prot.	33	21	46
"Pupils in Protestant and Catholic schools should be able to meet and mix more."	Cath.	71	12	17
	Prot.	57	16	27
"I believe that in Northern Ireland members of the two religions should be kept apart."	Cath.	28	22	50
	Prot.	36	19	45
"I would welcome the chance of learning more about the beliefs of people of the other religion."	Cath.	47	26	27
	Prot.	42	23	35

What seems to be the attitude of the religious groups towards each other? Can you think of any explanations for the Protestant attitudes?

[1] From the *Journal for the Scientific Study of Religion*

→ Option 4: The background to the Troubles

1 Unfortunately, Northern Ireland is not the only crisis area in the world today. Newspapers report almost daily about individuals, groups of people or nations that are in conflict. One of the main reasons for conflict is the +tension between people of different races, different political opinions, social classes or different religions. +Misunderstandings, ignorance, +intolerance, +lies, half-truths, clichés, +propaganda, prejudice and +discrimination often cause serious problems and make it impossible for people to live together peacefully.
How could such problems perhaps be solved? When the American magazine *Newsweek* asked some Belfast teenagers how they would solve their country's problems, they got some unexpected answers. Here are three of them:

If I were Prime Minister ...

I would divide Northern Ireland into two parts, and I would put Protestants on one side and Catholics on the other side.
(Peggy, age 13, Catholic)

I would make things so bad for Catholics that they would rush to the border to get out of Northern Ireland. This is Protestant country, so Catholics should not be in it.
(Derrick, age 15, Protestant)

I would pass a law that any Catholic who set foot on the street to start trouble would be shot. I would starve them like rats until there wasn't one left in Northern Ireland.
(David, age 14, Protestant)

Discuss these "solutions" in class.
Why do you think young people like Peggy, Derrick and David give such radical answers? Use the information you have about Northern Ireland to give possible explanations.

2 Take the word "conflicts" as the starting word and use key words like "reasons" to develop a network in your exercise book. You can start like this.

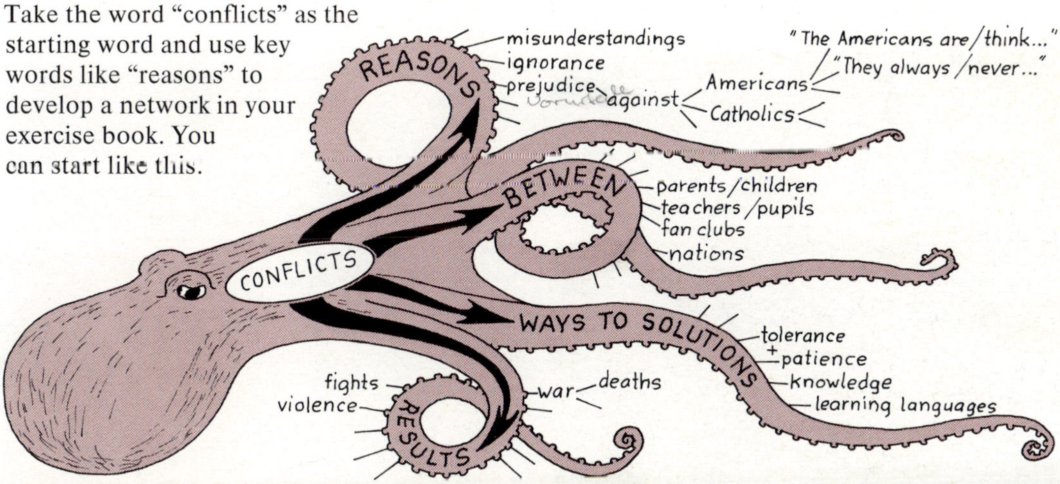

3 Choose a key word from your own network and write a short essay on it, e.g. "Discrimination – reasons, results and ways to solutions". You could begin like this: *The topic I'm going to write about is discrimination. There are many kinds of discrimination . . .*

4 Wherever people live or work together there are conflicts – even if they don't necessarily end in fights or violence. Describe a conflict you had in your class and how you solved it, or why you weren't able to solve it.

The Irish Voice

There is not a family in Northern Ireland that has not been affected one way or another by the violence in the country, and yet people continue to live there, even to enjoy living there. What keeps them, and what do they love about Northern Ireland?

The friendliness of the Irish is legendary – even across social and religious borders. After years of terror and violence, many Catholics and Protestants still remain friends and refuse to let the conditions in their country come between them.

A popular tourist area is the Antrim coast, whose quiet roads and little fishing villages are far away from the stress of the modern world. It seems strange, but in a country that knows no peace, it is the peace of the country that people love.

At its closest point, Northern Ireland is only 13 miles from the Scottish coast. Legends say that, long ago, giants used these stones to cross the sea to Scotland. Whether this is true or not, The Giant's Causeway is certainly one of nature's wonders.

The countryside is just as famous. Untouched and unspoiled, there is more variety over a hundred miles in Northern Ireland than over a thousand miles in North America.

Now that you know a bit more about Northern Ireland, would you like to go there on holiday, or even like to live there? Give reasons for your opinion.
Do you know anybody who has been to any part of Ireland? What did they say about it?
Try and write a letter in English and say why you would like to visit the country or not.

→ Option 5: Two poems and a song from Northern Ireland → Option 17: How to write a summary

1 Revision: Gerunds

Lagan College, Belfast *Use gerunds where possible.*

a bring together – Protestant – Catholic children – peaceful environment – the aim – Lagan College / today – several hundred Protestant – Catholic pupils – all kinds – background – chance – learn together – from each other – this school / since 1981 – children – enjoy – be together there / every year – more parents – be interested in – send – children – Lagan College – school can accept / this – how – begin / 1970s – group – Christian parents – start – make plans – future – their children / worried – send – them – schools – Protestants – Catholics only / finally – 1981 – succeed – start – school – 28 Catholic and Protestant pupils / so successful – few years later – several other schools – start – accept – Protestant – Catholic children, too

b *Try to explain what Lagan College wants to express by its crest* (Wappen).

2 Revision: Defining relative clauses

a **Linda Stewart's weekends** *Complete the sentences. Use "who", "that", "which" or a contact clause.*

1. The train service . . . runs between Belfast and Helen's Bay is very good. I often take the train at weekends and visit friends . . . live in Belfast.
2. In Belfast I have a group of friends . . . I see quite regularly at weekends. Sometimes we go to a disco or a concert . . . is organized by one of the churches or even by both churches.
3. There are some church youth clubs . . . are trying to bring Protestant and Catholic youths together. I think that's a good idea.
4. And sometimes we just spend a Saturday evening at a friend's. We listen to records . . . one of us has brought along, or we talk about all the things . . . have happened during the week.

b **Linda talking about herself and her family** *Make defining relative clauses with prepositions.*

Remember: In informal speech the preposition is the word (which) the verb is followed by.
In formal speech the preposition is the word with which you begin the relative clause.
⚠ If you use that as a relative pronoun, you must put the preposition after the verb.

Example: My parents and I talk quite often about the political situation in Ireland. (topic)
The political situation in Ireland is a topic my parents and I talk quite often about.

1. I've been thinking about joining one of the peace groups for a long time. (something) 2. I've always tried to believe in a peaceful solution to the troubles. (something) 3. I wouldn't want to emigrate to America, but I might go to England one day. (a country) 4. I also worry about the pollution of the environment. (problem) 5. Too many people just don't care about the environment. (something)

3 Belfast – from a small town to a major economic centre

Use non-defining relative clauses with "who", "whose" or "which".

a The 19th century was an eventful period in the history of Belfast, ... had been an unimportant town before. During that time it became a major centre of the British shipbuilding industry. One of the many ships built in Belfast was the "unsinkable" *Titanic*, ... wreck still interests many people today.
But since the end of the Second World War shipbuilding has become less and less important. Fewer and fewer people are employed in the shipbuilding industry, ... has been in a crisis all over Europe for many years now. Especially since the 1960s and 70s, foreign firms and business people, ... have been attracted by low taxes and low wages, have settled in and around Belfast. The city has become an attractive place for computer and other high-tech companies, for example, ... products have to face the competition of products from Asia. – These special tax rights, ... have helped the development of the town a lot, go back to the beginning of the 17th century. At that time only one third of the usual tax had to be paid for importing certain products into Belfast, ... attracted business people, as you can imagine.
But in spite of low wages and low taxes, Belfast, ... has seen so many troubles since 1969, finds it more and more difficult to offer enough jobs to its citizens.

b *Make a time line and add, in note form, important information for the different periods in the history of Belfast. Then tell the class about the development of Belfast with the help of your notes only.*

c *Make a similar time line for a town of your choice and tell the class about this town without telling them the name of the town. See if they can guess what town it is.*

4 Jokes – a mirror of Irish-English relations?

a *Read the text, then add the information in the box by using relative clauses in the right places.*

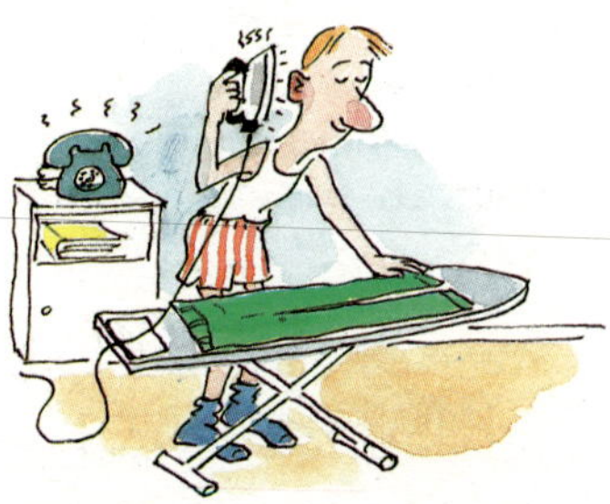

Irish jokes[1] are common in England. And often the English[2] are quite rude towards the Irish[3]. This has not helped to improve relations[4] between Protestants and Catholics in Northern Ireland.
In these jokes Irishmen[5] are shown as not very intelligent, or, to be honest, as completely stupid. Take, for example, this kind of joke[6]: How do you make Paddy burn his right ear?
– Phone him while he is ironing his trousers.

Or there's the following joke about Mick O'Hare[7]: "When he plants potatoes, he puts them in plastic bags to keep the dirt out of their eyes." – No wonder a certain bitterness[8] has found its way into jokes when they are told by the Irish. This one tells you what the Irish think of the English: "An Irishman was asked for £1 for the funeral *(Begräbnis)* of an Englishman. 'Here's £10,' he said, 'but please bury *(beerdigen)* ten of them.'"

1. be never very polite 2. be mainly Protestants 3. be almost all Catholics 4. have traditionally been bad 5. be often called "Mick" or "Paddy" 6. be not uncommon 7. be once given the prize for the kindest farmer in Ireland 8. be felt by the Irish

b What jokes about national groups can you think of? Are they totally harmless or are they perhaps not as harmless as they seem?

5 The "British character"? (Based on "The British Character", cartoons by Pont in *Punch*, 1934-40)

a The British . . .

1

. . . keep calm in all situations.

2

. . . just love open fires.

3

. . . never go without tea.

4

. . . love facing the weather.

Say what the pictures show and what you think of them. Use one or more relative clauses.

Example: Picture No 1 shows that the British keep calm in all situations, which I find quite strange. *Or:* . . . , which is admirable. *Or:* . . . , which is sometimes quite stupid.

b *These pictures illustrate, of course, opinions about the British that have become clichés. Do you know of any others? What do you think of them? – What do people say is typical of the Germans (or groups of people in Germany)? What do you think yourself?*

6 "Desert Island Discs"

Write an essay

Imagine your ship has sunk and you find yourself on a lonely island somewhere in the South Seas. You are the only person there. If you had been able to take your three favourite records, your favourite book and one more object of your choice, what would you have chosen? Write down what your choices would have been and explain why.

Here is how you could start: If I had been able to take . . . , I would have . . .

P.S.: "Desert Island Discs" is a weekly radio programme on BBC Radio 4 which has been popular with listeners for over 40 years. A famous person is interviewed on this programme and she/he is allowed to take eight records, a book and one more object of her/his choice to the island.

○ **7 Listening comprehension: Fatal mistakes**

Listen to the cassette, then answer these questions.

1. What were the soldiers going to do one evening? 2. Where did they park their van? 3. What did some IRA men do while the race was taking place? 4. What was the soldiers' mistake when they returned to their van? 5. What should soldiers do for security reasons? 6. Why do soldiers sometimes forget security?

8 WORDS WORDS WORDS

a Trouble spot: Words which sound similar

(to) accept [ək'sept] – aspect ['æspekt] – except [ɪk'sept] – (to) expect [ɪk'spekt] – expert ['ekspɜ:t] – extract ['ekstrækt] – respect [rɪ'spekt]

Use the words from the box in the following sentences:
1. You needn't read the whole book. An ★★★ will be enough. 2. I can't go to the meeting tonight. We're ★★★ing exchange students from abroad. 3. Tom is very good at repairing broken TV sets. In fact, he's a real ★★★. 4. Cheques are ★★★ed in many hotels and shops these days. 5. The way Jenny behaved is really un★★★able. 6. If people had more ★★★ for nature, all of us could lead a better life. 7. Everybody ★★★ed Arthur as the real king, ★★★ the Black Knight *(Ritter)*. 8. At our next meeting all ★★★s of this problem should be discussed.

b Personal nouns in English

In English only a small group of personal nouns clearly refer to male or female persons, e.g. *girl – boy, wife – husband, mother – father.* Find the corresponding partner for the following personal nouns and write them down as pairs in your exercise book.

uncle – widow – king – madam – son – gentleman – mum – Mrs/Ms – sister

Unlike German, which makes use of the suffix *-in* with many personal nouns, most personal nouns in English like *friend, pupil, teacher, doctor, manager, politician, Indian, cousin* can refer to male or female persons, according to the context:

My *cousin* Linda goes to Birmingham University. ("Cousine")
My favourite *cousin* lives in Bristol. He's called Dave. ("Cousin")

Sometimes, of course, it may be necessary to say clearly whether a noun refers to a male or female person in order to avoid misunderstandings. There are two ways of doing this in English:

Lynn to her father: "I spent the evening at a friend's."

1. You can add *male* or *female* to make the meaning clear:
   Most *female readers* found that article quite enjoyable, but some *male readers* didn't.
2. In a few cases the suffix *-ess* can be used to refer to a woman or a girl: *waiter/waitress, manager/manageress.* But be careful: Most speakers of English today try to avoid personal nouns ending in *-ess,* and many women do not like them.

Translate the following sentences into English. Use *male/female* only where they are needed.

1. Tina Turner ist eine sehr berühmte Rocksängerin. 2. Die Zahl der Studentinnen ist seit 1960 überall in der Welt gestiegen. 3. Janes Mutter ist Rechtsanwältin, aber Jane möchte Tänzerin werden. 4. Unser Krankenhaus beschäftigt 14 Krankenpfleger und 38 Krankenschwestern. 5. Unser Nachbar ist Inder. Er arbeitet als Krankenpfleger in unserem Krankenhaus. 6. Obwohl es heute mehr Politikerinnen gibt als vor zwanzig Jahren, werden viele politische Entscheidungen nur von Männern getroffen.

→ Option 15: Translation practice, p. 110

A little Indian and a big Indian are walking down a path. The little Indian is the big Indian's son. The big Indian is *not* the little Indian's father. Who is it?

A new life

Suddenly, without warning, the door was kicked in, and out of the darkness of the night soldiers stormed into the quiet house. Upstairs in his bedroom Michael lay terrified in bed, unable to move or call for his parents, while outside on the street the heavy noise of diesel engines could be heard and the shouts of neighbours who had come out of their houses to protest. He knew what it meant, and now it had happened to them.
The door of his bedroom flew open and a soldier pulled him out of his bed. "Hurry up and get dressed," he said. Michael climbed quickly into his trousers and pulled a pullover over his pyjamas.
Soldiers were in every room. They were opening cupboards, pulling things off shelves and putting them into large boxes which they carried out to their vehicles. His mother, he noticed, was alone. She was confused and frightened, not sure that what was happening was real. She saw Michael and held him to her. Together they were led out of the house and into an army vehicle.
More neighbours were now in the street. Their voices were loud and angry over the sound of the engines.
"What's happening?" he asked.
"I don't know," she said. "I just don't know."

They were taken to an apartment somewhere in the city, just Michael and his mother. They didn't know where they were, and there was no explanation why they were there, until a man came in and introduced himself as Mr Nolan. He took Michael's mother into the kitchen, where they talked quietly. Michael, alone in the living-room, once heard his mother cry loudly, "Oh, no! It's not true." He supposed something had happened to his father. But before the man left he came to Michael, smiled warmly at him and said, "Don't worry, Michael. Your father is fine. We had to do it this way to protect him and you."
"What's happened?" Michael asked.
"I'll explain everything soon," said the man in his warm, friendly voice. Mr Nolan came again and again. But once Michael heard his mother say, "You tell him. I can't." So Mr Nolan sat down on the sofa next to Michael, and they talked for a while about his friends, his school, his hobbies. Michael felt that he liked him, although he was sure he was from the police or the army. Then Mr Nolan became serious. "Michael, we're taking you and your parents out of Ireland. We're taking you away from here to a new life – and a new identity." Michael didn't realize what that meant until he looked at the passport which Mr Nolan was holding out to him.
Mr Nolan began to talk quickly, so that Michael had no time to interrupt or protest. "You're going first to England to meet your father and then, after a few days, to Canada. You will keep your Christian name, but your family name has changed. It is now Dunlop.

We organized the raid that night so that we could get you and your furniture out quickly." Michael looked into the open passport, which now had his photograph, his date of birth, but a different name. "It's necessary," said Mr Nolan. "We have to take you where nobody will find you. I'm sorry it has happened this way. Your father will explain everything to you. He is a brave man. You can be proud of him."
After that short meeting he sat day after day in a small room with groups of two or three men until he believed he was the person they had invented for him. What's your name? they asked. Where are you from? Where were you born? Which school did you go to? Wasn't there a family called Curtis that lived in your street? Did you know them? They had a dog. Who was your best friend at school? Until one day, tired and fed up, he said, "Sean O'Brien." And one of the men shouted angrily. "Your best friend's name was Paul Johnson. Remember that. Listen, Michael, there are guys out there looking for you. You make one mistake and they'll find you. Do you know what that means?" Michael nodded. Then the man smiled and took the boy's hand. "You're doing fine. Shall we try again?"

When it was time to leave, Mr Nolan went with them to the airport, and he sat with them on the plane. "At first it'll be difficult," he said, "but believe me, it'll get easier." Michael hardly listened until Mr Nolan said, "Do you think of your friends a lot?" Michael nodded. "Don't write to them," said Mr Nolan. "And don't ever try to phone them. Promise me." Michael had to fight back the tears. Even his friends had been taken from him.

His father was waiting inside a car at the airport. As soon as Michael climbed in he took him in his arms, and the tears ran down Michael's face.

Mr Nolan was right. It *was* difficult. His parents argued a lot with each other. But then the evening before they left for Canada, Michael's father took him for a walk and they sat together in a park. "What happened?" asked Michael, still waiting for the key to the mystery. His father looked down at the ground. "I helped the police. I gave them the names of the top IRA men in Belfast. I couldn't be with you because I had to identify the men in court." Michael froze. It wasn't possible. His own father!

"You grassed!" he screamed.

His father held his arm so that he couldn't run away. He talked quickly. "Those people are murderers. They'll kill women and children if it's necessary. Michael, I know them. I know what they're like. When you grow up where we live, it's too easy to become part of it all. But it's very difficult to get out. Can you understand that? And I wanted to get out. I wanted you to get out. Michael, those people put a bomb in a church. I saw it with my own eyes. This isn't about heroes and a love for Ireland, it's about murder."

But Michael wasn't listening. He turned away. His father was a grass, an informer, the worst kind of person alive. Their name was dirt. He could never return to Ireland, never see his friends again.

"Michael!" He had broken away and run across the park. His father followed him, but soon stopped. Michael ran on, along streets he hardly knew, until he found himself in front of a telephone box. He had to speak to somebody. Nervously he felt the coins in his pocket. He dialled the number and listened to a phone ring in a small house in Belfast. A voice answered and he recognized Sean's father. "Hallo, Mr O'Brien." "Michael!" said the voice warmly. "It's good to hear from you. How are you? We were all worried about you. Sean keeps saying he hopes you'll phone or write. I hope you're well." Michael smiled. It wasn't as bad as everybody had said. Sean was still his friend. "I'm fine, thanks, Mr O'Brien." "Listen, Michael, Sean isn't here just now, but I know he'd love to talk to you. Can he phone you back? Where are you staying?" And Michael almost told him when he remembered what the soldier had shouted at him. "Just one mistake and they'll find you."

He stopped and looked at the phone in his hand. He could hear Sean's father on the other end of the line. "Are you still there? Michael!" He put the phone back and ran back to his father.

Working with the text

a A first look at the text

Describe each picture and try to put it into its context in the story.
Picture 1 shows . . . . The two men are asking Michael questions about . . . . A few days before Mr Nolan had given Michael . . . .

b Understanding details of the story

1. He knew what it meant . . . (p. 39, l. 9). What does Michael think it means?
2. Michael felt that he liked him, although he was sure he was from the police or the army. (p. 39, l. 51). Explain why the conjunction "although" is used in this sentence.
3. "We organized the raid . . ." (p. 40, l. 1). Why do the soldiers have to raid the house?
4. "Dunlop" (Michael's new family name) and "Johnson" (the name of Michael's best friend) are both "Protestant" names. Why do you think these names were chosen?
5. He could never return to Ireland . . . (p. 40, l. 69). Why not?
6. "Where are you staying?" (p. 40, l. 90). Why do you think Mr O'Brien asks this question?
7. "Just one mistake and they'll find you." (p. 40, l. 93). What would be a mistake? Who must be meant by "they"? And what might happen if Michael made a mistake?

c Analysing the development of the story

1. Go through the story and complete the following table.

page/lines	setting	characters	action
(39) 1-29	Michael's home	Michael, his mother, soldiers	. . .
(39) 30-46	. . .	. . .	
. . .			

2. Try to explain – from your notes – how the story develops towards its climax.
3. Look at the pictures at the top of the page again. Why are the situations shown there important for the development of the story?

d What do you think?

1. Why is Michael so upset about the way his father behaved?
2. Was it right or wrong of Michael's father to become an informer?

e Writing a diary

Put yourself in Michael's place and write down the events in the way he might have written them. Add thoughts and feelings about what happened where you think it is necessary.

→ Option 6: An extract from a novel: 'The fight'

Unit 4

Whenever I go out Dad asks: "Where are you going? Who are you meeting? What time are you going to be back?"

I've got no idea what I want to do when I leave school.

Growing up in Britain

Sometimes I don't know what to do. I feel so lonely.

I can't wait till I get some wheels!

Pocket-money on Friday, broke on Monday! I never have enough money.

It's important to look right, have the right clothes and the right hairstyle.

Which of these statements can you identify with? What other problems do teenagers complain about?

By the time you are 15 you probably feel it is time you were allowed to do what you want, and that people should stop telling you what to do and what not to do. However, in the eyes of the law, there are still limits to what you are allowed to do.

You can ...	at the age of						at the age of					
	13	14	15	16	17	18	13	14	15	16	17	18
get a part-time job	●						●					
buy and drink beer or wine in a pub						●				●		
vote in an election						●						●
marry (with your parents' permission)				●						●		
buy and smoke cigarettes				●						●		
drive a car					●							●
ride a motorbike					●							●
ride a moped				●						●		
leave school and get a full-time job				●					●			

Which are the German laws and which are the British? Compare what teenagers in Britain and Germany can and can't do at different ages. Which laws do you think British teenagers dislike most? Which German laws do you dislike? Which British laws do you prefer?

Teenage life

The following facts are taken from a government survey of the problems and interests of 14 to 19-year-olds in Britain.

Part-time work

Almost 50 per cent of British teenagers have a part-time job. The most popular jobs are working in shops and stores (usually on Saturdays), doing a paper round (mornings, before school), or babysitting.

Helping at home

Nearly all teenagers (91 per cent) claim they help with the housework. But most admit they only do it because they have to.

Sport

Two thirds of those interviewed take part regularly in one or more sporting activities. Swimming is very popular with both sexes (53 per cent), while 40 per cent of boys play football. Other popular sports include ice-skating, table-tennis and darts.

Money

Money is seen as a problem by most teenagers. Without it they can't buy clothes or records, pay for transport, or go to concerts, cinemas or discos.
The majority of girls spend their pocket-money on clothes; half the boys spend it on records and cassettes. Three quarters try to save at least some money.

Parents

Most teenagers get along with their parents quite well. Although 50 per cent believe their parents are too strict, most agree that their parents offer help and support in times of crisis. When there are arguments, however, they are usually about what time they should come home at night, where they are going, and who they are going with.

Politics

About three quarters of 14 to 19-year-olds admit that they are not interested in politics. Only 2 per cent ever attend any political meetings, while over 60 per cent believe their interests and concerns are ignored by politicians.

Social concerns

The majority of all teenagers agree that it is important to help old or disabled people and to improve the environment. About half want to help poor people in the Third World. However, only a small minority (10 per cent) actually *do* anything themselves.

Worries

Over half of all teenagers – boys and girls – are concerned about how they look or worried about the clothes they wear. Many are annoyed that they're often treated like children, not adults. Possible unemployment was a major worry for nearly two thirds of those still at school.

What is most surprising/interesting to you? Write down what you think would be the results of such a survey in your area. Then prepare a questionnaire (either yourself or in a group) and do a survey with pupils from your class/school. Compare the results.

Part-time work (model questions)

Do you have a part-time job?
Where do you work?
What kind of job do you do?
When do you work?

Free time

When the teenagers in the survey were asked what they did in their free time, this is how they replied:

At home

Listen to music	92%
Watch TV	92%
Read	74%

Outside home

Visit friends	85%
Go out with friends	80%
Go to discos	56%
Go out with boy-/girlfriend	47%
Go to a sports centre	42%
Go to a youth club	32%
Do voluntary work	10%

Do a survey in your class and compare the results with those from Britain.

A big problem for teenagers can be knowing who to ask for advice when they need it: parents, teachers, the youth club leader, a sister or brother, or a friend. In some cases, if it is a very personal problem, teenagers write to a magazine for help or advice.

ADVICE

FROM MELANIE

Once a week I help to look after a group of old people. My boyfriend thinks I am silly and says I should spend more time with him. What should I do? I like him very much and don't want to lose him.
(Cathy, 15, Glasgow)

Your boyfriend is silly. I think that what you are doing is wonderful. Too many people in this country think only of themselves and never of others. Show this letter to him, or invite him to go with you one day. Perhaps then he might realize how wrong he is!

There is a girl in my class that I fancy. But I'm sure she fancies another boy. Two of my friends say that this girl likes me a lot and is dying to meet me at the next school disco. I don't believe them. I'm quiet and shy, and they're lively and very popular. I don't believe what they say, because they played this same trick last Christmas and made a fool of me. What should I do?
(Chris, 15, Oxford)

Stop listening to your friends and listen to yourself. You say you like this girl. Well, go and talk to her at the next school disco. You'll soon notice whether she likes you or not.

A gang of youths have been attacking our house for weeks because we are Asians. The police come when we call them, but the gang only comes back again the next night. What can we do?
(Rita, 15, London)

My suggestion would be to write to your MP. She or he can ask the police for a report and make sure that you are protected better. I am also sending you a list of addresses of different groups who help minorities if they feel they are threatened.

Write your own letters. They can be about imaginary or real problems, funny or serious. Then exchange letters with somebody in your class and write a reply to the letter you have received. Read out one of the letters and replies in class.

Focus on WORDS: People in contact

Although we are all individuals we are +linked in many ways with other people. We belong to a certain race, a nation, a social class, perhaps a religion. We are members of a club, a choir, a political +party or other groups. But there are many more +links between people than the same nationality or common interests. Each of us lives in a network of human relations. Every day we meet lots of people in different situations: other members of the family, neighbours, classmates and teachers at school or +colleagues at work. With all these people we +communicate: with some we have friendly conversations, with others we argue.
How we get along with each other +depends largely on our own character and how we behave towards each other. Kind, +punctual, +easygoing and +outgoing people are easy to get along with. +Arrogant, selfish, unreliable and ignorant people often make others feel miserable.

1 Collecting and arranging words: Here is a list of words you can use to describe people. Put the words in the groups a-d. (Some words may go in more than one group!) Add more words from your memory.

adults afraid alone angry argue Asians bored classmates disappointed employees encourage excited fed up fight force frightened gang generous hate honest immigrants intolerant neighbours party pleased protected respectful rude shy uncomfortable unfair unprejudiced unsafe worried

a **Groups of people**
Europeans, Jews, +Muslims, Whites, . . .
Friends, relatives, teenagers, . . .
Class, club, family, team, . . .

b **How people feel in the company of others**
They are/feel
– comfortable, confident, relaxed, safe, . . .
– bitter, lonely, nervous, sad, . . .

c **People's attitudes towards other people**
They
– like, love, admire, . . . other people.
– dislike, . . . other people.
They can be
– +just, polite, tolerant, +understanding, . . .
– +aggressive, +hostile, mean, strict, . . .

d **How people treat other people**
They
– apologize to, defend, help, support, . . . other people; make other people feel good, tell other people the truth, . . .
– +beat up, +cheat, +discourage, lie to, +offend, threaten, . . . other people.

2 Words in use

a Write a short text about Cathy, aged 15, using the information given below.

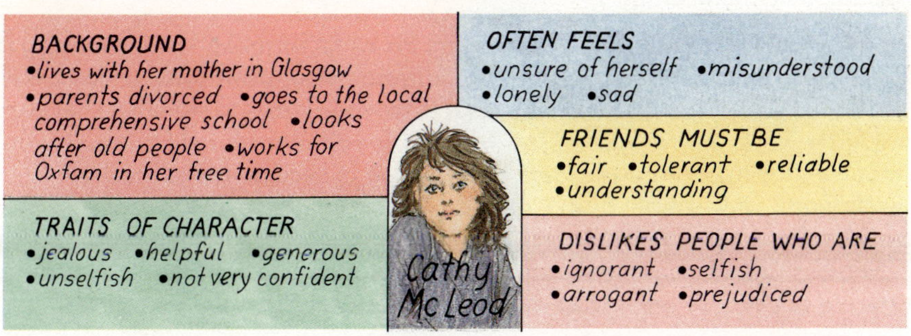

b Make a similar "network" for yourself or somebody you know very well.

c Invent a love story with a sad or happy ending. Or: Write about two strangers who have become very good friends. You could start like this: *When Angela first met Tony, she didn't like him at all. In fact, she thought he was the most ignorant . . . . But one day . . .*

4 A

Britain: a multi-cultural society

Have you noticed from the pictures you have seen that a lot of British people are not white? In fact there are about 2.4 million non-white people living in Britain, out of a total population of about 56.9 million. And of these 2.4 million, about 43% were born in Britain. Of course, the different ethnic groups are not equally distributed throughout the country. Most live concentrated in certain areas of large towns and cities, such as London, Birmingham or Bradford.
Since the Race Relations Act of 1976 it has been illegal in Britain to discriminate against people because of their colour, race, nationality or ethnic origin.

Of Britain's total non-white population of c. 2.4 million the biggest groups have the following countries of origin:

India	*c. 760,000*
West Indies	*c. 534,000*
Pakistan	*c. 397,000*
Bangladesh	*c. 103,000*
Africa	*c. 103,000*

What do the figures and the photos tell you about the population in Britain?

→ Option 7: From mighty monarchs to powerful parliaments → Option 8: The British system of government

Focus on GRAMMAR: Partizipialkonstruktionen anstelle von Nebensätzen
(Participle constructions instead of subordinate clauses)

Immigrants from the Commonwealth

a In the 1950s Britain needed large numbers of workers for its factories and industries. So the government decided to encourage people **living** in Commonwealth countries to come to Britain to work. Tens of thousands came, but what many of them didn't realize was that they would have to do hard, dirty work on low wages. However, the conditions **offered** by British companies were usually much better than those they had experienced in their home countries. **Having** British passports, immigrants from Commonwealth countries had the right to live in Britain permanently. For a time, things went quite well – until the immigrants began to bring their families. **Noticing** that more and more immigrant families were settling in Britain, many white people started to become worried or aggressive. **Convinced** that the foreigners were taking away their jobs, some whites insisted that the immigrants should be sent back to where they had come from. But this was hardly possible. **Having encouraged** them to come, the government couldn't force them to return. **Though protected** by the law, many immigrants found they were often attacked, or couldn't get jobs, or rent flats and houses. In 1976, Parliament passed the Race Relations Act, and so made it illegal to discriminate against people from other countries.

ev. b **Partizipialkonstruktionen anstelle von Relativsätzen**
(Participle constructions instead of relative clauses)

Present participle (active meaning)

Immigrants **coming** to Britain hoped to find a better life.
= Immigrants **who came** . . .

Past participle (passive meaning)

Many jobs **offered** by British companies were badly paid.
= Many jobs **which were offered** . . .

→ Ex 1

c **Partizipialkonstruktionen anstelle von Nebensätzen der Zeit, des Grundes oder der Einräumung**
(Participle constructions instead of clauses of time, reason or concession)

Present participle	*Past participle*
1. **(When) leaving** their home countries, the immigrants were full of hope. = **When the immigrants left** their home countries, they were full of hope.	**(When) invited** by the British government, they accepted the offer. = **When they were invited** by the British government, they accepted the offer.
Having left their home countries, many faced new problems. = **After they had left** . . .	
2. **Being** Commonwealth citizens, they all had British passports. = **As/Because they were** . . .	**Convinced** that the immigrants were taking away their jobs, some whites protested. = **As/Because they were convinced** . . .
3. **Although knowing** that they were no longer welcome, more immigrants arrived. = **Although they knew** . . .	**Although protected** by the law, immigrants were often discriminated against. = **Although they were protected** . . .

Wie die Beispiele zeigen, kann eine Partizipialkonstruktion anstelle eines adverbialen Nebensatzes stehen. Beachte, daß Partizipialsatz und Hauptsatz ein gemeinsames Subjekt haben, das aber nur im Hauptsatz genannt wird. Am häufigsten sind Partizipialsätze

1. der Zeit (manchmal zur Verdeutlichung durch *when* oder *while* eingeleitet, vor einem Partizip Präsens auch durch *after, before*),
2. des Grundes,
3. der Einräumung (immer durch *though/although* eingeleitet).

Solche Partizipialsätze werden vor allem im formellen – besonders im geschriebenen – Englisch und im literarischen Englisch verwendet. Sie stehen meist am Satzanfang und werden dann oft durch ein Komma vom Hauptsatz abgetrennt.

→ Ex 2-°5

d **Partizipialkonstruktionen zum Ausdruck von Begleitumständen**
(Participle constructions to express accompanying circumstances)

Most immigrants refused to be sent back, **pointing out** that it was illegal. . . ., und machten darauf aufmerksam, . . .

Immigrant leaders defended their rights, **reminding** politicians of their promises. . . ., wobei/indem sie die Politiker . . . erinnerten.

Eine Partizipialkonstruktion kann auch die Begleitumstände einer Handlung ausdrücken. Sie steht dann hinter dem Hauptsatz, von dem sie in der Regel durch ein Komma abgetrennt wird. Im Deutschen verwenden wir dafür häufig einen (durch „und" eingeleiteten) Hauptsatz oder einen Nebensatz mit „wobei/indem".

→ Option 15: Translation practice, p. 111

Focus on GRAMMAR: Das Partizip Präsens nach bestimmten Verben
(The present participle after certain verbs)

Rita Patel

a When Rita Patel is with her friends, she feels and behaves like any other British teenager.
"You don't usually think about the fact that you're Asian. After all, I was born in Britain and I grew up here. For us the problems really started when my parents bought a shop in a mainly white area. My father is a tailor, and he wanted to start his own business: Patel & Son, Quality Tailors. We put a special sign above the shop in bright fresh colours. But on the first evening after we had moved in, we **heard** people **shouting** outside. We **saw** a gang of youths **standing** on the street. Suddenly a stone **came flying** through the shop window. At first we couldn't believe it, but then we knew we were in danger. We **remained sitting** in the darkness of the room, broken glass on the carpet. We were terrified. The shouting didn't stop, so we called the police. But the youths came back night after night, always after the pubs had closed, and they threatened us on the phone. Sometimes we were so frightened that we didn't answer the phone, but **left** it **ringing**. Finally, we decided to buy a dog. One evening Dexter saved our lives when he **found** the carpet **burning** in the hall. Somebody had thrown a petrol bomb through our letter box."

b **Verben der Sinneswahrnehmung** (verbs of perception) **+ Objekt + Partizip Präsens**

The Patels **heard** people **shouting**.	Die Patels hörten Menschen schreien.
A neighbour **saw** a man **throwing** a bomb.	Ein Nachbar sah, wie ein Mann eine Bombe warf.
He **watched** somebody **hiding** behind a car.	Er beobachtete, wie sich jemand . . . versteckte.
Rita **felt** her heart **beating**.	Rita spürte, wie ihr Herz schlug.
Dexter **smelt** something **burning**.	Dexter roch, daß etwas brannte.

Nach Verben der Sinneswahrnehmung wie *hear, listen to; see, look at, watch, notice; feel; smell* kann ein Objekt + Partizip Präsens stehen. Im Deutschen verwenden wir dafür einen Infinitiv oder einen Nebensatz mit „wie" (oder „daß").

⚠ Vergleiche jedoch: Rita **saw** people **leaving** the house.
She **saw** a man **shut** the front door, **walk** to his car and **drive** away.

Das Partizip Präsens drückt aus, daß ein Geschehen wahrgenommen wird, das gerade im Verlauf, also noch nicht zu Ende ist. Vergleiche: *People were leaving the house.*
Der Infinitiv drückt aus, daß das Geschehen vollständig (von Anfang bis Ende) wahrgenommen wird. Vergleiche: *The man shut the front door, walked to his car and drove away.*

c ***find, leave, catch*** **+ Objekt + Partizip Präsens**

R

Dexter **found** the carpet **burning**.	Dexter entdeckte, daß der Teppich brannte.
The Patels **left** the phone **ringing**.	Die Patels ließen das Telefon läuten.
The police **caught** a man **breaking** into the shop.	Die Polizei erwischte einen Mann beim Einbruch . . .

d **Verben der Ruhe und Bewegung** (verbs of rest and movement) **+ Partizip Präsens**

The Patels **remained sitting** in the darkness.	Die Patels blieben im Dunkeln sitzen.
A neighbour **stood watching** the gang.	Ein Nachbar stand da und beobachtete die Bande.
The Patels **lay wondering** what to do.	Die Patels lagen da und überlegten, . . .
A stone **came flying** through the window.	Ein Stein kam durchs Fenster geflogen.

Nach Verben der Ruhe wie *remain, stand, sit* und *lie* sowie nach einigen Verben der Bewegung wie *come* und *go* kann ein Partizip Präsens stehen.

→ Ex 6

→ Option 25: The articles

R = Die mit „R" gekennzeichneten Abschnitte sind rezeptiv. Sie beschreiben Sprachmuster, die du verstehen, aber nicht selbst anwenden mußt.

1 Revision: Present and past participles

Indian girls and young women in Britain

a *Decide if you need a present or past participle.*
The ideas expressed in an article about young Asians living in Britain annoyed Suki Parekh so much that she wrote this letter saying how she sees the situation.

Dear Sir or Madam,

It seems to me that the author of your article about the Indian community in Britain still has not realized that the situation for Indian girls and young women (live) in Britain has changed a lot, especially since the beginning of the 1980s.
The ideas (express) by a number of white British people about our situation are totally wrong. Many people (talk) about the Indian community in Britain still say things like "Arranged marriages are very common among Indians". In fact, things are quite different today. It is no longer unusual to see an Indian girl (walk) down the street with her boyfriend. Some Indian teenagers will even tell you that the freedom (give) to them by their parents is greater than that of their white friends. A lot of white British girls (ask) by the BBC in a recent programme said that their parents were stricter than those of their Indian friends.
I would be very pleased if, in future numbers of your magazine, you could give a picture (show) what it is really like for us here in Britain.

Yours faithfully, Suki Parekh

b *Imagine you have received this letter. Write to Suki and apologize for what has happened. Express the hope that white British people and Indians will mix more in future, so that there will be fewer misunderstandings. Try to use some participles in your letter.*

2 A violent society? Results of a survey on violent behaviour among young people in Britain

Change the subordinate clauses into participle constructions.

When they heard about the results of the survey, many adults were shocked. But when they read the survey, they soon saw possible explanations for the results. Here are some of the things found out by the survey:

When they talk to each other, adults usually look at each other and smile. But when they talk to children, many adults don't smile. And because they often ignore their children's questions, adults don't have proper conversations with their children. A number of adults even beat their children because they remember that they were once beaten by their parents. Although they know that it doesn't really help, they pretend that beating children is necessary. And because they see all this violence in their families, young people often behave violently outside their home.

Example: <u>Hearing</u> about the results of the survey, many adults were shocked. But . . . *Go on.*

20/6

3 Race relations in Britain

Use the past participles of the following verbs to complete the sentences below.

fascinate ask employ protect encourage

In spite of the problems one hears about, many people of different races, white and non-white, get along quite well with each other. Here are some things that were said on a radio programme about race relations:

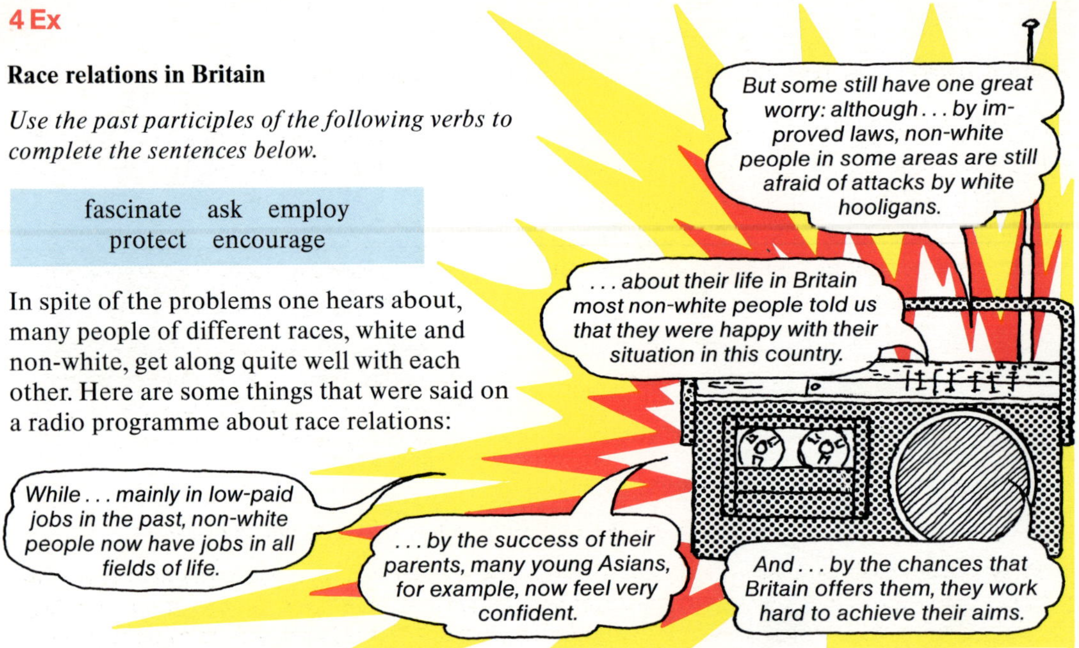

4 Tell the Mehta family's success story. *Complete the sentences with the correct forms of the verbs. Use "having + past participle" where possible.*

1. (arrive) in Britain in the late 1950s, Mr Mehta (be) unemployed for a short time. 2. (sell) Indian food in the streets of London for some time, he (open) a restaurant in London. 3. (decide) to start a factory for Indian food in Britain, he and his family (plan) and (build) a small factory. 4. (sell) their products successfully in the London area, the Mehtas (start) to sell their products in the north of England, too. 5. (find) the right place, they soon (build) a bigger factory in the north.

Today the Mehtas are one of the most successful business families in the whole of Britain.

Example: 1. Having arrived in Britain in the late 1950s, Mr Mehta was unemployed for a short time. . . . *Go on.*

○ 5 In English, please: A notice board at a German school

Tell an English friend what the pupils have written. Use participle constructions in your English sentences.

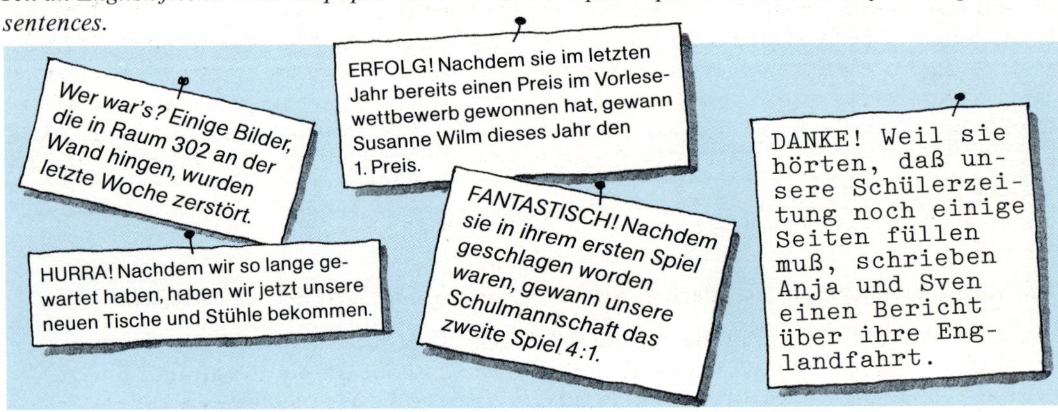

6 Trouble in different places *Complete each sentence with a participle construction.*

1. I could smell something burning. Then I heard people shouting for help. A lady came ... She asked me to call the fire brigade.	people/shout for help; run to my front door; something/burn
2. I watched ... Seconds later the old man opened his front door and I saw ... Then, very suddenly, they ran away ...	hold something in their hands; the boys/talk to him excitedly; two boys/stand outside an old man's house
3. I was listening to ... I heard ... Suddenly I heard ... Then there was the terrible noise of a crash. I ran out of my front door and saw ...	several cars/drive past quite slowly; a child/lie in the street/scream in pain; some children/play in the street; a car/race down the street

7 Revision: A mixed bag *Complete the sentences. In some you will have to add some words.*

1. Sorry I'm late, Susan. How long (you wait) for me? – ... 5 o'clock. 2. Do you remember who (write) "Fool on the hill"? – Sorry, at the moment I just (not remember) who (write) it. 3. I (buy) a rabbit for Tommy yesterday. – But you said (buy/hamster). 4. My cassette-recorder is broken. – Oh, if you (tell) me, I (bring) mine along. 5. When I started the car, I (know) at once that they (not repair) it properly. 6. I (not see) John for months. I (really/look forward/see) him at your party. 7. (you/enjoy) yourselves at the party? – Yes, we did. It was super.

8 Revision: Tenses, participles and conjunctions

Frankenstein's monster *Complete the text with the correct forms, using the conjunctions below.*

when but (2×) where because after

The name "Frankenstein" (remind) many people of horror stories and dark cellars ... monsters (create) by unfriendly scientists. ..., not many people (know) that Victor Frankenstein (be) the main character in a book often (call) one of the best horror stories of all times, even today. The book (write) at the beginning of the 19th century by Mary Shelley ... she (be) only 20 years old. Four years earlier, at the age of 16, she (run) away from home with the writer Percy B. Shelley. ... they (live) on their own in Switzerland for some time, they (join) a group of English writers (live) in Switzerland. During that time the character of Frankenstein (invent). In the story we (hear) about Victor Frankenstein, who, as a scientist, (fascinate) by the idea of creating a human being. ... the being he (create) is no more than an ugly monster. Still, (have) feelings like a "real" human being, the monster (want) to be loved by people. But ... nobody (like) him, he (start/kill) people. Full of hate for the man who (put) him into the world, he finally also (kill) Victor Frankenstein.

Remember: When you talk about a text, you use the simple present as the basic tense.

○ **9 Listening comprehension: The attack** *Listen to the cassette, then answer these questions.*

1. What are the Patels doing at the beginning? 2. Why does Mrs Patel send her children upstairs? 3. What's Mr Patel's reaction? 4. Would you describe the police's attitude towards the Patels as helpful? 5. Why do the police officers want to see the Patels' passports?

10 WORDS WORDS WORDS

Trouble spot: "lassen"

a German: "jemanden etwas tun lassen"
English: 1. **make** sb. **do** sth. (lassen = veranlassen, dazu bringen, zwingen)
2. **let** sb. **do** sth. } (lassen = zulassen, erlauben)
3. **allow** sb. **to do** sth.

⚠ No *to* after *let* and *make*!

Examples: My parents always **make** me **switch off** the light at 10 o'clock.
My parents would never **let** me **watch** TV after 10 o'clock.
My parents would never **allow** me **to watch** TV after 10 o'clock.

1. Peter's boss is very strict. She doesn't . . . anybody smoke in the office. 2. I thought you were my best friend. Why don't you . . . me read your letter? 3. The film was so sad that it . . . me cry. 4. Surprisingly my father . . . me to use his car. 5. Gary doesn't . . . anybody else ride his new moped. 6. The criminals tried to . . . the crime look like an accident. 7. What . . . you think I'm German? 8. The little money I've saved doesn't . . . me to go on holiday this year. 9. I wanted to go to that rock festival but my parents wouldn't . . . me to go. 10. Come on, . . . me buy you a drink. 11. My parents always . . . me wash our car. I hate it!

b German: "etwas (von jemandem) tun lassen" (= es nicht selbst tun)
English: **have** something **done** (by somebody)

Here are some examples of this structure. Read them carefully and translate them.

	have	object	**past participle**	
I	**have**	my hair	**cut**	once a month.
We're	**having**	a swimming-pool	**built**	in our garden.
I haven't	**had**	the film	**developed**	yet.
I	**had**	my coat	**cleaned**	only yesterday.
We **will**	**have**	our tyres	**checked**	before our trip.
We **must**	**have**	our school reports	**signed**	by our parents.
Why **did** you	**have**	a fence	**put up**?	
Do you	**have**	your car	**washed**	regularly?

⚠ I **have washed** the car, it's clean now. (= present perfect of *wash*)
Ich habe das Auto gewaschen, ...
I **have** the car **washed** twice a month. (= simple present of *have something washed*)
Ich lasse das Auto . . . waschen.

Translate the following sentences.

1. Joan must have her computer checked; it doesn't work properly. Or perhaps she should have a new one installed. 2. She could have it repaired at the "Chip Shop". They are not too expensive. 3. Now that Steve has had a second disk drive installed he can use much better programs than before. He's having a few special ones written at the moment.

1. Wenn ich du wäre, würde ich den Fernseher von einem Fachmann reparieren lassen. 2. Wir können uns nicht bei mir treffen. Wir lassen gerade unsere Wohnung streichen. 3. Nachdem die Bombe ihr Haus beschädigt hatte, ließen die Carlins neue Fenster einsetzen. 4. Ich habe gestern einen Brief aus Spanien bekommen. Ich werde ihn übersetzen lassen.

An eye for an eye

They were there again, as they were most evenings. Rita could hear them shouting outside in the dark street, “Pakis out! Pakis out!” She got out of bed and went to the window. Five youths, five stupid ignorant yobs. They were standing on the pavement outside their shop, beer cans in hand, ruining their nights, destroying their lives. Because of them her family was being forced to live in fear and even think of moving away.

She went back to bed. In the next room, behind the thin wall, she heard her younger brother, Sumit.

“Go to sleep,” she said. “I can’t,” said the young voice. “Pull the blankets over your head,” she said.

Soon a window belonging to the shop downstairs was broken and she heard her father talking quietly on the phone.

“The name is Patel. 26 Redwood Road. A gang of hooligans is attacking our house again. Can you please do something about it?” Leaving the house the next morning, Rita saw her mother cleaning away the broken glass from the pavement. Their shop, once fresh and blue with its new sign “Patel & Son, Quality Tailors”, was now covered in graffiti; several of the windows were covered with boards where the Patels had given up repairing them.

“There must be something we can do,” Rita thought as she walked to school. She had written to the town council, even to her MP, but all she had got back were letters saying that they were waiting for replies from the police, etc. – which meant nobody was doing anything. She wondered if the groups the magazine had mentioned could help.

In history that morning Rita fell asleep. At the end of the lesson her friend Leela had to wake her up. “Oh, my God,” said Rita. “He sends everybody to sleep. What have we got now?”

“What’s wrong with you?” asked Leela. “You look terrible.” Rita sighed. “We’ve had visitors again.” “Oh no,” said Leela, “How long has this been going on?” “Almost four months.”

“Listen,” said Leela. “I know some people who can help you.”

That evening a group of young men, some white and some Asian, came to their house. They knocked on the door after the Patels had just eaten their evening meal.

“Mr Patel?” said their leader. “We are friends of Leela’s. We call ourselves the PAR, People Against Racism. We’ve heard you are having trouble.” “Yes,” said Mr Patel, surprised, not knowing who had asked them to come or why they were there. But the PAR were very nice and friendly, and soon the Patels and the young men were sitting together relaxed in the living-room. For the first time in weeks there was laughter in the Patels’ home. It was almost like a party as they drank, ate sandwiches and played cards.

“If you feel tired,” said one of the PAR, “you can go to bed. We’ll stay all night if necessary.” “But we can’t possibly go to bed while you wait here,” said Mrs Patel. “It’s unfair.”

“I shall stay with them,” said Mr Patel. “The rest of you can go to bed.”

They came at midnight.
"Switch the lights off," said Jeff, the PAR leader, as soon as they heard the shouting in the street outside. They had brought a powerful light and together the PAR opened the window and held the light out. The gang stopped. As the light fell on their faces, some turned and ran away.
"Come on," shouted one of the PAR. "Show us who you are." Most had now run away, except one youth who stood alone on the pavement. "Do you recognize him?" asked Jeff. "Rita calls him Flatface," said Mr Patel. "He's their leader. "You," shouted Jeff. "Come on, give us your name!" The youth turned and ran away.

It was over. It had been as simple as that. Rita and her family were suddenly able to sleep. It was a wonderful feeling to lead a normal life again. In the mornings she felt so great she almost ran to school. Her parents became much healthier and argued less. They were happy and friendly as they had always been before.
Then Sumit was attacked and thrown from a railway bridge on his way from school one afternoon. When Rita found the note at home that he was in hospital, she went there at once. She found her parents sitting at the bed. Sumit was not moving, his head covered in bandages. That night the shouting started outside their house again.
Sumit died two days later. A feeling of deep sadness and emptiness entered their home and their lives. The person they had all loved the most had gone for ever. Nobody in the family looked at each other. Nobody talked. The mother moved weakly around the home, like an old woman. "Why didn't I go and meet him that day?" she said again and again. "You couldn't have done anything," said Rita. "They might have attacked you, too. Take your tablets and go to bed, Mum, please."
"I don't want to take any tablets," said Rita's mother and walked slowly out of the room.
"Why don't you *do* something?" Rita suddenly shouted at her father after her mother had gone to bed. "What more can I do? I have talked to the police. I have talked to the headmaster, I have talked to the teachers. Nobody saw anything." "Nobody ever sees anything," said Rita, angry and frustrated. "Why don't they arrest somebody?"
"They can't just arrest anybody." "Dad, they can arrest Flatface." "There are laws in this country, Rita. The police need proof." "But those people don't care about laws." "Rita, *we* cannot behave like them." "You're useless!" she screamed and ran to her room.

Rita had made her preparations. She waited until her parents were in bed before she left the house. They always came at the same time and from the same direction. At midnight she walked quietly down the stairs and opened the front door. She was carrying a shopping bag. Inside was a piece of cloth from her father's shop, a box of matches, and a bottle filled with petrol. At quarter past, the gang arrived in two cars, music coming loudly from their stereos.
They were laughing as they walked along the street, past a row of garages, towards the Patels' house. From the roof of one of the garages, Rita suddenly shouted, "Flatface!"

The gang stopped. Looking up, they saw only a dark figure and a flame coming from a burning cloth. Not understanding what it was, they stopped. At that moment Rita threw the bottle.

(Based on *The Diary of Rita Patel*
by Carole Boyer, a film shown on BBC 2, 14. 9. 1988)

Working with the text

a First impressions

1. Write down in no more than five or six short sentences what happens in the story.
2. Compare what different people in your class have written. (If you can't agree on some points, note down the points and check after you have done task b what is right or wrong.)

b A closer look at the story

1. Try to reconstruct the events that lead to Rita's violent behaviour. Go through the text carefully and make notes for each of the following questions. Use your notes to retell the story. What has been going on for nearly four months? How has this affected the Patels' lives (the parents' and the children's lives)? What has Rita done to try and solve the problem? Has she had any success? How does Rita's friend Leela try to help the Patels? How does the help of the PAR affect the Patels' lives? When and why do things get worse again? Why is Rita so angry with her father? What does she finally do?

c Explaining details

1. . . . several of the windows were covered with boards where the Patels had given up repairing them. (p. 53, l. 27) – How must the Patels have reacted when the hooligans first broke the windows? Why do you think they have given up?
2. "We've had visitors again." (p. 53, l. 43) – What does Rita really mean and how does she know Leela will understand?
3. As the light fell on their faces, some turned and ran away. (p. 54, l. 7) – Why do some of the hooligans run away?
4. Nobody in the family looked at each other. (p. 54, l. 35) – What do the members of the Patel family express by this behaviour?
5. "Nobody ever sees anything." (p. 54, l. 50) – What does Rita really mean?
6. "Rita, *we* cannot behave like them." (p. 54, l. 56) – Why does Mr Patel say this?

d Looking at Rita's behaviour

1. Describe how Rita's behaviour changes in the course of the story. Go through the text and find out what causes the changes.
2. In what way might her parents', especially her father's, behaviour have influenced Rita's final decision?
3. What are possible endings for the story as the result of Rita's violent behaviour?
4. What effect on the family's and on Rita's own life might her violent behaviour have? Was it worth having "an eye for an eye"?

e What do you think?

1. Could this have happened in Germany? 2. Why do some people make life difficult, sometimes even unbearable, for minorities? 3. How should the state (the police/the government) react in such situations? 4. What advice would you have given Rita if she had asked you?

f Son of Mine by Kath Walker

My son, your troubled eyes search mine,
Puzzled and hurt by colour line.
Your black skin as soft as velvet shine;
What can I tell you, son of mine?

I could tell you of heart-break, hatred blind,
I could tell you of crimes that shame mankind.
Of brutal wrongs and deeds malign,
Of rape and murder, son of mine;

But I'll tell instead of brave and fine
When lives of black and white entwine.
And men in brotherhood combine –
This would I tell you, son of mine.

Compare this adult reaction to discrimination with Rita's reaction. Where do you see the main reason for Rita's behaviour?

→ Option 9: A one-act play: 'Neighbours with Long Teeth' → Option 18: Talking about non-fictional texts

Unit 5

Australia – the continent "down under"

Aborigine claims Britain

27.1.88

Wearing tribal paint and an anorak to protect himself against the English weather, Burnum Burnum, an Australian Aborigine, planted a flag on Folkestone beach and claimed Britain for his people. "I, Burnum Burnum," he said to television cameras, "a noble man of ancient Australia take possession of Britain for the Aboriginal people. In claiming this land, we wish no harm to you natives."
Mr Burnum looked a lonely figure with his black, red and yellow flag. No invaders followed him, and the English did not come out to defend their country.

Why do you suppose Burnum Burnum came to England in January 1988?

On the same day on the other side of the world it was the Australian national holiday, Australia Day, and white Australians were celebrating the 200th birthday of their country. In Sydney harbour, an estimated two million people welcomed the eleven ships that re-enacted the arrival of the first English colonists, mostly prisoners, who landed there on January 26th, 1788.
At the other end of the city more than 20,000 Aborigines and their supporters marched through the streets with spears and boomerangs to protest about the way their society and culture have been almost destroyed since the arrival of the first Europeans. January 26th is known as "Invasion Day" by the Aborigines.

Why do two groups of Australians use different expressions for the same things, e.g. Australia Day and Invasion Day?

Sydney Harbour during the celebrations – in the middle: the famous Opera House

→ Option 10: The settlement of Australia → Option 11: The story of Henry and Susannah

Australia: facts and figures

Population	c. 16 million
Aboriginal population	c. 230,000
Area	7.7 million sq. km
Distance from west to east	c. 4,000 km
Distance from north to south	c. 3,200 km
Capital	Canberra (population 285,800)
Largest city	Sydney (population 3,430,600)
National language	English
Currency	Australian dollar

Compare these figures with those above:

Holland	Population: c. 15 million Area: 40,800 sq. km
USA (without Alaska)	Population: c. 240 million Area: 7.8 million sq. km
Europe (without Russia)	Population: c. 500 million Area: 4.9 million sq. km

Australia is the world's largest island, with a coastline of about 30,000 km. It is the driest and flattest of all the continents. It is also the emptiest. Eighty per cent of the population live in only five per cent of the country.
Australia became an independent country in 1901 but is still a member of the British Commonwealth. The British Queen is also the Australian head of state. The country's symbols, the kangaroo and the emu, were chosen because they are the only two animals which cannot run backwards. Like their country, they can only go forwards!

→ Option 12: From Empire to European Community

Life "down under"

most Australians – live – work – towns – cities – coast, mainly – south-west – south-east / warm climate – mean – enjoy – active outdoor life / many houses – outdoor swimming-pool – barbecue / summer – not unusual – see – doctors – office workers – wear - shorts

It's not unusual to see Father Christmas on the beach in Australia

Use the information on this page to give the class a short talk about Australia. Try and explain the advantages of living there.

Australia's native people

The interior of the continent is known as the bush, or the outback. Few people live there, as there is not enough water to support much life. Yet the "dead heart", as white Australians call it, is the natural home of many Aborigines. They have always known how to find food and water in areas where white explorers died.

The Aborigines have lived on the continent for probably at least 40,000 years. But in less than 200 years their traditional way of life and culture have been almost completely destroyed. Sadly, most white settlers were interested neither in the Aborigines themselves nor their culture.

INFO BOX

- *Like Native Americans, Aborigines have been given land in the form of reservations.*
- *They suffer from unemployment (30% compared to 7% for whites), poverty, and alcoholism.*
- *Aborigines are only 1.5% of the population, but they form 30% of the country's prisoners.*
- *A white person can expect to live for 72 years, an Aborigine for only 56.*
- *Many Aborigines no longer live according to the traditional ways of their ancestors. Almost all now depend on financial help from the government.*
- *Aborigines were not given full equality till 1967.*

The Aborigines have many holy places, and they believe the land near those places should not be touched. This belief often brings them into conflict with state governments and the mining companies. Australia is one of the world's biggest suppliers of minerals and raw materials. Indeed, about 46% of Australia's exports come from mining. Unfortunately, many of these minerals happen to lie under ground that the Aborigines claim is theirs.

Ayers Rock, in the Uluru National Park, now belongs to the Aborigines. It is one of their holiest sites.

A young Aborigine man

Compare the situation of the Aborigines with that of Native Americans. What is different/similar in the historical development of Australia and the USA?

Focus on WORDS: Leaving one's home

In her letter to her sister Sarah in Australia Helen gave mainly economic reasons for her decision to leave England. Do you remember what they were?
People may also have personal or political reasons – or a +mixture of reasons – for leaving their home temporarily or +for good. A school leaver may go abroad as an +au pair or as a student, for example. Employees of multinational firms may be +transferred to another branch, and their families may have to move with them. Unemployed or badly-paid people may move to another region or to another country, e.g. within the +EC, where the job situation is better. Others apply for jobs in developing countries. People in love with somebody of a different nationality may decide to live in their partner's home country. And people persecuted for political or religious reasons may leave and ask for political +asylum in another country.

Most people have certain +expectations of what their new home will be like: a healthier climate, no nuclear power stations, better working conditions, higher wages, cheaper houses, a good university, etc.
But, of course, nobody leaves without anxieties. People may ask themselves: Will I have language problems? Will I be welcome? Will people be prejudiced? Will I have enough money? Will my children have problems at school? Will they make new friends soon?
Before people can leave, a lot of preparations have to be made. Perhaps they will have to have their passports +renewed. They might have to apply for a visa and get a work +permit. They may have to sell their house and furniture – or +give notice to their +landlord or landlady and rent a new flat. But however carefully they prepare their move, there will always be something they have not thought of.

1 Collecting and arranging words

Make a network using the four underlined words from above as starting points.

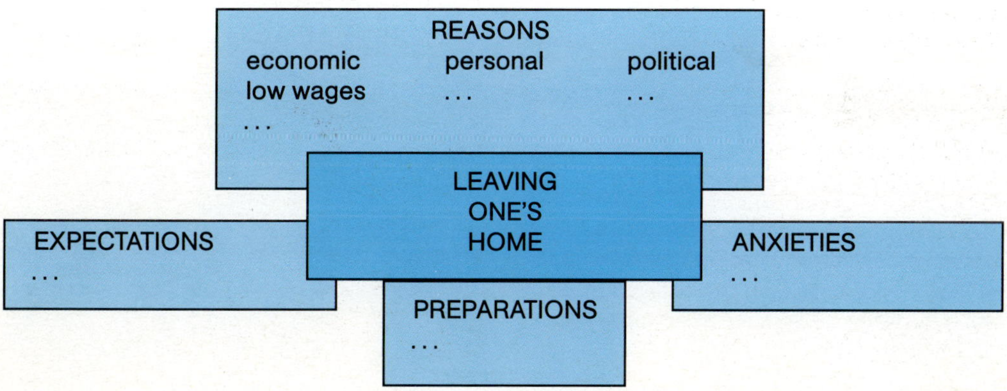

2 Words in use

a What is your dream country? Give reasons for your choice.

b Imagine your parents have decided to move to the USA. Write a letter to an American friend of theirs to find out more about the place, the people and the living conditions.

c Choose one of the following topics to write about:

1. Life in Germany as seen through the eyes of a foreign worker.
2. My first day (week/year) as an immigrant child in Germany.

Life on a sheep station

Where it is possible to live in the outback, you can find huge sheep and cattle farms (or "stations" as the Australians call them). Wool is still one of Australia's main exports.
Helen's sister Sarah has been living in Australia for ten years. She emigrated from Britain after she had married Lyle. Together with Lyle's uncle they run a sheep station in the outback of Queensland. Helen and her daughter Olivia visited them before they moved into their new home in Brisbane. In a letter to a friend, Olivia described what it was like.

The station is unbelievably big (300 square miles – that's half as big as the whole of London!). The only other family here lives seven miles away, so it can be very lonely. The nearest town (if you can call it that) is an hour away. It has two shops and a garage. If you want to go shopping properly, it means an eight-hour trip by car. Lyle and Sarah use the station's plane if they have to travel long distances.
Sarah took me for a trip over the station. As we flew over the bush, we could see thousands of sheep, the men on their motorbikes, and now and again a kangaroo which had been frightened by the noise of our plane.
Sarah's children can't possibly go to school, so the school comes to them. Every morning Melvin and Carrie sit down at their desks in their room, put on their headsets, check the microphones, switch on the radio and their computers – and lessons begin. They are taught via radio and satellite by the School of the Air. They can talk both with their teachers and other pupils and listen to what they say. They never miss a lesson – it's the only chance they have of talking to other children.
Without radios and planes people would find life here very difficult. A few days ago one of the men was injured in an accident. Lyle called for help and very soon the Flying Doctor landed outside the house. He couldn't treat the man, so he took him to hospital.

How would you like to live on an Australian sheep station and be taught – like Melvin and Carrie – by the School of the Air? What do you see as advantages/disadvantages?

Did you know . . .

. . . that there are ten times more sheep than people in Australia?
. . . that there are many forms of life – plants as well as animals – which can be found only in Australia?

The koala is one of Australia's most famous animals

Focus on GRAMMAR: *Present progressive* und *simple present* mit futurischer Bedeutung
(Present progressive and simple present with a future meaning)

a Helen and Olivia enjoyed staying on the sheep station, but like all good things, their visit soon came to an end. Lyle had been away on a business trip for a week. When he got back, Helen and Sarah were talking about Helen's travel arrangements.
"When **are** you **leaving**?" asked Lyle.
"Tuesday morning," said Helen. "Sarah **is driving** us to Cloncurry airport."
"When **does** your plane **leave**?"
"11.15. Sarah says we should leave at 7 am. Or need we leave earlier, do you think?"
"Yes, I think you need to leave by 6.30 at the latest. It's a four-hour drive to Cloncurry, don't forget. – What time **do** you **arrive** in Brisbane then?"
"Well, we **change** planes at Townsville, **wait** there for three hours and **catch** the plane to Brisbane at 4.20. It's a 90-minute flight, so we **get** there about six o'clock."

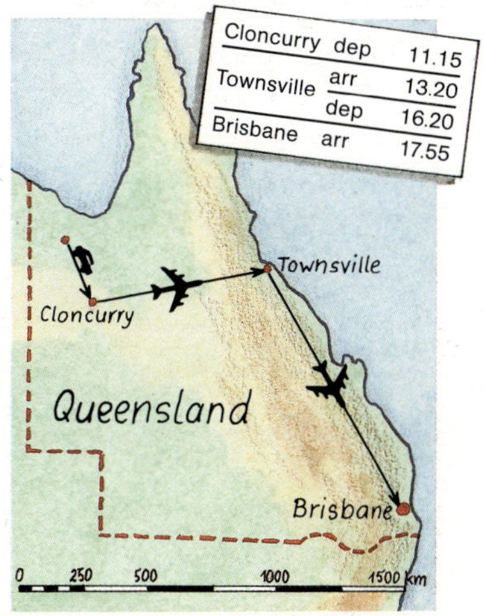

b Es gibt im Englischen verschiedene Möglichkeiten, über die Zukunft zu sprechen. Wir verwenden z.B. das *will-future, going to-future, present progressive* oder *simple present*. Welche Verbform man wählt, hängt davon ab, was man ausdrücken will (ob man z.B. eine Vorhersage macht, eine Absicht äußert oder über eine Vereinbarung spricht). → Option 26: Ways of expressing the future

c **Das *present progressive* mit futurischer Bedeutung**

Helen and Olivia **are leaving** the sheep station next Tuesday morning.
How **are** they **getting** to the airport? – Sarah **is driving** them there.

Mit dem *present progressive* drücken wir aus, daß etwas Zukünftiges konkret geplant oder persönlich vereinbart wurde. Daß sich das *present progressive* hier auf die Zukunft bezieht, muß durch Zeitbestimmungen (z.B. *next Tuesday morning*) oder aus dem Zusammenhang deutlich werden. → Ex 1

d **Das *simple present* in Hauptsätzen mit futurischer Bedeutung**

Helen's plane **leaves** at 16.20.
It **arrives** in Brisbane at 17.55.

When **do** Helen's holidays **begin/end** this year?
Christmas Day **falls** on a Wednesday this year.

Mit dem *simple present* in Hauptsätzen drücken wir aus, daß etwas Zukünftiges durch einen Zeitplan (z.B. Fahrplan, Kalender, amtliche Bekanntmachungen) festgelegt ist *("timetable future")*. Diese Verwendung ist häufig bei Verben wie *leave, arrive, begin, end, open, close*.

⚠ Ansonsten kann das *simple present* in der Regel nicht mit Bezug auf die Zukunft verwendet werden. → Ex 2

e **Das *simple present* in Nebensätzen mit futurischer Bedeutung**

Helen and Olivia will have a farewell party on the Saturday before they **leave**.
When they **arrive** in Brisbane, they'll ring up Sarah and Lyle.
If they **leave** for the airport at 6.15 in the morning, they'll have enough time.

In Nebensätzen der Zeit (nach *before, when, while, as soon as, as long as, till/until*) oder der Bedingung (nach *if, unless*) wird ein zukünftiges Geschehen mit dem *simple present* (⚠ nicht mit dem *will-future*) ausgedrückt. Daß sich das *simple present* in diesem Fall auf die Zukunft bezieht, wird aus dem Hauptsatz deutlich, in dem eine Form des Futurs (meist das *will-future* oder das *going to-future*) stehen muß.

1 Revision: The present progressive with a future meaning

Helen and Olivia's last days on the sheep station *Complete the questions and the answers with the correct form of the verbs and find the correct answer to each question.*

1. *Lyle:* Have you invited the Tanners to Helen and Olivia's farewell party?
2. *Lyle:* (they/stay) overnight or (they/drive) back after the party?
3. *Helen:* Olivia, (you/come) to the shops with Sarah and me tomorrow?
4. *Lyle:* What (you/prepare) for Saturday evening?
5. *Olivia:* How (we/get) to the airport on Tuesday?
6. *Helen:* (you/come) to the airport with us, Melvin?
7. *Olivia:* (we/spend) Christmas with Sarah and Lyle this year?

"Yes, Charlie – I'm pretty sure she is giving me a cordless telephone."

a) *Helen:* Sarah (take) us there after breakfast.
b) *Melvin:* No, I (stay) at home. I don't want to miss my lessons.
c) *Sarah:* Yes, and they (bring) one of their sons along, too.
d) *Helen:* No, I would like to spend it on the beach in Brisbane this year.
e) *Olivia:* No, Lyle (drive) out to look after some sheep, and Carrie, Melvin and I (go) with him.
f) *Sarah:* We don't have to prepare much. I (go) shopping with Helen tomorrow.
g) *Sarah:* They (sleep) here and (go) home early on Monday morning.

2 What's on next weekend?

135th Year, No 41,739 — **THE AGE** — 108 pages, 40 cents

PLAYBOX THEATRE
Last two shows!
THE KID
by M. Glow
Fri. 8 PM; $7 (all seats)
Sat. 8.15 PM; $9 (all seats)

CARLTON MOVIE-HOUSE
Tonight all seats $5
5.30 PM
WORKING GIRL
9.15 PM
TWINS

COBURG DRIVE-IN
Tomorrow, Friday, 13th
All places 1/2 price
6.45 PM, 8.30 PM, 10.15 PM
YOUNG EINSTEIN

THE WEEKEND AUSTRALIAN — **TV on Saturday**

CHANNEL 2
10.25 Roby On The Road
10.35 Cartoon Show
11.00 Saturday Morning Live
12.50 Movie: Friend or Enemy?
A teenager must decide between stealing to help a friend or protecting an old lady.

WOLLONGONG WIN 4
8.25 PM News
8.30 PM Movie: Perry Mason Returns. (1985)
Perry defends his secretary Della Street when he hears people say she has murdered her present boss.
10.30 PM Night Football

a *Ask each other questions about the next weekend. Use the simple present with a future meaning. Examples:*
What time is *Young Einstein* on? What's on at the Carlton tonight? When does the Perry Mason film finish? What's on Channel 2 this Saturday?
Go on.

b *Make up some mini-dialogues in which you use the simple present with a future meaning. Example:*
Can you go shopping for me before *Friend or Enemy* starts? – When does it start?
Go on.

3 Revision: Simple present or simple past, active or passive?

Do you know the answers to these questions? – You will find them at the bottom of the page.

1. Why (the Middle Ages/often/call) the "Dark Ages"? 2. What letter (never/find) in the alphabet? 3. What (go) up and down the hill but never (move)? 4. If (mother's day/father's day/invent) as special days, why (they/not invent) a son's day? 5. Why (be) the letter "a" like a sweet-smelling flower? 6. What (happen) when people (dial) 666?

4 Amy Johnson (1903-41) – airwoman

Write a text with the information given. In the boxes on the right you will find some help.

born – Kingston upon Hull – July 7th, 1903 – oldest daughter – fish importer John Johnson and his wife Amy / secondary school – Hull – student – Sheffield University – take – final exam – 1925

> Amy Johnson was . . . in . . . on . . . as . . . . She went . . . and later . . . at . . . where . . . in . . . .

finish – university course – move – London / work there – secretary – all her free time – London Aeroplane[1] Club / become – first woman – Britain – ground engineer's licence[2] – licence – fly

> Soon after . . . , she . . . . While she . . . , she . . . at . . . . She . . . who . . . and a short time later . . . .

never – fly further – London-Hull – start – long-distance solo-flight – Australia – May 5th, 1930 / take six days – Karachi, Pakistan – record for that distance / have to face – difficulties – flight / force – land – Rangoon, Burma – bad weather / May 24th, 1930 – Darwin, Australia

> Although . . .than from . . . , she . . . to . . . on . . . . It only . . . , which . . . . But from there on . . . . She . . . in . . . , for example, because of . . . . However, on . . . she finally . . . .

two more record-breaking long-distance flights: 1931 London-Tokyo-London; 1932 London-Cape Town-London

> In the following two years . . . ; In . . . and in . . . .

beginning of the Second World War – start working – British government / June 1941 – one of her flights – plane – crash – the Thames / die – accident / not known – plane – crash

> At . . . . In . . . , on . . . , . . . into . . . . She . . . in . . . . It . . . why . . . .

[1] aeroplane ['eərəpleɪn] = *plane* [2] ground engineer's licence ['laɪsəns] *Zulassung als Bodeningenieur/in*

○ **5 Listening comprehension: Life on the sheep station** *Listen to the cassette, then answer these questions.*

1. Do Carrie and Melvin like having lessons via radio? 2. Who helps them with their homework? 3. What's a "flying doctor"? 4. What was Olivia surprised about? 5. Why aren't the dogs allowed in the house?

1. There (be) so many „knights" *(Ritter)*. 2. The one that (lose) in yesterday's post. 3. A road. 4. There (be) a „Sunday" every week. 5. It (follow) by a „bee" *(Biene)* in the alphabet. 6. The phone (answer) by a police officer standing on her/his head.

How to emphasize words (Möglichkeiten, etwas hervorzuheben)

Remember: You already know two ways of emphasizing words:

a) Only a small number of settlers were able to understand an Aboriginal language, but even fewer were able to speak one.

The simplest way is to stress the words that are of importance when you speak.

⚠ Compare: Alan understands some Aboriginal words. (But Tony doesn't.)
Alan understands some Aboriginal words. (But he can't speak an Aboriginal language.)

b) The Aborigines **themselves** spoke at least one other language than their own. I would like to learn some Aboriginal words **myself**.

To emphasize a noun or pronoun, you can use a *-self/-selves* pronoun. Put the *-self/-selves* pronoun after the noun or pronoun that you want to emphasize or at the end of the sentence.
The main stress is on the *-self/-selves* pronoun.

→ Ex 6a

c) Here is another way of emphasizing a statement:

1. Today you can meet many Aborigines who speak English. But some of them **do** have problems with some of the sounds of English.
2. Although it was difficult, a few settlers **did** understand and speak an Aboriginal language.
3. **Do** go to Yirara College in Alice Springs if you want to get some more information about Aboriginal languages and culture.
4. In Aboriginal languages you don't find many words for buildings or furniture. But Aborigines **do** have a lot of words for all outdoor things.

To emphasize a statement (often to contrast it with a negative statement), you can stress the auxiliary verb. In simple present sentences use *do/does (+ infinitive)*, in simple past sentences use *did (+ infinitive)*, and before an imperative use *do*.

→ Ex 6b

6 What people say about Aboriginal life and history

a *Complete the sentences with a -self/-selves pronoun.*

1. Scientists say we've lived here for at least 40,000 years, but we . . . believe we've lived here since the beginning of time. 2. Many people speak of the "discovery" of Australia by Cook. As an Aborigine, I . . . prefer to call it an invasion. 3. At first the British said that we didn't have a culture. It took a long time before they . . . began to understand that we have a different culture. 4. Fortunately, the Prime Minister . . . has now promised to help us. 5. I'm very glad . . . that one leading white politician called the 1988 celebrations "tasteless". 6. You white Australians can't understand our situation because you've never been in a similar situation . . .

b *Emphasize the following statements. Use a form of "do".*

1. I'm pleased that the Aborigines finally achieved equality in 1967. 2. As a politician I can only say: Let's help the Aborigines to live the life they want to live. 3. Not long ago a white friend said to me that he finds it difficult to accept that there are two nations within this country. 4. Today at least our teachers tell their pupils how unjustly Aborigines were and in some ways still are treated. 5. It's hard to believe how our ancestors treated the Aborigines in the 19th century. 6. It's a sign of hope, I think, that more and more white people accept what the Aborigines are asking for.

→ Option 15: Translation practice, p. 111

7 WORDS WORDS WORDS

a Adjectives and participles used as nouns

1. Adjectives and participles used as nouns **to refer to people:**
In German many adjectives and participles can be used as nouns to refer to people (e.g. *tot – der/die Tote*). In English you usually have to add *man, woman, people* etc. Compare:

dieser Arme	this poor man	eine Arbeitslose	an unemployed woman
diese Armen	these poor people	mehrere Arbeitslose	several unemployed people
die Armen, Arme	(the) poor people	die Arbeitslosen, Arbeitslose	(the) unemployed people

In English we can use a few adjectives as nouns, too, but only if we want to refer to **a whole group of people**. We must use them **with the definite article** ***the*****: the poor – die Armen** (= alle Armen dieser Stadt, dieses Landes usw.), **the unemployed – die Arbeitslosen** (= alle Arbeitslosen dieser Stadt, dieses Landes usw.). They have no plural *-s* but are followed by a plural verb:

The deaf usually attend special schools.

Further examples: *the blind, the dead, the disabled, the healthy, the homeless, the hungry, the injured, the living, the lonely, the old, the rich, the sick, the weak, the young.*

Note: Adjectives like *black, white, native, Catholic, Protestant, Conservative* have become "real" nouns. They can be used with the indefinite article and have a plural ending in *-s*.

2. Adjectives used as nouns **to refer to things or ideas:**

In most films the good wins over the bad in the end.
(In den meisten Filmen siegt am Ende das Gute über das Böse.)

Adjectives can be used as nouns **with the definite article** to talk about things or ideas **in general**. In this case they are followed by a singular verb.
If we have a particular aspect in mind, we must add *thing:*

The good thing about this new computer is that it works twice as fast.
(Das Gute an diesem neuen Computer ist, daß er doppelt so schnell arbeitet.)

In English, please

1. Einige Arbeitslose geben zu schnell die Hoffnung auf. 2. In den letzten Jahren haben viele Städte besondere Busse für Behinderte angeschafft. 3. Das Wichtigste ist, daß du bald wieder gesund wirst. 4. Viele Kirchen laden Obdachlose und Einsame ein, gemeinsam Weihnachten zu feiern. 5. Die Regierung kann nicht alle Probleme der Arbeitslosen lösen. 6. Das Faszinierendste an dieser Stadt ist der Kontrast zwischen dem Alten und dem Neuen. 7. Viele Organisationen versuchen, den Kranken und Schwachen in der Dritten Welt zu helfen. 8. ‚Die Frau, die keine Augen hatte' ist die Geschichte einer Blinden. 9. Als Gesunder kann man oft nicht verstehen, wie Kranke sich fühlen. 10. Viele Menschen haben Angst vor dem Unbekannten. 11. Das Schöne an diesem Beruf ist, daß ich viel reisen kann. 12. Gestern abend gab es eine interessante Radiosendung: ‚Die Jungen und die Alten'.

b Missing words

⚠ *The following sentences are* ***wrong as they stand****. In each sentence one word is missing. Find the word and put it in the right place.*

1. Can I speak Mrs Jones, please? 2. There are a lot people out of work in this country. 3. When we came home a stranger was waiting in front the house. 4. The city Heidelberg has a very famous university. 5. Could I have a glass water, please? 6. This problem can only be solved with help of computers. 7. Could you explain me why these disks are so expensive? 8. This book isn't mine, I think it belongs Peter. 9. I haven't made mistakes in my test.

Friday, 12th January. The three boys, Harry, Wallace and Graham, had escaped from the city for a week of freedom in the bush. They had never done it before. The boys caught a morning train to the hills, got out at Barkley station and started walking. They felt wonderful. They were on their own. No one to say 'Do this', 'Do that'. They wouldn't have wanted to be anywhere on earth but where they were, walking up the road from Barkley towards Tinley. The north wind blew, a hot summer wind, and there was not a cloud in the sky. Here a boy could be king of the earth, thought Graham. He often wondered why Wallace and Harry accepted him. Wallace was a big, strong boy. Harry, on the other hand, was clever, but also the best runner in the school. Graham was neither strong nor clever. He was unusually gentle for his fifteen years.

Bush Fire

For their lunch they dug a small hole and collected sticks and made a small fire at the side of the road to cook their sausages and boil water for coffee. Coffee, they felt, good and strong, was the kind of drink a man would have when he was on his own. The water hadn't even started to boil in the billy-can when a car stopped and a woman called to them: "Put that fire out!"

The boys looked at her, surprised. She was like an angry school teacher. "You heard me," she said. "Put it out."

"We're only havin' our lunch, lady," said Wallace. "What's wrong with that?"

"You boys are old enough to know better. Put it out at once, or I'll report you to the police. There's a $200 fine and you can go to prison for making a fire outside on a day like this."

"It's only a little fire," complained Wallace. "We've dug a hole. We're watchin' it."

"Put it out quickly. Throw your water over it."

"Be fair, lady," said Wallace. "What do we drink? It's a hot day."

It was Harry who lifted the billy off with a stick and emptied the water into the hole. He had suddenly noticed how hot and strong the north wind was, how it blew the flames and the smoke.

"Now stand on it," the woman called. "Get it out. Put it all out."

She watched them with a strict expression on her face until they had done it; then she said, "If you want hot water on a day like this, go into a house somewhere and ask for it nicely. Fire is a dangerous toy at this time of year. Don't forget it."

She drove on, and the boys were left looking at each other sadly. "Toy, my fat aunt," said Wallace.

"Wouldn't it make you sick?" said Graham.

"I suppose she was right, though," said Harry.

"We were watchin' it. It couldn't have done any harm." Wallace was very upset. "If we can't make a fire, what are we goin' to eat and drink? What about our sausages?" "I don't know," said Graham.

"It's *stupid*. All right for her. She can go home and switch on the stove. Grown-ups. You can't get away from them. Two hundred dollar fine for cooking your lunch. Go to prison for drinkin' coffee. I suppose we're expected to die of hunger."

"We've got some buns," said Harry.

"*Buns*!"

"And we can drink water."

"Whose side are you on? I want *coffee* and *sausages*."

Another car going in the opposite direction stopped. At the wheel was a man who looked like a farmer. "You boys aren't making a fire, are you?" he said. "No," said Wallace. "Make sure you don't."

They had buns for lunch, and water. Much of the magic of the day had already gone sour on them. The north wind blew, hot and hard and dry. Behind it lay two thousand miles of land, brown in the burning sun. The wind itself was like fire without the flame.

When they got to Tinley they bought pies and cokes and ice-creams and more sausages to take away with them, and a tiny heater that burned methylated spirits with a hot blue flame and no smoke. They hadn't gone much more than a mile from Tinley towards the hills when Wallace said, "I'm tired. Let's find somethin' and camp."

Wallace was half-asleep. He thought he could smell methylated spirits. He even thought he could see Graham.

"What are you doin'?" "Making coffee," said Graham. "Do you want a cup?" Wallace sat up. "What's the time?" "Twenty past one." "Yeah. I'll have a cup." Wallace opened his sleeping bag and felt better. "Funny in the bush at night, isn't it? Awful dark."

"Noisy, too. I heard a tree fall down. Not far away either. Woke me up." "It's the wind." "Guess so." "Hot, isn't it?" "You can say that again. But this water's awful slow in boiling."

"The wind, I suppose. Have you got the lid on?" "Can't see when it boils if you've got the lid on." "Put the lid on, or it'll never boil."

"Don't know where the lid is, do you?"

"*Feel* for it. It's there somewhere. Use your torch." "The battery's flat. *Now* look what I've done. The metho bottle has fallen over." "Pick it up quick," cried Wallace. "Or we'll lose it all."

"It's *burning*," shouted Graham.

A blue flame raced from the little stove up through the rocks towards the bottle in the boy's hand: or at least that was how it seemed to happen. It happened so quickly. To protect himself, Graham threw the bottle away. There was a shower of fire from its neck. "Oh no," shouted Wallace and jumped out of his sleeping bag. "Harry!" he screamed. "Harry, wake up."

They tried to jump on the fire, but they couldn't find their shoes. They tried to put it out with their sleeping bags, but it seemed to be everywhere. Harry couldn't even escape from his bag; and for a few awful moments he thought he was in his bed at home and the house was in flames around him.

"Put it out," shouted Graham. "Put it out."

The fire was getting away from them in all directions, burning through the bush downwind. Even the ground was burning; grass, roots and fallen leaves were burning. There were flames on the trees. The heat was awful to breathe.

"We can't, we can't," cried Wallace. "What are we going to do?" They beat at it and beat at it and beat at it. "Oh no," sobbed Graham. He was crying, and he hadn't cried since he was twelve years old.

"What have I done? *We've got to put it out!*"

Harry was running around wildly, picking up all their things. He screamed at them. "Get your stuff and run." But they didn't hear him or didn't want to hear him. They were black, their feet were cut, even their hair was burned. They beat and beat and the fire was everywhere, in the tree-tops, and there was no darkness left, only bright light, red light, yellow light, light that was hard and cruel and very frightening, and there was smoke, smoke like a hot red fog.

"No," cried Graham. "No, no, no." His arms dropped to his sides and he shook with sobs and Wallace pulled him away. "Oh Wally," he sobbed. "What have I done?"

"We've got to get out of here," shouted Harry. "Take the things and run."

They ran down a path back towards Tinley; at least they thought it was towards Tinley, they didn't really know. Perhaps they were running to save their lives, running because they were afraid, running away from what they had done. When they thought they were safe, they hid in the bush. They could hear sirens; lights were going on here and there; the lights of cars along the roads. They could hear shouts on the wind, they heard a woman cry, they heard Graham sobbing. Over all was a red glow.

(Adapted from *Ash Road* by Ivan Southall)

Working with the text

a **First impressions**

1. What do you think the area looks like where the story takes place?
2. What is suggested by the last paragraph of the text?

b **A closer look at the text**

1. Look at the way in which the three boys behave and what they say. Make notes about them.
2. How do the boys react to what the woman tells them in the first part of the text? How do they comment on what she tells them to do when they speak to each other? How do you explain the difference between their behaviour and their comments?
3. Why do you think the boys bought a stove in Tinley?
4. What do these sentences tell you? Explain each of them in at least two sentences.
   a) "There's a $200 fine and you can go to prison for making a fire outside on a day like this." (p. 66, l. 17)
   b) "Fire is a dangerous toy at this time of year." (p. 66, l. 35)
   c) Much of the magic of the day had already gone sour on them. (p. 66, l. 63)
   d) "Funny in the bush at night, isn't it? Awful dark." (p. 67, l. 14)
   e) "Oh Wally," he sobbed. "What have I done?" (p. 67, l. 71)
5. Have a look at Option 17 (How to write a summary) and then write a short summary of the story.

c **Beyond the text**

1. Imagine that after the fire the woman in the car is questioned by the police. Write the dialogue.
2. Write a newspaper report: "Bushfire in Tinley area".
3. Do you think Ivan Southall has succeeded in presenting the boys' behaviour realistically (their wish to be free; making the fire; hiding when they can't put out the fire)? Why/Why not?

→ Option 19: Extensive reading

○ Song: Click go the shears

1. Out on the board the old shearer stands,
   Grasping his shears in his thin bony hands;
   Fixed is his gaze on a bare-bellied yoe,
   Glory if he gets her, won't he make the ringer go.

Chorus
Click go the shears boys, click, click, click,
Wide is his blow and his hands move quick.
The ringer looks around and is beaten by a blow,
And curses the old snagger with the bare-bellied yoe.

2. In the middle of the floor in his cane bottomed chair
   Sits the boss of the board with his eyes everywhere,
   Notes well each fleece as it comes to the screen,
   Paying strict attention that it's taken off clean.

3. Now the shearing is all over, we've all got our cheques,
   So it's roll up your swags and it's off down the track,
   The first pub we come to it's there we'll have a spree
   And everyone that comes along it's 'Have a drink with me.'

English: A world language

Have you ever thought how much English you actually see and hear around you every day – maybe real English, or simply English words being used in German? Here are some examples:

- Comment on the pictures. Say where and why English is used quite often in Germany.
- Make a list of English words that you regularly see or hear and put them into groups, e.g. cornflakes, grapefruit, toast, ... (food); jeans, T-shirt, ... (clothes); ... (pop music); ... (computers), etc.
- Many English words have been taken over into German and are used in everyday conversations, such as 'OK', 'super'. Can you think of more examples?
- Can you think of any jobs in Germany for which you need English? Give examples of how you might use it.
- Have *you* ever used English in situations outside the classroom? If so, describe them.

English around the world

The population of Britain is only about 57 million. But throughout the world English is spoken by over 700 million people.

- *About 350 million people speak English as their first or native language in countries such as the USA, Canada, Australia, New Zealand and South Africa.*
- *A further 300 million use English as a second or official language in over 60 countries (e.g. India), usually when doing business, or when completing official documents and forms.*
- *It is estimated that at least 100 million people throughout the world use English fluently as a foreign language.*

Maritsa Heiden (16)
Amsterdam, Holland
Native language: Dutch

"Holland is only a small country. Hardly anyone outside Holland wants to learn Dutch, so we use English as a *lingua franca*. If we didn't, we'd have nobody to speak to when we travel to other countries and meet people of other nationalities."

Ana da Gama (36)
Rio de Janeiro, Brazil
Native language: Portuguese

Ana – a doctor / her profession – English – necessary – if – keep up to date – latest techniques – developments in medicine / medical articles – often written – English

- Say in which countries English is used as a native language or as an official language.
- Use the prompts to make texts similar to Maritsa's about these different people.

Why English?

There are over 3,000 languages in the world. So why has English become so widely spoken?

From about 1600, explorers, adventurers, settlers and soldiers went out from Britain to found settlements and colonies overseas. They took the English language with them. At the height of their power, during the 19th century, the British could claim that the sun never set on their Empire. Today almost all the countries of the old Empire have become independent. However, most of them are now members of the Commonwealth of Nations, and English continues to be an important language for them.

Nginga Ibon (15)
Accra, Ghana
Native language: Ga

In many countries – knowledge of English – essential – if – want – a good job / Nginga – work – international bank – leave school / exams – English

Mijo Tochita (33)
Tokyo, Japan
Native language: Japanese

company – Mijo – work for – plan big deals – Arab world / nobody – Arabic – Arabs – not know Japanese – meetings – English

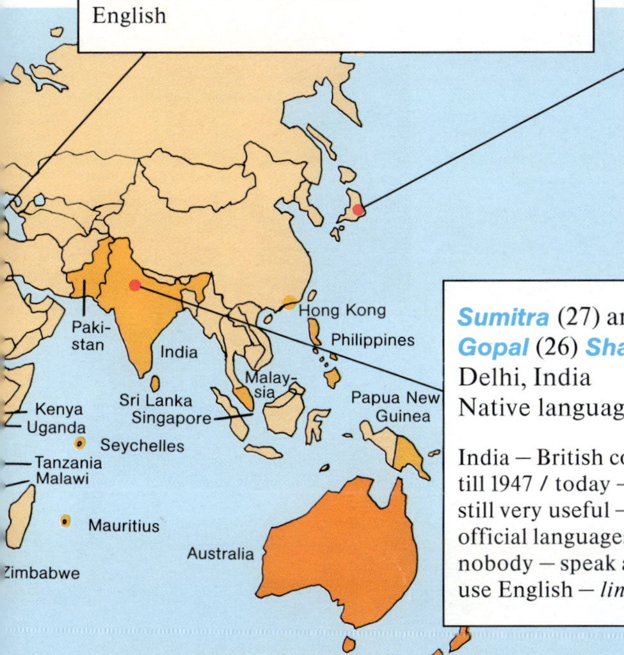

Sumitra (27) and **Gopal** (26) **Sharma**
Delhi, India
Native language: Hindi

India – British colony – 1858 till 1947 / today – English – still very useful – 15 other official languages – India / nobody – speak all of them – use English – *lingua franca*

- Why is English important for these people?
- Can you think of any jobs in which Germans might need English to work abroad?

After the Second World War the United States became what Britain had been in the 19th century: politically and economically the most powerful nation in the world. As its power spread, so the English language spread.
In Germany, many teenagers improve their English by listening to AFN radio.

Finally, with the development of computer technology and the explosion of information, English truly became a global language. Today over 80 % of the information stored in the world's computers is written in English. Over two thirds of the world's scientists write in English and three quarters of the world's mail is written in English.
English is the main language of the business world, of international travel, airports and air-traffic control, of electronics and computer technology; it dominates international politics, medicine, sports, pop music and advertising.

→ Option 13: The development of the English language

6 A

Different "Englishes" . . .

. . . around the world

Although 'English' is spoken throughout the world, there are, of course, many varieties of English, for example, British English, American English, Australian English or Indian English. People speaking these varieties of English can understand each other with no great difficulty, and you should have few problems understanding them. But there are a number of differences. The most important, obviously, is pronunciation, but vocabulary and grammar can also vary.

Listen to the people on the cassette.
Make notes about what they say about themselves, the countries they come from and the kind of English they speak.

. . . and in the UK

Different kinds of English can also be heard within the UK. Most native speakers speak English with a regional accent. This can often tell you where they are from, for example whether they are Welsh, Scots, Northern English, or whether they come from cities like Birmingham, Liverpool or Newcastle.

Listen now to these young people as they talk about themselves and where they live.

Fiona McKay, 16, Edinburgh

Sudhamani Parekh, 18, Leeds

Kirsty McCall, 17, Belfast

Gwyneth Thomas, 16, Bangor

Oliver Weaver, 15, St Albans

Jeff Turner, 21, Wigan

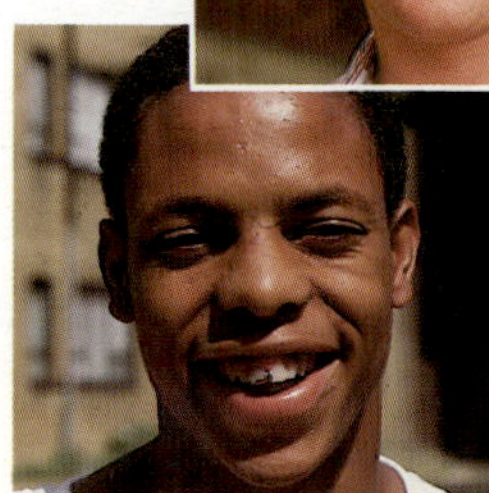

Vance Johnson, 17, London

INFO BOX

Most people in Britain speak Standard British English with a regional accent. Few people in Britain today speak a broad dialect, although dialects were once spoken in many parts of the country. A dialect is a variety of a language that is spoken in a certain part of the country and whose grammar, pronunciation and vocabulary are different from other forms of the same language. For example, "I ain't done nothing" for "I haven't done anything", or "I wants" for "I want". Dialects should not be confused with accent or slang.

- *What do you know about other languages in the UK?*

→ Option 20: A question of style: formal, neutral, informal

Focus on WORDS: Language and language learning

Why do people all over the world learn foreign languages? Perhaps because the world is getting smaller, in a way: nations are more closely linked with each other than ever before, companies +operate world-wide, scientists of different nationalities +co-operate, and tourists travel practically everywhere. The ability to communicate with people from other countries is getting more and more important. And learning foreign languages broadens your +horizons, too!
Before learners of a foreign language are able to communicate, they have to +acquire many +skills. They must learn to produce +unfamiliar sounds, like [θ] in English. They must build up a vocabulary. They must learn grammar rules and how to use them. And, +last but not least, they must develop listening, speaking, reading and writing skills and learn how to react in a variety of situations.

1 Collecting words: Add more words related to language learning to the following groups.

a **What can a language or a language variety be like?**

It can be
- clear, easy to learn, simple, . . .
- +artificial, formal, nonstandard, slang, . . .
- dirty, +offensive, polite, . . .

b **What do we do with language?**

We
- speak, understand, +master, . . . a language.
- describe things, ideas, . . .
- express expectations, feelings, needs, . . .
- apologize, complain, defend ourselves, protest, . . .

c **Where is language used?**

It is used
- in adverts, +instructions, notes, signs, warnings, . . .
- in books, magazines, . . . , on TV, . . .
- in +novels, plays, reports, stories, . . .
- in conversations, speeches, . . .

d **How do we master a foreign language?**

We
- learn how to combine, pronounce, spell, . . . words.
- learn how to ask questions, get information, give advice, . . .
- listen to cassettes, work in the language +lab, write essays, . . .

2 Arranging words: Make a network with *speak* as the starting word.

3 Words in use

a Besides English you are probably learning French or Latin at school. What were the reasons for your choice? Which language do you think is easier, English or your second foreign language? Should more foreign languages, such as Spanish, Russian or Japanese, be taught at school? Do you think that a basic vocabulary and basic grammar would be enough? Give your opinion.

b If German is a second language for you, tell your classmates about the difficulties you had or still have, and about some of the main differences between your native language and German.

c In 1874, a 15-year-old Polish boy, Ludwig Zamenhof, had the idea of creating an international language which was easy to learn: Esperanto. Collect information about Esperanto from your school library and write a short essay discussing its advantages and disadvantages.

Focus on GRAMMAR: Das Nomen (The noun)

1 Die Einteilung der Nomen (Noun classes)

a **Eigennamen** (Proper names or proper nouns): Tim, Mrs Brown, New York, Europe, the Thames, ...

b **Gattungsnamen** (Common nouns): book, knife, air, child, clothes, nature, idea, independence, ...
Gattungsnamen können zählbar *(countable)* oder nicht zählbar *(uncountable)* sein.

2 Unterschiede zwischen zählbaren und nicht-zählbaren Nomen
(Differences between countable and uncountable nouns)

This song is great. – **These songs are** great.
I'm looking for **a job**.
I need **two eggs/some eggs/a few eggs**.
How many £1 coins do you need?

Zählbare Nomen
– haben einen Singular und einen Plural,
– können mit *a/an* oder mit Zahlen verwendet werden,
– stehen mit *some* (+ Plural), *few, a few, many, how many, a number of, several, every, each.*

This music is great.
I'm looking for **work**.
I need **some salt/a little salt**.
How much money do you need?

Nicht-zählbare Nomen
– haben keinen Plural, und das zugehörige Verb steht immer im Singular,
– können nicht mit *a/an* oder mit Zahlen verwendet werden,
– stehen mit *some, little, a little, much, how much, a (little) bit of.*

Einige Nomen sind je nach Bedeutung zählbar oder nicht zählbar:

Mary drank **two glasses** of milk.
I bought **a paper** (= eine Zeitung).

I cut my hand on **some** broken **glass**.
I bought **some paper** (= etwas Papier).

3 Nicht-zählbare Nomen (Uncountable nouns)

a **Die Angabe bestimmter Mengen bei nicht-zählbaren Nomen**

some milk → **a bottle of** milk
some bread → **three loaves of** bread
some toast → **two pieces of** toast
some ham → **200 grams of** ham

Wenn wir eine bestimmte Menge eines nicht-zählbaren Nomens bezeichnen wollen, müssen wir eine zählbare Mengenbezeichnung wie *a bottle of, two pieces of* usw. vor das nicht-zählbare Nomen setzen.

Bei Bestellungen in Gaststätten werden nicht-zählbare Nomen oft wie zählbare verwendet, z. B.:
A tea and **two coffees**, please. = A cup of tea and two cups of coffee, please. → Ex 1

b **Die nicht-zählbaren Nomen *news, damage* usw.**

This/That	**news**	**sounds** interesting.	Diese Nachricht/en ...
Much	**damage**	**was** caused by the floods.	Viel Schaden/Viele Schäden ...
Some	**progress**	**has** been made so far.	Ein gewisser Fortschritt/Gewisse Fortschritte ...
Whose	**homework**	**hasn't** been checked yet?	Wessen Hausaufgabe/n ... ?
All this	**furniture**	**is** made of plastic.	Alle diese Möbel(stücke) ...

News, damage usw. sind im Gegensatz zu ihren deutschen Entsprechungen nicht zählbar. Sie können also nicht mit *a/an* verwendet werden und haben keinen Plural. Das zugehörige Verb steht immer im Singular. Ebenfalls nicht zählbar sind *advice* (Rat/schläge), *information* (Information/en, Auskunft/Auskünfte), *evidence* (Beweis/e), *knowledge* (Kenntnis/se), *housework* (Hausarbeit/en), *hair* (Haar/e).

Wir können *a piece* (oder: *two pieces*) *of news/information/advice/evidence/furniture* verwenden, um zu sagen, daß eine oder mehrere bestimmte, einzelne Nachrichten usw. gemeint sind, z. B.:
I've got **two** important **pieces of news** to tell you. – Let me give you **a piece of advice.**

4 Nomen, die nur als Plural stehen (Plural nouns)

a Die Pluralformen *clothes, handlebars, stairs, outskirts*

	Clothes	**are** quite expensive here.	Kleidung ist hier ziemlich teuer.
The	**handlebars**	**are** still too high.	Der Lenker ist immer noch zu hoch.
These/Those	**stairs**	**lead** to our flat.	Diese/Die Treppe führt zu unserer Wohnung.
The city's	**outskirts**	**are** very beautiful.	Die Außenbezirke der Stadt sind sehr schön.

⚠ Obwohl *the United States (the USA)* eine Pluralform ist, steht das zugehörige Verb im Singular:
The United States/USA consists of 50 states. = Die USA bestehen aus 50 Staaten.

b Die Gruppenbezeichnungen *police, people, cattle* sowie *the young, the poor* usw.

The	**police**	**have** caught the criminal.	Die Polizei hat den Verbrecher gefaßt.
A few	**people**	**were** very upset.	Einige Leute waren sehr bestürzt.
These/Those	**cattle**	**aren't** ours.	Dieses/Das Vieh gehört uns nicht.
The	**poor**	**get** poorer.	Die Armen werden ärmer.

c „Paarwörter"

I can't find my **glasses**. Have you seen **them**? — I think **they're** on the table.
Ich kann meine **Brille** nicht finden. Hast du **sie** gesehen? — Ich glaube, **sie ist** auf dem Tisch.

„Paarwörter" *(pair nouns)* bezeichnen Dinge, die aus zwei gleichen Teilen bestehen. Sie werden daher nur im Plural gebraucht. Sie dürfen nicht mit *a/an* oder mit Zahlen verbunden werden. Weitere Beispiele:

	Shorts	**are** cheaper this summer.	Kurze Hosen sind ...
My	**trousers**	**are** made of cotton.	Meine Hose ist ...
These/Those	**pyjamas**	**aren't** mine.	Dieser Schlafanzug gehört ...
A lot of	**binoculars**	**are** imported from Japan.	Viele Ferngläser werden ...

Wenn wir eine bestimmte Anzahl eines Paarwortes angeben wollen, müssen wir *a/one pair of* oder *two/three/several pairs of* vor das Paarwort setzen, z.B.:
I've only got **one pair of** clean **trousers**. — Luckily I've got **two pairs of glasses**.

→ Ex 2, 3

Problems when using a noun? — Why not use a dictionary?

As you have seen, it is important to know whether an English noun is countable, uncountable or can only be used with a plural verb. If you are not sure, an English dictionary can help you. Here are some noun entries from the *Oxford Student's Dictionary of Current English*. What abbreviations are used to mark countable, uncountable and plural nouns?

but·ter /ˈbʌtə(r)/ *nu* **1** a yellow fatty food substance made from milk, used on bread, in cooking etc. **2** a food substance similar to butter, made from other materials: *peanut butter*.

child /tʃaɪld/ *nc* (*pl* **children** /ˈtʃɪldrən/) **1** a young human being. **2** a son or daughter.

paint·ing /ˈpeɪntɪŋ/ *n* **1** *nu* the practice, art, of using paint. **2** *nu* the occupation of a painter. **3** *nc* a painted picture.

mys·tery /ˈmɪstərɪ/ *n* (*pl* **-ies**) **1** *nc* something of which the cause or origin is impossible to explain or understand: *The murder is an unsolved mystery*. **2** *nu* the quality, state, of being mysterious: *Agatha Christie's books are filled with mystery*.

in·for·ma·tion /ˌɪnfəˈmeɪʃn/ *nu* news, facts or knowledge given: *That's a useful piece/bit of information*.

glass /glɑːs/ *n* **1** *nu* a kind of hard substance (as used in windows): *made of glass*. **2** *nc* a drinking container or its contents: *drink a glass (of milk)*.

glass·es /ˈglɑːsɪz/ *n pl* (also *a pair of glasses*) two pieces of special glass in a frame, used by some people to see better.

po·lice /pəˈliːs/ *n pl* (the —) an official group of men and women whose job is to protect people and property, catch criminals etc: *The police have not made any arrests*.

1 Eating and drinking *Complete the dialogues with words from the cloud. In some cases there is more than one possibility.*

several – much – it – loaves – some – a glass of – many – lump – kilo of – bottles

1. How . . . bread do you want me to buy? – Two . . . , please. 2. How . . . sugar do you take? – Just one . . . , please. I don't like my coffee too sweet. 3. Can I have . . . orange juice, please? – Sorry, we've only got water. Would you like . . . ? 4. How . . . milk shall I buy? – Get three . . . , please. 5. I need . . . cups of tea with my breakfast every morning. – I don't drink . . . tea, I prefer coffee. 6. I like sweets so much that I always eat too . . . . – Is that why you've got so . . . trouble with your teeth? 7. I'm going to get a . . . beef at the butcher's. – I hope . . . won't be so much more expensive than at the supermarket.

2 From a local newspaper *Try to make one or two complete sentences from each extract.*

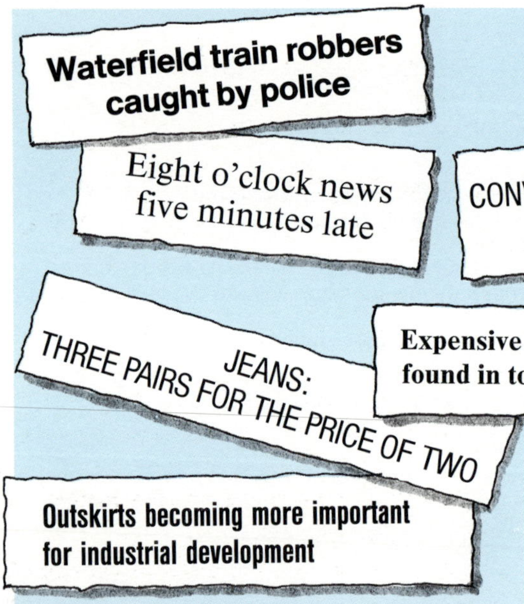

Examples:
1. The Waterfield train robbers were caught by the police. *or:* The police caught the Waterfield train robbers.
2. The eight o'clock news . . .
Go on.

3 In English, please

1. Hast du deine Haare selbst geschnitten?

2. Dieser Schlafanzug gefällt mir.
3. Kannst du mir die notwendigen Informationen geben?
4. Weil ich in unserem Haus nie eine Schere finden kann, habe ich vor kurzem fünf neue gekauft.
5. Entschuldigung, aber ich weiß nicht, was diese Nachricht bedeutet.
6. Du hast ja schon wieder deine Hausaufgaben nicht gemacht.
7. Ich weiß, daß die Polizei sofort am Unfallort war.
8. Deine neue Brille war sicher sehr teuer.

4 Revision: Question tags (Deutsch: nicht wahr?, nicht?, oder?, ja?)

Remember: As an engineer **you can't** get along without English, **can you?**
A third of all **people** in the European Community **speak** English, **don't they?**
Let's see what our encyclopedia says about the use of English, **shall we?**

a **From conversations about the English language** *Add the right question tag.*

1. All over the world people have got a need for English, . . . ? 2. Today most scientists write their books in English, . . . ? 3. Until the end of the 16th century English wasn't a very important language, . . . ? 4. Today the majority of pop songs are in English, . . . ? 5. Some countries don't allow the use of English so freely, . . . ? 6. English has become what Latin was in the Middle Ages, . . . ? 7. English began as a little known language about 1200 years ago, . . . ? – I don't know. But let's ask Mrs Jones, . . . ? 8. Mr Hastings told us to learn at least ten new words a day, . . . ? 9. We could ask Anne to explain the new grammar rules again, . . . ? 10. You didn't find it easy to understand your Australian relatives, . . . ?

b **In English, please**

1. Heutzutage sprechen mehr Menschen Chinesisch als Englisch,
2. Weil sie perfekt Englisch spricht, bezieht Susi ein höheres Gehalt,
3. In der Computertechnologie kannst du ohne Englisch nicht auskommen,
4. Auf Speisekarten findet man häufig Englisch,
5. Politiker in Frankreich wollten den Gebrauch des Englischen aufhalten,
6. Englisch Lehren ist ein Millionen-Dollar-Geschäft geworden,
7. Thomas hat die Stelle in England nicht bekommen,
8. Als Diskjockey muß man Englisch können,
9. Katrin wird in Indien oft Englisch sprechen müssen,
10. In Deutschland lernen nur wenige Kinder Englisch in der Grundschule,

. . . nicht wahr?

More about the gerund

Remember:
Swimming can be fun. Do you **like swimming?** – No, not really. I'm not very **good at swimming**.

Now compare: I don't like being late. — I don't like my **boyfriend/him** being late.
Ich komme ungern zu spät. — Ich habe es nicht gern, wenn mein Freund/er zu spät kommt.

A personal noun or pronoun can be put before a gerund to say who the gerund refers to.
In formal English the possessive form of the noun *(boyfriend's)* or a possessive adjective *(his)* is preferred.
Example: I dislike Peter's/his being late.

5a *Make a few sentences in which you say what you like/don't like doing and what you like/don't like other people doing. Examples:* I like getting up late. I don't like my brother waking me up early. *Go on.*

b Here are some more verbs and adjectives to make sentences with gerunds, with and without a personal noun or pronoun:

apologize for — dream of — look forward to — talk about — tired of — worried about

Examples: My parents were worried about me failing my exam.
My little brother dreamt of (his dog) running away. *Go on.*

6 WORDS WORDS WORDS

a A colourful mixture

Over the centuries the rivers of various languages have flowed into the large reservoir of English. As you are learning French or Latin as a second foreign language, you will easily see that the six underlined words have been borrowed from one of the two languages. In fact, modern English vocabulary is a mixture in which about 30% of the words are of Germanic and about 60% of French or Latin origin. As a result, English has become a very rich and powerful language. But sometimes new words forced their way into word families, splitting them up and making English more difficult to learn.

Compare German *sehen*, English *see*, French *voir* and their "relatives":

Fern**sehen**	(An–)**Sicht**	kurz**sicht**ig	Ge**sicht**	Ge**sicht**spunkt	**Sicht**(weite)	(un)**sicht**bar
television	**sight**/view	short-**sight**ed	face	point of view	visibility	(in)visible
télévision	vue	myope	visage/face	point de vue	visibilité	(in)visible

b Same stem in German, different stems in English

Look at the following lists of words and find the pairs that go together in each group, e.g. *end* and *final*, . . . (group 1), *(to) believe* and *superstitious*, . . . (group 2), etc. It might be helpful to translate them into German first!

1. Noun and adjective	*end enemy fruit king law man mouth need*	*(in)fertile final hostile (il)legal male necessary oral royal*
2. Verb and adjective	*(to) believe (to) eat (to) last (to) see*	*(in)edible obvious permanent superstitious*
3. Noun and noun	*book cup foot knowledge murder state town water word world year*	*century citizen environment ignorance library pedestrian saucer sewage suburb suicide vocabulary*
4. Verb and verb	*(to) come (to) know (to) live (to) speak (to) tell (to) write*	*(to) arrive (to) describe (to) predict (to) pronounce (to) recognize (to) survive*

c Related sounds and spellings

Compare the following lists of words with their German translations. Do you notice any regularities?

1. *holiday holy once one only soap stone*
   Why do you think *only* has been included here? Use an English-German dictionary if you are not sure.
2. *thick thin thing think third thirst this*
3. *eight light night right weight*

When Christopher Wren had completed St Paul's Cathedral, King George I told him that he found his work "amusing, awful and artificial" – and that, of course, was meant as a compliment. What do these words mean today, and what do you think they meant 300 years ago?

The language expert

Tony Stevens left the arrivals building at Munich airport and walked towards the long line of taxis. It was a hot summer morning and not a very busy time of the day. Drivers were standing in groups or sitting in their cars reading books and magazines. Tony went to the front of the line and a smiling taxi driver took his bags and put them in the boot.

"Die Uni, bitte," Tony said. "Oh, are you English?" the driver asked. "That's right," Tony replied, surprised he had been recognized so quickly as an Englishman. "I thought you were," the driver said as he started the engine and drove away. "I can usually tell. The clothes you wear, or the way you speak."

"I've hardly said anything," said Tony.

"I can still tell. The university. You're the third person I take there today." "*Have* taken," said Tony automatically and thought, the Germans always make the same mistakes. "Okay, okay," said the taxi driver. "A real expert. You're the third person I have taken there today. So what's happening? A big meeting?"

"An international conference," said Tony. "It's about teaching English as a foreign language."

"Is that right?"

They left the airport and turned onto the motorway. Within seconds they were driving at top speed towards the city, overtaking every vehicle on the road. Tony had the feeling they were going to take off again.

"You know something?" said the driver. "No teacher has taught me English." "Really? Where did you learn it then?" "Here in this taxi. I teach myself. When I have no passengers, I learn English." He pointed to a book and a number of cassettes. "English is good. I like it. It's easy. Not like German." "How do you mean?" asked Tony. "Well, look at German: 'der', 'die', 'das'. It's crazy. Who needs three words? You've just got one word. 'The'. And that's it. It's much better."

"Yes," said Tony. "I'd be much happier myself if you only had one word for 'the'."

"And what about 'du' and 'Sie' and 'ihr'? Who needs them? Why not one word, like in English? 'You'. It's great. No problems. And we've got so many long words. Take 'Wochenende'. Wo-chen-ende. What do you say? 'Weekend'. It's short. It's good. 'Weekend'."

Tony looked out of the window. What do you say to that, he wondered? As they came towards the end of the motorway, the traffic got heavier and heavier. Vehicles were coming from all directions. The driver already had his window open, now he started shouting at every other driver on the road. Tony began to think he was in a tank.

"Don't kill anybody," he said. The taxi driver threw his cigarette out of the window. "The people here can't drive," he said. "They're all sleeping. They sit in their cars and sleep." He shouted at another driver, blew his horn a few times, and their speed got slower and slower. As they entered the city, they finally stopped. They were in the middle of a Munich traffic jam.

"I get a lot of passengers from other countries. Sometimes I learn a little bit of their language. It's fun. I tried to learn Hungarian once. They talk backwards."

Tony looked at him, surprised. "They do *what*?"

"They really have a crazy grammar. They don't say 'on my table', they say 'table on my'. Instead of saying 'on Tuesday', they say 'Tuesday on'." He laughed. "Isn't that crazy?"

"I don't know a lot about Hungarian," said Tony.

"Lovely people. Just a crazy language. But do you know what's wrong with the English language?"

"Tell me," said Tony, realizing that they were going to be in the traffic jam for a while, so he might as well pass the time in a conversation with the taxi driver. “I’ll tell you. The tenses. They’re crazy. I once had a university professor in the taxi and she said you can speak English easily if you know a lot of words. You just put them together in a long line. You don’t need a lot of grammar. But the tenses. ‘I wait’, ‘I’m waiting’, ‘I have waited’, ‘I have been waiting’. Oh boy, what a language. Why don’t you say: ‘I wait now’, ‘I wait every day’, ‘I wait tomorrow’, ‘I wait for two hours’? Basta.”

“Why don’t you say ‘der Fenster’ or ‘das Frau’?” “Das Frau? Oh boy. I like it. Just imagine. ‘Das Frau’. But we say ‘das Mädchen’. You know, when you think about it, Germans are even crazier than the Hungarians. In our language the moon is male, the sun is female, but our girls are neither male nor female.”

Slowly the traffic moved forwards as they followed a route over the river and through the city centre towards the university. “But it’s a good question,” said the driver. “Why don’t we say ‘der Fenster’?”

“Because grammar is crazy,” said Tony.

“It isn’t logical. Languages don’t have logical grammars. But we all accept our own grammars as normal and think that those of other languages are silly.”

The taxi driver stopped outside the university entrance. “Twenty-six marks,” he said. “You know something? Perhaps we’re all crazy people because we have crazy grammars. What do you say?” Tony got out of the taxi. “Don’t drive away. This door is ajar,” he said. The driver looked at him confused. “It’s what?” “It’s ajar.” “I learn a jar of coffee. How can a door be a jar? It’s made of metal.”

“Not a jar, ajar.”

“Sounds the same to me.”

“Look it up in a dictionary,” said Tony with a smile. “Like you said, languages are crazy.” He waved to the driver and went into the building. Inside he looked for the rooms where the conference was taking place. That afternoon at two o’clock he had to give a talk on how to make the teaching of English tenses easier. He wondered whether he should invite the taxi driver to give the talk instead.

Working with the text

a **A first look at the text**

Munich German language airport take a taxi by plane talk about conference about university taxi driver hot summer day

Use the words in the box to say in a few sentences what happened to Tony Stevens in Munich. Start like this:
Tony Stevens had come to Munich by plane. He wanted to . . . Go on.

b **A closer look at the text**

1. Go through the text and find what the driver likes/doesn’t like about German and English.
2. Why does/doesn’t he like these aspects of the two languages?
3. What does the adjective ‘crazy’ mean for the driver?
4. How does Tony confuse the driver when he gets out of the taxi? Try to explain Tony’s joke.

c **Beyond the text: The ‘crazy’ English language**

1. ‘Crazy’ pronunciation: blood – good – boot / although – through – enough. Find more words in which letters or combinations of letters are pronounced differently.
2. ‘Crazy’ spelling: the famous Anglo-Irish writer George Bernard Shaw (1856-1950) fought against English spelling all his life. To show how ‘crazy’ the English spelling is, he made up the ‘word’ *ghoti*. That’s how you could spell [fɪʃ] if you applied the spelling you find in the words *cough, women* and *nation*. Make up a few funny words like *ghoti* and see who can read them properly.

The United Kingdom – facts and figures[1]

The United Kingdom is very small compared with many other countries in the world. However, only 15 other countries have more people, and only 12 other cities are bigger than London. Here is a summary of important facts and figures about the UK. (For further information see the map at the front of the book.)

Population and area

The UK:	*57 million*	*244,000 sq. km*
England:	*47.4 million*	*130,000 sq. km*
Scotland:	*5.1 million*	*79,000 sq. km*
Wales:	*2.8 million*	*21,000 sq. km*
N. Ireland:	*1.6 million*	*14,000 sq. km*
Germany:	*78 million*	*357,000 sq. km*

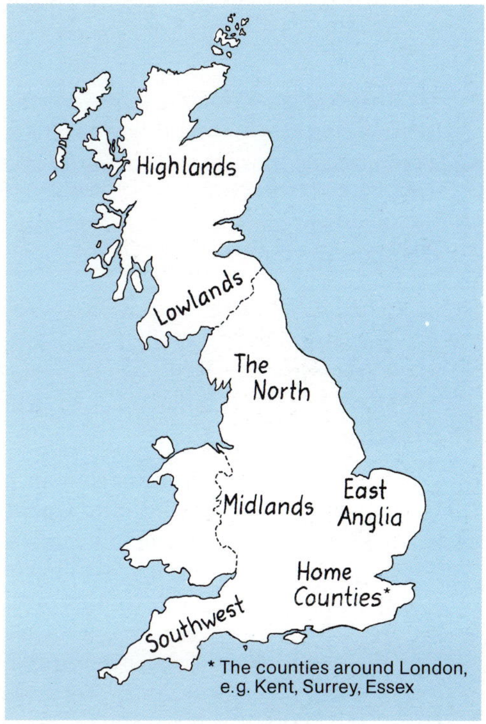

The largest cities

London:	*6,770,000*
Birmingham:	*998,000*
Glasgow:	*716,000*
Leeds:	*709,000*
Sheffield:	*532,000*
Liverpool:	*476,000*
Berlin:	*3,400,000*
Hamburg:	*1,600,000*

The islands

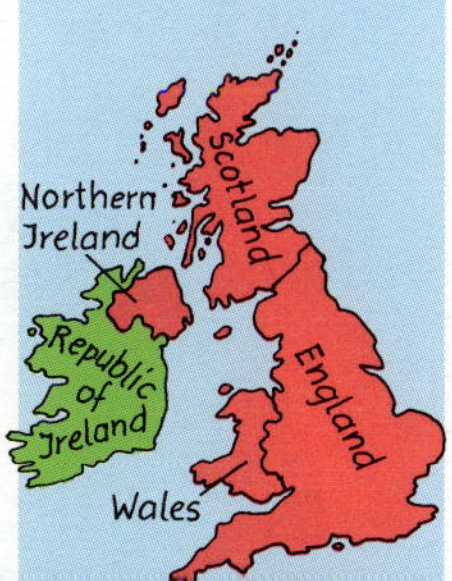

The countries

The highest mountains

Ben Nevis:	*1,343 m*
Snowdon:	*1,085 m*
Zugspitze:	*2,963 m*

The longest rivers

The Severn:	*354 km*
The Thames:	*338 km*
The Rhine:	*1,320 km*

Did you know?

- *The population density[2] of England is six times that of Scotland. (You can work out the exact[3] number of people per sq. km from the figures on this page.)*
- *About one third of the UK population lives in the south-east of England.*
- *The main areas of high land and mountains are in Scotland, Wales and the north of England. The flattest area is East Anglia.*

- Take some of the information from this page which you find interesting and give a talk to the class. This is how you could begin: The United Kingdom is part of a group of islands. . . .
- Find pictures of different regions of Britain and describe them to the class.

[1] figure ['fɪgə] *Zahl* [2] population density ['densɪtɪ] *Bevölkerungsdichte* [3] exact [ɪg'zækt] *genau*

British humour

The British are famous for their sense of humour,[1] and if you live in Britain – or are only a visitor for a short time – you certainly need one. Things often go wrong,[2] but the British are much too polite to complain. "Can't complain, I suppose," is a popular English saying, and also "Look on the bright side" or "Keep your chin up.[3]"

A true story

Mr Brown was on holiday in the south of France. The hotel had at least three stars in all the travel guides, but this time Mr Brown was unlucky. It was early in the season, there weren't many tourists staying in the hotel, and the food was not of the standard Mr Brown expected. So what did he do? – Nothing, of course. Back home he told his friends: "Hotel was excellent. But the food was terrible and, unfortunately, there weren't any Germans to complain about it."

A joke

The British are also very fond of making fun[4] of each other. Or rather[5] the English enjoy jokes about the Welsh, the Scots or the Irish, the Scots make fun of the English, and so on. Many jokes begin, like this one, with the line: "An Englishman, a Scotsman and an Irishman . . ."

An Englishman, a Scotsman and an Irishman were alone on a desert island.[6] One day the Englishman found an old bottle. He broke it and out came a genie.[7] "Oh master," said the genie, "for ten thousand years I have been a prisoner in that bottle. I will give you and your friends three wishes. But choose well, because you may have only one wish each."

"My wish is quite simple," said the Englishman. "I wish to be taken home." "Your wish is my command,[8]" said the genie, and the Englishman disappeared.[9] "Yes, I'd like the same," said the Scotsman. "I wish to be taken home too." And the Scotsman, too, disappeared. "And your wish, oh Master?" the genie said to the Irishman. "I'm very lonely without the other two," said the Irishman, "I wish they were back here with me."

A sense of fun

Another characteristic of the British is treating a serious topic with a sense of fun. On March 11th 1989, for example, thousands of British people bought and wore red plastic noses to raise[10] money for homeless and hungry people. Many even put big ones on their cars. Can you imagine a "Red Nose Day" in Germany?

1 sense of humour [ˌsens‿əv ˈhjuːmə] *(Sinn für) Humor* 2 go wrong *schiefgehen*
3 Keep your chin up. *Kopf hoch!* chin *Kinn* 4 make fun of sb. *sich über jn. lustig machen*
5 rather [ˈrɑːðə] *vielmehr* 6 desert island [ˌ--ˈ--] *einsame Insel* 7 genie [ˈdʒiːnɪ] *Flaschengeist*
8 command [kəˈmɑːnd] *Befehl* 9 disappear *verschwinden* 10 raise [reɪz] *hier: aufbringen, auftreiben*

Class Four-D's trip to the British Museum

The following text about a class trip to London is from the best-selling book *The Secret Diary of Adrian Mole Aged 13 3/4* by Sue Townsend. The diary is written by Adrian Mole, a serious boy who dreams of becoming a poet. He is in love with the strong-willed[1] feminist Pandora Braithwaite.

7 am Boarded[2] coach.
7.05 Ate packed lunch, drank low-calorie drink.
7.10 Coach stopped for Barry Kent to be sick.
7.20 Coach stopped for Claire Neilson to go to the Ladies.
7.30 Coach left school drive[3].
7.35 Coach returned to school for Ms Fossington-Gore's handbag.
7.45 Coach stopped for Barry Kent to be sick again.
8.10 Coach driver loses temper,[4] refuses to drive on motorway until "bloody[5] teachers control kids".
8.20 Ms Fossington-Gore gets everyone sitting down.
8.25 Drive onto motorway.
8.30 Everyone singing "Ten Green Bottles".
8.35 Everyone singing "Ten Green Snotrags".[6]
9.40 Barry Kent sick in coach.
9.50 Two girls sitting near Barry Kent are sick.
9.51 Coach driver refuses to stop on motorway.
9.55 Ms Fossington-Gore covers sick in sand.
9.56 Ms Fossington-Gore sick as a dog.
11.30 Fight breaks out on back seat as coach approaches[7] end of motorway.
11.45 Fight ends. Ms Fossington-Gore finds first-aid[8] kit and sees to wounds.[9]
11.50 Coach breaks down[10] at Swiss Cottage.
12.30 Class Four-D catch London bus to St Pancras.
1.30 Enter British Museum. Adrian Mole and Pandora Braithwaite awestruck[11] by World Culture. Rest of class Four-D run berserk[12], laughing at nude[13] statues and dodging[14] curators.[15]
2.15 Ms Fossington-Gore in state of collapse.
3 pm Curators round up[16] class Four-D, and make them sit on steps[17] of museum.
3.05 American tourists photograph Adrian Mole, saying he is a "cute[18] English schoolboy".
3.15 Ms Fossington-Gore recovers[19] and leads class Four-D on sightseeing tour of London.
4 pm Barry Kent jumps in fountain at Trafalgar Square, as predicted by Adrian Mole.
4.35 Police arrive, arrange coach back. Phone parents about new arrival time. Phone headmaster at home. Claire Neilson has hysterical fit.[20] Pandora Braithwaite tells Ms Fossington-Gore she is a disgrace[21] to teaching profession.[22] Ms Fossington-Gore agrees to resign.[23]
7 pm Coach leaves police station with police escort.
7.35 Coach driver begs[24] Pandora Braithwaite to keep order.
8 pm Ms Fossington-Gore drafts[25] resignation.
8.30 Coach driver afflicted by[26] motorway madness.
8.40 Arrive back. Tyres burning. Ms Fossington-Gore led off by headmaster. Parents up in arms.[27]

Would you like to have been on this trip? Why/Why not?

[1] strong-willed *willensstark* [2] board [bɔ:d] *einsteigen* [3] drive *Einfahrt*
[4] lose your temper *die Beherrschung verlieren* [5] bloody *verdammt* [6] snotrag *„Rotzfahne"*
[7] approach [ə'prəʊtʃ] *sich nähern* [8] first-aid *Erste Hilfe* [9] wound [wu:nd] *Wunde*
[10] break down *eine Panne haben* [11] awestruck ['ɔ:strʌk] *von Ehrfurcht ergriffen*
[12] run berserk [bə'zɜ:k] *Amok laufen* [13] nude [nju:d] *nackt* [14] dodge [dɒdʒ] *ausweichen*
[15] curator [kjʊ'reɪtə] *Wächter/in* [16] round up *zusammentreiben* [17] step *Stufe* [18] cute [kju:t] *niedlich, süß*
[19] recover [rɪ'kʌvə] *sich erholen* [20] fit *Anfall* [21] disgrace [dɪs'greɪs] *Schande*
[22] profession [prə'feʃn] *Beruf(sstand)* [23] resign [rɪ'zaɪn] *kündigen* [24] beg *anflehen* [25] draft *entwerfen*
[26] afflicted by [ə'flɪktɪd] *heimgesucht von* [27] up in arms *empört*

The background to the Troubles

To understand the Troubles between Protestants and Catholics in Northern Ireland today, it is necessary to go back a long way in history.

a English-Irish relations up to 1690

The English have been in Ireland for over 800 years, but the problems really have their origin in the 17th century. Between 1603 and 1625 King James I of England gave Protestant English and Scottish settlers land in Ireland, especially in the northern parts. This became known as the "Ulster Plantation".[1]

In 1649 Oliver Cromwell, ruler of England between 1649 and 1658, conquered the whole of Ireland. He was strongly anti-Catholic and took all political power away from the Irish. From this time on, most landowners in Ireland were of Scottish or English origin, and were Protestants.

Oliver Cromwell

In 1688 King James II, a Catholic, was forced to leave England and give the Crown to the Protestant King William of Orange. King James went to Ireland and was defeated in 1690 at the Battle of the Boyne by the English and Protestant Irish. Even today the Protestant Orangemen in Northern Ireland (King William's colours were orange) celebrate this battle every year on July 12th with parades and music.

King William of Orange

b English-Irish relations from 1801 to 1921

In 1801 Ireland became part of the United Kingdom and was ruled directly from London.

Between 1845 and 1848 the potato crop[2] failed, which led to the Great Famine[3]. The situation was made worse by English landowners who sent what little food there was to England and left the Irish to starve or emigrate. In just 13 years the population of Ireland fell from 8 million to 4 million.

Irish children searching for potatoes

[1] plantation [plæn'teɪʃn] *Verpflanzung* [2] crop *hier: Ernte* [3] famine ['fæmɪn] *Hungersnot*

A street in Dublin during the Easter Rising

On Easter Monday 1916 a Republican rebellion to form an independent Ireland was put down[1] in Dublin by the British army. Over 500 people lost their lives in the so-called Easter Rising. Its leaders were executed, but the Irish Republican Army (IRA) was born. A very cruel War of Independence followed. In 1921 the southern part of Ireland became independent as the Irish Free State, while six counties in the north (part of the original province of Ulster), remained British with their government and parliament in Belfast.
The majority of people in Northern Ireland were, of course, Protestants, and they discriminated against[2] Catholics in all fields of life. For example, Protestant firms employed only Protestants, so unemployment among the Catholics was very high. The police and the courts were also controlled by Protestants.

c Northern Ireland today

In 1968 and 1969, influenced by Martin Luther King and events in the United States, Catholics in Northern Ireland organized civil rights marches[3]. They wanted equal rights in voting[4], housing[5] and employment. During one march in 1969 Catholics were attacked by Protestant extremists. Riots and violence followed. The government in Northern Ireland made changes to improve the situation for Catholics, but peace did not return to the country. That year British soldiers were sent to keep the peace. They were welcomed by the Catholic population.
In January 1972 during a civil rights march, British soldiers shot 13 people. This day became known as "Bloody Sunday". In March of the same year the British suspended[6] the Northern Ireland parliament and introduced direct rule from London.
During the 1980s the British government realized that a military[7] solution to Northern Ireland's problems would never be possible. In November 1985 the British and Irish Prime Ministers signed the Anglo-Irish agreement and promised to work together to end the violence in the province. By meeting regularly to discuss policies and problems in Northern Ireland, both countries hoped that the way to peace had finally been found.

Civil rights march in 1969

1. Make a time line with the dates from these two pages. Add a few notes for each date. Then use the time line and the notes to give a talk to the class: "Historical reasons for the present troubles in Northern Ireland".
2. If you look at the history of Ireland, what might be the fears[8] of the Catholic population in Northern Ireland? What might be the fears of the Protestants?
3. Find out if there have been any recent developments which have helped to bring peace to Northern Ireland.

[1] put down *hier: niederwerfen* [2] discriminate against [dɪˈskrɪmɪneɪt] *diskriminieren* [3] march [mɑːtʃ] *Marsch*
[4] voting [ˈvəʊtɪŋ] *Stimmrecht* [5] housing [ˈhaʊzɪŋ] *Wohnungen* [6] suspend [səˈspend] *auflösen*
[7] military [ˈmɪlɪtrɪ] *militärisch* [8] fear [fɪə] *Befürchtung*

Two poems and a song from Northern Ireland

The situation in Northern Ireland has affected the lives of almost everyone who lives there. Here are three examples of people expressing how they feel about the Troubles:

1. They talk, the older folks[1],
   And paint a rosy[2] past.
   Oh! I am tired of hearing
   How things were in Belfast.

2. They talk and tell me stories
   Of the good times they once had
   And the more they talk about it all
   The more it makes me sad.

3. For I cannot remember
   A childhood[3] free from strife,[4]
   To me the bombs and bullets
   Are just a way of life.

4. So I have just one question
   To ask our violent men:
   What about my wasted childhood,
   Can you bring it back again?

Fionnuala Bogues (16), Dominican Convent, Belfast

1. Practise reading the poem aloud in class and discuss how it should be read.
2. Why do you think the old people talk about Belfast's "rosy past"? – Don't forget how the past changes for people as they get older.
3. Why do you think the girl sees her childhood as a "wasted childhood" and as "lost years"?

The winds are singing freedom

(by Tommy Makem from County Armagh)

Chorus:
The winds are singing freedom,
They sing it everywhere,
They sing it on the mountain side
And in the city square.
They sing of a new day dawning,[5]
When our people shall be free;
Come and join the song of freedom,
Let it ring from sea to sea.

1. In the battle streets of Belfast,
   You can hear the people cry
   For justice[6] long denied[7] them,
   And their cry will fill the sky.
   But the winds of change are blowing,
   Bringing hope from dark despair;[8]
   A new day is dawning,
   You can feel it in the air.

2. Too long our people suffered
   In misery[9] and in tears,
   And foreign rulers used our land
   For about 800 years.
   It's a long road has no turning,
   And I know that soon will be
   A day of justice dawning,
   When our people shall be free.

3. There's a time laid out[10] for laughing,
   And there's a time laid out to weep,[11]
   There's a time laid out for sowing,[12]
   And a time laid out to reap.[13]
   There's a time to love your brother,
   There's a time for hate to cease;[14]
   If you sow the seeds[15] of justice
   Then you'll reap the fruits of peace.

1. What, in general, is Tommy Makem trying to say?
2. Three key words in this song are "freedom", "justice" and "peace". How are the three related to each other according to the song?
3. Which do you prefer: the poem or the song? – Why?

[1] folks [fəʊks] = *(infml.) people* [2] rosy [ˈrəʊzɪ] *rosig* [3] childhood [ˈtʃaɪldhʊd] *Kindheit*
[4] strife [straɪf] = *troubles; opposite of peace* [5] dawn [dɔːn] *(herauf)dämmern*
[6] justice [ˈdʒʌstɪs] *Gerechtigkeit* [7] deny [dɪˈnaɪ] *verweigern* [8] despair [dɪˈspeə] *Verzweiflung*
[9] misery [ˈmɪzərɪ] *Elend* [10] lay out *hier: vorsehen* [11] weep [wiːp] *weinen* [12] sow [səʊ] *säen*
[13] reap [riːp] *ernten* [14] cease [siːs] *aufhören* [15] seeds [siːdz] *Samen, Saat*

IRA Victim

by Siobhan[1] Aiton, 14

A second splits[2] before the bullet
Enters the brain,[3]
Exploding in the mind[4]
Like the shattering[5] of a window
Or a waterfall crashing on rocks.

In that split second
He heard his wife putting the peas on to boil,
Saw his children arrive home from school
And throw their coats down in the hall
Just as he had told them not to.
He smelt the dew-scented[6] roses
Colouring his garden,
And the rosehip[7] wine
He had bottled last summer.
He thought of his mother,
Just visiting her neighbour
For a cup of tea,
As she did every afternoon,
And of the tapestry[8] his daughter was making.
And just before the bullet splintered[9] his skull[10]
And dropped him into the past tense,
He thought of his slaughterers.[11]

The sun shone down on Belfast that day,
Herding[12] black-bodied flies
Around the sticky[13] blood
Spilt[14] like milk on the pavement.
And it's no use crying over spilt milk [15]

(This poem won the third prize in the 11-14 years age group of the *Observer* National Children's Poetry Competition 1987.)

1. First try to imagine and then to describe the situation which Siobhan presents in her poem.
2. Why has Siobhan divided her poem into three verses?[16]
3. What is the victim's last split second like? How does Siobhan try to express what goes through his mind?
4. What opinion on the conflict in Northern Ireland is expressed in the poem? (Pay attention especially to the last two lines.)
5. Compare this poem with "The Lost Years". Which poem affects you more? Which one do you prefer? Try to give reasons.

[1] Siobhan [ʃɪˈvɔːn] *irischer Vorname (weiblich)* [2] split *sich spalten*; split second *Bruchteil einer Sekunde* [3] brain *Gehirn* [4] mind *Verstand, Kopf* [5] shatter *zerspringen* [6] dew-scented [ˈdjuːˌsentɪd] *taufrisch duftend* [7] rosehip [ˈrəʊzhɪp] *Hagebutte* [8] tapestry [ˈtæpɪstrɪ] *Wandteppich* [9] splinter *zersplittern* [10] skull *Schädel* [11] slaughterer [ˈslɔːtərə] *Schlächter* [12] herd *zusammentreiben* [13] sticky *klebrig* [14] spill, spilt *verschütten, vergießen* [15] (letzte Zeile) *engl. Redensart, etwa: Was geschehen ist, ist geschehen.* [16] verse [vɜːs] *Strophe*

The fight

(From *The Twelfth Day of July* by Joan Lingard)

The story so far: Sadie Jackson (13) and her brother Tommy (14) live in a Protestant working-class family in Belfast, Kevin McCoy (14) and his sister Brede (15) in a working-class Catholic family several streets away. Sadie and Kevin are the main characters in the book. The action takes place in 1969 during the week before July 12th (Orangeman's Day), an important public holiday for all Northern Irish Protestants. Sadie and Kevin have both been taught to mistrust[1] all members of the "other" religion; in the days before July 12th they and other teenagers have been busy at night painting graffiti on the walls of their "enemies'" houses. On one of these expeditions[2] into the Catholic area Sadie has met Brede, a peace-loving girl who doesn't think much of "war games." The tension has been rising until the evening of July 11th, the time when the following extract takes place.

For a moment all was quiet. They could hear the city traffic in the distance, but they were only interested in what was going to happen here, in this street. This is what they had been waiting for all week: to stand face-to-face, on opposite sides of the road. One or two shivered[3], either with fear[4] or expectation. But none moved away. It was as if a magnet held them there.

The moment of quiet passed. Now the voices were raised, soft[5] to begin with.

"Dirty Micks!"[6]

"Filthy[7] old Prods!"[8]

The voices grew louder.

"Kick the Pope!"[9]

"To hell[10] with King Billy!"

No one knew who threw the first stone. One seemed to come from each side at the same time. It was as if a whistle[11] had been blown. Suddenly children appeared from every direction; they came out of side streets, shouting, cheering, booing[12], looking out for any ammunition[13] they could find, large stones, small ones, pieces of wood, half-bricks[14]. They moved forward on to the road. The distance between the two sides narrowed.

Sadie was in the front line. Her heart beat fast with excitement. She felt as if a fever[15] possessed[16] her. And then for a second she stopped, a shout trapped[17] at the back of her throat. She had seen Brede's face. Brede stood behind the Catholics, not shouting, or throwing, just standing.

At that moment a brick flew high over the heads of the crowd. Sadie saw Brede duck[18]. But she was too late; the brick caught her full on the side of the head.

Brede went down and disappeared among the moving bodies of the Catholics. "Brede!" shouted Sadie.

Brede was hurt. Brede . . .why Brede? Inside Sadie felt cold. There was no fever now, no excitement, only a need to get across and find out what had happened to the fallen girl. With another shout Sadie rushed forward.

"Come back, Sadie," someone shouted behind her. "They'll murder you." Sadie fought through the lines, pushing children out of her way. She felt hands trying to hold her, but the strength[19] in her body was so great they could not stop her. She reached the group round Brede's body.

A boy caught hold of[20] her roughly. "Leave her be," said Kevin McCoy quietly, looking up from where he knelt[21] beside his sister. Sadie knelt beside him.

"Is she bad?"

"Think so."

[1] mistrust sb. [mɪsˈtrʌst] *jm. mißtrauen* [2] expedition [ˌekspɪˈdɪʃn] *Expedition* [3] shiver [ˈʃɪvə] *zittern; schaudern* [4] fear [fɪə] *Furcht* [5] soft [sɒft] *weich* [6] Mick [mɪk] *Schimpfwort für Katholik/in* [7] filthy [ˈfɪlθɪ] *dreckig* [8] Prod [prɒd] *Schimpfwort für Protestant/in* [9] pope [pəʊp] *Papst* [10] hell [hel] *Hölle* [11] whistle [ˈwɪsl] *Pfeife* [12] boo [bu:] *buhen* [13] ammunition [ˌæmjʊˈnɪʃn] *Munition* [14] brick [brɪk] *Backstein* [15] fever [ˈfi:və] *Fieber* [16] possess [pəˈzes] *besitzen* [17] trapped [træpt] *eingeschlossen* [18] duck *sich ducken* [19] strength [streŋθ] *Kraft* [20] catch hold of sb. *jn. packen* [21] kneel, knelt, knelt [ni:l, nelt] *niederknien*

Brede lay still, her arms lifeless at her sides, her eyes closed. There was blood on her head. The sound of a police siren screamed further along the road. Children flew to right and left, dropping their ammunition as they ran. By the time the police car arrived, the street was almost empty. Only four children remained. Tommy crossed the road to join Sadie and Kevin. He knelt beside them, looking down at Brede. "Stupid," he said. "Stupid, stupid, stupid!" The car doors closed loudly; two policemen got out and came towards them. "Now then, what's been happening here?" "We'll need an ambulance," said Kevin.

An ambulance was called, and arrived within minutes with its blue light flashing[1]. The men covered Brede with a blanket and carried her into the ambulance.

Sadie, Tommy and Kevin went into the back of the police car. They drove through the late-night streets behind the ambulance, watching its flashing light, listening to its siren. The sound made Sadie shiver.

At the hospital the lights were bright and blinding. Brede was taken away; doors closed behind her.

The waiting-room was warm, but Sadie could not stop shivering. Kevin took a bar of chocolate from his pocket and broke it into three pieces. They ate in silence, sitting side by side.

After a few minutes a police officer appeared to take down their statements. He shook his head. "Why can't you kids keep to your own sides of the road?" "Will she die?" Sadie shouted out, unable to control the question any longer. "We don't know yet."

The door opened, and in came Mr McCoy looking white and shaken. He began to shout when he saw Kevin. "I can't trust[2] you kids an inch. I knew you'd end up in trouble."

"Come on," said the police officer to Sadie and Tommy. "I'll get someone to take you home." "Can't we wait and see how she is?" asked Tommy. "Your parents will be worrying about you. Don't you think you've caused enough trouble for one night? But I'll see if there's any news before you go."

Sadie looked back at Kevin. "I hope she'll be all right." Kevin nodded.

They left him with his father. As soon as the door closed they heard Mr McCoy starting to shout again. They waited in the corridor while the policeman went off. "If I got my hands on the one that did it!" said Tommy. "Does it matter?" said Sadie tiredly.

"You mean it could just as easily have been me?"

"Yes. Or me."

The policeman returned. "They're going to do an emergency[3] operation," he said. "They're getting her ready now."

(Slightly adapted)

Questions

1. Try to say what happens in this excerpt in about five sentences.
2. How do the children, especially Sadie, feel before the fight?
3. How do you explain what happens after Brede has been hurt? Look at Sadie's, Kevin's, Tommy's and all the other children's behaviour.
4. Looking at this excerpt from the novel, what do you think are the author's feelings and hopes for the situation in Ireland?
5. Imagine the following situation: Sadie has come home and is trying to explain to her parents where she and Tommy have been and why they went to the hospital. Write the dialogue.

[1] flash [flæʃ] *blinken* [2] trust sb. [trʌst] *jm. trauen* [3] emergency [ɪˈmɜːdʒənsɪ] *Notfall*

From mighty[1] monarchs[2] to powerful parliaments

Do you recognize the frightening lady in the picture? It's the Queen of Hearts from *Alice's Adventures in Wonderland*. In Lewis Carroll's book this monarch had power over life and death. Of course, a modern monarch in Britain no longer has such power. But it was centuries before the people and their Parliament ruled[3] in Britain and not the monarch. The scenes from history which follow tell the story and show how things changed.

King John and Magna Carta (1215)

King John (1199-1216), for example, must have seemed like a dictator[4] to the Englishmen of the time: he interfered with[5] the Church and with trials[6] in courts, closed large areas of forest so that he could hunt the deer in them alone, and took more and more taxes from the barons[7], the "freemen"[8] and the London merchants[9]. He even murdered[10] his twelve-year-old nephew[11] when he stood in his way. As a king, he wasn't even successful, and his leading barons lost not only their money but also half of their French lands in the King's wars in France.

That did it[12]. The chief barons wrote down a list of English customs which had been kept by the rulers before John and which the King should follow in future. They forced him to meet them on an island in the Thames called Runnymede[13]. Here John had to listen while "Magna Carta" was read out to him. Angry but helpless, he signed his name.

Remember Robin Hood lived around this time; what do you know of his activities?

So the monarch was reminded that Parliament ("parleyment" is French for "talking-place") wanted to help to rule the country. Not longer after John, some common people[15] joined the barons in Parliament, which divided into the House of Lords and the House of Commons. But over the following centuries, the monarch didn't always listen to Parliament.

[1]mighty [ˈmaɪtɪ] *mächtig* [2]monarch [ˈmɒnək] *Monarch/in* [3]rule [ruːl] *regieren* [4]dictator [dɪkˈteɪtə] *Diktator/in* [5]interfere with [ˌɪntəˈfɪə] *sich einmischen in* [6]trial [ˈtraɪəl] *(Gerichts-)Verfahren* [7]baron [ˈbærən] *Baron* [8]freemen [ˈfriːmən] *Freie* [9]merchant [ˈmɜːtʃənt] *Kaufmann/Kauffrau* [10]murder [ˈmɜːdə] *ermorden* [11]nephew [ˈnevjuː] *Neffe* [12]That did it. *Das hat gereicht.* [13]Runnymede [ˈrʌnɪmiːd] [14]property [ˈprɒpətɪ] *Eigentum* [15]common [ˈkɒmən] people *das einfache Volk*

Crisis: A king is executed

When in 1625 Charles I became king, he made it quite clear that he believed in his "divine right"[1]. Parliament, however, believed that "Law is King". Charles and Parliament argued endlessly about taxes and other things. When the King started to use the army to punish Members of Parliament, Parliament decided they must form their own army. A civil war began, and the King lost. On 30th January 1649, Charles' head was cut off in London in front of a huge crowd.

For the next eleven years, Britain was a republic. The new ruler was the Puritan[2] leader of Parliament's army, Oliver Cromwell. But under Cromwell, it was the army and not Parliament that held the power. Parliament didn't want to have a dictator, so when Cromwell died, King Charles II was called home from his exile[3] in Holland.

Parliament couldn't work with either Charles I or with Oliver Cromwell. Explain why not.

A bloodless revolution

The British were glad to have Charles II after the Puritan rule of Cromwell. But when Charles died in 1685, his brother James II became king, a man who had become a Roman Catholic. England had been Protestant[4] for over 100 years now, but James started helping Catholics into positions of power. The English were nervous that France or Spain, both of them Catholic countries, might invade the country. King James had two children; his daughter Mary, married to Protestant William of Orange, but also a Catholic son, who would be the next king unless something happened to stop him. Something *did* happen. A small group of leading Englishmen wrote to William in Holland and asked him to invade England. William and Mary arrived with an army. But the revolution of 1688 was a bloodless one; James escaped to France and was never seen in England again.

And this time, Parliament made sure that no English monarch should try to rule against Parliament again. This is what William and Mary had to agree to before they became king and queen (Bill of Rights[5], 1689).

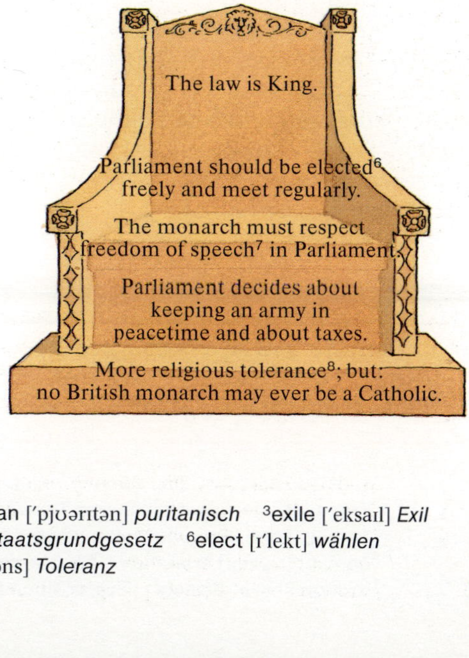

- Make a family tree with the names of the royal people on this page.
- Option 4 tells you more about Oliver Cromwell and James II. Find out what they did in Ireland.

[1]divine [dɪ'vaɪn] right *Königtum von Gottes Gnaden* [2]Puritan ['pjʊərɪtən] *puritanisch* [3]exile ['eksaɪl] *Exil*
[4]Protestant ['prɒtɪstnt] *protestantisch* [5]Bill of Rights *brit. Staatsgrundgesetz* [6]elect [ɪ'lekt] *wählen*
[7]freedom of speech [spiːtʃ] *Redefreiheit* [8]tolerance ['tɒlərəns] *Toleranz*

The British system of government

Since the revolution of 1688, the British system of government hasn't changed much at all. But there have, of course, been some important changes:
– More people, e.g. women, are allowed to vote[1].
– Important Government decisions are made mainly by the Cabinet[2] Ministers; each of these politicians is the head[3] of a Government department (health, trade, etc.).
– The Prime Minister[4], leader of the strongest party[5] in the House of Commons[6] and head of the Cabinet, is the most powerful politician in Parliament.

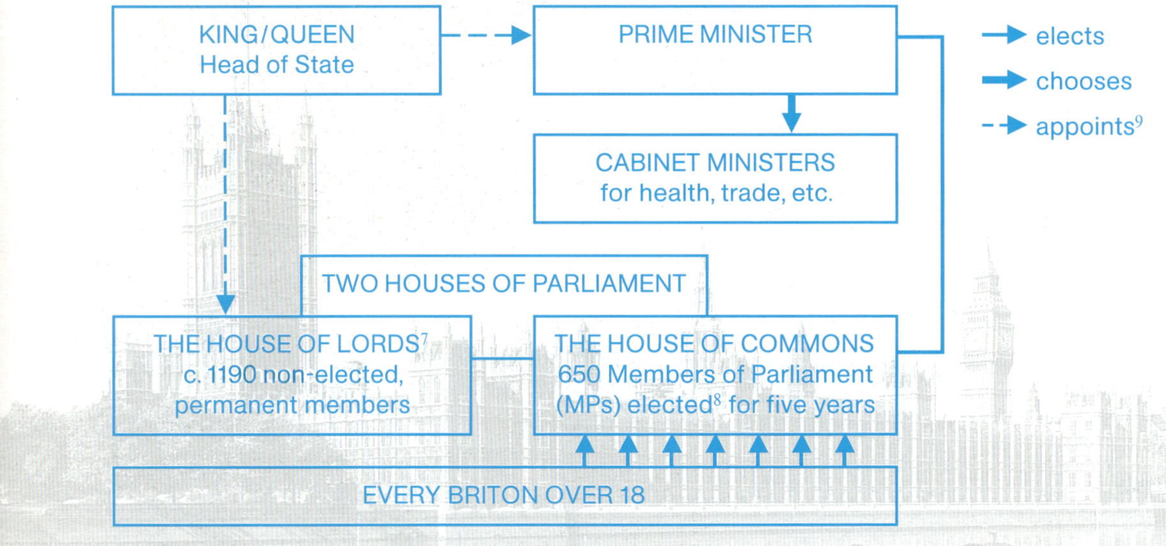

A note on . . .

. . . the monarch[10]:
She or he has no real power today. The laws she or he signs have been decided by the House of Commons, and even the speech[11] she or he makes each year when Parliament is opened is written by the Prime Minister.

. . . the House of Lords:
Lords, bishops[12] and people who have been made lords for life sit in the less important House of Lords.

. . . the House of Commons:
It is the most important part of Parliament; all the members of the Government party sit on one side of the House and the Opposition[13] MPs face them on the other.

- Use the facts you have just learnt and try to describe the British system of government.
- In Germany you have a Bundespräsident, a Bundestag and a Bundeskanzler. Who does their jobs in Britain?
- Find out the names of some top British politicians and some information about them.

[1]vote (for sb.) [vəʊt] *(jn.) wählen* [2]Cabinet ['kæbɪnɪt] *Kabinett* [3]head [hed] *Leiter/in; Oberhaupt* [4]Prime Minister [ˌpraɪm 'mɪnɪstə] *Premierminister/in* [5]party ['pɑːtɪ] *Partei* [6]House of Commons ['kɒmənz] *brit. Unterhaus* [7]House of Lords *brit. Oberhaus* [8]elect (sb.) [ɪ'lekt] *(jn.) wählen* [9]appoint [ə'pɔɪnt] *ernennen* [10]monarch ['mɒnək] *Monarch/in* [11]speech [spiːtʃ] *Rede* [12]bishop ['bɪʃəp] *Bischof* [13]Opposition [ˌɒpə'zɪʃn] *Opposition*

Changing things through politics[1]

If you're unhappy about the way something is organized in your country, you can try to change it. In this advert, which was in all the leading British newspapers together with a shocking picture of some dead dogs, the RSPCA (= **R**oyal **S**ociety[2] for the **P**revention[3] of **C**ruelty[4] to **A**nimals, the same as the German "Tierschutzbund") is trying to win people's support[5] for such a change.

Read the text carefully to find out what the problem is and what exactly the RSPCA says the readers should do to help to solve it.

When the Government killed the dog licence[6] they left us to kill the dogs.

One thousand dogs are killed in Britain every day. They are usually healthy dogs with years of life left in them. The killings take place at local vets[7] and in RSPCA centres throughout the country. We hate the killing. We are sick of doing the Government's dirty work behind closed doors. Please help us to get a law on dog registration[8]. The dogs we kill are homeless, unwanted and left to run around the streets and parks. There are at least 500,000 of them out there right now. Left to themselves, there would be close to 4 million in ten years' time. But we can't blame[9] the dogs, for we live in a society that makes it more difficult to own a television than a living, breathing animal. Homeless dogs cause road accidents, attack farm animals and foul[10] our parks and pavements. The Government abolished the licence last year and we can now see the results.

The RSPCA wants to see the introduction of dog registration. If there was a registration fee, it would encourage dog-owners to be responsible[11]. Write to your MP and fight for dog registration. If you're not sure what to do, call free on 0800 400478 and we'll add your name to our petition[12]. Do it now, for every day that goes by sees another 1,000 dogs put down[13]. And what kind of society kills healthy dogs?

RSPCA

Registration, not extermination[14].

Explain why the RSPCA put this advert in the newspapers and what it hopes will happen now. Follow the RSPCA's suggestion and write a letter to an MP. You could begin: "Dear Mrs Pilkington-Smythe, I am writing to ask you as my MP to support dog registration . . ."

[1]politics [ˈpɒlɪtɪks] *Politik* [2]society [səˈsaɪətɪ] *Gesellschaft* [3]prevention [prɪˈvenʃn] *Verhütung* [4]cruelty [ˈkrʊəltɪ] *Grausamkeit* [5]support [səˈpɔːt] (n., v.) *Unterstützung; unterstützen* [6]dog licence [ˈlaɪsəns] *Hundemarke* [7]vet [vet] *Tierarzt(praxis)* [8]registration [ˌredʒɪˈstreɪʃn] *Anmeldung* [9]blame [bleɪm] *die Schuld geben* [10]foul [faʊl] *beschmutzen* [11]responsible [rɪˈspɒnsɪbl] *verantwortungsvoll* [12]petition [pəˈtɪʃn] *Unterschriftensammlung; Petition* [13]put down [ˌ–ˈ–] *einschläfern* [14]extermination [ɪkˌstɜːmɪˈneɪʃn] *Ausrottung*

How Parliament makes laws

This page shows you how the RSPCA's suggestion might become law.

Private people or interest groups write or talk to MPs, sign a petition or start a campaign[1].

An MP or a Minister drafts[2] a new law (a bill[3]) and presents[4] it in Parliament.

The House of Commons discusses the bill. The debate is led by "Mr Speaker" in the central chair. Usually, a smaller number of MPs will form a committee[5] to study the bill carefully. Then the MPs vote on it.

The House of Lords also discusses the bill and can suggest changes to it. The Lords cannot stop it from becoming law in the end. Then they send it back to the Commons for a final vote.

It is a formality[6], but the bill still needs the monarch's signature[7] and the Grand Seal[8] before it becomes law.

How about having a discussion on animal registration in class? First, make a list of the disadvantages (cost, impractical, too many forms[9], etc.) as well as the advantages of the idea. Elect a Speaker to keep order. Then exchange your views before you finally vote.

[1]campaign [kæmˈpeɪn] *Kampagne* [2]draft [drɑːft] *entwerfen* [3]bill [bɪl] *Gesetzentwurf* [4]present [prɪˈzent] *vorstellen, präsentieren* [5]committee [kəˈmɪtɪ] *Komitee* [6]formality [fɔːˈmælɪtɪ] *Formsache* [7]signature [ˈsɪgnɪtʃə] *Unterschrift* [8]seal [siːl] *Siegel* [9]form [fɔːm] *Formular*

Neighbours with Long Teeth

Excerpts[1] from a one-act play[2] by Peter Griffith

Scene 1
Outside a house in an English suburb

(Enter Mr Smith and Mrs Smith)

Mr Smith: Good morning.
Mrs Smith: Good morning.
Mr Smith: We are Mr and Mrs Smith. I am Mr Smith, and this is my wife . . .
Mrs Smith: Mrs Smith.
Mr Smith: We have one son – Richard.
Mrs Smith: We are proud of our son.
Mr Smith: When he grows up he will go to university, and then he will get a good job.
Mrs Smith: When he grows up he will marry a nice girl, and have two nice children – or three.
Mr Smith: But first he will get a good job. Perhaps he will be a chartered accountant[3] . . .
Mrs Smith: . . . or a bank manager . . .
Mr Smith: . . . or a doctor . . .
Mrs Smith: . . . or a solicitor[4] . . .
Mr Smith: . . . or the boss of a big industry, with a great big office and a huge desk and a secretary . . .
Mrs Smith: . . . and a lovely wife at home.
Mr Smith: Yes.
Mrs Smith: We will do everything we can to help our son Richard.
Mr Smith: After all, he is our only child.
Mrs Smith: He is all that we have.
Mr Smith: Good day.

(Exit[5] Mr and Mrs Smith. Enter Rick)

Rick: Hi. My name's Rick. Rick Smith. Yeah, I know, you know all about me already, don't you? You've met my parents. And they've been talking about me. They're OK, my parents. They want the best for me, and they try hard to help me. But they don't really understand me. And especially, they don't understand my friends. And especially especially, they don't like my girlfriend. You see, my girlfriend really is a bit different. It's not just that she's not English or German or even European. No, it's worse than that. My girlfriend's not even a human being. She's – a vampire.[6] But let me tell you how it all began. One day I was in our garden . . . when I noticed that new people were moving into the house next door.

(Next door, a figure with a hood[7] is carrying boxes, etc. The figure then takes off hood to show her face)

Rick: Hi.
Phylthia: Hi.
Rick: Er . . . I'm Rick.
Phyl: Phylthia.[8]
Rick: What?
Phyl: My name – Phylthia. Phylthia-Jane Spatula.[9]
Rick: Oh.
Phyl: Nice to meet you.
Rick: You . . . er . . . moving in here?
Phyl: Certainly looks like it, doesn't it?
Rick: Yeah well, I mean – don't come too close.
Phyl: What?

[1] excerpt [ˈekss:pt] *Auszug* [2] one-act play *Einakter* [3] chartered accountant [ˌtʃɑ:təd əˈkaʊntənt] *Buchhalter/in, Buchprüfer/in* [4] solicitor [səˈlɪsɪtə] *Anwalt/Anwältin* [5] exit (A and B) *(A und B) gehen ab (von der Bühne)* [6] vampire [ˈvæmpaɪə] *Vampir* [7] hood *Kapuze* [8] Phylthia [ˈfɪlθɪə] *(erfundener Mädchenname, phonetisch identisch mit 'filthier' = dreckiger)* [9] Spatula [ˈspætjʊlə] *(erfundener Familienname, = Spachtel, Spatel)*

Rick: I mean, lovely to have new neighbours. But, I mean, you're a . . . a . . .

Phyl: I'm a vampire. Is that what you're trying to say?

Rick: Well . . . yes.

Phyl: And?

Rick: What?

Phyl: And? What's the trouble? Haven't you ever met a vampire before?

Rick: Well . . . no.

Phyl: And is it so terrible? Am I really so ugly?

Rick: Well no . . . you're really pretty attractive actually . . . it's just . . .

Phyl: Yes?

Rick: I mean . . . your teeth . . .

Phyl: Are they dirty?

Rick: No no, very clean, I think, I just mean . . .

Phyl: Yes?

Rick: Well, aren't you a bit . . . dangerous?

Phyl: Dangerous? Me?

Rick: Er . . . yes. I mean you . . . don't you . . . ?

Phyl: Yes?

Rick: I thought that vampires . . . bite[1] people . . . don't they?

Phyl: You've been seeing too many Hollywood horror films. Of course some vampires, a few hundred years ago, used to drink human blood. But we don't do that sort of thing any more. We get our blood in bottles now, and keep it in the fridge. You're quite safe with me.

Rick: Oh . . . good.

Phyl: Do you trust[2] me?

Rick: Oh . . . er . . . yes, of course. I feel . . . perfectly safe.

Phyl: Great! I can tell that we're going to be good friends. Perhaps you can show me round the town a bit. Show me where it all happens.

Rick: Er . . . yes, fine . . . I'd love to.

Phyl: Wonderful. Let's make it this evening then. I've just got a couple more things to bring in, then our move's complete.

Rick: Er . . . can I give you a hand?[3]

Phyl: Well yes, if you like. Can you carry this for me, or is it too heavy?

Rick: I can manage.[4] What is it?

Phyl: My grandmother – ashes.[5] She was . . . burnt.

Rick: Oh. Right. Where shall I put it – her?

(Exit Phylthia, enter Mr Smith)

Mr Smith: Richard, come here.

Rick: Eh?

Mr Smith: Richard, I hope you will have nothing to do with these . . . people . . . things . . . whatever they are.

Rick: Vampires, Dad.

Mr Smith: Yes. Vampires. I hope you will have nothing to do with them.

Rick: Why not?

Mr Smith: They are different from us. They . . . live . . . differently. They don't understand our ways, and we don't understand their ways. It's a disgrace,[6] their moving into this neighbourhood.

Rick: They've got to live somewhere, Dad.

Mr Smith: Of course they have. But not in a respectable part of the town like this. It's a disgrace.

Rick: I think Phylthia is very nice.

Mr Smith: Do you? I must say, I don't think "nice" is the word I would choose.

Rick: Anyway, I've promised to take Phylthia out tonight. To show her around the town a bit.

Mr Smith: I see. She's getting her teeth into you already . . . so to speak. I'm sorry. Richard, you're of an age now where I can't force you to see only friends that your mother and I approve of.[7] But I want to say again, I hope you will have as little as possible to do with these . . . with our new neighbours.

(Exit Mr Smith)

Rick: And so, it all began. That evening, as arranged, Phylthia and I met. I put on a shirt with a high collar[8] – there's no point in taking chances.

(Exit Rick)

Scene 2 A pub

(Enter Phylthia and Rick)

Rick: What would you like to drink, Phyl?

Phyl: I'll have a tomato juice.

Rick: Right. Pint[9] of bitter[10] and a tomato juice please. Thanks. Here we are. Cheers.[11]

Phyl: Cheers. – Thanks for the drink, Rick.

Rick: That's all right.

Phyl: Rick . . .

Rick: Yeah?

Phyl: Why are all the people in this pub looking at us so strangely?

Rick: . . . Are they?

Phyl: Yes. Look at them. They're all staring[12] at us.

[1] bite, bit, bitten *beißen* [2] trust *vertrauen* [3] give sb. a hand = help sb.
[4] manage [ˈmænɪdʒ] *zurechtkommen* [5] ashes [ˈæʃɪz] *Asche* [6] disgrace [dɪsˈgreɪs] *Schande*
[7] approve of [əˈpruːv] *billigen, gutheißen* [8] collar [ˈkɒlə] *Kragen* [9] pint [paɪnt] *(engl. Maß = 0,568 l)*
[10] bitter *engl. Biersorte* [11] Cheers. [tʃɪəz] *Prost.* [12] stare at [steə] *anstarren*

Rick: Well, you see . . . I shouldn't think they get many vampires coming in here.

Phyl: It's putting me off[1] my drink – the way they're all looking at us. *(Raising her voice, to the other customers)* All right you lot,[2] you don't have to stare at us. Just get on with[3] your own drinks.

Rick: Phylthia, be quiet.

Phyl: What's the matter?[4] Haven't you ever seen a vampire before?

Rick: Phylthia . . .

Phyl: Are you afraid I'm going to bite you all? Can't I even enjoy a bloody[5] tomato juice without you all staring at me?

Rick: Phyl, come away.

Phyl: All right, I'm going. Yes, you lot. I'm a vampire and I live around here, and you're going to have to get used to it. I'm going now, and so you can get on with your drinks in peace, and all stare at each other instead of having to stare at me. Goodbye – till we meet again! *(They leave the pub)*

Rick: For God's sake[6], Phylthia, are you drunk?

Phyl: On one tomato juice? You must be joking.

Rick: Why did you have to do that?

Phyl: It really annoys me, the way these idiots all look at me, as if I were some creature[7] in the zoo. Why shouldn't I tell them what I think of them?

Rick: They'll drive you from the neighbourhood if you're not careful.

Phyl: I'm not ashamed[8] of being a vampire. I'm not going to hide my face behind a scarf[9] and pretend to be alive, just to please[10] them. They must learn to accept me.

Rick: Come on, let's get back home, before they come out and follow us.

Phyl: Rick – it's done me good to come out with you. I don't have many friends. As soon as people see that I'm a vampire they don't want to have anything to do with me. Look, before you go home, come into our place for a cup of coffee – will you?

Rick: Well, if you think it's safe, OK.

Scene 3 Phylthia's house

Phyl: So, here we are. This is it. What do you think of it?

Rick: Er . . . well it's nice . . . er . . . don't you have any furniture?

Phyl: Furniture?

Rick: You know. Chairs. Tables. You don't even have a bed.

Phyl: What would a vampire want with a bed?

Rick: Er . . . I see.

Phyl: A coffin[11] is all we need. You can sit on it, you can use it as a table, and when you're tired you can lie in it. Would you like to look in mine?

Rick: Oh, no thank you, that's quite all right.

Phyl: You can if you like.

Rick: No really . . . I'd rather not.[12]

Phyl: OK, please yourself.[13] Now, what would you like to drink? Coffee?

Rick: Thanks. What are you drinking – another tomato juice?

Phyl: No.

Rick: Oh, I see. Right. Cheers.

Phyl: Cheers. Let's sit down. This is my father's coffin. He won't mind. Rick . . . I'm sorry I made such a fool of myself in the pub.

Rick: That's all right. It was quite funny really.

Phyl: No, it wasn't fair on you. When I go out alone I can do what I like. But it was thoughtless of me to make a scene when I was with you.

Rick: That's all right. I enjoyed going out with you, anyway. – Oh God, what time is it?

Phyl: Just gone midnight. The best part of the day.

Rick: Past midnight? Oh God, my parents, I forgot. They lock up the house and go to bed at eleven. I'll have to wake them up. They'll be really angry.

Phyl: Haven't you got a key?

Rick: My parents won't give me one. They say they like to know when I'm back. They say they can't sleep if I'm not there. My father will be furious.[14] I've got to get back straight away. Look . . . will you come with me?

Phyl: Me come with you? Why?

Rick: My father's so polite with strangers. If you're with me he can't shout at me or do anything.

Phyl: Well, if you really think it'll help. OK.

Scene 4 Rick's house

(They knock at the door of Rick's house. Enter Mr Smith)

Rick: Hallo, Dad.

Mr Smith: Richard. What sort of a time do you call this? It's after midnight. Your mother and I have been worried out of our . . . oh. Good evening, Miss . . . er . . .

Phyl: Spatula.

[1] put sb. off sth. *jm. etwas verleiden* [2] you lot (infml.) *ihr alle* [3] get on with *weitermachen mit*
[4] What's the matter? *Was ist denn (los)?* [5] bloody (⚠ infml.) *verdammt; (im wörtlichen Sinne) blutig*
[6] for God's sake (infml.) *um Gottes willen* [7] creature [ˈkriːtʃə] *Geschöpf, Wesen*
[8] be ashamed of [əˈʃeɪmd] *sich schämen für* [9] scarf [skɑːf] *Schal* [10] please *gefallen* [11] coffin *Sarg*
[12] I'd rather not. [ˈrɑːðə] *Lieber nicht.* [13] Please yourself. *Wie du willst.* [14] furious [ˈfjʊərɪəs] *wütend*

Mr Smith: Er, yes, Miss Spatula. Good evening.

Phyl: Good evening, Mr Smith. You must excuse my bringing your son home so late.

Mr Smith: That's quite all right.

Phyl: Rick has been so kind to me. We were having such a lovely time that we never noticed how late it was.

Mr Smith: Really? Well, goodnight, Miss . . . er . . . Spatula.

Phyl: Goodnight.

Rick: Oh Dad, I promised Phylthia she could come in. She's terribly keen[1] to see what our house is like.

Phyl: Yes. Yes. Terribly keen.

Mr Smith: You want to come in?

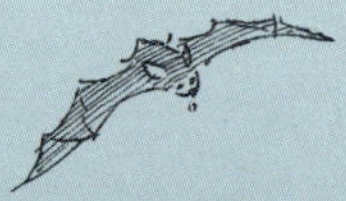

Rick: Yes.

Mr Smith: At this time of night?

Phyl: Yes.

Mr Smith: Oh. Well, perhaps it's not so bad. It gives me a chance to say something I've been wanting to say to the two of you. Do come in. Let me take your coat.

Phyl: No, thank you.

Mr Smith: Oh well, please yourself. Do sit down. Richard, find Miss Spatula a chair.

Phyl: I don't mind standing.

Mr Smith: Please yourself. Now you two . . . Your mother and I – that is Richard's mother and I – have been talking . . . Richard, you're now of an age . . . when we can talk to you – I hope we can talk to you? . . . Well, and your new . . . relationship[2] with Miss Spatula . . . leads me to say something which, perhaps, should have been said before . . . I hope you understand what I mean.

Rick: I've no idea, Dad.

Mr Smith: Well . . . When two young people . . . get together . . . spend time together . . . there are some things that you might need to know about. Maybe you know about them already, I don't know . . . with young people these days it all seems to happen so much earlier than with . . . with us older people . . . In my younger days, when I spent an evening with a young lady – with your mother, for example, before we were married – the most I could expect was to hold her hand . . . and it was only after we were married that . . . we . . . needed to know about . . . the sorts of things that perhaps you need to know about already . . . or perhaps not, I don't know. Anyway, seeing that the two of you have . . . begun this relationship . . . your mother and I – Mrs Smith and I – felt that we should . . . that I should perhaps make sure that the two of you do in fact . . . know about the things that you need to know about. I hope I'm making myself quite clear. . . . Where was I? Ah yes, you see, if you do . . . if you . . . decide to . . . then I hope you know what you have to . . . er . . . use. Er . . . do you?

Rick/Phyl: Yes.

Mr Smith: Good. Good. Well I'm so glad that's all out of the way. So nice that we were able to discuss it so sensibly[3] together. Good heavens[4] – is that really the time? Now I'm afraid it really is time we all went to bed – to our own beds, I mean. Miss Spatula, it's time you were going home. I do hope you've enjoyed seeing inside our house.

Phyl: Well, thank you for entertaining us, Mr Smith. You'll be all right, Rick?

Rick: I'll be all right. Good night, Phyl.

Phyl: Night, Rick. Bye.

(Exit Phylthia)

Rick: Good night, Dad.

Mr Smith: I don't know what to say.

Rick: What?

Mr Smith: I don't know what to say, what to think. That girl . . . that thing, whatever she is. You're breaking your mother's heart, you know – and mine. Coming home with her in the small hours of the morning. Bringing her in here, into our house.

Rick: Dad, you're talking about someone who, in the short time that I have known her, I've grown to like.[5]

Mr Smith: That's just it. You like her. You like that . . . thing.

Rick: Dad, don't call her that.

Mr Smith: After all we've done for you. Moving to this neighbourhood so that you could go to a good school. Paying out our money to buy you things. And this is how you thank us. Bringing us this . . . creature into our house.

Rick: Don't talk about her like that. I didn't ask you to buy me things. I'd rather you just tried to understand me as I am. I happen[6] to have taken a liking[7] to our new neighbour. So what? What's the harm?[8]

Mr Smith: What's the harm? Don't you know what she is?

[1] keen *neugierig, versessen* [2] relationship [rɪ'leɪʃnʃɪp] *Beziehung* [3] sensibly ['sensɪblɪ] *vernünftig*
[4] Good heavens! [ˌɡʊd 'hevnz] *Du lieber Himmel! Du liebe Zeit!*
[5] grow to like sb. *jn. lieben, schätzen lernen* [6] happen to do sth. *zufällig(erweise) etwas tun*
[7] take a liking to sb. *jn. gut leiden mögen, gern haben* [8] harm (n., v.) *Schaden; schaden*

Rick: She's a vampire, yeah. So what? She comes from a family of vampires. Am I supposed[1] to hate her just because of what her parents are?

Mr Smith: Your mother and I have done everything we could to bring you up[2] the right way – to bring you up to understand the decent[3] things in life – goodness, Christianity, love . . .

Rick: Love? What do you know about love? Isn't that just what I'm showing to Phylthia? You're the one that's unloving and un-Christian, the way you talk about her.

Mr Smith: You don't know what you're saying, Richard. I tell you I'm not going to stand by[4] and watch my son being . . . taken over by a vampire. I know it's hard for you, but I see that I must act now, before this thing goes any further. Richard, you must not see her again.

Rick: Dad, I'll see anyone I want to see. You can't lock me up like a princess in a tower. If I want to see Phylthia, I'll go and see her.

Mr Smith: No, Richard.

Rick: All my life you've been trying to make me into what you want – to make me into a younger version[5] of you. I'm a person in my own right[6], and you can't stop me from making friends with whoever I want to.

Mr Smith: I can certainly try. Listen to me, Richard . . .

Rick: I've listened to you enough.

Mr Smith: Don't be silly, Richard. I'm doing this for your own good.

Rick: You couldn't care less[7] about my good. You're doing it because you have the same lousy[8] prejudices about vampires as everyone else in this town, and you're worried about what the neighbours will think if they see me with a vampire . . .

Mr Smith: Richard, be quiet . . .

Rick: I won't be quiet. I've had enough of you. You can't control me. I'm old enough to know my own mind,[9] and if you try to stop me seeing Phylthia, I'll leave home.

Mr Smith: I have to stop you seeing her. It's for your own good.

Rick: What's for my own good is for me to decide. I'm going.

Mr Smith: Come back . . .

Rick: I'm off.[10] Good night!

(Richard leaves the house, slamming[11] the door. Exit Mr Smith)

Scene 5 Outside Phylthia's house

(For a moment Rick is alone. Then enter Phylthia)

Phyl: Rick?

Rick: Leave me alone.[12]

Phyl: Rick, what is it?

Rick: Go away. Leave me alone.

Phyl: What's the matter? What's happened? Rick . . .

Rick: Don't touch me!

Phyl: Rick . . .

Rick: So it's true. It's true what they all say. You only want to suck[13] my blood.

Phyl: No.

Rick: You wait till I can't resist[14] and then you take hold[15] of me, ready to sink your teeth . . .

Phyl: No Rick, it's not true.

Rick: I haven't got any friend I can turn to.

Phyl: I'm your friend, Rick. Don't you realize? I'm in the same state[16] as you. I don't have any friends either. I'm the only vampire in town – apart from[17] my father. I've never had anyone I can call a friend. And then you came along. You're the first person who's ever taken notice of me – who's been kind to me. I'd never harm you, Rick. I know what – I'll swear[18] to you.

Rick: Oh.

Phyl: Put your hand here. Now. I swear by my grandmother, Mildred the Mildewed[19], Arch-vampire and Fanged Terror[20] of Kensington Gore,[21] that I will never harm you, and never bite you, as long as I live. There. How's that? And now you must come inside. You're frozen, and tired out. I'll look after you.

(Exit Rick and Phyl)

Scene 6 Rick's house

(Enter Rick)

Rick: And so that's the story so far. As I said at the beginning, my parents don't like my

[1] be supposed to *sollen* [2] bring up *großziehen, aufziehen* [3] decent [ˈdiːsnt] *anständig*
[4] stand by *tatenlos zusehen* [5] version [ˈvɜːʃn] *Version, Ausgabe* [6] in my own right *hier: eigenständig*
[7] You couldn't care less . . . *. . . ist/sind dir doch völlig gleichgültig!* [8] lousy (infml.) [ˈlaʊzɪ] *lausig*
[9] know one's own mind *wissen, was man will* [10] be off (infml.) = go away, leave
[11] slam *zuschlagen, zuknallen* [12] leave sb. alone *jn. in Ruhe lassen* [13] suck *saugen*
[14] resist [rɪˈzɪst] *widerstehen* [15] take hold of sb. *jn. packen* [16] state *Situation, Zustand*
[17] apart from *außer* [18] swear [sweə] *schwören* [19] the Mildewed [ˈmɪldjuːd] *(erfundener Name, = die Verschimmelte)* [20] Fanged Terror [ˈfæŋd ˈterə] *(erfundener Titel, von 'fang' = Vampirzahn, Fang)*
[21] Kensington Gore *Straße in London ('gore' = auch 'Blut')*

girlfriend. So, you must be wondering, how does the story end? How could it end? Several things might happen. I could leave home, and go and live with Phylthia, and never see my parents again. Or I could decide that my father is right about vampires, go back to my parents, and never see Phylthia again. Or maybe my father could decide that vampires aren't so bad after all, and we could all be friends. What do you think? In real life there are no easy answers to questions like this. But this isn't real life – it's a play. So I'm OK: we can make the third ending – the happy one – happen.

(Enter Mr Smith and Phylthia)

Mr Smith: Richard, son, I'm sorry I ever doubted[1] you. Miss Spatula, you may be a vampire, but you're honest and loyal,[2] and I'm delighted[3] to have you as a neighbour. I hope that you and Richard will be good friends, and that you will visit us as often as you like.

Phyl: Everything's turned out right[4] in the end. Let's all sing a song to celebrate.

Mr Smith: A song?

Phyl: Yes. Come on, Rick.

Phyl/Rick: Vampires are OK –
Don't care what they say.
Pointed[5] teeth are fine –
Red eyes look divine.[6]
Coffins in your living-room –
Furnish[7] your house like a tomb.[8]
Vampires are OK.
Vampires are the best –
North south east and west.
Vampires are the thing –
Summer autumn winter spring.
Black cloaks[9] flying in the night –
Give your kids no cause for fright.[10]
Vampires are the best!

Mr Smith: I like vampires too –
They're just like me and you.
Vampires can be fun –
My next-door-neighbour's one.
I think pointed teeth are cute[11] –
If they want my blood they're welcome to't.
I like vampires too!

(End)

These excerpts from *Neighbours with Long Teeth* have been reprinted[12] by kind permission of the author, Peter Griffith. Peter Griffith is the founder of the White Horse Theatre Company, a group of professional actors[13] who tour Germany and put on plays for schools.

Some discussion points

1. Why do you think the author chose to make Phylthia a vampire?
2. What do you think the author is trying to say in this play?
3. What problems in real life are similar to the one in the play? Why?
4. Why do you think problems like the one in the play keep happening in real life, too?
5. Are there circumstances[14] in which parents have the right to stop their children from developing a particular[15] friendship or relationship?
6. How should children behave if they disagree with their parents on moral[16] or political questions?

- Try to act the play or parts of the play.

[1] doubt sb. [daʊt] *jm. nicht glauben; an jm. zweifeln* [2] loyal [ˈlɔɪəl] *loyal, treu* [3] delighted *hocherfreut* [4] turn out right *gut ausgehen* [5] pointed *spitz* [6] divine [dɪˈvaɪn] *göttlich* [7] furnish *möblieren* [8] tomb [tu:m] *Grab(kammer)* [9] cloak [kləʊk] *Umhang* [10] fright *Schreck(en)* [11] cute [kju:t] *niedlich* [12] reprint [ˌri:ˈprɪnt] *nachdrucken* [13] actor [ˈæktə] *Schauspieler/in* [14] circumstances [ˈsɜ:kmstənsɪz] *Umstände* [15] particular [pəˈtɪkjʊlə] *bestimmt* [16] moral [ˈmɒrəl] *moralisch*

The settlement[1] of Australia

Cook claiming Australia for Britain

1770	1776		1783	1788
James Cook claims Australia	Declaration of Independence[2] in America	American War of Independence	The 13 colonies become the United States of America	First prisoners arrive in Australia

When Captain James Cook landed on the east coast of Australia, he called the place he found Botany Bay[3] because there were so many beautiful flowers there. However, for seventeen years after Cook had discovered Australia, the English did nothing with their new colony. They could see no use for it. It was too far away. It was empty, uncultivated[4], and only Aborigines lived there. And they already had richer colonies in America, Canada and India. However, events in America soon made the English change their policy[5].

During the eighteenth century unemployment, poverty and crime were great social problems in England. Many families lived in dark, unhealthy homes. Children often died of illnesses and, if they survived, all they could expect from life was hard work and little to eat. Many people stole what they needed. As the prisons got fuller, the judges[6] became stricter and more cruel. Men and women were hanged for stealing sheep or even bread, or they were sent to work in one of the prison colonies in North America.

A public execution, 1780

After the War of Independence, the English lost their American colonies. But they still had an unexplored[7] and undeveloped continent at the other side of the world, which might bring them the kind of wealth the American colonies had brought. So the English turned their attention to Australia. But at first they only used it as a prison. Within a few years Botany Bay became the name of one of the most feared prison colonies in the world. It wasn't until the middle of the next century that regular settlement began.

Find out what sort of people settled in Australia in the nineteenth century.

[1] settlement ['setlmənt] *Besiedlung* [2] Declaration of Independence [ˌdekləˈreɪʃn‿əv‿ˌɪndɪˈpendəns] *Unabhängigkeitserklärung* [3] Botany Bay [ˌbɒtənɪ ˈbeɪ] [4] uncultivated [ˌʌnˈkʌltɪveɪtɪd] *unbebaut* [5] policy [ˈpɒlɪsɪ] *Politik* [6] judge [dʒʌdʒ] *Richter/in* [7] unexplored [ˌʌnɪkˈsplɔːd] *unerforscht*

The story of Henry and Susannah

Poor families in 1800

The year is 1783. In a small village in England a father went out one evening with his young son to find food. Like many families in England they were very poor, and the father had no work. They decided to go to a farm and steal a rabbit or any other wild animal they could find. It was a dark night. The two moved quietly through the trees, but they weren't careful enough, and they were seen. They tried to run away and hide, but they were caught and taken to prison.

When they appeared in court, Henry and his father had little hope, and the judge[1] made his decision quickly.

"This isn't the first time you have been here," said the judge. "But it will be the last. This time you will hang. Both of you."

But Henry's mother cried out, "Please have mercy[2], my Lord[3]. My son is only 14. He still has his whole life before him. He is too young to die. Please don't let him hang." The judge looked at the two prisoners: the father, miserable and poor like so many he had seen before, and the young boy, thin, dirty and hungry, his clothes like rags[4]. "The father will hang," said the judge. "The boy will go to prison for 14 years." And so Henry was taken away to one of the worst prisons in England, Norwich Jail[5].

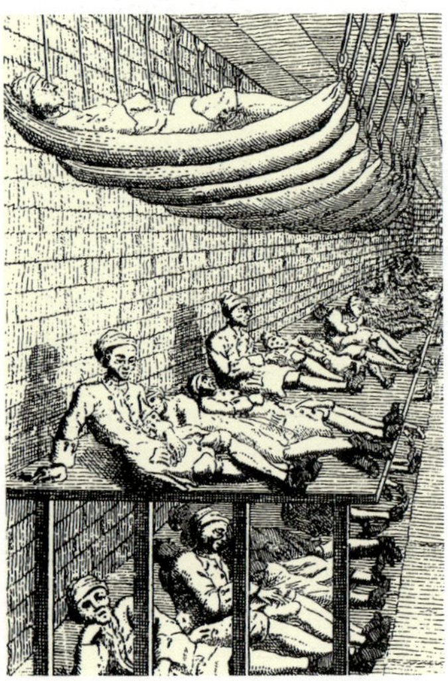

A crowded prison in London

In Norwich Jail the prisoners, men, women and children, were all together. It was dirty, crowded and dangerous. Only the fittest could survive. Henry stayed there for three years, and during this time he met and fell in love with a young girl called Susannah. She was in prison for stealing two silver[6] spoons from her mistress[7]. Susannah had wanted to run away from her cruel and miserable life as a serving girl, but she now found herself in a situation that was even worse than the one before.

"I don't think I'll ever come out of here alive," she said, keeping close to Henry for protection[8].

"You're lucky you're here," said an older prisoner. "Prisoners are usually sent to America. But now they've lost that country in the war, so there's nowhere they can send us."

"Why send us anywhere?" asked Susannah.

"Because the prisons are full. Half the nation is behind bars[9]. Food and money are only for the rich, my dearest. The poor can die in prison. But as I said, the prisons are full, so now they'll have to hang everybody."

"You can't hang the whole population," said Henry angrily. "Just the poor," said the prisoner. "Just the poor."

The same year that Henry and Susannah were sent to Norwich Jail, the United States of America officially became an independent country. In May 1787, the English decided to send the first group of prisoners to establish[10] a settlement at Botany Bay. Captain Arthur Phillip, who sailed with the First Fleet, had eleven ships, about 600 male passengers and 180 female passengers.

[1] judge [dʒʌdʒ] *Richter/in* [2] mercy [ˈmɜːsɪ] *Gnade* [3] my Lord [lɔːd] *Euer Ehren* [4] rags [ræɡz] *Lumpen*
[5] jail [dʒeɪl] *Gefängnis* [6] silver [ˈsɪlvə] *silbern, Silber-* [7] mistress [ˈmɪstrɪs] *Herrin*
[8] protection [prəˈtekʃn] *Schutz* [9] bar [bɑː] *Gitter* [10] establish [ɪˈstæblɪʃ] *gründen*

They had food for two years as well as pigs, chickens and sheep. One of the female passengers was Susannah.

During those four years in prison Susannah and Henry had had a child. They had wanted to marry while in prison, but it hadn't been possible. To make things worse, Susannah had had to leave Henry and go to Portsmouth.

"Please, let me go with her," Henry begged[1].

"She and the child go alone," said the guard and pushed him away from her.

For hours Susannah and two other women prisoners rode through the cold November weather towards the coast where the ships were waiting. When Susannah arrived at the harbour, the captain saw the child and refused to take it.

"I have no orders to take babies," he shouted. "Take it away from her." "No, you can't," Susannah screamed. "He's mine. You can't take him away from me." "Who brought them here?" asked the captain. "Where's the driver?" "They have come from Norwich Jail," the driver said. "The baby was born there."

"Well, you can ride back to Norwich Jail and take the baby with you. The woman stays here, but the baby goes back to prison."

Convicts in chains in the port of London

The coach[2] driver was horrified[3]. Feeling sorry for Susannah, he rode instead to London and carried the baby to the house of Lord Sydney, a very important man in the British government. Lord Sydney was a kind man and, although shocked that a coach driver should run into his house with a baby in his arms, he listened to what had happened and decided that the baby should go with the mother and that Henry should be allowed to marry Susannah and go with them.

And so Henry, Susannah and their baby son sailed on one of the first ships that left Britain for the new prison colony in faraway Australia. The journey took eight months, until they finally arrived at the place where James Cook had landed 18 years earlier, at Botany Bay. The captain did not want to walk through the sea from the boat to the coast, so Henry offered to carry him on his back. As he walked out of the sea onto the beach, Henry became the first prisoner to stand on the new colony. And two weeks later, on February 10th, Henry and Susannah finally got married in the first British marriage ceremony ever held on the Australian continent.

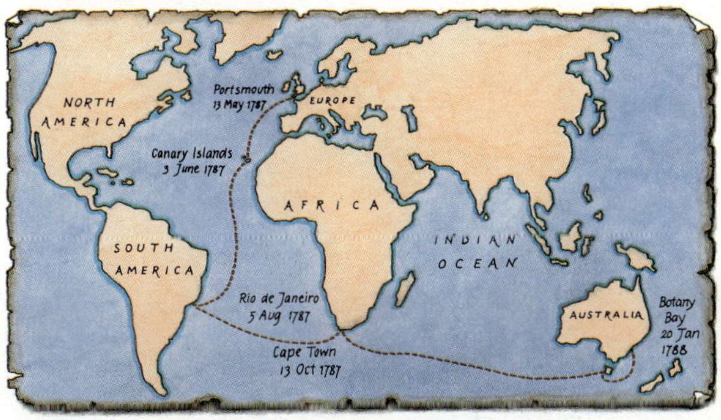

The system of transportation[4] stopped in 1853, but up to that time thousands of women and men were put in ships and sent to the other side of the world. When their sentences[5] were over, Henry and Susannah Cable[6] stayed in Australia as farmers. Henry was 82 when he died, Susannah died before him. But their children and grandchildren[7] lived on. Today there are many Australian families like the Cables who can say that their ancestors first came to Australia as prisoners.

Imagine that Henry Cable's great-grandchildren want to hear the story of Susannah. Tell the story for them.

[1] beg [beg] *(dringend) bitten* [2] coach [kəʊtʃ] *Kutsche* [3] horrified ['hɒrɪfaɪd] *entsetzt*
[4] transportation [ˌtrænspɔː'teɪʃn] *Verschiffung* [5] sentence *Strafe* [6] Cable ['keɪbl]
[7] grandchildren ['græntʃɪldrən] *Enkelkinder*

From Empire[1] to European Community

A cup of tea – the national drink – is something the British got used to a long time ago. So this packet of Indian tea from an English supermarket can look back on a long history. By 1700, England was importing 50,000 kg of tea a year. It was just one of the products coming into the country from its fast-growing trading empire, which reached from China to America. Wherever new lands were discovered, private companies moved in to develop trade, and many became fantastically rich. In India, the British Government gave the East India Company the monopoly[2] on trade. The picture below shows General Robert Clive (left), who was once an official[3] of the East India Company, after his famous victory at Plassey in 1757.

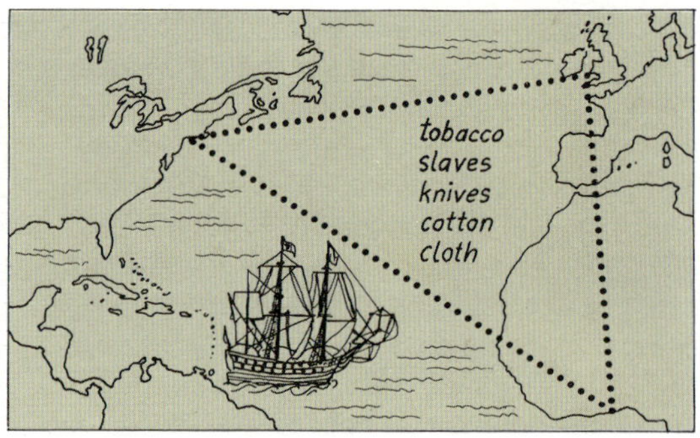

The Trade Triangle[4]: this was the richest trading route in the world until 1815. Say what was traded between the three continents.

Other people left Britain not only to trade but simply to settle in a new country. They were unhappy with poor living conditions at home, or sometimes they wanted to escape religious discrimination. After America and Canada many more countries, for example Australia or one of the African colonies, became new homes for the British. From 1815-60, about 7 million people left the British Isles.

In the 19th century, the British Government took over direct political control of the Empire. With the help of a large and modern navy[5], new lands were won and British interests protected. In the end, the British Empire covered a quarter of the world's land surface[6] and English was spoken on every continent. Queen Victoria was called "Empress"[7] to show her power. A popular song expressed the feelings of the British Empire-builders in its first two lines: "Rule Britannia, Britannia rule the waves, Britons never, never, never shall be slaves!"

[1] Empire [ˈempaɪə] *brit. Weltreich* [2] monopoly (on sth.) [məˈnɒpəlɪ] *Monopolstellung (auf etwas)*
[3] official [əˈfɪʃl] *Funktionär/in* [4] triangle [ˈtraɪæŋgl] *Dreieck* [5] navy [ˈneɪvɪ] *Kriegsflotte*
[6] surface [ˈsɜːfɪs] *Oberfläche* [7] empress [ˈemprɪs] *Kaiserin*

Controlling its huge Empire was an expensive and difficult business. And soon the British Government had to face powerful movements[1] for self-government.

Mahatma Gandhi (1869-1948)
In India, it was Mahatma Gandhi who led the 300 million people in his country out of the British Empire and into independence. It was a long struggle[2], but through it all his rule was: use no violence! Gandhi was a Hindu[3] and a strong believer in the simple life. He ate no meat, had few possessions, and, in his later life, wore only a simple cloth which he spun[4] himself.
Gandhi didn't see much of India as a young man. He was trained as a lawyer in England and then found a job in South Africa, where he stayed for 21 years. Having fought injustice[5] there, he was in a good position to help to free India from foreign government.
One of the many things the Indians hated about the British was their tax on salt. Everybody used salt, anybody could easily make it, but the British said only they were allowed to make and sell it. This was because they wanted the Indians to pay tax on it. Gandhi had an idea for a peaceful protest[6] that would still have an effect. One day, he started out with a few followers to "steal" salt – from the sea. It was a 241-mile-march, on foot. Everywhere they passed, new supporters joined the marchers. When he reached the sea, Gandhi had several thousand followers. The crowds on the beach watched as he picked up some salt left by the waves. He was breaking British law by being in possession of salt which hadn't been sold and taxed by the British. It was a signal. Soon Indians all over the country were following his example and making salt from seawater.
With tactics[7] like this, Gandhi won the respect of the Indians and of world opinion, but also of British people. The year was 1930 and he still had a long way to go before India was finally given independence in 1947. Often he was put in prison and often he went on a hunger strike to achieve his aims.
His end was tragic[8]: just a few weeks after his nation had become independent, a Hindu fanatic[9] shot Gandhi dead as he was going to say his prayers.

- Find out why Gandhi was shot.
- The pictures on this page are from a very successful Gandhi film. They show you scenes mentioned in the text. Write some captions[10] for them.

[1] movement [ˈmuːvmənt] *Bewegung* [2] struggle [ˈstrʌgl] *Kampf* [3] Hindu [ˈhɪnduː] *Hindu*
[4] spin, spun, spun [spɪn, spʌn] *spinnen* [5] injustice [ɪnˈdʒʌstɪs] *Ungerechtigkeit*
[6] protest [ˈprəʊtest] *Protest* [7] tactics [ˈtæktɪks] *Taktik* [8] tragic [ˈtrædʒɪk] *tragisch*
[9] fanatic [fəˈnætɪk] *Fanatiker/in* [10] caption [ˈkæpʃn] *(Bild-)Unterschrift*

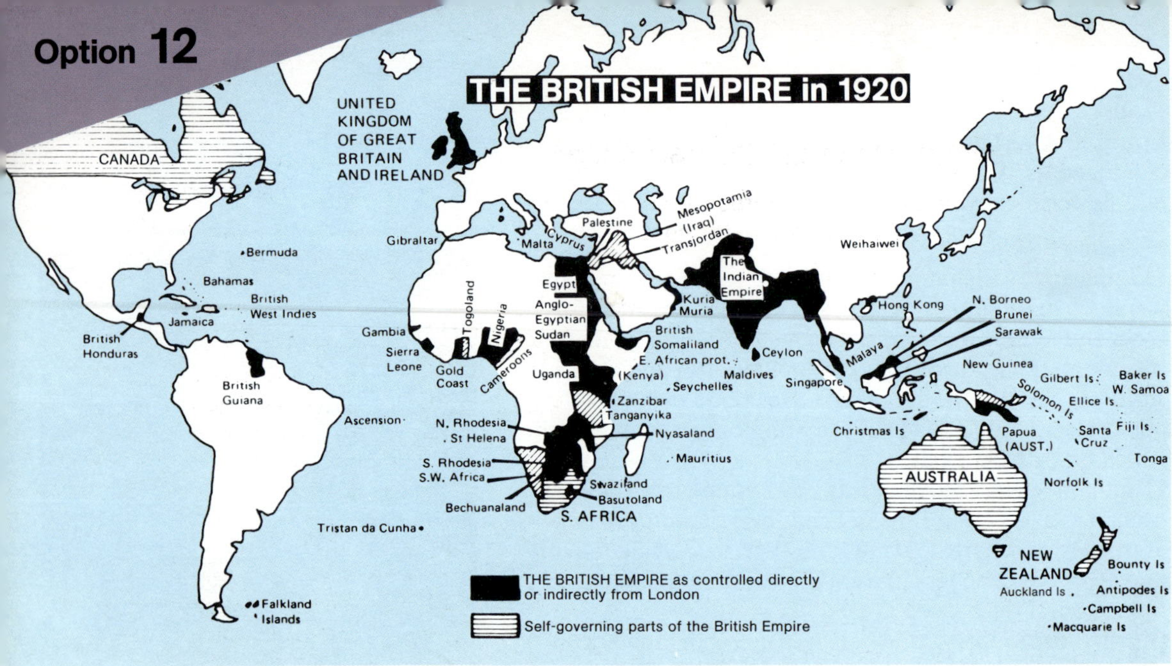

Wealthy[1] Britons used to go on a "grand tour" round the world, stopping at many of the British colonies. Imagine you were such a "tourist" – which route would you choose? Which countries would you visit?

Commonwealth[2] and European Community

Canada, Australia and other colonies became independent long before India. Between 1945 and 1965, nearly all the rest were given self-government, and all in all, the change was peaceful. Most nations chose to keep special connections to Britain by staying in the "Commonwealth of Nations"[3]. The British monarch[4] is the head of this organization, but the former[5] colonies which join are free and equal members. When the 48 leaders of these countries meet every two years, they represent[6] all kinds of different states. The meetings help them to keep in contact economically and politically, but there is also an important sporting contact: the Commonwealth Games.

Britain tried to keep its international influence through the Commonwealth, but decided to work more within Europe, too. It joined the European Community in 1973.

Now Britain is trying with the other members to take away the political and trading barriers[7] and to create a real European Community. However, many Britons are worried about these changes and feel that their country is losing some of its independence.

Proportion of British exports[8] . . .

	to the Commonwealth	*to the European Community*
in 1972	*19%*	*34%*
in 1987	*11%*	*49%*

What do the statistics tell you about Britain's trade with the Commonwealth and the European Community?

[1] wealthy ['welθɪ] *wohlhabend* [2] Commonwealth ['kɒmənwelθ] *Commonwealth* [3] British Commonwealth of Nations *die brit. Völkergemeinschaft* [4] monarch ['mɒnək] *Monarch/in* [5] former ['fɔːmə] *früher* [6] represent [ˌreprɪ'zent] *vertreten* [7] barrier ['bærɪə] *Schranke* [8] exports ['ekspɔːts] *Exportgüter*

The development of the English language

English			
cow	mouse	beef	defend
German		**French**	
Kuh	Maus	bœuf	défendre

A lot of English words are easy for Germans to learn as they are similar in both languages. But the same could be said by the French. Why is this?

When the Romans left Britain after almost 400 years, the country and the Celtic people who lived there were unprotected. Soon the island was invaded by different tribes from northern Germany and Denmark – the Angles and Saxons.

c. AD 400

From the Romans came a lot of place names ending in -chester, -cester, -caster.

The Angles and Saxons settled in large areas of Britain. These tribes spoke similar Germanic[1] dialects. And a new language, Anglo-Saxon, replaced[2] Celtic as the native language of Britain.

c. 650

From the Angles and the Saxons came: mother, brother, father; eat, sleep, drink; cow, cat, fish, field.

During the 9th century Vikings[3] from Denmark and Norway started settling in Britain. They introduced many of their words, but the language remained basically Anglo-Saxon.

c. 800

The Vikings added: law, skin, sky, knife, take, hit, same, ugly, they, them, their.

The Normans were the last people to conquer Britain. For 300 years their language, French, was the official language of the country. However, Anglo-Saxon remained the language of the native people. Most of them never even learned French. In the 14th century English became a kind of "mixture" of Anglo-Saxon and Norman French.

1066

The Normans introduced: government, parliament, minister, officer, science, religion, judge, court, crime, defend.

Over the centuries the English language continued to develop and show a great ability to accept words from other languages. As British explorers came back from different countries in the 15th and 16th centuries, they introduced words such as 'shampoo' and 'pyjamas' from India, 'tea' and 'tobacco' from America. And it has continued to accept more and more new words: 'anorak' from the Eskimos[4], 'moccasins'[5] from the American Indians, 'rucksack' and 'kindergarten' from the Germans. Today, the English language has over 800,000 words – more than any other language in the world.

Here are lists of 1. Latin, 2. French words.
Try to find the English words corresponding to them.

1. absens, accipere, Britanni, certo, destruere, difficilis, Germania, machina, pagina, parens, persona, persuadere, promittere, serius, signum, theatrum, violentia
2. activité, adresse, appartement, automne, citoyen, commun, dictionnaire, découvrir, grandmère, hôpital, idée, introduire, leçon, littérature, prix, prononciation, produire, survivre, véhicule, vocabulaire

[1] Germanic [dʒɜˈmænɪk] *germanisch* [2] replace [rɪˈpleɪs] *ersetzen* [3] Viking [ˈvaɪkɪŋ] *Wikinger*
[4] Eskimo [ˈeskɪməʊ] *Eskimo* [5] moccasin [ˈmɒkəsɪn] *Mokkasin*

Language: the humorous[1] side

"Crazy" spelling

You remember G. B. Shaw's "ghoti" as a spelling for "fish" (page 80)? – Well, here's a poem about the "crazy" way sound and spelling disagree in English:

When the English tongue[2] we speak
Why is *break* not rhymed with *weak*?
Won't you tell me why it's true
We say *sew*,[3] but also *few*?
And the maker of a verse[4]
Cannot rhyme his *horse* with *worse*?

Think of *blood* and *food* and *good*;
Mould[5] is not pronounced like *could*.
Why is it *done*, but *gone* and *lone*[6] –
Is there any reason known?
To sum it up,[7] it seems to me
That sounds and letters don't agree.

Puns[8]

A lot of English jokes are based on puns, or plays on words, i. e. words which sound the same but have a different meaning.

A limerick

There was a young fellow named Hall,
Who fell in the spring[13] in the fall;
'Twould have been a sad thing
Had he died in the spring,
But he didn't – he died in the fall.

Tongue twisters[14]

Try to say six times quickly: Greek grapes[15] · Mixed biscuits · Red lorry, yellow lorry
And this is almost impossible: The sixth sick sheik's[16] sixth sheep's sick.

[1] humorous [ˈhjuːmərəs] *humorvoll* [2] tongue [tʌŋ] *Zunge*; hier: *Sprache* [3] sew [səʊ] *nähen*
[4] verse [vɜːs] *Vers, Reim* [5] mould [məʊld] *Gußform* [6] lone [ləʊn] *einsam*
[7] sum sth. up *etwas zusammenfassen* [8] pun [pʌn] *Wortspiel* [9] bright *auch: intelligent*
[10] upside down *verkehrt herum* [11] pasteurized [ˈpɑːstjʊraɪzd] *pasteurisiert* [12] lay *legen;* lay the table *den Tisch decken* [13] spring *Quelle* [14] tongue twister *Zungenbrecher*
[15] grape [greɪp] *Weintraube* [16] sheik [ʃiːk] *Scheich*

Translation practice

Remember: When you have to translate a text, you should keep to the original as closely as possible and at the same time produce a "correct" text in the other language. For a good translation you need to know all the words in a text. Whenever you find new words on the following three pages, try to guess their meaning. If you don't understand a word and if you can't find it in the mini-dictionary, use a dictionary.

Unit 1:

Translate the following text.

The Archers – the longest-running daily radio serial in the world

In January 86 The Archers celebrated its 35th birthday and on May 26th, 1989 the 10,000th episode of the serial was broadcast. It is heard by a growing number of people on the Continent. Around the world the events in the small village of Ambridge, the made-up setting for the programme, can be listened to on BFBS, the British Forces Broadcasting Service. So The Archers is probably the only thing that is still left from the British Empire. It is a programme "on which the sun never sets". It can be heard 48 times every 24 hours around the world.

Not long ago a respectable English newspaper wrote: "The programme makers know that The Archers is a national institution, listened to by the great and the good and even the Royals, as well as four million others – it is the most successful programme of its kind. They also know that it is increasingly popular among younger listeners."

But let us go back for a moment into "pre-history". Not quite to the Ice-Age, but to about 1950, the days when Britain had only one television channel, which operated for only a few hours each evening – in black and white of course. It was then that the idea for The Archers came up at a meeting between farmers, the BBC and the government. Farmers were not listening to BBC farming programmes as often as the BBC and the government wanted them to; and farmers were not interested enough in modern methods of farming. Someone made a comment that a kind of soap opera was needed. Everybody laughed, but the programme was born: The life of a small English farming village with all its ups and downs was and still is at the centre of this unbelievably successful radio serial, although today the programme is no longer intended to inform farmers about methods of farming.

(Based on: W. Smethurst, *The Archers – The New Official Companion*)

Unit 2:

Remember: Some verbal expressions in English can be translated into German as adverbs.

Examples:

I'd like to go to the swimming-pool.	Ich würde gern ins Schwimmbad gehen.
I told him to stop, but he still continued shouting.	..., aber er schrie trotzdem weiter.
I know that she used to go sailing a lot.	..., daß sie früher oft segeln ging.

⚠ *Used to* (to describe a past habit) needn't always be translated:
When they lived at the seaside, they used to go sailing every weekend.
Als sie an der See lebten, gingen sie jedes Wochenende segeln.

→ Vocabulary p. 143

Heard at a party where some people didn't know any German and others didn't know any English

Translate the sentences. Use adverbs in German and verbal expressions in English.

1. Hoffentlich regnet es morgen nicht. 2. I hate going for walks in the rain. 3. Ich verbringe meinen Urlaub lieber in den Bergen als am Meer. 4. Früher habe ich viel Sport getrieben. 5. Until not so long ago my wife and I used to go to Spain twice a year. 6. I suppose Tom will stay at home tomorrow. 7. Susan seems to have gone to town. 8. I'm very sorry I can't go to the cinema with you on Friday.

Unit 3:

In English you quite often find the construction[1] adjective/noun + *for* + object + *to*-infinitive. The translation into German varies[2] according to the context.

Examples:

At first it was impossible for Christopher to express himself.	Anfangs war es unmöglich für Christopher, sich auszudrücken.
His parents bought a typewriter for him to use.	Seine Eltern kauften eine Schreibmaschine, die er benutzen konnte.

Now translate the following text about Christopher Nolan, a young Irish writer.

Christopher Nolan was eleven years old before anybody knew he could write. It was hardly possible for his family to communicate with him in any way. His extreme physical handicap – caused by a difficult birth – was so bad that it was hard for people to believe that there was a perfectly normal mind inside this body. To most people Christopher just seemed a totally disabled person sitting in his wheelchair and staring at the grey Dublin sky. He was a person to pity, no more.

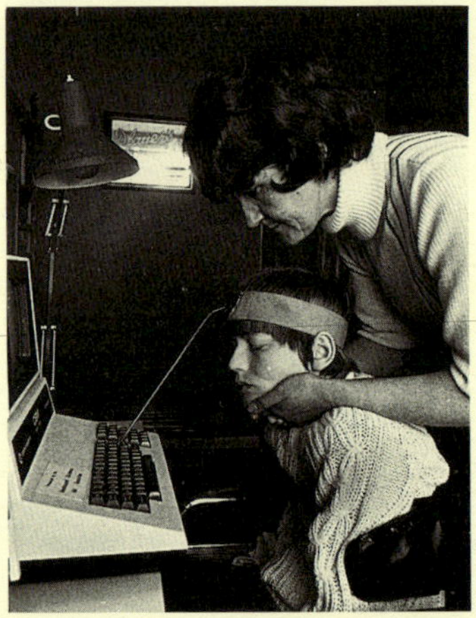

But in his eleventh year Christopher's life changed completely: a new drug made it possible for him to control the movements of his head for short periods of time. His doctors made a "unicorn" stick for him to fit on his forehead. To the surprise of everybody he soon learnt to use a typewriter with this stick. His doctors had found a way for him to express himself, to write down everything he had had to keep inside himself for so many years. And although at first it took ten to fifteen minutes for him to type just one word, he kept on working.

Only five years later, in 1981, Christopher's first book, *Dam-Burst of Dreams*, was published and made him known as a talented young writer. His life story *Under the Eye of the Clock* won the Whitbread Book of the Year Award in 1987. Today it is almost unthinkable for educated people in the British Isles not to have heard of Christopher Nolan. His work has been compared to that of the greatest modern Irish writers.

(Based on the introduction to C. Nolan, *Dam-Burst of Dreams*)

[1] construction [kən'strʌkʃn] *Wortfügung* [2] vary ['veərɪ] *sich (ver)ändern*

Unit 4:

Remember: In written English – in newspapers, magazines and encyclopedias[1], for example – and in radio and television news programmes participle constructions are quite common. When translating participle constructions into German, we almost always use subordinate clauses.

Translate the following text into German using subordinate clauses for the participle constructions where possible.

Magazines advertising computers sometimes suggest that computers have human characteristics. But, as anybody working with computers will tell you, computer hardware, consisting of the keyboard, the screen, disks and the central processing unit, is neither friendly, clever nor intelligent.

The human characteristics referred to in these adverts are to be found in another part of the computer system: the software. Being "invisible", software is often a mystery to people who only have little knowledge of computer systems.

However, having come a long way since Harvard Mark I (1943), the first fully automatic computer, the computer today no longer needs a computer expert to operate it. Early computers, programmed in machine code and therefore demanding a lot of expert knowledge, could not be operated by people simply wanting to use a computer for their work. In the meantime, many computer languages have been invented and developed, and one main characteristic of computer software today is that it can be used much more flexibly than ever before. These days one person, without needing to know in detail a program written by someone else, can easily incorporate this program into one written by himself or herself. It is enough to know how to call the program into action and to know about the conditions under which it will not work.

(Based on Hutchinson's *Encyclopedia of Modern Technology,* "Computer Software")

Unit 5:

a

Brits find better use for books

In some southern African countries there is a shortage not of food, but of books. Chris Martin, a British headmaster, discovered the lack of textbooks in schools in Malawi,[2] Zambia[3] and in Tanzania,[4] for example.

Now he is collecting books all over the country to send them there.
The first shipment consisted of more than 20,000 books.

Translate this text into German for your school magazine.

b *Imagine some German teachers have heard about this project and are talking about it. Translate their conversation. Be careful: In the English sentences you will have to use modal auxiliaries with a perfect infinitive.*

Herr Hubig: Unsere Schule hätte auch Englischbücher nach Afrika schicken können.

Frau Meier: Schade, wir hätten das früher wissen müssen.

Frau Stück: Ich hätte vielleicht eine Sammlung von Deutschbüchern organisiert.

Herr Fink: Hätten wir wirklich so viele Bücher sammeln können?

Frau Siegel: Wir hätten fragen und uns besser informieren können.

[1] encyclopedia [ɪnˌsaɪklə'pi:dɪə] *Lexikon* [2] Malawi [mə'lɑ:wɪ] [3] Zambia ['zæmbɪə] [4] Tanzania [ˌtænzə'nɪə]

Explaining grammar in English

There was a young pupil of Garmisch
Who just loved the English language.
She used words like "subject"
And "indirect object"
To talk about grammar – in English.

1 The following sentences from a pupil's exercise book all have mistakes in them. Look at how the first three mistakes have been explained. Then try to correct and explain mistakes 4, 5 and 6. The grammatical terms on pages xxi and xxii and the phrases on the next page will help you.

This bike used to belong to me. Now it is belonging[1] to my younger sister. [I]

I have been[2] at the youth club last night. If I would have known[3] about the football match on TV, I had stayed[3] at home. [II]

Why did you get a firm to do that work for you? You two could have done it yourself.[4] [I]

I feed my rabbits regular[5] every morning. I give them very often carrots.[6] [II]

1 *Belong* can't be used in the progressive form because it is a state verb. So you have to use the simple form *belongs* in spite of the signal word *now*.

2 *Have been* is the wrong tense here. The simple past *was* must be used in this sentence because *last night* tells us when the speaker was at the youth club.

3 The verb forms in this conditional sentence are incorrect. The speaker is talking about consequences[1] of a past situation that did not happen. The condition can no longer be fulfilled.[2] For conditional sentences of this kind ("conditional III") a past perfect form (= *had* + past participle) should be used in the *if*-clause. In the main clause the form to use is *would have* + past participle.

4 . . .

2 In order to explain grammar in English you should be able to identify[3] and name[4]
– grammatical forms like simple present, past participle, active, etc.
– parts of speech[5] like noun, adjective, preposition, etc.
– parts of a sentence like subject, indirect object, adverbial, etc.
– clause types[6] like main clause, relative clause, etc.

But, most importantly, you should be able to say *why* a particular[7] word, grammatical form or word order is used or not used in a given sentence.

Ex *Read the following sentences and try to explain the use of the underlined grammatical forms. (Look at the phrases in 3c first.) This is something you may be asked to do in an English test.*

1. When were you born? 2. Jane sings very well. 3. The man talking to John is my brother. 4. If you came back tomorrow, we would have more time to talk. 5. This is the book ____ I was looking for. *(Why no relative pronoun?)* 6. This isn't your pen. Yours is over there. 7. I'm looking forward to going to your party. 8. I was in Brighton yesterday. *(word order)*

[1] consequence [ˈkɒnsɪkwəns] *Folge, Konsequenz* [2] fulfil [fʊlˈfɪl] *erfüllen*
[3] identify [aɪˈdentɪfaɪ] *identifizieren, erkennen* [4] name *benennen* [5] part of speech [spiːtʃ] *Wortart*
[6] type [taɪp] *Typ, Art* [7] particular [pəˈtɪkjʊlə] *bestimmt*

3 Phrases which will help you to talk about grammar in English

a Questions

Can I say *She has died yesterday*? What's wrong with (saying) . . . ?
Why is this tense wrong? Why do I have to use the simple past?
Why can't I use the present perfect in this sentence?
Which tense do I need?/do I have to use?/should I use?
Shouldn't the verb *die* be in the simple past? (⚠ *Not:* ~~stand~~ in the past)

Could you use Would it be wrong to use	the past progressive/the passive here?

b Saying what is wrong

Martin has confused[1] the tenses.
The word order is wrong.
Sandra has left out/omitted[2] the indefinite article.
Sandra should have used the indefinite article.
The indefinite article is missing.

It's wrong/incorrect to You can't	say *these informations.* use *information* in the plural.

c Explaining forms and functions[3]

(Try and put in the missing grammatical terms.)

We use . . . **You use** . . . . . . **is used**	**to say** what was going on at a particular time in the past. **to refer to**[4]**/express/describe** an activity in progress in the past.

We/You form . . . **with** *have/has + past participle.*

The past participle of regular verbs **is formed**	**by adding** *-ed* **to** . . . . **in the same way as** . . . .

We/You use *do* **to form/make/ask questions** in the simple present or . . . .

The object **must follow** the verb.
The subject **must come before/must be followed by** . . . .
Prepositions **are** usually **put at the end of** . . . , not **at the beginning**.

The simple past in *If I saw her* **refers to** . . . or . . . , not to . . . .
A conditional sentence **consists of** . . . and . . . .
In *the man sitting over there* the present participle **stands for** . . . with an active verb.
The adverb *heavily* in *It was raining heavily* **modifies**[5] . . . .
A relative clause **is** usually **introduced by** . . . .
The relative pronoun **can be left out/omitted** if it is . . . of the relative clause.
In indirect questions . . . **is the same as** in statements:[6] S-V-O.

I'm going to see him tomorrow **is similar to** *I'm seeing him tomorrow.*
I must go **has a slightly**[7] **different meaning to** *I have to go.*
She looked angry **means something different to** *She looked angrily.*

Fast (as in *run fast*) **is an exception.**[8] **Normally/As a rule**[9] . . . **end in** *-ly.*

[1] confuse [kən'fju:z] *verwechseln* [2] omit [ə'mɪt] *auslassen* [3] function ['fʌŋkʃn]
[4] refer to [rɪ'fɜ:] *sich beziehen auf* [5] modify ['mɒdɪfaɪ] *näher bestimmen*
[6] statement ['steɪtmənt] *Aussage(satz)* [7] slight [slaɪt] *leicht, geringfügig*
[8] exception [ɪk'sepʃn] *Ausnahme* [9] as a rule *in der Regel*

Option 17

How to write a summary

In *Round Ireland in Low Gear*[1] Eric Newby, a well-known writer of travel books, tells his readers about the trips he and his wife Wanda made through different parts of Ireland.

Return to Kilmakilloge[2] (Adapted from Eric Newby, *Round Ireland in Low Gear*, London 1987)

In 1968, two or three years after our first visit, just before Christmas, we decided that the only thing to do, in order to avoid a hectic Christmas in England, was to forget it and leave the country. My daughter said she would like to come, too.
I rang Ted O'Sullivan's pub at Kilmakilloge where we had stayed the last time. Ted's wife reacted surprisingly unenthusiastically. Still, I arranged a crossing to Cork for our Land Rover and the three of us on the 23 December. On the morning of Christmas Eve I asked the tourist office at Cork to telephone the O'Sullivans and tell them of our decision to arrive on their doorstep. "They will take you," we were told, "but they don't sound very excited about it."
It was dark when we arrived. Mrs O'Sullivan looked at Wanda, surprised and happy, when we entered the bar of their pub. "Oh," she said, "I thought it was another Mr and Mrs Newby. We had another woman with a name something like that. She was a terrible woman, the kind of woman who has forty dresses."
We had a fantastic time with the O'Sullivans that Christmas and did a lot of walks in the area. One afternoon we met an old farmer with a brand new car, something pretty unusual in the Kilmakilloge area at that time. "Can you please turn it round for me?" he asked, "if not I will have to drive it all round the Beara Peninsula and over the Healy Pass, about eighty miles. I haven't yet got the trick of going backwards."
When we went back to England, we knew that wherever we might go in the world, this was one place to which we would want to return.

The aim of a summary is to give someone who does not know a text an idea what it is about without retelling[3] every detail of the original. You only state the main points. A summary must be without any personal comment. Leave out such things as examples, comparisons and direct speech. Now read the following steps[4] very carefully.

1. Read the text several times – at least twice. Then try to say in one sentence what the whole text is about. It will help if you ask yourself questions with *who, what, where* and *when.* The title may help you, too. You could start your summary like this: The text is about . . . (see summary on the next page).

2. Examine the structure[5] of the text by looking for changes of time, of place or of characters. The above text contains many adverbials of time so it can easily be structured[6] according to the changes of time.
   a. Underline the adverbials of time in the text.
   b. Divide the text into its different parts according to the changes of time.
   c. Write down key words for each part or summarize the content of each part in one or two sentences. Be careful to use your own words.

If you choose to structure this text according to changes of place, you'll get exactly the same parts (cf. the key words in brackets).

Example:
1st part: ll. 1-9: in 1968, just before Christmas (Newbys' home in England)
a. decision to go to Kilmakilloge / get away from hectic time in England
b. preparations[7]: phone O'Sullivans' pub / unfriendly answer

[1] gear [gɪə] *Gang (eines Autos oder Fahrrads)* [2] Kilmakilloge [ˌkɪlməkɪˈləʊg] [3] retell [ˌriːˈtel] *nacherzählen*
[4] step *Schritt* [5] structure [ˈstrʌktʃə] *Struktur* [6] structured [ˈstrʌktʃəd] *gegliedert, strukturiert*
[7] preparation [ˌprepəˈreɪʃn] *Vorbereitung*

2nd part: ll. 10-20: Christmas Eve (Cork / O'Sullivans' pub at Kilmakilloge)
   a. morning: arrival in Cork / phone O'Sullivans / again unenthusiastic
   b. evening: arrival at Kilmakilloge / warm welcome[1] by Mrs O'Sullivan / misunderstanding reason for unfriendliness on phone
3rd part: ll. 21-28: Christmas time (area around Kilmakilloge)/walks in area
4th part: ll. 29-31: home in England

3. Write a text with the help of your notes. Use words like *but, although, however, nevertheless*[2], *therefore*[3], *since,* etc. to connect the sentences. As a rule, use the simple present tense.

The text is about the writer Eric Newby's second visit to Kilmakilloge with his wife and daughter in December 1968. The Newbys decide to spend Christmas in Kilmakilloge because Christmas at home is usually very hectic. They phone the O'Sullivans' pub where they want to stay, and are surprised that Mrs O'Sullivan does not seem very pleased, although they have been there before. After their arrival in Cork on Christmas Eve they phone the O'Sullivans again, and again they get an unenthusiastic answer. But when they finally get to Kilmakilloge, they are warmly welcomed by Mrs O'Sullivan, who had expected a different couple to arrive. During their stay, the Newbys go for a lot of walks in the area and enjoy themselves very much.
Back home in England, they know they will return to Kilmakilloge one day.

Now you can practise writing a summary yourself. This text is about the Newbys' third visit (this time by bike) to Kilmakilloge in January 1986.

When we arrived at Kilmakilloge Bay, we were greeted, as if by magic, by a brilliant orange sunset. It was our first cloudless sky of the whole trip, although the mountains and Healy Pass behind us were still covered in black clouds. Across the road there was a yellow and white painted pub and a sign which said it was Teddy O'Sullivan's. Frozen, we parked our bicycles outside and opened the front door, and there was Mrs Joan O'Sullivan selling a little girl some sweets. She looked up and slowly she began to smile. She had recognized us.
"You've been a long time away," she said. "You missed a fine funeral today – Mrs Lyons from the shop at Lauragh[4]. Lots of people were there. Some came all the way from Dublin in a Mercedes. Some are still in the bar; they won't go home. You'll stay the night, of course."
That night we had fish fresh from the sea, followed by a 1985 Christmas pudding. Overhead a full moon swam in a star-filled sky.
The next morning, a Saturday, was as unfriendly and dark as the evening before had been clear and golden. We had to force ourselves to get up and pack.
"How far do you think we're going on this trip?" Wanda said, while we were eating an O'Sullivan breakfast. "And when do you think we're going to get there?"
"I don't know," I said. "It's difficult to say. I'd really like to go round the Ring of Kerry. That's about seventy miles. (I was hopelessly wrong – it is more than a hundred.) And then there's the Dingle[5] Peninsula. And there's Killarney[6], too. With luck we might be in Tralee[7] by next Saturday."
"Do you really have to go round all these bloody peninsulas?" she asked. "They all look about the same in this kind of weather."

[1] warm welcome ['welkəm] *herzliches Willkommen* [2] nevertheless [ˌnevəðə'les] *nichtsdestoweniger, trotzdem*
[3] therefore ['ðeəfɔ:] *deshalb, deswegen* [4] Lauragh ['lɔ:rə] [5] Dingle ['dɪŋgl] [6] Killarney [kɪ'lɑ:nɪ]
[7] Tralee [trə'li:]

Talking and writing about non-fictional texts

Computer future

Computer technology has developed unbelievably quickly. Fifty years ago a simple computer filled a room, could only be operated by experts and sometimes made mistakes. Now, with microelectronics, computers can store vast amounts of information in a small area.

They're no longer just super adding machines – they're a vital part of business, science and industry. The latest computers are even becoming more intelligent than the scientists who make them. Impossible? Well, in Japan and America there are computers which can diagnose illness more accurately than a doctor, write stories and even design other computers. In a recent TV programme, one computer scientist predicted that computers in the future will be so much more intelligent than us that they will take over and keep us as pets.

But until that happens, computer scientists are still in control of their computers. Recently, the *Sunday Times* newspaper held a competition to find the Young Computer Brain[1] of the Year. Students up to the age of 18 were asked to write computer programs which would help society. Fifteen-year-old Derek Reynolds from Newcastle won the competition.

Derek spends most of his free time programming computers and says: "I decided to write a program which would help disabled people to use computers." He designed a simplified keyboard with just two keys. One is round, the other square. By pushing the round key the user can choose which answer he or she wants, and by pushing the square key the choice is entered[2] into the computer. If it is correct, a smiling face appears on the screen, but if the user chooses the wrong answer, a crying face appears. Derek's idea is simple and very practical.

Other entries included a computerized identikit[3] program for the police. Thirteen-year-old Rachel Gooberman's idea was to store thousands of possible noses, mouths, chins,[4] eyes, etc. in a computer, then use them to help in the identification of criminals.

The judges[5] in the Young Computer Brain of the Year competition were impressed with[6] the hundreds of excellent programs they received. And the prizes for the competition winners? – Computers, of course.

1 Expressing your first reactions to a text

Basically there are three ways of reacting to a text:

a Say in general what the text is about:

The text	is about deals with[7] presents	...	The author[8] The writer	says/states[9]/points out/asks explains believes/thinks/doubts[10]	...

b Express your opinion on the text as a whole or on certain aspects of it:

I think/feel that the text is ... I can't agree with ... It seems to me that ...
I can't (really) believe that ... I don't think one can say that ... As far as[11] I know/can see ...

c Ask questions if you don't understand or aren't quite clear about certain things in the text, or if you aren't so sure about the meaning of some words or expressions:

I don't really understand what the author/the text says in line ...
I can understand ..., but I'm not sure what ... means.
I'm not sure what ... means/is in German. What does ... mean?/Does ... mean ... ?
Is ... (something) similar to ... ? Is ... the noun/the verb which goes with ... ?

[1] brain [breɪn] *Gehirn;* (hier:) Genie [2] enter [ˈentə] *eintragen* [3] identikit [aɪˈdentɪkɪt] *Phantombild*
[4] chin [tʃɪn] *Kinn* [5] judge [dʒʌdʒ] *Richter/in* [6] impressed with [ɪmˈprest] *beeindruckt von*
[7] deal with [diːl] *handeln von* [8] author [ˈɔːθə] *Schriftsteller/in* [9] state [steɪt] *feststellen*
[10] doubt [daʊt] *anzweifeln* [11] as far as *soweit*

Of course there are different ways to find out by yourself what certain words or expressions mean:

– think of the word family;
– use your knowledge of word building;
– look for similar words/ expressions in German, French or perhaps Latin;
– read the context carefully in which the word appears. It's not always necessary to know the exact translation.

New Vocabulary	English G, A1-A5	German	French	Latin
l. 2 (to) operate	operation	operieren	opérer	
l. 4 (to) store	store, n.			
l. 4 vast			vaste	vastus, a, um
l. 10 (to) diagnose		diagnostizieren	diagnostiquer	
l. 10 accurately		akkurat		accuratus, a, um
l. 11 (to) design	designer, design, n.	der Designer das Design	dessiner	
l. 33 identification	identity, (to) identify	Identifikation/ Identifizierung	identification	

2 Getting more out of a text

If you want to get more out of a text you should have a closer look at it. You can, for example:

a Divide the text into its main parts to see how it develops.

b Study each part of the text and write down key words to get a better picture of the main ideas.

Example: l. 1: introduction/development of computer technology
ll. 1-14: historical outline[1] of this development:
a fifty years ago: computers very large/only for experts/sometimes mistakes
b now: . . .
c the future: . . .
ll. 15-34: examples (computer competition): . . .
ll. 35-38: final remarks:[2] . . .

Write down the missing key words and complete the table.

c Mark the parts that contain examples, illustrations, statistics, etc. and use them to explain the key words.

d Use your notes to write a summary (see "How to write a summary", pp. 114-115).

e Ask yourself questions about the text and try to answer them.

Examples: Who operated computers fifty years ago? (ll. 1-3) How big was the room that one computer filled? (ll. 1-3)

f Try to find out the author's intention.[3] The following questions will help you:

Who do you think the text was written for? What is the author's attitude towards computer technology? How much information does he/she give on the subject?

3 Discussing and questioning certain aspects of the text and giving personal comment[4]

Examples: Are computers really a vital part of business, science and technology? (ll. 6-14). Will computers replace[5] doctors, writers, scientists and even take over the leading role in everyday life? (ll. 6-14) Do you think that young people should be encouraged to spend most of their free time programming computers? (ll. 15-34) . . .

[1] outline ['aʊtlaɪn] *Umriß* [2] remark [rɪ'mɑːk] *Bemerkung* [3] intention [ɪn'tenʃn] *Absicht*
[4] comment ['kɒment] *Kommentar* [5] replace [rɪ'pleɪs] *ersetzen*

Extensive reading[1]

Reading and understanding texts is without doubt[2] one of the most important skills[3] to be learnt in English lessons. It is a skill which will probably be valuable[4] to most of you in later life, whatever your plans are.

In recent years you have read a great number of texts in English. However, most of them were quite short and usually with vocabulary notes to help you.

This Option aims to teach you to read and understand longer texts without such vocabulary annotations[5], and so help you to understand stories, novels[6], plays and all sorts of non-fictional texts in English which have *not* been written especially for English schoolbooks. Of course it is only fun reading these texts if you can read them quite fast, without stopping and thinking whenever a new word or expression comes up. With this kind of reading (often called "extensive reading") it is quite normal for people, even when they read texts in their own language, not to understand every single word. The aim is simply to enjoy the text and get a general idea of its content.[7] In our mother tongue we use certain skills, quite subconsciously[8], to guess the meaning of words ("intelligent guessing"). It is possible to learn to apply the same strategies[9] in a foreign language (see the notes on the following pages). – All that is important for extensive reading is to get a general idea of what you have read.

Now read the following lines from Ivan Southall's *Ash Road* and try to understand what they are about without any additional help. New words are marked with⁺.

They who run away

The fire that Graham had started through his accident with the cooker is now out of control. The boys have decided to run away in another direction over the hill to the next town. On their farm on the other side of the hill, some miles from the fire, Lorna and her father are working in the fields. It has become a very hot day and the sun is burning on them as they work. Suddenly, her father falls to the ground with a heart attack. Lorna is alone, as her brother John has gone to the town on his motorbike.

Lorna sat on the ground between the ⁺raspberry rows, ⁺nursing her father's head in her hands, fighting to keep the panic off her face.

Her father was looking at her, ⁺speechlessly. It was frightening, but there was something special about it, like a ⁺sacred ⁺bond between them. He hadn't spoken a word for minutes. His only ⁺communication with her was through his eyes. It was hard to read them because they were no longer very clear, but she knew they were asking her not to leave him. She wanted to run for help, to ring the doctor or an ambulance, but his eyes asked her to stay. She wanted to get out of his sight, out of his hearing so that she could let herself go.

"What is it, Dad?" she said. "Where does it hurt?" He couldn't tell her.

"Dad," she said, "I must try and get John." But his eyes wouldn't let her go. "Please, Dad. Let me go for the doctor." "In a little while," his eyes seemed to say.

So she held his head and tried to ⁺shade him from the sun. When she went for the doctor, she would have to leave him in the sun because she was afraid that if she tried to move him she might kill him. She mightn't be able to move him, anyway, even though she wasn't a weak girl: she cut the wood sometimes, when there wasn't a man around.

[1] extensive reading [ɪkˌstensɪv ˈriːdɪŋ] *extensives Lesen* [2] doubt [daʊt] *Zweifel* [3] skill [skɪl] *Fertigkeit* [4] valuable [ˈvæljʊəbl] *wertvoll* [5] annotation [ˌænəʊˈteɪʃn] *Anmerkung* [6] novel [ˈnɒvl] *Roman* [7] content [ˈkɒntent] *Inhalt* [8] subconsciously [ˌsʌbˈkɒnʃəslɪ] *im Unterbewußtsein* [9] strategy [ˈstrætədʒɪ] *Strategie*

She thought of herself cutting wood, and, strangely, that made her feel even more miserable. How lonely it would be with only John and herself to cook for. She thought of all the nice things her father had done, forgot the bad times, thought of his lifelong battle to survive in the outback. She thought, too, of the terrible fear she had felt when she had believed he was dead.

"Dad, I must go. I don't want to lose you. I'd never forgive myself if I could have saved you by trying. Please let me try to get some help."

It was one of the few times in her life when she had reached him wholly and completely with her heart. She knew he was ready to let her go, so she ran towards the house, crying a little, confused because she wasn't exactly sure what to do.

When she got to the telephone she couldn't remember the doctor's number, and when she tried to +turn over the pages of the +directory, she could hardly see the names, didn't even know what page she was looking at. She couldn't read the +print. She had been in the bright sunlight for so long that she could not see in the gloom of the house. She +stumbled to the nearest window, found the number and with a +painful +effort of will +dialled it slowly and carefully.

It rang and rang and there was no answer. She +hung up because she knew there wasn't going to be an answer. She +fumbled with the directory again, turning to Miltondale, as that was where the ambulance had to come from. Again she dialled carefully, though she was shaking from head to foot.

Stop reading for a few minutes at this point and try to say in no more than three or four sentences what this part of the text is about. If you can answer the following four questions, you have understood the text well:
– What is the situation at the beginning of the text?
– Why doesn't Lorna run for help at once?
– How does she feel in this situation?
– Why is it so difficult for her to dial the doctor's number?

Before you go on reading let's consider[1] why you could understand so many words you had never seen before. What are the skills you have to apply when trying to read a text fast?

1. Sometimes the context in which a word appears gives us clues to its meaning. You probably understood the noun "directory" (l. 28) because of the context and words like "telephone", "the doctor's number", "pages of the ~, "names".
2. Some words are similar to German words, for example "fumble" (l. 34), or words from another language which are used in German, like "communication" (l. 5).
3. You will also have recognized new words whose meaning is clear to you because you know other words of the same word family and you have learnt some word-building rules.
   Examples: "nursing" (l. 1) – present participle of the infinitive "(to) nurse"; noun: "a nurse". "speechlessly" (l. 3) – adverb which goes with the adjective "speechless"; noun: "speech"[2] + "less" (without) = adj. "speechless"
4. Sometimes you will know the meaning of a word because you have learnt a similar word in another foreign language.
   Example: "sacred" (l. 4) from Latin "sacer" or French "sacré"

Whenever you read a text there will certainly also be words whose meaning you don't understand, but which are not really important for an understanding of the text. An expression like "raspberry rows" (l. 1) is a good example in this part of the text; or a verb like "stumble" (l. 31), where you know that it has something to do with "move towards", but where the exact meaning is unimportant.

[1] consider [kən'sɪdə] *überlegen* [2] speech [spiːtʃ] *Sprache*

In the next part of the text some new words are marked. Please check if their meaning is clear to you and which of the above skills you have applied.

"Civil Ambulance Station," said the woman's voice. "Oh," cried Lorna. She could hardly get her thoughts straight. "Oh, thank goodness. I want an ambulance please. I'm all on my own. It's my father." "I'm sorry." The voice was firm, but not unkind. "You'll have to wait." "Wait?"

"I'm sorry. We have an emergency here. Where are you ringing from?" "From Prescott. I can't even get the doctor." "I'm very sorry, my dear, but it's the fires. You'll have to try to make other arrangements. We've really got troubles enough of our own." "But my father –" Lorna was shocked.

"Every doctor in the hills is there, my dear, and every ambulance. There have been an awful lot of injuries, snake bites and burns and broken legs and heart attacks. All sorts of things. The fire's got to come first this morning." "But my father –" "Can you drive a car?" "I'm only *fourteen*." "But can you drive?" "No, of course I can't." "What's wrong with your father?"

"I don't know. I don't know anything about these things. I think he's dying." "Listen to me, dear. If you want to help your father you must be very brave and very calm and very sensible. I'll try hard to get a car for you, but it's not going to be easy. Everyone's gone to the fires. Just about everyone. We're evacuating the town. The fire is only a mile away. I'm not certain that a car could even get through to you or that you could get through to the hospital. You mustn't count on me. It will be much better, much surer, if you call one of your neighbours. They're so much closer."

"But we live on a farm," cried Lorna. "I'm near the end of the road. I'm three miles from the town. It's a quarter of a mile to the nearest neighbours, and even they're on holidays. I'm all alone. There isn't anybody, anywhere."

"There must be someone, my dear. Even if they're half a mile away they're much closer to you than we are. Now you really must control yourself. Give me your name and address quickly and I'll do my best, but you must not count on me. Please, please don't –" Suddenly that was all. The line died. "Hallo," shouted Lorna. "Hallo, hallo. Don't go away . . . Hallo . . ."

The line was dead. Desperately, she dialled the number again. There was no ring. Something had happened to the line between Prescott and Miltondale and the ambulance didn't even have her address.

She dialled the Fire Station. The line was still open there, but no one answered, not even the radio officer. She dialled the taxi service, but no one answered. She dialled the Buckinghams, but no one answered.

She put the phone down, and for a few moments covered her face with her hands. There was a fear in her, a feeling such as she had never known before. Now it was more than fear for her father lying down there in the cruel sun. Now it reached out to the fire near Miltondale. What were they talking about? What sort of a fire was that? And then the fear came right back to herself, to her aloneness.

Now read the text to the end. Perhaps you can write a possible ending for the story.

She ran outside and looked into the sky in the west and the north. There was no smoke, nothing that really looked like smoke, only the smell of smoke and of dust, and the burning sun. Perhaps she could get help at the Fairhalls or from Grandpa Tanner. But Grandpa was so old and the Fairhalls were so slow and they didn't have telephones, anyway. She looked at her father's old car in the shed. How she wished she could drive it.

But it was a one-man car; her father had always made that clear. It was "very hard" to drive, he said. Even John was not allowed to use it. Only one person could drive it properly and that was her father, her stubborn father, who should have bought a better one years ago. And even the tyres of her bicycle were flat. There was always something wrong with her bike. Everything was worn out. Nothing worked.

She ran back to her father. He lay in the full sun, covered with dust and sweat. She felt so sad for him, for a man so proud, lying there like that. Even if it hurt him, she would have to move him. She dried his face on her dress, put her hands under his arms, and pulled him into the bushes out of the sun. "Won't be long now, Dad," she said. "They're coming."

She ran back up the hill. She was beginning to feel sick. She did not believe that she was strong enough to run as far as the Fairhalls' or to Grandpa Tanner. Her legs wanted to give way at the knees.

Suddenly she thought of Bill Robertson. He was young and strong and had a big truck and was only a mile and a bit up the road and was on the telephone and should have brought some oil to her father that morning anyway. She hadn't spoken to Bill Robertson more than three or four times in her life, but at once he seemed very close to her. She ran inside, looked up his number, and dialled it. She couldn't believe it. There was no answer. Where was everybody? What was the use of a telephone in an emergency if no one ever answered it? For an awful moment she felt that perhaps her father was meant to die. There were people who said that when one's number was up, it was up, and nothing could be done about it; that trying to stop the passage of destiny was like ordering a river to run backwards. There was a knock on the door. It frightened her terribly, because there wasn't anyone, she thought, within miles. All sorts of dark images went through her mind, things she had never thought of before. The knock seemed at this moment like a signal, telling her that time was up for her father, or even like a signal from her father himself, as if his spirit as it passed by had stopped for one last moment of contact with her. The knock came again. It was, after all, an earthy, ordinary knock. How could it have been anything else? She felt ashamed, then wildly excited. Now it seemed like an answer to a prayer. She went to the door, and there, in the brilliant light, were the heads and shoulders of two real live men. One of them said, "Do the Pinkards live here?"

Then she saw they weren't men, but boys, strange boys, and that there were three of them. She pushed the door open, but didn't know what to say. When at last she spoke, her words flooded out, and the third boy, the one standing back, said in a low voice, "It's the wrong place. I told you it was. Let's go." "Don't go," she said quickly, suddenly afraid again.

The nearer two looked at each other uncomfortably, and the third continued to move away. "Come on," he said. "It's not Pinkards'. I said it was at the bottom of the hill." "Do stay," cried Lorna. She couldn't believe that anyone would leave her now. "I can't get a doctor and my father's ill. I can't get anybody. Nobody answers the phone." The boy at the back said, "Do we look like doctors? Come on. Let's get out of here." "You wouldn't *leave* me," cried Lorna. "You couldn't do that. He's out in the sun. Can't you even carry him up to the house for me?"

"Look," said the boy at the back, not to Lorna but to the others. "We – can't – get – involved."

Lorna looked at him. He didn't seem that sort of boy. He looked tired and dirty, terribly dirty; they all did; but he had a nice face. The face didn't go with the words that came out of it. Nothing fitted. She couldn't understand that the others seemed to do as he said. They were so much bigger than he was. The biggest was like a man, except for his face. It didn't seem right that the most boyish of them should be their spokesman, should decide their actions. Lorna was desperate. She had to hold them.

"There's an old door in the shed," she said. "We can carry him on that. We can each take a corner." She looked angrily at the boy at the back. "You're a fine sort of gentleman, you are!" "Come on, Graham," said the big one. "We've got to do it. Haven't we?" [. . .]

They put the door down at the back of the house, and Lorna dropped on one knee beside her father. She didn't know what to do next. She ran her fingers nervously across his face and said, "I'll get a pillow."

As soon as she had disappeared into the house Graham hissed at the others: "You're crazy. You're completely crazy. Now look what you've done. How are we supposed to get out of this lot?"

Harry and Wallace glanced at each other and at the sick man at their feet. Harry said, "It's just one of those things." Lorna came back with the pillow in her hand. "Here, give it to me," said Harry, anxious to get her out of the way again for a moment. "You'd better get a blanket, too." "It's too hot for that," said Lorna.

"We don't know for sure, do we? We don't know what's wrong with him. At least we're on the safe side if we cover him." "All right," said Lorna and went inside again. Graham mumbled, "We were safe. I just know we were safe." "We still will be," growled Wallace, "if you'll shut up." "We'd got all this way," sighed Graham.

Not one of them really knew how he was managing to stand up or how he had managed to walk more than fourteen miles. What a nightmare the hours of darkness had been, hiding from passing traffic, sometimes running with their packs jolting and chafing at them. Their feet were like balls of fire.

Lorna brought the blanket and Harry took it from her. At that moment Pippa came round the side of the house.

She met Graham's eyes first. "He's nice," she thought. But Graham didn't notice Pippa for what she was or wasn't; he saw her as just one more danger to be overcome, one more person who might take news of what he had done to the police or to his parents, one more reason why he had to get away by himself. He didn't want even Harry or Wallace. Much of what had happened was Harry's fault, anyway. "We're going to stick together," Harry had said, while they were still hiding not far from the fire. "We'll make for the Pinkards' now. No one's there. All we've got to do is find the place. Jerry said if we got there before he did to make ourselves at home. That's good enough for me. It's the perfect place to hide." [. . .]

When Pippa saw old man George she cried, "Lorna, what's happened to him?" Lorna stared at her. "Where'd you come from? I've been ringing your number. Everybody's number. I couldn't get an answer anywhere."

"Mum's there," said Pippa, not fully understanding. "Dad's there. Stevie, too, I think." "But no one answered. I rang and rang. Oh, Pippa, my dad's awfully sick. I don't know what I would have done if these boys hadn't turned up. I thought your dad could drive him to hospital, but I couldn't get an answer. They're not home, Pippa. Honest, they're not –" "But they are [. . .] you must have dialled the wrong number."

"But I didn't." "Well let me try." "Try if you want to, but I'm telling you they're not there." The boys, prompted by a single thought, found themselves looking at one another, for the girl called Pippa followed the girl Lorna indoors. "Right!" said Harry. As one, they ran round the side of the house and took a short cut across a garden bed towards the path.

(From *Ash Road* by Ivan Southall, slightly adapted)

A question of style: formal, neutral, informal

a Most of the English you have heard or read so far is neither particularly formal nor especially informal. The English most often used in writing or speaking is **neutral**[1] in style. A **formal** style is impersonal. It is used in business letters, public notices and official documents, for example. An **informal** style, on the other hand, is often a sign of a personal relationship.[2] It is used in friendly, everyday conversation (between friends, colleagues, among family members), in personal letters and also in advertising.

⚠ As a speaker of English as a foreign language it is usually best to use a neutral style – especially if you are not sure. Used in the wrong situations, a very informal style may easily sound impolite or even rude. A formal style in the wrong situation will sound strange, too.

b *Compare the corresponding sentences from two letters and a telephone conversation. There are grammatical differences as well as differences of vocabulary. Look at the formal structures and words in the first letter and say how these are expressed in neutral or informal style.*

formal:	**neutral:**	**informal:**
Having read your advertisement[3] in the Sunday Times, I would like to inquire[4] ...	I read your advertisement in our local newspaper and would like to ask ...	Hi, Bob. – I read your advert in our paper and I'd like to know ...
Unfortunately, I have been unable to obtain[5] the required[6] information.	I have not been able to find the information I need.	I haven't been able to find out what I want to know.
My son, who is fifteen years of age, would like to ...	My son is fifteen years old and he would like to ...	Tom is fifteen now, you see, and he'd like to ...
I trust[7] you do not mind my asking, but ...	I hope you do not mind me asking, but ...	Hope you don't mind, but I'd like to ask ...

c *Decide which of the following sentences are formal and which are informal. Then try and rewrite each sentence in a more neutral style.*

1. ... I look forward to receiving your reply. Yours faithfully, ... 2. Thanks a lot. 3. Is this the girl whom you met at the party? 4. Should you be interested in the book, I shall be pleased to lend it to you. 5. The pop singer Penny Davis, who wanted to visit South Africa, has been refused permission to enter the country. 6. More potatoes, Tina? 7. Hey, you guys, have you got the time? 8. Having damaged several parked vehicles, the two men were arrested by the police. 9. Whom might we ask? 10. Carol got real mad with her kids.

[1] neutral [ˈnjuːtrəl] [2] relationship [rɪˈleɪʃnʃɪp] *Beziehung* [3] advertisement [ədˈvɜːtɪsmənt] *Anzeige, Inserat*
[4] inquire [ɪnˈkwaɪə] *(fml.) sich erkundigen* [5] obtain [əbˈteɪn] *erlangen, erhalten*
[6] required [rɪˈkwaɪəd] *erforderlich* [7] trust [trʌst] *(fml.) zuversichtlich hoffen*

Conditional sentences

Revision

In these sentences the speakers state[1] conditions and talk about their possible consequences.[2]
Say – in which part of the sentences the conditions/their consequences are expressed,
- what verb forms are used,
- which conditions can/cannot be fulfilled.[3]

⚠ The *if*-clause can come before or after the main clause. A comma is often used when the *if*-clause comes first. There is usually no comma when the *if*-clause follows the main clause.

Conditional sentences I

If you **see** Professor Clever,	he**'ll talk** about his latest invention.
(this is possible and	you **must ask** him about his new magic drink.
will probably happen)	**don't drink** any of his magic drink.
if + present tense	will-future
	modal auxiliary + infinitive
	imperative

If + present tense is used if the speaker thinks that the condition will probably be fulfilled (it is a "real condition").

⚠ Don't use *will* in the *if*-clause (even if the condition refers[4] to the future)!

Instead of the simple present, other tenses may be used in the *if*-clause, according to the context:[5]

If Prof Clever **is** still **working** on his invention,	don't go into his room.
If he **hasn't invented** anything useful yet,	he ought to give up trying.
If you **should drink** any of his magic drink,	you'll certainly feel ill soon.
(this is possible, but not very probable)	

The simple present is used in the *if*-clause and the main clause to talk about things that are always true:

If the temperature **falls** below zero,	water **freezes**.
(if = whenever)	

[1] state *nennen, angeben* [2] consequence [ˈkɒnsɪkwəns] *Folge, Konsequenz* [3] fulfil [fʊlˈfɪl] *erfüllen*
[4] refer to [rɪˈfɜː] *sich beziehen auf* [5] context [ˈkɒntekst] *Kontext, Zusammenhang*

Ex 1 Adverts

1. SPLASH bubble bath – feel like a new-born baby
2. WIZARD vacuum cleaner – spend less time on the housework
3. SOFT shampoo – shiny hair
4. GENTLE soap – softer[2] skin
5. HURRICANE toothpaste – fresh all day long
6. PIRATE, the new camera – fantastic pictures

a *Make adverts for the products on the right.*

Example: WHIRL washing powder[1] – cleaner clothes
If you wash with WHIRL washing powder, your clothes will be cleaner.
or: If you want cleaner clothes, use WHIRL washing powder.

b *Make up some adverts yourself. Choose real products or invent your own.*

Conditional sentences II

a) If I **invented** a magic drink, (this is possible, but <u>improbable</u>)	I **would be** happy and I **could make** a lot of money.
b) If I **was** twenty years younger, (this is <u>impossible</u>)	I **might marry** the young woman.
if + past tense	*would/could/might* + infinitive

If + past tense is used if the speaker thinks that
a) it is improbable that the condition will be fulfilled, or
b) it is impossible that the condition can be fulfilled (this is an "unreal condition").
The past tense in the *if*-clause does not refer to the past, but to the present or future.

⚠ Don't use *would* ("würde") in the *if*-clause!
In more formal English you can use *were* instead of *was* after *I/he/she/it*: If I **was/were** rich, . . .
Only *were* is used in the expression *if I were you*: If I **were** you, I would . . .

Ex 2 If pigs could fly . . .

– Do you think pigs (fly) if they (have) wings?
– I don't think so. If pigs (want) to fly, they (need) huge wings. But I'm sure pigs are far too heavy, no matter how big their wings are.
– I suppose if they (have) wings, it (not make) them much happier. They (probably be) locked up most of the time because they (fly away) from the farm if they (not be locked up). And if they (fly away), there (be) no chops[3] for dinner. There (really be) more disadvantages than advantages if pigs (have) wings. But a flying pig is a funny idea, don't you think?
– It certainly is. But I think I (prefer) it if I (have) wings myself. Because if I (have), I (fly) to a sunny island right now and I (not have to) do my homework.
– Yes, 'If wishes (be) horses, beggars (ride)'.

Ex 3 I often wish I was a king, and then I could do anything

Say what you would or could do
– if you were a king/queen, a politician, a famous sportsman/sportswoman, James Bond, the headmaster/headmistress of your school, a bird, . . .
– if you had a million dollars, a motorbike, magic powers, a time machine, . . .
Write a short text.

Ex 4 Life without cars

In what ways would our lives be different if we didn't have cars?
Think of advantages and disadvantages.

[1] washing powder ['wɒʃɪŋ ˌpaʊdə] *Waschpulver, -mittel* [2] soft [sɒft] *weich* [3] chop [tʃɒp] *Kotelett*

Conditional sentences III

If Prof Clever **had invented** a magic drink,	he **would have become** famous.
If the young woman **had drunk** the new drink,	she **might have stayed** young for ever and
(this is no longer possible)	she **might** still **be** beautiful.
if + past perfect	*would/could/might* + *have* + past participle *would/could/might* + infinitive

If + past perfect is used if the condition can no longer be fulfilled (this is an "unreal condition" referring to the past). The speaker speculates[1] about possible consequences of things that did not happen in the past.

Ex 5 If I had lived a hundred years ago, ...

If you had lived a hundred or even more years ago, what would your life have been like?

Ex 6 If history had been different, ...

Just imagine some of the consequences – then and now. You needn't be too serious!

1. If the Romans had had planes, ...
2. If Columbus hadn't had a compass,[2] ...
3. If Guy Fawkes hadn't been caught, ...
4. If Britain hadn't had so many colonies, ...
5. If the wheel hadn't been invented, ...
6. If I had been on the moon on July 21st, 1969, ...

Example: If William the Conqueror hadn't invaded Britain, he would never have seen the beautiful British Isles. He wouldn't have been called 'the Conqueror'. The Angles and Saxons could have lived in peace. British history and the English language would be totally different. We couldn't visit the castles the Normans built. Pupils wouldn't have to remember the date '1066'.

Conditional sentences without "if"

If you **should wish** to complain, **Should** you **wish** to complain,	speak to the headmaster.
If the young woman **had drunk** the magic drink, **Had** the young woman **drunk** the magic drink,	she might have stayed young for ever.

In *if*-clauses with *should* or *had* the *if* can be left out in formal English. The clause must then begin with *should* or *had* + subject.

Ex 7 What have you learnt about if-clauses?

Put in the correct tense of the verbs. Be careful, sometimes there is more than one solution.

1. If I (be) you, I (accept) this offer. 2. If you (learn) your words well, you (not have to) be afraid of the vocabulary test. 3. I (meet) Mary this morning. I'm sure she (come) to your party last night if you (invite) her. 4. If you (enjoy) the party, (not go) home yet. 5. If your brother (drive) more carefully, the accident (not happen). 6. I (tell) Alan about it yesterday. (you/tell) him the truth if he (ask) you? 7. If air (get) warmer, it (rise). 8. I think life (be) very boring if we (have) nothing to do. 9. I (not suppose) Jack (call) while I (be) away, but if he (do), tell him I (ring) him back later. 10. If you (not forget) the map, we (not lose our way). 11. If I (live) in Australia, I (probably be) a sheep farmer. 12. Take my advice! If you (give up) smoking, you (feel) a lot better.

[1] speculate ['spekjʊleɪt] *nachdenken, Vermutungen anstellen* [2] compass ['kʌmpəs] *Kompaß*

Revision

Preparing for a trip to Britain

Many of you will probably go to Britain this year or next year, either with your class on a class trip, or on an exchange with a British school. You needn't be worried about such a trip. You have now learned enough English to get along very well in Britain. However, it might be helpful to practise again the language for some of the situations you could experience[1] and to make your own **phrase-book** before you leave. This will make you more confident.

Meeting people

The first situation in which you will need your English is when you meet people for the first time. For example, your partner's family or friends. Listen to or read the following scene. Marion Ostermann from Moers has just arrived in Kirkby by coach. Marion's partner, Gillian, is waiting to meet her . . .

Gillian: Hallo, Marion. Welcome to Britain.
Marion: Hallo, Gillian. Thank you.
Gillian: Marion, this is my mother.
Marion: How do you do,[2] Mrs Barnett.
Mrs B.: Hallo, Marion. Pleased to meet you.[3]
Gillian: And this is my father.
Mr B.: How do you do. I hope you had a good journey.
Marion: Yes, thank you. I enjoyed it. But it was very long and very tiring.[4] I'm glad we're here at last.
Gillian: Where's your luggage?[5] Is it still on the coach?
Marion: Yes, I think so. The driver is just unloading it. Then I must look for my suitcase.
Mrs B.: What time did you leave Germany?
Marion: Oh, the coach left Moers at 2 o'clock yesterday afternoon . . .

Some questions to help you to find expressions for your phrase-book:
1. How does Gillian greet[6] Marion? 2. How does she introduce her mother? 3. What does Marion say to Mrs Barnett? 4. How does Mrs Barnett reply? 5. How does Mr Barnett greet Marion after he has been introduced?

⚠ The British don't shake hands with each other nearly as often as the Germans. It is only usual when you first meet somebody, or haven't met for a long time. Young people often just say "Hi" or "Hallo". "How do you do" is *not* a question. It is a formal way to say "Hallo".

Ex 1 Work in groups and practise introducing each other. Your partner can be a brother, sister or friend of Gillian's, or an adult.

⚠ When you meet people for the first time, it is important to talk. Meeting somebody is often an awkward[7] situation and silence[8] makes things worse. If somebody asks a question, don't just answer "yes" or "no". Look again at how Marion answers the questions about her journey, her luggage and when she left Germany.

Ex 2 Work with a partner. Ask each other questions about the journey: what the crossing was like, how long it took, whether you have been to Britain before. The answer to each question should be more than one sentence.

Ex 3 Now take Marion's part in the second dialogue on the cassette.

[1] experience [ɪk'spɪərɪəns] *erleben* [2] How do you do. (formal) *Guten Tag, Angenehm* [3] Pleased to meet you. (formal) *Angenehm, Sie kennenzulernen.* [4] tiring ['taɪərɪŋ] *anstrengend* [5] luggage ['lʌgɪdʒ] *Gepäck* [6] greet [gri:t] *begrüßen* [7] awkward ['ɔ:kwəd] *peinlich* [8] silence ['saɪləns] *Schweigen*

Meal times

If you stay with a family in Britain, you will certainly have some of your meals with them. You will not only find the food different, but also some of the customs.

Mrs B.: We've prepared a typical English dinner for you, Marion, roast beef and Yorkshire pudding.[1] We've never had a German guest before, so I hope you like it.
Marion: I'm sure I will. It looks delicious.
Mr B.: Would you like something to drink? We've got fruit juice, mineral water or lemonade.
Marion: Can I have fruit juice, please?
Mr B.: Of course. And help yourself to potatoes and vegetables. Gillian, pass the potatoes to Marion, will you?
Mrs B.: Well, please start, Marion. Don't let it get cold. . . .

—

Marion: Mmm, this is very nice, Mrs Barnett. I'm really enjoying it.
Mrs B.: Oh good. I'm glad you like it.

—

Marion: That was lovely. I really enjoyed it.
Mrs B.: Thank you, Marion. There's lots left. Would you like some more?
Marion: No, thank you. It was delicious, but I really couldn't eat any more.
Mr B.: Well, I hope you've left some room for dessert. It's apple pie[2] and cream.

Some questions to help you to find expressions for your phrase-book: What does Marion say . . . 1. when Mrs Barnett says she hopes she'll like the meal? 2. when Mrs Barnett offers her something to drink? 3. to compliment Mrs Barnett on the meal? 4. to explain she's feeling full?

⚠ **Thank you – No, thank you.**
The British say "Thank you" to a compliment or when you give them something. They say "No, thank you" to refuse an offer politely.

⚠ **Please**
The British say "please" when they ask for something. They *never* say "please" in reply to "thank you". They usually then don't say anything at all, but if you want to be especially polite you can say "That's all right", "Don't mention it" or "Not at all".

⚠ The British have no expression for "Guten Appetit". Look again at what Mrs Barnett says to Marion before the meal.

Ex 1 Work with a partner.
– Compliment somebody after a meal, or after you have eaten some cakes or sandwiches.
– Imagine you are Marion and you're still hungry. Ask politely for some more roast beef, potatoes or vegetables. Imagine you can't reach the orange juice. How would you ask for it?

Ex 2 **Role play** Write a dialogue:
It's breakfast time. Gillian asks Marion what she would like to eat (cornflakes, toast, jam, marmalade[3]) and offers her something to drink (tea, coffee, juice). Mr Barnett asks Marion how she slept. Mrs Barnett wants to know what people have for breakfast in Germany.

Ex 3 Now take Marion's part on the cassette.

[1] Yorkshire pudding [ˈjɔːkʃə ˈpʊdɪŋ] *Teiggericht* [2] pie [paɪ] *Torte*
[3] marmalade [ˈmɑːməleɪd] *Orangenmarmelade*

Going into town Most of the time you will be with other young people, but sometimes, of course, you will want to do things on your own.

Marion: I'd like to go into town this afternoon, Mrs Barnett, and change some money. Can you tell me the best way, please?
Mrs B.: Yes, of course. It's a bit far to walk, though. Why don't you take the bus? The bus stop is only a couple of minutes away.
Marion: Can you tell me how to get there?
Mrs B.: Go to the end of the road, turn right and go straight on until you come to the garage. Turn right again and you'll see the bus stop. It's in front of a pub called *The King George*. Look for the number 27 bus. It'll say "Town Centre" on the front.
Marion: Do I have to change?
Mrs B.: No. But if you want to come back on the bus, they leave from the bus station every half hour at 7 and 37 minutes.
Marion: I'm sorry. I didn't understand that. Could you repeat it, please?

Mrs B.: A bus leaves from the bus station at 7 minutes past the hour, and then again at 37 minutes past.
Marion: Oh, I see. Thank you. Can I bring anything back for you?
Mrs B.: It's very kind of you to ask, Marion, but no thanks. I've got everything I need.
Marion: Should I be back at any particular[1] time?
Mrs B.: Well, we want to have dinner at six o'clock. So try and be back by then, please.

Some questions to help you to find expressions for your phrase-book:
1. How does Marion ask for directions?[2] 2. How does Mrs Barnett give Marion directions to the bus stop? 3. How does she tell Marion about the times of the buses back? 4. How does Marion react when she doesn't understand what Mrs Barnett has said? 5. What does Mrs Barnett say when Marion offers to do some shopping for her?

⚠ Traffic drives on the left in Britain, so be careful when you cross the road. You must first look right, then left before you cross. When you ride a bike, you must be particularly careful when you turn right.

Ex 1 Work with a partner and
– ask for and give directions to a bank, post office, the nearest telephone, the bus station.
– make or use timetables to explain when a bus or train leaves.
– practise asking your partner to repeat something until you have understood it.

Ex 2 **Role play**
Marion and Gillian are talking about a day trip to Chester. Here is some information you can use in the dialogue: The train times from Liverpool are: *dep 8.34, arr 9.12*. Return from Chester: *dep 17.35, arr 18.15*. In Chester they want to go shopping and visit the zoo. Write a dialogue.

Ex 3 Now take Marion's part again.

[1] particular [pəˈtɪkjʊlə] *speziell, besondere/r/s*
[2] ask for/give directions *nach dem Weg fragen; den Weg erklären*

Option 22

Apologizing and asking for permission

Marion was late back from town and the Barnetts had already started their evening meal.

Marion: I'm sorry I'm late. I missed the bus and had to wait another half an hour.

Mrs B.: Don't worry. Come and sit down. We've already started, I'm afraid, because I have to go out soon.

Mr B.: You can always give us a ring,[1] Marion. You've got our number, haven't you? Liverpool 548 1359.

Marion: Yes, how silly of me. I didn't think. I hope I didn't cause any problems.

Mrs B.: Not at all. Now, pass me your plate.

———

Gillian: I thought Marion and I could go on a bike ride tomorrow. Could Marion borrow your bike, Mum, please?

Mrs B.: Yes, of course. I won't need it tomorrow. You know where it is.

Marion: Thanks a lot, Mrs Barnett.

Mrs B.: That's okay. Well, I must hurry. I've got a pottery class this evening.

Mr B.: We can do the washing up.[2] Leave everything where it is.

Mrs B.: Right, thanks.

Marion: Can I do anything to help?

Gillian: Well, you can either wash or dry. Which would you prefer? . . .

Some questions to help you to find expressions for your phrase-book:
1. How does Marion apologize and what excuse does she give? 2. How do Mr and Mrs Barnett react? 3. How does Gillian ask for permission to borrow her mother's bike? 4. How does Marion thank her? 5. How does Mr Barnett offer to do the washing up? 6. How does Marion offer to help?

> ⚠ It can be useful to have a phonecard in Britain, as many public telephones accept them instead of coins. You can buy a phonecard from a newsagent's[3] or a post office.

Ex 1 Work with a partner and practise
– apologizing because you are late, you don't like a certain meal, you are tired and don't want to stay up/watch TV, you didn't understand what somebody said.
– asking for permission to use the phone, to get a drink from the fridge, to watch TV, to stay out late because you want to go to a disco, to wash some clothes.
– offering to help with the housework or in the garden.
– finding out and saying phone numbers in English.

Ex 2 Write a dialogue:
Marion and Gillian want to go to a party at a friend's house on Friday evening. Gillian asks her parents for permission. As the party will probably finish late, there will be no bus to bring them home. Gillian asks her father if he will pick them up. He wants to know the friend's address and at what time he should pick them up.

Ex 3 Now take Marion's part.

[1] give sb. a ring *jn. anrufen* [2] do the washing up *abwaschen*
[3] newsagent's ['nju:z,eɪdʒənts] *Zeitungsladen*

Feeling ill Everybody hopes that it won't happen, but it is always possible that you will become ill while you are away from home.

Mrs B.: Are you all right, Marion?
Marion: I don't feel very well, Mrs Barnett.
Mrs B.: Oh dear! I'm sorry. What's wrong?
Marion: I don't really know. I feel sick.[1]
Mrs B.: It's probably just an upset stomach.[2] But you should go back to bed. I'll call the doctor's surgery[3] and try and get an appointment[4] for you.

—

Receptionist[5]: Dr Featherstone's surgery. Can I help you?
Mrs B.: Hallo. Susan Barnett speaking. A young German girl is staying with us, and she isn't feeling very well. Could she possibly see Dr Featherstone today?
Receptionist: Well, let me see. What about 11 o'clock?
Mrs B.: Yes, that'll be fine.
Receptionist: What's her name, please?
Mrs B.: Ostermann. O-s-t-e-r-m-a-double n.
Receptionist: And the first name?
Mrs B.: Marion.
Receptionist: Thank you, Mrs Barnett. Goodbye.

Some questions to help you to find expressions for your phrase-book:
1. How does Marion tell Mrs Barnett that she is ill? 2. How does she explain to Mrs Barnett what is wrong with her? 3. How does Mrs Barnett ask for an appointment with the doctor?

> ⚠ Every British family has a family doctor. As a visitor to Britain, you can phone any doctor and ask for an appointment. Treatment[6] by a doctor is free in Britain, but you might have to pay if you go to a dentist.[7] You should, of course, check with your health insurance[8] in Germany what the situation is before leaving home.

Ex 1 Work with a partner and practise
- explaining that you feel ill (e. g. you have a headache, a sore throat, a bad cold, etc.) or that you have had an accident and hurt yourself.
- phoning to make an appointment and spelling your name in English.

Ex 2 Write a dialogue:
You are staying with a family in Britain and you don't feel well one morning when you come down to breakfast. You don't want to upset anybody, so you try to eat your breakfast. Your partner notices that something is wrong with you and asks how you feel. You say that you feel ill and describe what is wrong (a sore throat, a bad cough, a headache). You wonder whether your partner should phone the doctor.

Ex 3 Now take Marion's part.

[1] I feel sick *mir ist übel* [2] upset stomach *Magenverstimmung* [3] surgery [ˈsɜːdʒərɪ] *Praxis(räume)*
[4] appointment [əˈpɔɪntmənt] *Termin* [5] receptionist [rɪˈsepʃənɪst] *Sprechstundenhilfe*
[6] treatment [ˈtriːtmənt] *Behandlung* [7] dentist [ˈdentɪst] *Zahnarzt/-ärztin*
[8] health insurance [ɪnˈʃɔːrəns] *Krankenversicherung*

Past tense and present perfect

We can use different tenses to talk about past events.
Say – what tenses are used here.
– how they are formed.

1 The simple past is used:

to say that something happened at a particular[3] point of time in the past, or during a period of time that finished in the past. This point or period of time is either given (e.g. *yesterday, at the weekend, last Friday, two weeks ago, in 1980, during the holidays, as a child*) or understood from the context.[4]
The simple past is often used to tell a story or to report something.

The past progressive is used:

to express that something was in progress, i.e. not completed at a particular point or period of time in the past.

2 The present perfect is used:

a to say that something has happened, but we do not know or want to say exactly[5] when. Typical adverbials with the present perfect are *just, recently, ever, never, often, several times, always, before, so far, already, yet?, not . . . yet.*

b to talk about something that began in the past and continues up to the present. If we want to say how long something has gone on for, we use *since* (+ point of time) or *for* (+ period of time).

⚠ With state verbs we use the **(simple) present perfect**, with activity verbs we use the **present perfect progressive** when we talk about things that have gone on up to the present:

I've known her since 1987. (state verb)	Ich **kenne** sie schon seit 1987.
I've been reading for two hours. (activity verb)	Ich **lese** schon seit zwei Stunden.

3 Past tense and present perfect in contrast

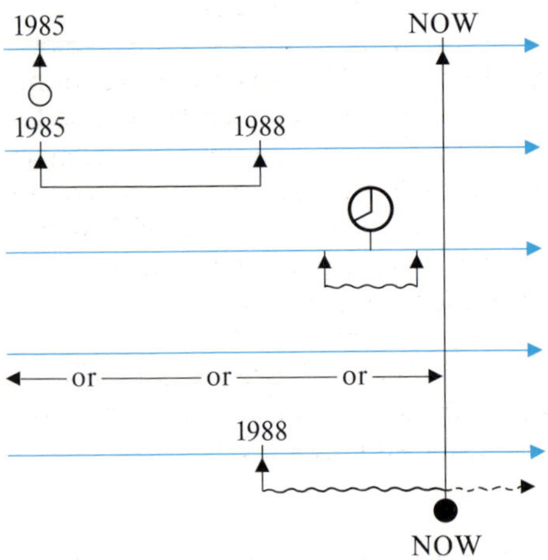

Janet **started** to learn French | in 1985. / . . . years ago.

She **learnt** French | from 1985-1988. / for three years.

She **was learning** Italian grammar at eight o'clock last night.

She **has learnt** Spanish, too.
(It does not matter when or for how long.)

She **has been learning** Russian | since 1988. / for . . . years.

[1] canary [kəˈneərɪ] *Kanarienvogel* [2] lame [leɪm] *lahm* [3] particular [pəˈtɪkjʊlə] *bestimmt*
[4] context [ˈkɒntekst] *Kontext, Zusammenhang* [5] exact [ɪgˈzækt] *genau*

Ex 1

Tiger free in precinct

Brighton, July 20 (AP). Yesterday afternoon a tiger (escape) from the local zoo. Nobody knows how it (get) out of its cage. The tiger (walk) into the precinct and (cause) great confusion[1] among the pedestrians. People (run) into shops, children (start) crying. Finally, the police (call) and after two hours they (catch) the animal in front of a butcher's shop. It (take) back to the zoo at once.

a *Put in the correct simple past forms. Be careful, sometimes you have to use a passive construction.*

b Imagine you are a reporter for a popular magazine and want to write a report about the tiger's escape.

1. *Interview one of the people who saw what happened. Add some extra information so that the interview is a bit more exciting.*
2. *Now write the report for your magazine.*

Ex 2 The job interview

a Sally has applied for a job in a bank. Mr Price, the bank manager, has asked her to come for an interview. *Put in the correct tense of the verbs.*

Mr Price: . . . Let me ask you a few questions about yourself. When (you/leave) school?
Sally: Two years ago.
Mr Price: What (you/do) these last two years?
Sally: Well, two years ago I (go) to France and I (work) in Paris for one and a half years. I (try) to get a job since the summer.
Mr Price: I see. So your knowledge of French must be pretty good. (you/learn) any other foreign languages at school?
Sally: I (learn) German at school and I (just/start) to learn Spanish in evening classes. Unfortunately I (not be) to Germany or Spain so far.
Mr Price: I suppose modern languages (be) your favourite subjects at school then?
Sally: Not really. I (enjoy) French and German, but in fact I (like) maths best. That's where I (get) my best marks, too. I (always/like) maths.

b What other questions might Mr Price have asked Sally (e.g. about other jobs, experiences, other applications,[2] hobbies)?

Ex 3

a
– Guess what (happen) when I (work) with my computer yesterday.
– (it/break down)[3]?
– Oh no, nothing as simple as that. I (try) to work with a new program when suddenly I (hear) a funny noise. It (sound) as if the computer was going to blow up.
– I hope you (switch) it off at once.
– Well, before I (can) do that, a strange voice (say), "How (you/find out) my private number? You (use) it several times before. So far I (not say) anything because at first I (think) it (be) just a mistake. But now I think you're only doing it to disturb[4] my peaceful afternoons." Of course I (be) totally surprised and (not know) what to say.
– What (happen) next?
– You won't believe it. While I (think) of an answer – oh, here's my bus now. I'll tell you the rest of the story tomorrow.

b *Can you continue the strange story of the computer voice?*
Have you had any exciting or funny dreams yourself? Try to describe them to the others in class.

[1] confusion [kən'fju:ʒn] *Verwirrung, Durcheinander* [2] application [ˌæplɪ'keɪʃn] *Bewerbung*
[3] break down *kaputtgehen* [4] disturb [dɪ'stɜ:b] *stören, durcheinanderbringen*

? ? ? ? ? ? ? ? Questions ? ? ? ? ? ? ? ?

1 The two main types[1] of questions are:

– **Yes/no questions**, which we can answer with *yes* or *no*, e. g. **Do you speak English**? – Yes, I do.
– **Wh-questions** (= questions with question words), e. g. **Where are you going**? – To the shops.

2 How to form questions

– Put an auxiliary verb (or modal) before the subject.
– Use *do/does* in simple present questions and *did* in simple past questions.

	Auxiliary	Subject	
	Have	**you**	read the book?
When	**can**	**Sally**	come?
	Does	**Linda**	live here?
What	**did**	**you**	say?

⚠ If *who, what, which* or *how many* is the subject of the question, do not use *do/does/did*:

Janet loves Gary. (Subject)
Who loves Gary? (= Wer?)

Janet loves **Gary**. (Object)
But: **Who** does Janet love? (= Wen?)
Whom does Janet love? *(formal)*

⚠ A preposition comes in the same place as in a statement,[2] i. e. after the verb or object.

Gary is looking **for** the newspaper.
What is Gary looking **for**?

He got the newspaper **from** Janet.
Who did he get the newspaper **from**?

Ex 1 Sorry, what did you say?
Imagine you didn't hear the underlined parts of the following sentences. *Ask the right wh-questions. Example:* Liz likes music. – Sorry, who likes music?/Sorry, what does Liz like?

1. Columbus discovered America in 1492. 2. Janet met Gary's parents on the bus. 3. Pat is travelling to Cuba by plane. 4. The electric light bulb was invented by Edison. 5. The accident caused a traffic jam. 6. Ms Black has lived in Oxford for 25 years.

Ex 2 The interview Julie works as a reporter for *Teen Life* magazine. Today she is going to interview Moira Best, a famous tennis player.

. . . when Moira started playing tennis / how often she practises / if she smokes / what other sports she is good at / how many competitions she has won / if she enjoys being famous.

What does Julie ask Moira? Start like this: Moira, when did you start . . . ?

Ex 3 At a party
Sigrid Blome from Bochum is on an exchange visit to Manchester. At a party she meets Brian, an English boy. What questions does he ask Sigrid? Here are her answers.

– Sigrid. – Bochum. – We arrived last Friday. – For twelve days. – At Carol's. – No, I've never been to England before. – Yes, I like it very much. – No, not yet. We're going there tomorrow. – Oh yes, please. I love dancing.

Ex 4 A quiz about Britain
Do a quiz about what you know about Britain. Work in groups. Each group finds questions for the quiz and then answers another group's questions.

[1] type [taɪp] *Typ, Art* [2] statement [ˈsteɪtmənt] *Aussagesatz*

Revision

The articles: *the* and *a/an*

1 **We do not use *the* with:**

a – abstract nouns[1] – material nouns[2] – countable nouns[3] in the plural } used in a general or unrestricted[4] sense[5] (even when there is an adjective before them).

Modern technology has made **life** easier.
Die moderne Technologie hat **das** Leben erleichtert.
Meat is becoming more and more expensive.
Cars have become faster and faster.
(Die) Autos . . .

b – personal names in the singular (not even when there is an adjective before them),
– the names of most streets and places (esp. parks, squares and bridges), and with some buildings,
– many geographical[7] names (e.g. countries, towns, lakes and mountains).

(Little) Jane lives here. **Die** kleine Jane . . .
in **Tree Road**, in **Hyde Park**, near **Oxford Station**
in **England**, near **Lake Erie**, on **Ben Nevis**

c *church, hospital, prison, court, university, school,* etc. when we think of their function.[8]

We went to **church** in Eastwood last Sunday.
. . . **zum** Gottesdienst . . .

d phrases of time such as *on Sunday, before Friday, next/last Monday; at night, by day; in June.*

We use *the* with:

– abstract nouns – material nouns – countable nouns in the plural } used in a specific[6] or restricted sense, e.g. when an *of*-phrase or a relative clause follows.

I've got a book about **the life** of Shakespeare.
Ich habe ein Buch über das Leben Shakespeares.
The meat I bought yesterday was expensive.
The cars which have been constructed in recent years use less petrol.

– family names in the plural,
– the names of some buildings (esp. museums, theatres, cinemas, hotels, and all names that consist of a noun and an *of*-phrase),
– some geographical names (e.g. plural place names, rivers and seas).

The Millers have bought a house. Millers . . .
near **the British Museum**, in **the White House**
from **the United States**, on **the River Thames**

church, hospital, prison, court, university, school, etc. when we think of the building.

The church in Eastwood is opposite **the school.**

phrases of time such as *on the Sunday before our holidays; during the night, in the morning/evening/. . .*

⚠ *Most* (= more than half, nearly all) is used with nouns in two ways:

most + noun without *the* (= general sense)
Most football spectators aren't hooligans.
Die meisten Fußballzuschauer . . .

most of the + noun (= more restricted sense)
Most of the spectators cheered **most of the time.**
Die meisten Zuschauer jubelten **die** meiste Zeit.

⚠ *All, half, both, twice* and *double* go before *the*: **all the food, half the cake, both (the) teams**

2 **We use *a/an*:**

a with jobs, also after *as* (German "als"):
Mrs Baker is **a landscape painter**. She also works **as a photographer**. . . . als Fotografin.

b in phrases of frequency,[9] speed, price, etc. In these phrases *a/an* means *per* (German "pro"):
Mrs Baker sometimes sells several pictures **a month.** . . . mehrere Bilder pro Monat.

⚠ *Quite, such* and *half* go before *a/an*:
Mrs Baker is **quite a** good **landscape painter**. . . . eine recht gute Landschaftsmalerin.

[1] abstract noun *abstraktes Nomen, Begriff (z.B. history, technology, life)* [2] material noun *Stoffname (z.B. meat, water, oil)* [3] countable noun *zählbares Nomen (z.B. car, bird)* [4] restrict [rɪ'strɪkt] *einschränken, eingrenzen* [5] sense [sens] *Sinn, Bedeutung* [6] specific [spə'sɪfɪk] *bestimmt* [7] geographical [ˌdʒɪə'græfɪkl] [8] function ['fʌŋkʃn] *Funktion, Zweck* [9] frequency ['fri:kwənsɪ] *Häufigkeit*

Ex 1 **Michael Hennessy** *Find the missing words and put in "the" where necessary.*

Michael Hennessy arrived in the US from Ireland in 1910. He was a very poor man. He had never gone to . . . , so he had never learnt to read or to write. Because he was so poor, . . . hadn't been easy for him. In America he had a better chance to make . . . and become rich. His idea was to buy a farm. He had been a farmer in Ireland, but he had never owned . . . he worked on. He hoped that . . . of a farmer in the New World might be better. He could then send his children to . . . , where they could learn properly. If his family became ill, he could send them to . . . . He had heard that . . . in America had very good doctors.
But . . . of an immigrant wasn't without its problems. Michael soon found that he couldn't afford a farm. . . . was expensive, especially in the east. So he decided to go west. For the first time in his life he felt free. In Ireland he had only been able to dream of . . . . Michael finally settled in Texas. There was no special reason to stop there. He just liked the countryside. But he was lucky. Ten years later . . . was found on his land. An oil-rig was built where his house had once stood, and Michael had no more money problems.

Ex 2 **Proverbs and sayings** *Explain in English what they mean, then translate them into German.*

1. Time flies. *2. While there's life, there's hope.* *3. Politeness costs nothing.*
4. Actions speak louder than words. *5. History repeats itself.* *6. Truth is stranger than fiction.*

Ex 3 **Billy Brown's childhood**[1] *Put in "the" or "a/an" where necessary.*

Billy Brown lived in • small village in • north of England in • early 19th century. Like • most people in • village, his parents were very poor. • poverty was • serious problem in those days. It meant that • children had to start • work at • early age. • work was even more important than • school. When Billy was only twelve, he had to work in • factory for nine hours • day. • working conditions in • factory were very bad. There was little light, • air was full of • smoke and • dust • most of • time, and • noise was terrible.
Of course, • young Billy wasn't happy with his situation. But what could he do? • situation was • same for • most children of his age. Some of his friends begged[2] in • streets in • evenings for • money or • food. • most of them were arrested by • police sooner or later and were sent to • prison. It was • quite • hard time.

Ex 4 **In English, please**

1. Die Lebensmittelpreise sind wieder gestiegen. Besonders der Kaffee ist viel teurer geworden.
2. Am letzten Montag brach in der Autofabrik in der Bahnhofstraße Feuer aus. Die Fabrikgebäude brannten völlig nieder, obwohl Polizei und Feuerwehr sofort alarmiert wurden *(call)*.
3. Die kleine Barbara interessiert sich für Bücher über die Natur, besonders für Bücher über Tiere. Ihre Lieblingstiere sind Pferde. Sie verbringt mehrere Stunden in der Woche mit den Pferden auf dem Bauernhof ihres Onkels. Später möchte sie auch Bäuerin werden.
4. Katzen fressen Mäuse. Aber mir scheint, die Katzen in unserer Straße bevorzugen das Futter, das wir im Supermarkt kaufen.

"We're seven dwarfs,[3] but not The Seven Dwarfs."

[1] childhood ['tʃaɪldhʊd] *Kindheit* [2] beg [beg] *betteln (gehen)* [3] dwarf [dwɔːf] *Zwerg*

Revision

Ways of expressing the future

There are several different ways of expressing future time in English. Sometimes the differences between them are very small. If you choose the wrong form, people will probably still understand what you are trying to say.

⚠ In German we most often use the "Präsens" to talk about something in the future. In English we almost always have to use the will-future, the going to-future or the present progressive to refer to future events.

1 The will-future is used:

a to talk about future events which we cannot influence or control.
Next July **I'll be** 18. . . . **werde** ich 18.
We **won't be** back before lunch.

b to predict future events or to express hopes, expectations, etc. In such sentences we often use *I'm sure, I believe, I expect, I hope, I suppose, I think, I guess* or *perhaps, possibly, probably, surely.*
I expect Tim **will get** the job.
Ich erwarte, daß Tim die Stelle **bekommt**.
Perhaps Jane **will come** later.
Vielleicht **kommt** Jane später.

c with *I/we* for spontaneous[1] reactions or to make promises.
Wait a minute. **I'll help** you.
Ich **helfe** dir.

I/we shall is sometimes used instead of *I/we will*. But in spoken English we usually use *I'll* and *we'll*.

2 The going to-future is used:

a to talk about things that people intend,[2] plan, or have decided to do in the future.
Sue **is going to study** medicine.
Sue hat vor, Medizin zu studieren.

⚠ Did you know that Sarah is in hospital?
– No, I didn't. **I'll visit** her this afternoon. (spontaneous reaction, *compare* 1c)
– Yes, **I'm going to visit** her next Monday. (intention,[3] planned action, *compare* 2a)

b to predict future events for which there is some evidence in the present (e.g. black clouds).
Look at those black clouds.
I think it**'s going to rain**.

3 The present progressive is used:

to talk about things that people have arranged or definitely[4] decided to do in the future. It must be clear from adverbials of time or from the context that the speaker is referring to the future and not to the present.
We**'re flying** to Spain next week.
Wir **fliegen** nächste Woche nach Spanien.
Another drink? – No thanks, **I'm driving**.

⚠ Sometimes the difference between the present progressive and the going to-future is very small, because in some situations there is little difference between an intention and an arrangement.[5]

4 The simple present is used:

a to talk about programmes or any kind of timetable ("timetable future"). In such sentences verbs like *begin, end, open, close, leave, arrive* are often used.
The next guided tour of the castle **starts** at 2 pm.
The next train **leaves** at 10.

b in subordinate clauses with *if/unless* or conjunctions of time like *when, while, before, until/till, as soon as, as long as*. In the main clause we have to use a future form (usually the will-future or the going to-future) or an imperative.
If you **come** later, I **won't see** you.
I **won't leave** till you **get** here.
I'm going to become an engineer when I **leave** school.

[1] spontaneous [spɒn'teɪnɪəs] *spontan* [2] intend [ɪn'tend] *beabsichtigen* [3] intention [ɪn'tenʃn] *Absicht*
[4] definitely ['defɪnətlɪ] *eindeutig* [5] arrangement [ə'reɪndʒmənt] *Vereinbarung*

Option 26

Ex 1 **Your horoscope**[1]

Ask your friends what their star signs are: What's your star sign? – I'm Taurus/Leo/...
Then write their horoscopes for next week. (The two examples will help you.)
Remember to use the will-future for predictions.[2]

Cancer (21 June–20 July)
There'll be a lot of extra work for you. But you'll make some extra money.

Scorpio (23 Oct–21 Nov)
You won't be able to keep your promises. A good friend will let you down.

Ex 2 **A trip to York** *Use the will-future for predictions and the going to-future for intentions. But remember to use the simple present in subordinate clauses.*

Jane: Tracy and I (spend) a few days in York.
Roger: Lucky you! I'm sure you (like) the town. I was there last summer. It's really beautiful. Where (you/stay)?
Jane: Well, Tracy thinks we (be) able to stay with her grandparents. She (write) to them this evening. She's also got a friend in York, and I think we (visit) her if she (be) at home.
Roger: What (you/do and see) in York?
Jane: Well, I'm not quite sure yet. I think we (decide) when we (get) there. But of course we (visit) the famous York Minster and the Castle Museum. And we (spend) a day in the Lake District if the weather (be) fine.
Roger: How long (you/stay)? I suppose you (be) back for the volleyball match on Tuesday, ... you?
Jane: Yes, I .... We (have) to be back on Monday.
Roger: That's good. We (need) our best team against Fane Street.

Ex 3 **Thinking about the future**

What do you think or hope life will be like in 50 years from now? How will the following be different: living conditions, the job situation, working hours, free time activities, the pollution of the environment, space travel, computers, TV, fashion, pop music, school, etc.? *Write a text about your expectations, hopes and ideas as well as your personal plans and intentions.*

Ex 4 **In English, please**

1. Bleibt ihr dieses Jahr in den Sommerferien zu Hause? – Nein, wir fahren für vierzehn Tage nach Spanien. 2. Susan hat eine Stelle in einer großen Firma in Liverpool angeboten bekommen. Ich bin sicher, sie wird das Angebot annehmen, obwohl es natürlich bedeutet, daß sie von Oxford wegziehen muß. Aber sie wird wahrscheinlich bald neue Freunde in Liverpool finden. 3. Der nächste Zug nach Exeter fährt erst um 14 Uhr. Aber ihr könnt auch den Bus nehmen. Er fährt um 11 Uhr ab. Wenn ihr euch beeilt, erreicht ihr ihn noch. Dann seid ihr viel früher in Exeter. 4. Ich rufe dich an, sobald ich nach Hause komme. 5. Es sieht aus, als ob es bald anfängt zu regnen. – Dann brauchen wir den Rasen heute abend wenigstens nicht zu sprengen *(water)*. 6. Ich gehe jetzt nach Hause. – Warte, ich komme mit.

[1] horoscope [ˈhɒrəskəʊp]: Aquarius [əˈkweərɪəs] Pisces [ˈpaɪsiːz] Aries [ˈeəriːz] Taurus [ˈtɔːrəs] Gemini [ˈdʒemɪnaɪ] Cancer [ˈkænsə] Leo [ˈliːəʊ] Virgo [ˈvɜːgəʊ] Libra [ˈliːbrə] Scorpio [ˈskɔːpɪəʊ] Sagittarius [ˌsædʒɪˈteərɪəs] Capricorn [ˈkæprɪkɔːn] [2] prediction [prɪˈdɪkʃn] *Vorhersage*

Vocabulary

Im folgenden Wörterverzeichnis *(Vocabulary)* sind die **neuen Wörter jeder Unit** aufgeführt. **Eingerückte Wörter** sollen mit dem vorausgehenden Wort mitgelernt werden, obwohl sie nicht an der betreffenden Stelle der Unit vorkommen. **Eigennamen** stehen nach dem *Mini-dictionary* auf der Seite xxi. Eine Übersicht aller in den Bänden A1 bis A5 benutzten **grammatischen Fachausdrücke** steht auf den Seiten xxi-xxii. Die neuen Wörter aus den *Options* sind im *Vocabulary* nicht aufgeführt, weil nur eine Auswahl an *Options* bearbeitet wird und der darin enthaltene neue Wortschatz in Band 6 nicht vorausgesetzt wird. Eine Auswahl wichtiger Wörter aus den *Options*, die zum Lernwortschatz hinzugefügt werden können, steht auf den Seiten 167-168.

Die **fett gedruckten Wörter** gehören zum produktiven, die **normal gedruckten Wörter** zum rezeptiven Wortschatz. In Bundesländern, in denen keine Unterscheidung zwischen einem rezeptiven und einem produktiven Wortschatz gemacht wird, sind alle Wörter als Lernwortschatz gleich zu behandeln.

Die **kursiv gedruckten Wörter** sind aus fakultativen Abschnitten. Sie werden außerhalb dieser fakultativen Abschnitte nicht als bekannt vorausgesetzt.

Die **mit einem ° versehenen Wörter** gehören zum sogenannten ‚Situationswortschatz'. Es sind Wörter, die zwar zum Thema einer bestimmten Unit gehören, aber weniger gebräuchlich sind und daher in den folgenden Units nicht als bekannt vorausgesetzt werden.

Die **rote Unterstreichung** bei einigen Wörtern soll auf die richtige **Schreibung** hinweisen, der **Rotdruck des Betonungszeichens oder eines bestimmten Lautes** soll auf die richtige **Aussprache** aufmerksam machen.

Die **Tilde** (~) in der dritten Spalte steht anstelle des Wortes oder der Wendung aus der ersten Spalte. Pro Tilde muß ein Wort eingesetzt werden.

sb. = somebody, sth. = something; jd. = jemand, jm. = jemandem, jn. = jemanden
adj. = adjective, adv. = adverb, conj. = conjunction, n. = noun, prep. = preposition, v. = verb;
sing. = singular, pl. = plural
AE = American English, Aust. E = Australian English, BE = British English
fml. = formal (förmlich), infml. = informal (umgangssprachlich), nonstandard (ungrammatisch), slang (Slang)

Unit 1: Introduction and Revision

The United Kingdom

p. 6	**past** [pɑːst]	vergangen	The number of unemployed young people has risen in the ~ few months.
	attractive [əˈtræktɪv]	anziehend, attraktiv, reizvoll	beautiful, good-looking Well, the flat is really nice, but the area isn't very ~. We live right next to a factory. Sarah is very beautiful. – Yes, she's a really ~ woman.
	revolution [ˌrevəˈluːʃn]	Revolution	time of sudden political, economic or social change
	general [ˈdʒenrəl]	allgemein, generell	Can you give me a ~ idea what the job will be like?
	generally [ˈdʒenrəlɪ]	im allgemeinen, im großen und ganzen	Michael ~ does well in English, but in his last test he did very badly.
p. 7	°minster [ˈmɪnstə]	Münster	
	aspect [ˈæspekt]	Aspekt, Gesichtspunkt, Seite	The discussion about pollution on TV last night showed many ~*s* of the problem.
	task [tɑːsk]	Aufgabe	a piece of work to be done
	(to) have sth. in common [ˈkɒmən]	etwas miteinander gemein haben	We're just not interested in the same things. In fact, we *haven't* anything ~ ~ at all.
	common	gemeinsam, gemeinschaftlich; üblich, normal	We've got ~ interests. We like doing the same things. Lots of men are called John. It's a very ~ name.

Unit 1

p. 8 Peace in danger?

security [sɪ'kjʊərɪtɪ]	Sicherheit; Sicherheitsvorkehrungen	Musicians are often unemployed. The job doesn't offer much ~. *S*~ has to be very strict at airports.
forward(s) ['fɔ:wəd(z)]	vorwärts	opposite of backward(s)
bay [beɪ]	Bucht	part of the sea surrounded on three sides by land 
°glow worm ['gləʊ wɜ:m]	Glühwürmchen	
(dis)satisfied (with) [(dɪ)'sætɪsfaɪd]	(un)zufrieden (mit)	I'm very *s*~ with your English. It's really improved. Mr Smith is very *dis*~ with his job. That's why he's applying for a new one.
satisfaction [ˌsætɪs'fækʃn]	Zufriedenheit; Befriedigung	Tim really enjoys his job. It gives him a lot of ~.
(to) **point** sth. **at** sb. [pɔɪnt]	etwas auf jn. richten *(Waffe usw.)*	*Don't* ~ your finger *at* me. It's rude. The police officers ~*ed* their guns *at* the criminal.
cigarette [ˌsɪgə'ret]	Zigarette	Do you smoke a lot? – Yes, 20 ~*s* a day.
clear (of) [klɪə]	frei (von)	I'll wait till the roads are ~ of traffic before I leave.
evidence (of) *(sing.)* ['evɪdəns]	Beweis(e) (für); Beleg(e) (für)	Graham has stolen my money. – Do you have any ~ of this?
shocked (by/at) [ʃɒkt]	schockiert, bestürzt (über)	Mrs Brown was ~ by her daughter's green hair. I was ~ at the news that she'd had an accident.

p. 9 A new start "down under"

down under [ˌdaʊn‿'ʌndə] (infml.)	*umgangssprachliche Bezeichnung für Australien*	an informal way of talking about Australia, as it's on the other side of the world
visa ['vi:zə]	Visum	You need a tourist ~ to visit some countries.
as soon as *(conj.)* [əz 'su:n‿əz]	sobald	I'll let you have the book ~ *soon* ~ I've read it.
salary ['sælərɪ]	Gehalt	money paid to an employee, usually once a month Ms Fox is on a ~ of £20,000 a year. ⚠ *wages* = (meist wöchentlich bar gezahlter) Lohn
alternative [ɔ:l'tɜ:nətɪv]	Alternative	If you don't like my suggestion you can think of an ~.
alternatively [ɔ:l'tɜ:nətɪvlɪ]	andererseits, als Alternative	Shall we go to the cinema tonight? Or ~ we could go out for a meal.
profession [prə'feʃn]	(freier/akademischer) Beruf	a job for which you need a special training Mary is a doctor by ~. She works in a large hospital.

if + <u>should</u> + infinitive

If you leave school, . . . *(possible and probable)*	Wenn du von der Schule abgehst, . . .
If you **should leave** school, . . . *(possible, but less probable)*	Wenn du von der Schule abgehen solltest, . . .
If you left school, . . . *(possible, but improbable)*	Wenn du von der Schule abgingest/abgehen würdest, . . .

jealous (of) ['dʒeləs]	eifersüchtig (auf); neidisch (auf)	Tim is so ~ when I go out with other men. John is ~ of his sister because she's good at school.
(to) **send/give one's love to sb.**	jn. grüßen (lassen)	If you see Richard, *give him my* ~ and tell him to call me.

(p. 9)	clue (to) [klu:]	Anhaltspunkt (für), Hinweis (auf)	The police are still looking for ~*s* to the death of three Bristol nurses last month.
	(to) **learn** (about)	herausfinden (über), erfahren (über)	We*'re* ~*ing* about the Romans in history. I ~*ed* about Ed's plans to move only yesterday.
	indirect [ˌɪndɪˈrekt, ˌɪndaɪˈrekt]	indirekt, mittelbar	opposite of direct
	(to) present [prɪˈzent]	präsentieren, darlegen	Mr Ward ~*ed* his idea to the boss. Susan Green ~*s* the nine o'clock news on TV. ⚠ *(to) present* [prɪˈzent] – *the present* [ˈpreznt] = das Geschenk
	oral [ˈɔ:rəl]	mündlich	spoken; not written

p. 10 Different cultures

sari [ˈsɑ:rɪ]	Sari	a long traditional dress that is worn by some Indian and Pakistani women, for example
(even) though *(conj.)* [ðəʊ]	obwohl	although *T*~ it rained a lot, we had a great holiday.
rich	kräftig *(Geruch, Farbton)*; schwer, nahrhaft *(Speise)*	What colour is your new car, Tim? – It's a deep ~ red. This cake is very ~. It's full of cream.
(to) **support** [səˈpɔ:t]	unterstützen, befürworten	*Did* you ~ the building of the Channel Tunnel?
support	Unterstützung, Beistand	Tom and I went to watch Sue play in her tennis match and to give her some ~.
supporter [səˈpɔ:tə]	Befürworter/in; Anhänger/in	Jim is a ~ of nuclear power. Liz is against it. Are you a ~ of Bayern München?

Two schools – two different worlds

	playing field [ˈpleɪɪŋ fi:ld]	Sportplatz	area of ground where football or cricket, for example, can be played
	scene [si:n]	Schauplatz, Ort; Szene	They found the thief at the ~ of the crime. The hero forgot his words in the first ~ of the play.
	afterwards [ˈɑ:ftəwədz]	später, nachher, hinterher	The film finishes at 8 o'clock, so we could go out for a meal ~.
	ordinary [ˈɔ:dənrɪ]	einfach, gewöhnlich, normal	normal; not unusual I'm not wearing anything special, just my ~ clothes.
	exclusive [ɪkˈsklu:sɪv]	vornehm, exclusiv	The Stewarts went out for a special meal at one of Belfast's most ~ restaurants.
	privileged [ˈprɪvɪlɪdʒd]	privilegiert, bevorzugt	Mr Woodbridge is the best maths teacher in the school. You're very ~ to have him as your teacher.
	privilege [ˈprɪvɪlɪdʒ]	Privileg, Bevorzugung	Juliet is an excellent singer. It was a real ~ to hear her sing last week.
p. 11	**the ..., the ...**	je ..., um so/desto ...	*The* more you practise, ~ better you'll become.
	(to) **get to know**	kennenlernen	*Did* you ~ *to* ~ any Germans on holiday?
	in this/that respect [rɪˈspekt]	in dieser/jener Hinsicht, Beziehung	Sue and her brother Paul are very shy. They are both very similar ~ *this* ~.
	(to) illustrate [ˈɪləstreɪt]	veranschaulichen, illustrieren	There was a film about Africa on TV last week. It ~*d* some of the problems of developing countries.
	on the one hand/ on the other hand	einerseits/andererseits	*On* ~ *one* ~, I enjoy living in a city because there's so much to do. *On* ~ *other* ~, I hate the pollution.
	wealth [welθ]	Reichtum, Wohlstand	Only families with ~ can afford to send their children to a public school.
	wealthy [ˈwelθɪ]	wohlhabend, reich	Sarah owns two houses and two cars. She's very ~.

(p. 11)	(to) **frighten** [ˈfraɪtn]	ängstigen	The film ~*ed* Tony. He couldn't sleep afterwards.
p. 12	fleet [fli:t]	Flotte	a group of ships, especially warships

German "hätte/wäre" in conditional sentences II and III

(II)	If I **had** (= **hätte**) a proper job,	I **would have** (= **hätte**) enough money.
	If I **was/were** (= **wäre**) your grandfather,	you **would be** (= **wärst**) my grandchild.
	if-Satz: **had; was/were**	Hauptsatz: **would have; would be**
(III)	If Patrick **had** asked me,	I **would have** helped him.
	Wenn Patrick mich gefragt **hätte**,	**hätte** ich ihm geholfen.
	If Debbie **had** come to the party,	I **would have** been happy.
	Wenn Debbie zu der Party gekommen **wäre**,	**wäre** ich glücklich gewesen.
	if-Satz: **past perfect (= had + past participle)**	Hauptsatz: **would have + past participle**

1 Ex 1	°pirate [ˈpaɪərət]	Seeräuber/in, Pirat/in	
	°admiral [ˈædmərəl]	Admiral	
	order [ˈɔ:də]	Befehl	The captain of the ship gave the sailors their ~*s*. . . .
	(to) **order** sb. **to** do sth.	jm. befehlen, etwas zu tun; jn. damit beauftragen, etwas zu tun	. . . He ~*ed* them *to* clean the ship.
2	DIY [ˌdi:‿aɪ ˈwaɪ] (BE, infml.) = Do-It-Yourself	Heimwerken	
3	(to) kick [kɪk]	treten	The football player ~*ed* the ball.
5	(to) transplant [trænsˈplɑ:nt]	verpflanzen, transplantieren	It was a successful operation. The heart *was* ~*ed* very quickly.
6	adapted from [əˈdæptɪd]	eine Bearbeitung von, frei nach	The film is ~ ~ a successful play.
	plastic [ˈplæstɪk]	Kunststoff, Plastik; Plastik-	Is that a leather jacket? – No, it's actually made of ~. I've forgotten my shopping basket. Can I have a ~ bag?

Unit 2: Schools in Britain

2 A Focus on WORDS

p. 16	(to) drive sb. mad	jn. wahnsinnig, verrückt machen	to annoy somebody a lot Jo listens to music late at night. It ~*s* me ~!
	science [ˈsaɪəns]	(Natur-)Wissenschaft	Biology, chemistry and physics are all ~ subjects.
	democracy [dɪˈmɒkrəsɪ]	Demokratie	The workers complain that they have no rights. There's no ~ at the firm.
	discipline [ˈdɪsɪplɪn]	Disziplin	Nobody pays any attention to our maths teacher, Mr Hill. He can't keep ~ at all.
	°(to) doodle [ˈdu:dl]	Männchen malen	
	otherwise [ˈʌðəwaɪz]	sonst, andernfalls	I'll probably see you tonight, Tim. *O*~ I'll call you.
	(to) **do without** (sth.)	ohne (etwas) auskommen, verzichten (auf etwas)	I forgot to buy a newspaper. We'll have to ~ *without* one today.
	entertainment [ˌentəˈteɪnmənt]	Unterhaltung, Belustigung	Cinema, theatre and television are all forms of ~. Simon made a real fool of himself yesterday, much to the ~ of his friends.

p. 16)	**point** [pɔɪnt]	Sinn, Zweck	What's the ~ of learning Latin? You can't even speak it.
	pressure [ˈpreʃə]	Druck, Zwang	Mr Sutton is under a lot of ~ at work at the moment. He has to work very long hours six days a week.
	network [ˈnetwɜːk]	Netz(werk); Vernetzung	A railway ~ is a system of railway lines which cover a certain area.

2 A Gary King: A profile of a young Liverpudlian

p. 17	profile [ˈprəʊfaɪl]	Kurzbiografie, -porträt; Profil	There's a ~ of the president's life in the paper today. the side view of something, especially a person's head 
	Liverpudlian [ˌlɪvəˈpʌdlɪən]	Liverpooler/in	a person who comes from Liverpool
	self-employed [ˌselfɪmˈplɔɪd, ˈselfɪmplɔɪd]	selbständig *(Geschäftsleute)*	Sarah is ~-~ [ˌ--ˈ-]. She owns a restaurant. Andrew and Simon are both ~-~ [ˈ---] businessmen. They have their own businesses.
	engineering [ˌendʒɪˈnɪərɪŋ]	Maschinenbau	the profession or science of an engineer
	design [dɪˈzaɪn]	Produktgestaltung, Design, Konstruktion(slehre); Entwurf, Skizze	I don't like the ~ of that chair. It's too traditional. The town planner looked at the ~*s* for the new shopping centre.
	designer [dɪˈzaɪnə]	Konstrukteur/in, Gestalter/in, Designer/in	My mother did the design for Sue's wedding dress. She's a professional dress ~.
	unlike *(prep.)* [ˌʌnˈlaɪk]	anders als, im Gegensatz zu	John hates jazz music. *U*~ her brother, Susan really enjoys listening to it.
	(to) dominate [ˈdɒmɪneɪt]	beherrschen	If Sarah comes, no one else will have a chance to say anything. She always ~*s* the discussions.
	by the time *(conj.)*	wenn, bis	Ms Smith works very long hours. *By* ~ ~ she gets home, she's usually very tired.
	(I) used to (do . . .) [ˈjuːstə]	Früher habe/bin (ich) immer . . .	John always ~ *to* go on holiday with his parents. But now he goes with his friends.

Über frühere Zustände und Gewohnheiten sprechen

Wir verwenden **used to + Infinitiv,**

– um über frühere Zustände zu sprechen:

We **used to live** in Leeds, but now we live in Norwich.	Früher haben wir in Leeds gewohnt, . . .
He **didn't use to be** so shy. Why has he changed?	Er war früher nicht so schüchtern. . . .

– um über frühere Gewohnheiten oder regelmäßige Handlungen in der Vergangenheit zu sprechen:

I **used to do** a lot of sport, but I haven't got the time now.	Ich habe früher viel Sport getrieben, . . .
He **didn't use to smoke** when I met him.	Er hat (früher) nicht geraucht, . . .
Did you **use to go** swimming a lot when you were a child?	Bist du als Kind oft schwimmen gegangen?

Beachte: Zum Ausdruck von früher regelmäßig wiederholten Handlungen wird statt **used to + Infinitiv** auch **would + Infinitiv** verwendet (mit Zeit- oder Häufigkeitsangaben wie *every day, often, from time to time* usw.):
My older sister **used to/would take** me to the zoo every Sunday when I was little.

2 A Focus on GRAMMAR

p. 18	(to) **serve** [sɜːv]	(be)dienen, servieren	A waiter ~*s* customers in a restaurant. Is anybody hungry? Shall I ~ the soup?

Unit 2

(p. 18)	**rush** [rʌʃ]	Ansturm, Andrang; Eile, Hetze(rei)	Before Christmas there's always a ~ to buy presents. It'll be a ~ but I'll try and be there by 8.30.
	(to) **rush**	eilen, hetzen	to hurry; to do something too quickly
	rush hour	Hauptverkehrszeit	when traffic is very busy because people are travelling to work or school, or back home again

p. 19

Verbs not normally used in the progressive form (state verbs)

1. *Zustandsverben (Verben, die Zustände, Eigenschaften oder Besitzverhältnisse beschreiben):* **appear (to be)** (scheinen), **be, belong to, consist of, cost, exist, have** (besitzen), **look** (aussehen), **matter, mean** (bedeuten), **need, own, seem, smell** (riechen, stinken), **sound** (klingen, sich anhören), **taste** (schmecken), **weigh**
2. *Verben des Meinens, Wissens und Vermutens:* **agree, believe, disagree, imagine, know, mean** (meinen), **realize** (einsehen, merken), **recognize, remember, see** (verstehen, einsehen), **suppose, think** (meinen, glauben), **understand, wonder**
3. *Verben der Sinneswahrnehmung:* **feel, hear, notice, see**
4. *Verben des Mögens, Nichtmögens und Wollens:* **dislike, hate, hope, like, love, mean (to do)** (absichtlich tun, tun wollen), **mind** (etwas einzuwenden haben), **prefer, want, wish**

2 A One kind of exchange: Twin towns

p. 20	twin [twɪn]	Zwilling; Partner-, Zwillings-	You look just like your brother Paul. Are you ~*s*? – Yes, he's my ~ brother. Nottingham and Karlsruhe are ~ towns. . . .
	(to) twin, -nn- [twɪn] (BE)	verschwistern *(Städte)*, eine (Städte-)Partnerschaft eingehen	. . . They *are ~ned* with one another.
	°borough ['bʌrə]	Stadtbezirk, Stadtteil	
	orchestra ['ɔːkɪstrə]	Orchester	a group of musicians who play different instruments together
	inland ['ɪnlənd]	Binnen-, inländisch	The Smiths spent their last holiday on Britain's ~ waterways. They hired a canal boat for a week.
	return (to) [rɪ'tɜːn]	Rückkehr, Wiederkehr (nach); Rück-	It didn't take us very long to get home. The ~ journey was very quick.
	pleasure ['pleʒə]	Vergnügen, Freude; Vergnügungs-	It was a ~ meeting Frank again. A ~ boat leaves for Greenwich every hour.
	(to) **depart** (from) [dɪ'pɑːt]	abfahren, abreisen (von)	to leave The Leeds train *will* ~ from platform 3.
	NB, nb [ˌen'biː] = nota bene (Latin)	bitte beachten	
	swimming costume (BE) ['swɪmɪŋ ˌkɒstjuːm]	Badebekleidung, Badeanzug	
	swimming trunks *(pl.)* [trʌŋks]	Badehose	
	farewell [feə'wel]	Abschieds-	John is emigrating to the USA tomorrow. We're having a ~ party for him tonight.
	relations (with) *(pl.)* [rɪ'leɪʃnz]	Beziehungen (mit)	International ~ are very tense because of the present crisis.

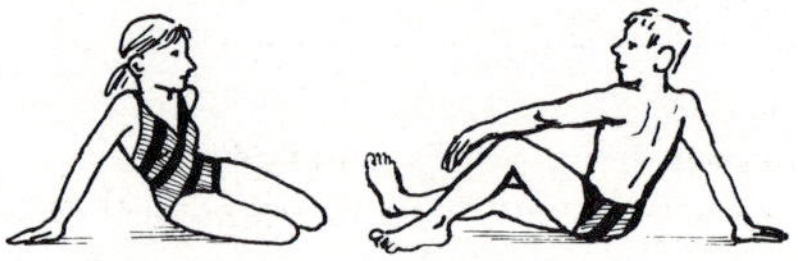

2 A A different kind of exchange

p. 21	**background** ['bækgraʊnd]	Hintergrund; Herkunft	Who's that in the photo? – That's the family I stayed with in the USA. You can see their house in the ~. Tom comes from a poor ~. His family is very poor.

). 21)	**well-off** [ˌwel‿ˈɒf]	wohlhabend, reich	opposite of poor; wealthy
	average *(n., adj.)* [ˈævərɪdʒ]	Durchschnitt; durchschnittlich, Durchschnitts-	Simon's results were pretty ~, but Ann's results were well above ~.
	prejudice (against) [ˈpredʒʊdɪs]	Vorurteil, Voreingenommenheit (gegen, gegenüber)	My brother has a ~ against women. He doesn't think they're as intelligent as men. . . .
	prejudiced (against) [ˈpredʒʊdɪst]	voreingenommen (gegenüber)	. . . He's ~ against women.
	°rabble [ˈræbl]	Pöbel, Mob	
	silver [ˈsɪlvə]	silbern; Silber	Is that ring ~? – No, it's made of some cheap metal.
	ignorant [ˈɪgnərənt]	unwissend, ungebildet, ignorant	I've no idea how cars work. I'm really ~ about them. He said he was ~ of the test, but I don't believe him.
	ignorance [ˈɪgnərəns]	Unwissenheit, Unkenntnis, Ignoranz	Prejudice is usually based on ~.
	producer [prəˈdjuːsə]	Produzent/in, Produktionsleiter/in	a person who organizes the making of a television programme or film, for example

2 A Rugby – a public school

fee [fiː]	Gebühr, Beitrag; Schulgeld; Honorar	money which you pay to go to a private school, to join a club, or for the services of a doctor

Income (= Einkommen)

income: [ˈɪŋkʌm] any money you receive regularly, not just money you get for your work
In most countries you pay tax on all your **income**, not just on your salary.

pay: the general word for the money that is paid for your work
I like the work, but the **pay** (= Bezahlung, Entgelt) is bad.

salary: usually paid once a month and directly into your bank account (= Konto)
We offer a **salary** (= Gehalt) of £18,000 a year.

wages: usually paid once a week and in cash (= bar), especially for manual work (= manuelle Arbeit)
Your **wages** (= Lohn) will be £140 a week.

fee: what doctors, lawyers, etc. get for their services
I had to pay a large **fee** (= Honorar) for my lawyer's advice.

	(to) be prepared (to do sth.) [prɪˈpeəd]	bereit sein, willens sein (, etwas zu tun)	to be willing (to do sth.)
	education [ˌedjʊˈkeɪʃn, ˌedʒʊˈkeɪʃn]	(Aus-)Bildung; Erziehung	Some people say you get a better ~ at a private school. Everybody in Britain has the right to a good ~.
	scholarship [ˈskɒləʃɪp]	Stipendium	My parents only pay half my school fees as I won a ~.
	academic [ˌækəˈdemɪk]	akademisch, wissenschaftlich	Tim is good at art and sport but he's not very good at more ~ subjects.
	standard [ˈstændəd]	Niveau; Standard	The ~ of your work has improved this year. In Europe there's a higher ~ of living than in Asia.
	entrance exam [ˈentrəns‿ɪgˌzæm]	Aufnahmeprüfung	To get a place at a public school you often have to pass an ~ ~.
	sixth former (BE) [ˈsɪksθ ˌfɔːmə]	*Schüler/in der Oberstufe in Großbritannien*	a pupil in the sixth form of a school
Ex 1	°GCSE [ˌdʒiː siː‿es‿ˈiː] (= General Certificate of Secondary Education) (BE)	*eine Art Mittlere Reife oder Hauptschulabschluß*	
	lower sixth (form)/ upper sixth (form) (BE)	vorletzte/letzte Klasse der Oberstufe	

2 Ex 7	ticket ['tɪkɪt]	Strafmandat, -zettel	something you might get for parking on the pavement
	fine [faɪn]	Bußgeld, Geldstrafe	the money you have to pay if you break the law
9	collocation [ˌkɒlə'keɪʃn]	Kollokation *(Wörter, die oft zusammen vorkommen)*	Words that often go together are a ~, e.g. to brush your hair, heavy rain.
	syllable ['sɪləbl]	Silbe	There are two ~*s* in the word ticket: [tɪk] and [ɪt].

2 T Changing places

p. 26	**wooden** ['wʊdn]	hölzern; Holz-	made of wood
	(to) sign out/in [ˌsaɪn‿'aʊt, ˌsaɪn‿'ɪn]	sich schriftlich abmelden/(wieder)anmelden, sich aus-/eintragen	Visitors must ~ *in* on arrival at the youth hostel.
	(to) **sign** [saɪn]	unterschreiben	Excuse me, sir, you've forgotten to ~ your cheque.
	(to) **put** sth. **down** [ˌpʊt 'daʊn]	etwas aufschreiben, eintragen	to write down *Put* your names ~ on the list if you're going.
	confinement [kən'faɪnmənt]	Eingesperrtsein, Gefangenschaft; Arrest, Haft	Prisoners often suffer from a feeling of ~. Tom spent two days in ~ for being rude to an officer.
p. 27	(to) **be/get used to** sth./ doing sth. [ˌbiː/ˌget 'juːstə]	an etwas gewöhnt sein/sich an etwas gewöhnen	Jan soon *got* ~ ~ driving on the other side of the road in the UK.

used to + infinitive ⟷ (to) be/get used to + -ing form (gerund)

Jim **used to go** to work by car, but now he goes by bike.	**Früher** ist Jim **(immer)** mit dem Auto zur Arbeit **gefahren**, . . .
At first he found it strange, but now he**'s used to going** to work by bike.	. . . , aber jetzt **ist** er **daran gewöhnt**, mit dem Fahrrad zur Arbeit **zu fahren**.
He soon **got used to going** to work by bike.	Er **hatte sich** bald **daran gewöhnt**, mit dem Fahrrad zur Arbeit **zu fahren**.

⚠ I used to do it. — Ich habe es früher immer getan.
I'm used to doing it./I'll get used to doing it. — Ich bin daran gewöhnt/Ich werde mich daran gewöhnen, es zu tun.

⚠ *pronunciation:*
I **used to** ['juːstə] walk. — I'm **used to** ['juːstə] walking.
Did you **use to** ['juːstə] walk? — I'll get **used to** ['juːstə] walking.

I **used** [juːzd] petrol. (Ich habe Benzin benutzt.)
The **use** [juːs] of petrol . . . (Der Gebrauch von Benzin . . .)

(to) **appreciate** [ə'priːʃɪeɪt]	schätzen, würdigen, zu schätzen wissen	Mr Johnson is a wine expert. He really ~*s* good wine. Thanks for helping me to move flat. I really ~ it.
vacuum ['vækjʊəm]	luftleerer Raum, Vakuum	an empty space with no air in it
(to) **live on** sth. [lɪv]	von etwas leben, sich von etwas ernähren	Unemployed people don't have much money to ~ *on*.
amazing [ə'meɪzɪŋ]	erstaunlich	It's ~ that Simon has won a scholarship to Rugby School. He really didn't expect to.
have got to	= (to) have to	I can't come because I ~ *got* ~ study for my exams. ⚠ *Have* you *got to* leave now? = *Do* you *have to* leave now?
(to) **be meant as** [ment]	gedacht sein als, gemeint sein als	I'm sorry, Tina, I didn't want to be rude. It *was* actually ~ ~ a joke.
punishment ['pʌnɪʃmənt]	Strafe, Bestrafung	Sally didn't do her maths homework, so she was given some extra work as a ~. . . .
(to) **punish** ['pʌnɪʃ]	bestrafen	. . . Her teacher ~*ed* her by giving her extra work.

p. 27)	He wouldn't let them go.	Er weigerte sich, sie gehen zu lassen. / Er wollte sie (einfach) nicht gehen lassen.	

"won't/wouldn't" zum Ausdruck einer Weigerung oder Ablehnung

I'm sure Steve knows where it is, but he **won't** tell me.	. . . , aber er **will** es mir **einfach nicht** sagen.
Could you help me, please? The car **won't** start.	. . . Das Auto **will einfach nicht** anspringen.
The children wanted to stay up late, but their parents **wouldn't** let them.	. . . , aber ihre Eltern **wollten** sie **nicht** aufbleiben lassen.
I tried again and again, but it **wouldn't** work.	. . . , aber es **wollte einfach nicht** funktionieren.

⚠ Sandra doesn't want to help Mike. — Sandra will Mike nicht helfen.
Sandra won't help Mike. — Sandra weigert sich, Mike zu helfen. / Sandra will Mike einfach nicht helfen.

Won't und *wouldn't* werden benutzt, wenn die Tatsache der Weigerung oder Ablehnung besonders stark hervorgehoben werden soll.

	vicious circle [ˌvɪʃəs ˈsɜːkl]	Teufelskreis	Unemployment can lead to alcoholism and alcoholism to unemployment. It's a ~ ~.
	(to) bully [ˈbʊlɪ]	schikanieren, drangsalieren	to be unkind to a weaker person
	ball [bɔːl]	Ball, Tanzfest	a formal party with dancing
	minister [ˈmɪnɪstə]	Minister/in	a politician at the head of a government department
	Conservative *(n., adj.)* [kənˈsɜːvətɪv]	Konservative(r); konservativ	Margaret Thatcher is a very famous ~. She was the first woman to become leader of the British ~ party.
	case [keɪs]	Kiste; Koffer; Behälter	word for a container, also short form for suitcase a ~ 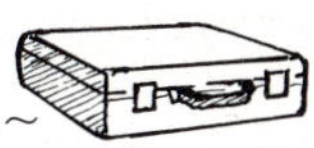  a ~ of oranges
	documentary [ˌdɒkjʊˈmentərɪ]	Dokumentarfilm, Filmbericht	a film, radio or TV programme which presents facts
p. 28	**detail** [ˈdiːteɪl]	Detail, Einzelheit	I enjoyed the film but I can't remember it in any ~.
	context [ˈkɒntekst]	Zusammenhang, Kontext	Do you know what "kind" means? – It has several meanings. I'll have to see the word in ~.

Unit 3: Northern Ireland

3 A Forty shades of green and two religions

p. 29	shade [ʃeɪd]	(Farb-)Ton, Schattierung, Nuance	What colour is your new dress, Anne? – It's a dark ~ of blue.
	°blossom [ˈblɒsəm]	Blüte *(eines Baumes oder Busches)*	
	°(to) wander [ˈwɒndə]	schlendern (durch), umherwandern (in)	
	°sorrow [ˈsɒrəʊ]	Kummer, Sorge; Trauer	
	wasteground [ˈweɪstgraʊnd]	Ödland	land which is empty and infertile
	Lord [lɔːd]	Herr(gott)	another word for God
	°mercy [ˈmɜːsɪ]	Gnade, Erbarmen	
	soul [səʊl]	Seele	Christians believe that a person's ~ never dies.

Unit 3

(p. 29)	**(Roman) Catholic** *(n., adj.)* [ˈkæθlɪk]	Katholik/in; (römisch-) katholisch	*~s* are in the minority in Northern Ireland. Juliet belongs to the *Roman* ~ Church.
	killing [ˈkɪlɪŋ]	Töten, Tötung; Mord	There were more *~s* in Northern Ireland at the weekend: ten people were killed.
	°the IRA [ˌaɪ‿ɑːr‿ˈeɪ] = the Irish Republican Army	die Irisch-Republikanische Armee *(antibritische militante Organisation irischer Nationalisten)*	
	Republican *(n., adj.)* [rɪˈpʌblɪkən]	Republikaner/in; republikanisch; *hier:* antibritische/r irische/r Nationalist/in	
	°Loyalist [ˈlɔɪəlɪst]	Loyalist/in; *hier:* probritische/r irische/r Protestant/in	

3 A One island – two countries

p. 30	province [ˈprɒvɪns]	Provinz	Northern Ireland is sometimes called a ~ because Ulster was originally one of the four *~s* of Ireland.
	from top to bottom [frəm ˌtɒp tə ˈbɒtəm]	von oben bis unten, von oben nach unten	The house was so dirty that I had to clean it *from ~ to ~* today.
	bottom [ˈbɒtəm]	Boden, Fußende, unteres Ende	opposite of top Look at the map at the ~ of the page.
	county [ˈkaʊntɪ]	Grafschaft, Verwaltungsbezirk	England and Wales are divided into 53 *~ies*. Each ~ has its own local government.
	race [reɪs]	Rasse	People of different nationalities and *~s* live in Britain. ⚠ *race* = 1. Rasse; 2. (Wett-)Rennen
	Protestant *(n., adj.)* [ˈprɒtɪstnt]	Protestant/in; protestantisch, evangelisch	In the Republic of Ireland there are many more Catholics than *~s*. Are you ~ or Catholic? ⚠ capital letters: Catholic, Protestant, Jewish, Christian
	currency [ˈkʌrənsɪ]	Währung	the kind of money used in a country
	Secretary of State [BE: ˈsekrətrɪ, AE: ˈsekrəteriː]	BE: Minister/in; Staatssekretär/in; AE: Außenminister/in	
	°punt [pʊnt]	Pfund *(irische Währung)*	the Irish pound (= IR£), Irish currency
	figure [ˈfɪgə]	Zahl, Ziffer	According to the sales *~s* the firm had a record year.

3 A A family from Northern Ireland

	manager [ˈmænɪdʒə]	Geschäftsführer/in, Filialleiter/in, Manager/in; Führungskraft	This meal is inedible. I'd like to speak to the ~. The *~s'* meeting lasted all afternoon.
	fashion [ˈfæʃn]	Mode	Long hair is out of ~ and short hair is in ~ again.
	normality [nɔːˈmælətɪ]	Normalität	After the war it was a long time before the soldiers' lives returned to ~.
	(to) **disturb** [dɪˈstɜːb]	stören	*Don't* ~ Julie. She's trying to work.

3 A Focus on GRAMMAR

p. 31	**bomb** [bɒm]	Bombe	In 1945 the USA dropped two nuclear *~s* on Japan. ⚠ Stummes *b*: bomb [bɒm], climb, comb, thumb
	whom [huːm] (fml.)	den, die das; dem, der, dem *(Relativpronomen)*	Ed, ~ Diana met on a train, is a really nice man. Ed is the man ~ she gave the flowers to.
	whom (fml.)	wen; wem *(Fragepronomen)*	*W~* did you meet yesterday?

(p. 31)

whom

Gewöhnlich wird statt *whom* eher *who* benutzt, besonders im gesprochenen Englisch:
Ed, **who** Diana met on a train, is a really nice man. Ed is the man **(who/that)** she gave the flowers to.
Who did you meet yesterday? **Who** did you go to the concert with?

⚠ Wenn man im sehr formellen Englisch die Präposition **vor** das Relativ- bzw. Fragepronomen setzt, **muß** man *whom* benutzen:
Ed is the man to **whom** she gave the flowers. With **whom** did you go to the concert?

3 A The Troubles

p. 32	(to) **rule** [ruːl]	(be)herrschen, regieren	Although Britain has a queen, the country *is* actually *~d* by the government.
	radical [ˈrædɪkl]	radikal	John is a very ~ Conservative. He thinks many of the party's policies need to be changed. Sally used to be very shy. But she's changed *~ly* since she left home.
	victim [ˈvɪktɪm]	Opfer	Jim was the ~ of an accident. He was hit by a car.
	anti-(British) [ˈæntɪ]	anti(britisch)	You behaved in a very ~-social way at the party.
	pro-(British) [prəʊ]	pro(britisch)	opposite of anti-
	(il)legal [ˈliːgl, ɪˈliːgl]	(un)gesetzlich, (il)legal	In Britain it's *il~* to drink alcohol in pubs if you are under 18.
	(to) **remain** [rɪˈmeɪn]	bleiben; übrigbleiben	When John emigrated to the USA, Sue *~ed* in England. Very little *~ed* of the theatre after the fire.
	°the UDA [ˌjuː diː‿ˈeɪ] = the Ulster Defence Association [əˌsəʊsɪˈeɪʃn]	der Ulster Verteidigungsverband *(protestantische, probritische militante Organisation in Nordirland)*	
	defence [dɪˈfens]	Verteidigung	The British government spends a lot of money on ~, especially on its nuclear weapons. The school football team can defend well. It's got a good ~.
	extremist [ɪkˈstriːmɪst]	Extremist/in; extremistisch	a person with very radical views; very radical
	extreme [ɪkˈstriːm]	extrem, äußerst	The UDA is an organization with very ~ views. The test was *~ly* difficult. I couldn't do any of it.
	behaviour (towards) [bɪˈheɪvjə]	Verhalten, Benehmen (gegenüber)	Tim is behaving very strangely. His ~ towards me has changed in the last few months.

3 A Belfast: Who lives where?

survey (of, on) [ˈsɜːveɪ]	Umfrage, Untersuchung (über)	The recent government ~ on smoking shows that more and more people are giving up cigarettes.
(to) **mix** (with) [mɪks]	(sich) mischen (mit); (miteinander) verkehren	Oil and water *don't ~*. Now that he's got a new job Bob doesn't want to see us any more. He doesn't want to ~ with us.
apart [əˈpɑːt]	getrennt, auseinander	We keep the cat and dog ~ as they always fight. Don't your parents live together any more, Anne? – No, they've been living ~ for about a year now.
attitude (towards) [ˈætɪtjuːd]	Haltung, Einstellung (gegenüber, zu)	He has a very strange ~ towards work.
explanation [ˌekspləˈneɪʃn]	Erklärung	Mrs Smith wanted to know why Simon was late to school. She wanted an ~. ⚠ *spelling:* (to) explain – explanation

Unit 3

3 A Focus on WORDS

p. 33	tension [ˈtenʃn]	Spannung(en)	The world leaders met to try to end international ~.
	misunderstanding [ˌmɪsʌndəˈstændɪŋ]	Mißverständnis	There's been some terrible ~. I didn't expect you till Monday. You must have misunderstood me.
	(in)tolerance (towards) [ˈtɒlərəns, ɪnˈtɒlərəns]	(In-)Toleranz (gegenüber)	Some people show no *t~* towards immigrants; they are intolerant towards them.
	lie [laɪ]	Lüge	I know that's not true, Marie. Don't tell *~s*.
	(to) **lie** (to sb.), *-ing-form:* **lying**	(jn. an-, be)lügen	That's not true, Jim. *Don't ~* to me. ⚠ *(to) lie – lied – lied* = lügen *(to) lie – lay – lain* = liegen
	propaganda [ˌprɒpəˈgændə]	Propaganda	information that is used, especially by a government, to influence the population
	discrimination (against) [ˌdɪskrɪmɪˈneɪʃn]	Diskriminierung (von)	There's ~ in our firm against women. Men get more money than women for the same job. . . .
	(to) **discriminate against** sb. [dɪˈskrɪmɪneɪt]	jn. diskriminieren, benachteiligen	. . . It's terrible that the company *~s against* women.
	prime minister (infml.: PM) [ˌpraɪm ˈmɪnɪstə]	Premierminister/in, Ministerpräsident/in	the head of the Government, e.g. in Britain and Australia
	(to) pass (a law) [pɑːs]	(ein Gesetz) verabschieden	The Government wants to ~ a law to stop people from smoking in public buildings.
	(to) **set** [set] – **set** – **set**, *-ing-form:* **setting**	setzen, stellen, legen	to put She carefully ~ the glasses on the table.
	(to) starve [stɑːv]	aushungern; (ver)hungern	In wartime enemies often ~ their prisoners. They don't give them enough to eat. In Africa millions of babies ~ to death every year.
	rat [ræt]	Ratte	an animal similar to a mouse but bigger 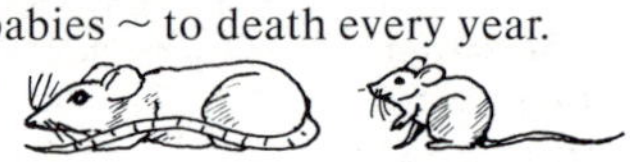 a ~ a mouse
	(im)patience [ˈpeɪʃns, ɪmˈpeɪʃns]	(Un-)Geduld	You have to be very patient to catch fish. I'm afraid I don't have the *p~*.

3 A The Irish Voice

p. 34	(to) affect [əˈfekt]	betreffen, sich auswirken auf; beeinträchtigen	Sue found the film very sad. She *was* really *~ed* by it. *Are* you *~ed* by the new tax laws? – No, I don't pay any tax. Alcohol *~s* your driving.
	yet [jet]	doch, dennoch	Nigel hadn't wanted to go to Sarah's party. *Y~* he was glad he went. He had a great time.
	legendary [ˈledʒəndrɪ]	berühmt; legendär	very famous
	terror [ˈterə]	Terror; Entsetzen	Our dog is a ~ to visitors. He always attacks them. The man was really afraid. There was ~ in his eyes.
	giant [ˈdʒaɪənt]	Riese; riesig	a legendary character of great size; very tall or big
	°causeway [ˈkɔːzweɪ]	Damm	
	(to) **spoil** [spɔɪl] – **spoiled, spoilt** [spɔɪlt] – **spoiled, spoilt**	verderben, verschandeln; verwöhnen, verziehen *(Kinder)*	Tim was mugged on his second day in Paris. It really *~ed* the rest of his holiday. Many of Britain's beaches *have been ~ed* by pollution. The Hills give their son whatever he wants. They really ~ him.
	variety [vəˈraɪətɪ]	Vielfalt; Abwechslung; Sorte	We have the dress in a ~ of colours. Rob hates his job because there's no ~ in it. He does the same thing every day. They sell 30 different *~ies* of ice-cream.

3 Ex 2	**speech** [spi:tʃ]	Rede, Vortrag; Sprache, Sprechweise	a formal talk given to a group of people; the way somebody speaks; spoken language ⚠ *eine Rede halten = (to) give a speech*
	°the troubles, the Troubles ['trʌblz]	die Unruhen *(Bezeichnung für den Konflikt in Nordirland)*	
4	(to) iron ['aɪən]	bügeln	I never ~ my clothes after I've washed them. – No, I can see that.
5	admirable ['ædmərəbl]	bewundernswert	I admire the way you behaved in the situation. Your behaviour was very ~. ⚠ *admirable* ['ædmərəbl] – *(to) admire* [əd'maɪə]
	cliché ['kli:ʃeɪ]	Klischee	an idea or expression that has been used so often that it doesn't say anything new
°7	*fatal (to)* ['feɪtl]	tödlich (für); verhängnisvoll, fatal (für)	
8	(to) **refer to**, -rr- [rɪ'fɜ:]	sich beziehen auf	Answer one of the following questions *~ring to* the text.
	male *(n., adj.)* [meɪl]	männlich; männliche Person; Männchen	We thought our hamster was ~ so we called him Henry. But then . . .
	female *(n., adj.)* ['fi:meɪl]	weiblich; weibliche Person; Weibchen	. . . "he" had six babies and we realized "he" was a ~.

3 T A new life

p. 39	diesel ['di:zl]	Diesel, Dieselöl	Some cars don't use petrol but ~.
	(to) **confuse** [kən'fju:z]	verwirren, durcheinanderbringen	Susan tried to explain the passive to her brother. But she only *~d* him even more.
	(to) **interrupt** [ˌɪntə'rʌpt]	unterbrechen	That man is so rude. He always *~s* other people when they're talking.
	Christian name ['krɪstʃən neɪm]	Vor-, Rufname	a person's first name, especially in Christian countries
p. 40	raid (on) [reɪd]	Razzia (in); Überfall (auf)	Did you hear about the ~ on the new hotel? The police were looking for stolen clothes. £50,000 was stolen during a ~ on the bank.
	mystery ['mɪstrɪ]	Geheimnis, Rätsel	something which can't be explained
	(to) identify (with) [aɪ'dentɪfaɪ]	(sich) identifizieren (mit)	to recognize; to put oneself in somebody else's situation and understand how they feel
	court [kɔ:t]	Gericht(shof), Gerichtssaal	a place where the law decides if a person has committed a crime ⚠ *in court* = vor Gericht – *at court* = am (königlichen) Hof, bei Hofe
	(to) take sb. to court	jn. verklagen, vor Gericht bringen	Mr Smith *was taken* ~ ~ last week for stealing clothes from a department store.
	°(to) grass on sb. [grɑ:s] (BE, slang)	jn. verpfeifen	a slang word for "(to) inform (the police)"
	°grass (BE, slang)	Spitzel, Informant/in	
	informer [ɪn'fɔ:mə]	Informant/in, Spitzel	somebody who informs the police, for example, about someone, often in exchange for money
	murderer ['mɜ:dərə]	Mörder/in	a person who kills somebody
	murder ['mɜ:də]	Mord	a killing ⚠ *murderer* = Mörder/in – *murder* = Mord
	(to) break away (from) [ˌbreɪk‿ə'weɪ]	sich losreißen (von)	The thief *broke* ~ from the police officer and ran into the crowd.
	(to) dial, BE: -ll- ['daɪəl]	wählen *(beim Telefon)*	If you give me the phone number, I*'ll* ~ it for you.
	line [laɪn]	(Telefon-)Leitung	Sue, phone for you! Your mother is on the ~.

p. 41	table ['teɪbl]	Tabelle	numbers and facts, arranged across and down the page

Same form – different word class

(to) **bomb**	bombardieren	(to) **order**	befehlen; beauftragen
bomb	Bombe	**order**	Befehl
(to) **check**	kontrollieren, (über)prüfen	(to) **raid**	eine Razzia durchführen (in, bei), überfallen
check	Kontrolle, Überprüfung	**raid**	Razzia; Überfall
(to) **defeat**	besiegen, schlagen	(to) **return**	zurückkommen, -gehen
defeat (of; by)	Sieg (über); Niederlage (durch)	**return**	Rückkehr, Wiederkehr
(to) **design**	entwerfen, konstruieren	(to) **rule**	(be)herrschen, regieren
design	Design; Entwurf, Skizze	**rule**	Regel, Vorschrift
(to) **exchange**	aus-, umtauschen, *(Geld)* wechseln	(to) **rush**	eilen, hetzen
exchange	Austausch	**rush**	Eile, Hetze
(to) **kick**	treten	(to) **shock**	schockieren
kick	Tritt	**shock**	Schreck, Schock
(to) **lie** (to sb.)	(jn. an-, be)lügen	(to) **storm** (into)	(hinein)stürmen
lie	Lüge	**storm**	Sturm, Gewitter
(to) **murder**	(er)morden	(to) **taste**	schmecken; kosten
murder	Mord	**taste**	Geschmack
past *(n.)*	Vergangenheit	(to) **welcome**	willkommen heißen
past *(adj.)*	vergangen	**welcome** (to Ireland)	willkommen (in Irland)

Unit 4: Growing up in Britain

p. 42	°wheels [wi:lz] (slang)	fahrbarer Untersatz	
	(to) be/go broke [brəʊk] (infml.)	pleite sein/machen, gehen	an informal way of saying that you have no money Mike lost his job because the firm *went* ~.

Das *past tense* in Wunschsätzen

I'm 15 now. **It's time I was allowed** to do what I want. ... Es wird Zeit, daß ich tun darf, was ich will.
It's (high) **time** we **left**. — Es ist/wird (höchste) Zeit, daß wir gehen.
I wish I knew how to answer this question. — Ich wünschte, ich wüßte ...

In Wunschsätzen mit *it's (high) time* und *I wish* steht das folgende Verb im *past tense*. Das *past* bezieht sich in diesen Fällen auf die Gegenwart oder Zukunft, nicht auf die Vergangenheit.

Vergleiche die Verwendung des *past tense* in *if*-Sätzen des Typs II und nach *as if*:
If I won £50,000, I could buy a house. — Wenn ich 50 000 Pfund gewinnen würde, ...
He talks **as if** he **was/were** the boss (, but he isn't). — Er redet, als ob er der Chef wäre ...

limit ['lɪmɪt]	(oberste) Grenze, Beschränkung	Okay, I'll give you £3,000 for the car, but that's my ~. I can't afford to pay any more. In Britain there's a speed ~ of 70 mph on motorways.
beer [bɪə]	Bier	a popular alcoholic drink
(to) **vote for** [vəʊt]	(ab)stimmen für, wählen	Which political party are you going to ~ *for* ...
election [ɪ'lekʃn]	*(politische)* Wahl	... in the next ~?
full-time [ˌfʊl'taɪm, 'fʊltaɪm]	ganztags; Vollzeit-, Ganztags-	Do you work ~-~ [ˌ-'-]? – No, I've got a part-time job. Ann has a ~-~ ['--] job. She works 38 hours a week.

4 A Teenage life

p. 43	teenage ['ti:neɪdʒ]	Teenager-; im Teenageralter	Not getting along with one's parents is a ~ problem. Mrs White has got two ~ daughters, aged 13 and 15.
	(to) do a paper round ['peɪpə raʊnd] (BE)	Zeitungen austragen	Jim *does* ~ *paper* ~ three mornings a week. He is paid to take papers to people's homes.
	(to) **claim** [kleɪm]	behaupten; fordern, Anspruch erheben auf	Bob ~*s* he did the work, but I don't believe him. *Does* anyone ~ this hat? It was left here yesterday.
	claim (for, on)	Behauptung; Anspruch (auf), Forderung (nach)	Do you believe Joe's ~ that he can eat fifty eggs? Jill made a ~ for some more money at work. You're my boyfriend, but you don't have any ~*s* on me.
	(to) **admit, -tt-** [əd'mɪt]	zugeben; zulassen, (hin)einlassen	Sue ~*ted* having stolen Jim's money. The college ~*s* 3,000 new students each year. Joe *wasn't* ~*ted* into the disco because he was wearing jeans.
	sex [seks]	Geschlecht; Sex	What ~ is your cat? – It's a "he". There's more danger of getting Aids if you have ~ with lots of different partners.
	(to) **include** [ɪn'klu:d]	(mit) einschließen, enthalten, beinhalten	Popular part-time jobs among teenagers ~ babysitting, doing a paper round and working in a shop. There'll be six of us, ~*ing* myself.
	politics ['pɒlɪtɪks]	Politik	Peter isn't interested in ~ at all. He's not even going to vote in the next election. ⚠ *politics* = (allgemeine) Politik, „Staatskunst" *policy* = Politik (als Taktik, Verfahren usw.); (Geschäfts-)Politik
	(to) **attend** [ə'tend]	besuchen, teilnehmen an *(Kurs, Schule usw.)*	to go to Why *didn't* you ~ school yesterday? – I was ill. *Did* you ~ the computer course last week? ⚠ *jn. besuchen* = (to) visit sb.
	concern [kən'sɜ:n]	Angelegenheit, Belang, Sache	What I do at the weekend is no ~ of yours, Mike.
	(to) **be concerned about** [kən'sɜ:nd]	sich Sorgen machen um, sich Gedanken machen über	to be worried about I*'m* really ~ *about* pollution.
	(to) **concern** [kən'sɜ:n]	betreffen, angehen	to affect Don't be so curious, Mike. It *doesn't* ~ you.
	(to) **treat** [tri:t]	behandeln	Tim ~*s* Jill badly. He's often very unkind to her. Dr Brown *is* ~*ing* Ann's broken finger.
	questionnaire [ˌkwestʃə'neə]	Fragebogen	a list of questions which are answered by a number of people so that information can be collected on a certain subject

4 A Free time

p. 44	voluntary ['vɒləntrɪ]	freiwillige(r, s)	Sue does ~ work; she visits old people twice a week.
	(to) fancy ['fænsɪ] (BE, infml.)	gern haben	Simon must really ~ you. He always wants to sit next to you.
	(to) be dying to do sth.; (to) be dying for sth. ['daɪɪŋ] (infml.)	etwas unbedingt tun wollen; etwas unbedingt haben wollen/brauchen	Pat has told me all about you, so I *was* ~ *to* meet you. I'm so thirsty. I*'m* ~ *for* a drink.
	MP [ˌem'pi:] = Member of Parliament (BE)	Mitglied des Unterhauses	a politician who has been voted by the people to be in parliament
	(to) **threaten** ['θretn]	(be)drohen	Mrs Simmons ~*ed* to stop Brian's pocket-money if he didn't work harder at school.
	imaginary [ɪ'mædʒɪnərɪ]	erfunden; eingebildet	something that is made up or exists only in the imagination

4 A Focus on WORDS

p. 45

(to) **be linked** (by/with) [lɪŋkt]	verbunden, verknüpft sein (durch/mit)	The two cities *will be* ~ with London by the new motorway.
link [lɪŋk]	Verbindung, Beziehung, Bindeglied	Police believe that there may be a ~ between the recent murders on the London Underground.
party [ˈpɑːtɪ]	Partei	Margaret Thatcher was the first woman in Britain to become the leader of a political ~. ⚠ *party* = 1. Partei; 2. Party, Fest, Fete
colleague [ˈkɒliːg]	Kollege/Kollegin	somebody who works in your office or firm ⚠ *colleague* [ˈkɒliːg] = Kollege/Kollegin – *college* [ˈkɒlɪdʒ] = Hochschule
(to) **communicate** (with) [kəˈmjuːnɪkeɪt]	kommunizieren (mit), sich verständigen (mit)	I was able to ~ with Uwe because we both spoke English.
(to) **depend on** [dɪˈpend]	abhängig sein von, abhängen von; sich verlassen auf	Can you come to the party? – I'm not sure. It *~s on* how much work I've got. You can ~ *on* Jill. She'll certainly help you.
punctual [ˈpʌŋktʃʊəl]	pünktlich	Roger is never ~. He usually arrives at least 15 minutes late.
easygoing [ˌiːzɪˈgəʊɪŋ, ˈiːzɪgəʊɪŋ]	gelassen, unbeschwert	Mike is a very ~ [ˈ----] man. Nothing seems to worry or annoy him. – I wish I was so ~ [ˌ--ˈ--].
outgoing [ˌaʊtˈgəʊɪŋ, ˈaʊtgəʊɪŋ]	gesellig, kontaktfreudig	Sally is a very ~ [ˈ---] girl. She doesn't mind talking to strangers at all. – I wish I was so ~ [ˌ-ˈ--].
arrogant [ˈærəgənt]	arrogant, überheblich	John thinks he knows everything. He's so ~.
Muslim *(n., adj.)* [ˈmʊzlɪm, ˈmʌzlɪm]	Moslem; moslemisch	Many *~s* live in Bradford. There's a large ~ community there.
(un)just [dʒʌst; ˌʌnˈdʒʌst, ˈʌndʒʌst]	(un)gerecht	(un)fair It was very *un~* [ˌ-ˈ-] of Ms Bright to send me out of the classroom for talking and not you. Mrs Hill is a very *un~* [ˈ--] boss. She doesn't treat her workers fairly.
understanding [ˌʌndəˈstændɪŋ]	verständnisvoll	Mrs White is a very ~ teacher. She's always prepared to listen to you if you have any problems.
aggressive (towards) [əˈgresɪv]	aggressiv (gegenüber)	Our dog is very ~. He always attacks strangers.
hostile (to) [ˈhɒstaɪl]	feindselig, feindlich (gegenüber)	Andrew is very ~ to me because I went out with the girl he fancies. He won't talk to me any more.
(to) beat sb. up [ˌbiːt‿ˈʌp]	jn. zusammenschlagen	Pete, what's happened to your face? – I *was ~en up* by a gang on the way home.
(to) **cheat** (sb. of sth.) [tʃiːt]	mogeln; (jn. um etwas) betrügen	Kai got a "6" in his maths test because he*'d ~ed.* Di lost her job for *~ing* the customers of money.
(to) discourage sb. (from doing sth.) [dɪˈskʌrɪdʒ]	jn. entmutigen; jn (davon) abhalten/abbringen (, etwas zu tun)	opposite of "encourage" Ann *~d* Ed by telling him the exam would be difficult. My parents tried to ~ me from leaving school at 16.
(to) offend [əˈfend]	kränken, beleidigen	to hurt somebody's feelings

Telling a story – useful adverbials of time and frequency[1]

One day, long ago, ... In those days	Eines Tages, vor langer Zeit, ... Damals . . . .
Now and again . . . , and from time to time	Hin und wieder . . . , und von Zeit zu Zeit . . . .
But over the years . . . , and in the past few years . . . . From then on	Aber im Laufe der Jahre . . . , und in den vergangenen Jahren . . . . Von da an . . . .
Nowadays [ˈnaʊədeɪz]/These days . . . , and from now on . . . . Sooner or later	Heutzutage . . . , und von nun an . . . . Früher oder später . . . .

[1] frequency [ˈfriːkwənsɪ] Häufigkeit

4 A Britain: a multi-cultural society

p. 46	multi- [ˈmʌltɪ]	mehr-, multi-	Cathy is really ~-talented. She's not only very intelligent but she's also very good at sport.
	cultural [ˈkʌltʃərəl]	kulturell, Kultur-	The ~ life in our town is terrible. There's no theatre and only one cinema.
	society [səˈsaɪətɪ]	Gesellschaft; Verein, Arbeitsgemeinschaft	British ~ consists of people of many different nationalities, religions and races. ⚠ No article: *British society = die britische Gesellschaft* Have you joined the school drama ~, Paul?
	equally [ˈiːkwəlɪ]	gleichmäßig; gleichermaßen	Liz and Helen are ~ good at German. They both get the same marks.
	equal [ˈiːkwəl]	gleich	There's an ~ number of boys and girls in our class: 15 boys and 15 girls.
	equality [ɪˈkwɒlətɪ]	Gleichheit	My boss doesn't believe in ~ of the sexes. I get paid less than a man for the same job.
	(to) **distribute** (sth. to sb.) [dɪˈstrɪbjuːt]	verteilen; (etwas) austeilen (an jn.)	Wealth *isn't* equally *~d* throughout the world. A free newspaper *is ~d* to all the houses in our area every Friday.
	act, Act [ækt]	Verordnung, Gesetz	In 1988 the British Parliament passed an *act* which changed pub opening times.

4 A Focus on GRAMMAR

p. 46	the Commonwealth (of Nations) [ˈkɒmənwelθ]	*Staatengemeinschaft aus ehemals zum britischen Weltreich gehörenden Ländern*	an organization which consists of the UK and 48 states which were once British colonies
	(to) **insist** (on) [ɪnˈsɪst]	bestehen (auf), verlangen	Jo *~ed* on paying for the meal, though it was his birthday.
	(to) **rent** [rent]	mieten, leihen	In Britain it's more common to buy than to ~ a house. ⚠ In BE you *rent* things for a long period of time, and you *hire* things for a short period of time.
p. 48	tailor [ˈteɪlə]	Schneider/in	a person whose job it is to make clothes, especially for men
	quality [ˈkwɒlətɪ]	Qualität; Qualitäts-	The last shoes I bought there were of such bad ~ that I threw them away after six months. We only sell the best; we only sell ~ products.
Ex 1	**author** [ˈɔːθə]	Autor/in	the writer of a book or a play, for example
	(to) **arrange** [əˈreɪndʒ]	arrangieren, vereinbaren	Bob can't come to the party because he*'s* already *~d* to go to the cinema with Ann.
	marriage (to) [ˈmærɪdʒ]	Ehe (mit); Heirat	Sue's ~ to Ed didn't last very long. They got divorced after 18 months. Where did their ~ (= wedding) take place? – In Kingswood Church.
10	structure [ˈstrʌktʃə]	Struktur, Konstruktion	Today we're going to learn a new ~: "to make sb. do sth."

4 T An eye for an eye

p. 53	°an eye for an eye	Auge um Auge	
	°Paki [ˈpækɪ] (BE, slang)	*(Schimpfwort für)* Pakistaner/in	

Unit 4

(p. 53)	°yob [jɒb] (BE, slang)	Rowdy	
	can [kæn]	Dose, Büchse	a metal container in which food and drinks are sold
	(to) **ruin** [ˈru:ɪn]	zerstören, ruinieren	to destroy, to spoil
	fear (of) [fɪə]	Furcht, Angst (vor)	Because of his ~ of flying Ed refuses to go by plane. ⚠ *Angst haben vor = (to) be afraid of, (to) be frightened of*
	(town/city) council [ˌtaʊn ˈkaʊnsl]	Stadtrat *(Gremium)*	a group of people who run the local government of a town
	(to) send sb. to sleep [ˌsend tə ˈsli:p]	jn. einschläfern, zum Schlafen bringen	The film was so boring that it *sent* everybody ~ ~.
	(to) **go on**	im Gange sein, vorgehen	to happen; to take place
	We can't possibly do it.	Wir können es beim besten Willen nicht/unmöglich tun.	*I ~ ~ go shopping* this evening. I've got to work until 8 o'clock.
p. 54	bandage [ˈbændɪdʒ]	Verband, Binde	something that you tie around a part of the body that has been hurt 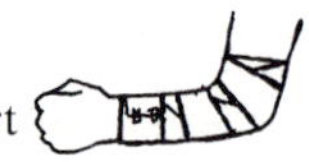
	frustrated [frʌˈstreɪtɪd]	frustriert, enttäuscht	Tom has been trying to do his maths for an hour now. But he still can't do it. He's really ~.
	(to) **arrest** [əˈrest]	verhaften, festnehmen	The police ~*ed* somebody for mugging tourists.
	proof [pru:f]	Beweis(e), Nachweis(e)	Do you have any ~ (= evidence) that you were at home on the night of the murder?
	preparation [ˌprepəˈreɪʃn]	Vorbereitung, Zubereitung	Can I help you with the ~*s* for the party, Sam? ⚠ *preparation* [ˌprepəˈreɪʃn] – *(to) prepare* [prɪˈpeə]
	cloth [klɒθ]	Stoff; Tuch, Lappen	a piece of material made of cotton, for example; something used to clean furniture, windows, etc. ⚠ *cloth, pl. cloths* [klɒθs] – *clothes (pl.)* [kləʊðz, kləʊz] = Kleidung
	match [mætʃ]	Streichholz	a ~ 
	stereo [ˈsterɪəʊ]	Stereoanlage	
	flame [fleɪm]	Flamme	The Turners came home to find their house in ~*s*. They still don't know the cause of the fire.
p. 55	(to) **note** sth. **down** [nəʊt]	(sich) etwas notieren, aufschreiben	to write something down
	(to) retell [ˌri:ˈtel]	nacherzählen	to tell a story again in a different way
	effect (on) [ɪˈfekt]	Wirkung, Auswirkung (auf)	Jenny hasn't been the same since her father's death. It has had a great ~ on her. ⚠ *the effect* [ɪˈfekt] – *(to) affect* [əˈfekt] = betreffen, sich auswirken auf
	(un)bearable [ˈbeərəbl]	(un)erträglich	The weather was *un*~ today. It was so hot.
	reaction (to) [ri:ˈækʃn]	Reaktion (auf)	What was Mike's ~ to the news? – He was very upset. I didn't expect him to react like that.
	troubled [ˈtrʌbld]	beunruhigt, bekümmert	worried, concerned
	(to) search (for) [sɜ:tʃ]	(durch)suchen (nach), (durch)forschen (nach)	I*'ve ~ed* everywhere for my bag, but I can't find it. The police ~*ed* the flat for bombs.
	puzzled [ˈpʌzld]	verwirrt	confused
	soft [sɒft]	weich; leise	Do you prefer sleeping in a ~ or a hard bed? You must speak louder. You've got such a ~ voice.
	°velvet [ˈvelvɪt]	Samt	
	(to) **shine** [ʃaɪn] – **shone** [ʃɒn] – **shone**	glänzen	The silver plate was so clean that it *shone*.
	hatred (of, for) [ˈheɪtrɪd]	Haß (auf)	I have a ~ of violence. Mr Brown feels a lot of ~ for the person who murdered his son.
	°(to) shame [ʃeɪm]	beschämen	

55) mankind [ˌmænˈkaɪnd]	(die) Menschheit	the human race ⚠ No article: A nuclear war would probably destroy *mankind.* = . . . würde *die Menschheit* wahrscheinlich vernichten. ⚠ A lot of people prefer not to use the word *mankind* to refer to men and women. Instead they speak of *the human race, human beings* or *people.*
°brutal [ˈbruːtl]	brutal, gewalttätig	
deed [diːd] (fml.)	Tat	Jim is very kind. He often does good ~*s* for others.
°malign [məˈlaɪn]	böswillig, boshaft	
°rape [reɪp]	Vergewaltigung	
°(to) entwine [ɪnˈtwaɪn]	(sich) ineinanderschlingen, (sich) verflechten	
°brotherhood [ˈbrʌðəhʊd]	Brüderlichkeit	
(to) **combine** (with) [kəmˈbaɪn]	(sich) verbinden (mit), kombinieren (mit)	Mrs Stewart ~*d* a business trip to Rome with a few days' holiday. ⚠ *(to) combine* [kəmˈbaɪn] – *combination* [ˌkɒmbɪˈneɪʃn]

Unit 5: Australia – the continent "down under"

5 A Aborigine claims Britain

Die Deutschen begriffen auch Besitz von fremden Ländern

56 °Aborigine [ˌæbəˈrɪdʒəniː]	austral. Ureinwohner/in	
°Aboriginal people [ˌæbəˈrɪdʒənl ˈpiːpl]	austral. Ureinwohner/innen	= Aborigines
noble [ˈnəʊbl]	adlig, edel, erhaben	A queen is of ~ birth.
ancient [ˈeɪnʃnt]	alt, historisch, antik	from a time long ago; very old
(to) **take possession of** [pəˈzeʃn]	Besitz ergreifen von, in Besitz nehmen	The English *took* ~ *of* Australia in 1788.
(to) possess [pəˈzes]	besitzen	to own
in doing sth.	indem; beim	*In learning* other languages, you usually learn a lot about your own language. *In crossing* the road, Jim fell over.
(to) do sb. harm [hɑːm]	jm. Schaden zufügen; jm. eine Verletzung zufügen	It *won't do* you any ~ to spend an evening at home. Be careful! You*'ll do* someone some ~ with that ball.
native *(n., adj.)* [ˈneɪtɪv]	Eingeborene(r), Einheimische(r); einheimisch, gebürtig, Heimat*(land)*, Mutter*(sprache)*	Someone who was born in New York is a ~ of that city. He/She is a ~ New Yorker. Although Louise often speaks French at home, English is her ~ language. She's an English ~ speaker.
°(to) re-enact [ˌriːɪˈnækt]	nachspielen, nachstellen, neu inszenieren	
colonist [ˈkɒlənɪst]	Kolonist/in, Siedler/in	a person who settles somewhere and founds a colony
(to) **march** [mɑːtʃ]	marschieren	The Aborigines ~*ed* through the streets to protest against discrimination.
°spear [spɪə]	Speer	
°boomerang [ˈbuːməræŋ]	Bumerang	a ~ 
invasion (of) [ɪnˈveɪʒn]	Einmarsch (in), Einfall (in), Invasion	It's more than 50 years since the ~ of Poland by Germany. Germany invaded Poland in 1939.
opera [ˈɒprə]	Oper; Opern-	An ~ is a play where the words are sung. You can hear *operas* in an ~ house.

Sie marschierten in ihre Nachbarschaft ein

Unit 5

5 A Australia: facts and figures

p. 57	head of state [ˌhed‿əv ˈsteɪt]	Staatsoberhaupt	Queen Elizabeth II is the ~ *of* ~ of the UK and Australia, among other countries.
	symbol (of, for) [ˈsɪmbl]	Symbol, Zeichen (für)	Red is a ~ of danger. On this map a star is the ~ for a tourist attraction.
	°emu [ˈiːmjuː]	Emu	

5 A Life "down under"

barbecue [ˈbɑːbɪkjuː]	Grill; Grillparty	something that you put coal in and use to cook food with outside; an outdoor party where food is cooked over a fire

5 A Australia's native people

p. 58	interior [ɪnˈtɪərɪə]	(das) Innere; Innen-	the area inside a house or a car, for example; the middle of a country or a continent
	°the outback *(sing.)* [ˈaʊtbæk]	der Busch, das Hinterland (Australiens)	
	neither . . . nor [ˈnaɪðə nɔː, ˈniːðə nɔː]	weder . . . noch	Jim doesn't smoke or drink. He ~ smokes ~ drinks.
	holy [ˈhəʊlɪ]	heilig, geweiht	The Bible [ˈbaɪbl] is sometimes called the *H*~ Book.
	mining [ˈmaɪnɪŋ]	Bergbau; Bergbau-, Bergwerks-	The ~ industry lost millions of dollars last year because of the miners' strike.
	supplier [səˈplaɪə]	Lieferant/in	a person or business that supplies products
	indeed [ɪnˈdiːd]	in der Tat, tatsächlich	Australia is ~ the world's largest island. Did he cry? – *I*~ he did.
	export [ˈekspɔːt]	Ausfuhr, Export	noun from the verb "to export"
	import [ˈɪmpɔːt]	Einfuhr, Import	opposite of export ⚠ *the export* [ˈekspɔːt] – *(to) export* [ɪkˈspɔːt] *the import* [ˈɪmpɔːt] – *(to) import* [ɪmˈpɔːt]
	(to) **happen to** do [ˈhæpən]	zufällig(erweise) tun	*Do* you ~ *to* know what's on TV tonight? I didn't plan to meet Mike last night, we just ~*ed to* be at the same party.

Verbal[1] expressions in English – adverbs in German (1)

You already know many verbal expressions like the following; they are translated as adverbs in German:

Jean **likes** ski**ing**, and she's very **fond of** swimm**ing**, too.	Jean läuft **gern** Ski, und sie schwimmt auch sehr **gern**.
Roger **prefers** cycl**ing** to walking.	Roger fährt **lieber** Rad . . . .
Sheila **hates** walk**ing**.	Sheila geht **ungern/überhaupt nicht gern** zu Fuß.
Keep (on) runn**ing**!	Lauf **weiter**!
Liz **used to** visit her aunt every Sunday.	Liz hat **früher** jeden Sonntag ihre Tante besucht.
I'm afraid I can't help you.	Ich kann Ihnen **leider** nicht helfen.
I **hope to** see you before you go on holiday.	**Hoffentlich** sehe ich Sie noch, . . .
Where's Sandra? – At home, I **suppose**. She **seems to** have left early.	. . . **Vermutlich** zu Hause. Sie ist **anscheinend** schon früh gegangen.

[1] verbal [ˈvɜːbl] = verbal, mit einem Verb gebildet

p. 58)

Verbal expressions in English – adverbs in German (2)

Here are some more examples of verbal expressions which are translated as adverbs:

Do you **happen to** know the way to Tinley?	Wissen Sie **zufällig** den Weg nach Tinley?
Sarah **is likely to** win.	Sarah wird **wahrscheinlich** gewinnen.
Simon **is unlikely to** come.	Simon wird **wahrscheinlich nicht** kommen.
You're **sure to** like the story, Pete.	Du wirst die Geschichte **bestimmt/sicher(lich)** mögen, Pete.
Gary **is known to** be afraid of spiders.	Gary hat **bekanntlich** Angst vor Spinnen.

site [saɪt]	Stätte, Stelle	place where an event has taken/will take place A camp ~ is a place where you can camp.

5 A Focus on WORDS

Es sprach eine Mischung aus Englisch u. Deutsch

p. 59 **mixture** [ˈmɪkstʃə]	Mischung	If you mix yellow and blue paint, you get a green ~.
for good [fə ˈgʊd]	für immer, endgültig	Tom left Sydney ~ ~ in 1964. He never went back. *Sie verloren ihr Haus für immer*
au pair [ˌəʊ ˈpeə]	Au-Pair(-Mädchen, -Junge)	
(to) transfer (to), -rr- [trænsˈfɜː]	versetzen, verlegen (nach, in)	Jill *has been ~red* to Sydney by her firm.
EC [ˌiː ˈsiː] = European Community	Europäische Gemeinschaft	Britain joined the ~ ~ in 1973. ⚠ In Britain, the EC is still often referred to as the "Common Market" or the "EEC" (= European Economic Community).
asylum [əˈsaɪləm]	Asyl	Anyone who is being persecuted in their own country may ask for ~ in another country.
expectation [ˌekspekˈteɪʃn]	Erwartung	what you expect something to be like
(to) **renew** [rɪˈnjuː]	erneuern; verlängern	I must ~ the tyres on my car. They're really old. Birgit *has ~ed* her visa so she can stay in Australia for another six months.
permit [ˈpɜːmɪt]	Genehmigungs(schein), Erlaubnis	You usually need a work ~ to be allowed to work in a foreign country.
(to) give (sb.) notice [ˌgɪv ˈnəʊtɪs]	(jm.) kündigen; (bei jm.) kündigen	You'll have to ~ four weeks' ~ when you want to move out of your flat. Bob *has been given* ~ by his boss. He's leaving next month.
landlord/landlady [ˈlændlɔːd, ˈlændleɪdɪ]	Hauswirt/in, Hauseigentümer/in; Gastwirt/in	the person who owns the room or flat you live in; a person who owns or is the boss of a pub or hotel

5 A Life on a sheep station

p. 60 **wool** [wʊl]	Wolle	the hair of a sheep used to make pullovers etc.
(to) **run** (a school, a farm etc.)	(eine Schule, Farm usw.) leiten, betreiben	Ms Taylor *~s* the youth club. A headmistress *~s* a school.
garage [ˈgærɑːdʒ]	Tankstelle mit Reparaturwerkstatt	a place where petrol and diesel are sold and/or vehicles are repaired
headset [ˈhedset]	Kopfhörer	something that you put on your ears to listen to music 
microphone [ˈmaɪkrəfəʊn]	Mikrophon	something pop stars sing into so they can be heard at the back of a concert hall
via [ˈvaɪə]	über, per, via	You can travel to Britain from Germany ~ Ostend.
satellite [ˈsætəlaɪt]	Satellit	
°koala (bear) [kəʊˈɑːlə]	Koala(bär)	

Unit 5

5 A Focus on GRAMMAR

p. 61	(to) **come to an end**	zu Ende gehen, ein Ende nehmen	to finish
	arrangement [əˈreɪndʒmənt]	Vereinbarung, Abmachung	What are your ~*s* for the weekend? Have you made any plans?
	Need we . . . ?	Müssen wir . . . ?	= Do we need to . . . ?/Do we have to . . . ?

"Need" als Voll- und als Hilfsverb

Vollverb	Hilfsverb
You **don't need to go** now.	You **needn't go** now.
Do we **need to go** now?	**Need** we **go** now?
⚠ *do*-Umschreibung; Infinitiv-Anschluß **mit** *to*	⚠ **keine** *do*-Umschreibung; Infinitiv-Anschluß **ohne** *to*

Need wird als Hilfs- und als Vollverb benutzt. Als Hilfsverb wird es nur im Präsens verwendet und steht hauptsächlich in verneinten Aussagesätzen, seltener auch in Fragesätzen. Als Vollverb steht es auch in bejahten Aussagesätzen: I think you **need to leave** by 6.30.

	at the latest [ət ðə ˈleɪtɪst]	spätestens	Our flight is at 7.30. We'll have to be at the airport by 6.30 ~ *the* ~.
5 Ex 4	**difficulty** [ˈdɪfɪkəltɪ]	Schwierigkeit	Phillip finds English very difficult. He has a lot of ~*ies* with the grammar. ⚠ Ich *hatte Schwierigkeiten*, ihn *zu verstehen*. = I *had difficulty (in) understanding* him.
6	(to) **emphasize** [ˈemfəsaɪz]	betonen, hervorheben	Their teacher ~*d* the importance of good exam results. Read the sentence again, but *don't* ~ the first word.
	discovery [dɪˈskʌvərɪ]	Entdeckung	Aborigines speak of Captain Cook's invasion of Australia. Europeans talk of his ~.
	(to) **contrast** sth. (with) [kənˈtrɑːst]	etwas kontrastieren (mit), etwas gegenüberstellen	*C*~ the Queen's behaviour at the beginning of the play with her behaviour at the end. ⚠ *(to) contrast* [kənˈtrɑːst] – *the contrast* [ˈkɒntrɑːst] = der Gegensatz, Kontrast
7	(to) **have** sth. **in mind** [maɪnd]	etwas im Sinn haben, an etwas denken	*Do* you *have* anything ~ ~ for John's birthday? – Yes, I thought I'd buy him a record.
	particular [pəˈtɪkjʊlə]	bestimmte(r, s), spezielle(r, s)	certain, special Do you want to get anything ~ at the shops?

5 T Bush fire

p. 66	**but** [bʌt, bət]	*(nichts, nirgends)* als, außer	I wouldn't want to live anywhere ~ here. I really like Germany.
	gentle [ˈdʒentl]	zart; sanft	opposite of rough or violent
	(to) **dig** [dɪg] – **dug** [dʌg] – **dug**	graben	to make a hole in the ground with a tool or one's hands
	(to) **boil** [bɔɪl]	(ab)kochen, sieden	I*'ll* ~ some water for a cup of tea. ⚠ *(to) boil* = *(Wasser, Eier, Reis)* kochen *(to) cook* = *(Essen)* kochen, zubereiten *(to) make tea/coffee* = Tee/Kaffee kochen
	°billy(-can) [ˈbɪlɪkæn] (BE, Aust. E)	(Camping-)Kochgeschirr	

p. 66)	**though** *(adv.)* [ðəʊ]	jedoch, (aber) doch	Rod promised to phone me yesterday. He didn't, ~. (= But he didn't.) ⚠ The adverb "though" (= jedoch, doch) can't be used at the beginning of a sentence, and there is always a comma before it.

Konjunktionen und satzverknüpfende Adverbien der Einräumung/des Gegensatzes

We decided to go for a walk **although/even though** it was raining.	. . . , **obwohl** es regnete.
John said he'd help me with the dishes. He didn't, **though**.	. . . **Aber** dann hat er es **doch** nicht getan.
We had thought about going to the cinema. **Yet** we decided to stay at home. *or:* But we decided to stay at home **after all**.	. . . **Aber** wir haben dann **doch** beschlossen, zu Hause zu bleiben.
I went to bed early last night. **However**, I still feel tired. *or:* I still feel tired, **however**.	. . . **Aber** ich bin **doch** noch müde./ **Trotzdem** bin ich noch müde.
The water didn't look very clean, but we went swimming **anyway**.	. . . , aber wir gingen **trotzdem** schwimmen.
It was raining, but I didn't want to go out **anyway**.	. . . , aber ich wollte **sowieso** nicht rausgehen.

	stove [stəʊv]	(Koch-)Herd; Ofen	another word for cooker; something in which you burn wood, coal or gas in order to keep a room warm
	grown-up [ˈgrəʊnʌp]	Erwachsene(r)	another word for an adult, usually used by or when talking to children
	bun [bʌn]	süßes Brötchen	a kind of round sweet roll
	°The magic of the day had gone sour on them.	Der Zauber des Tages war verflogen/war ihnen verdorben.	
	pie [paɪ]	(Fleisch-)Pastete; Obstkuchen	The baker sells both fruit and meat ~*s*.
p. 67	**tiny** [ˈtaɪnɪ]	winzig	very small
	heater [ˈhi:tə]	(Heiz-)Ofen; *hier:* (Camping-)Kocher	It's very cold in here. Can we switch the electric ~ on?
	heat [hi:t]	Hitze	I really suffer from the ~. I could never live in a hot climate.
	°methylated spirits (Aust. E infml.: metho) [ˌmeθɪleɪtɪd ˈspɪrɪts; ˈmeθəʊ]	Brennspiritus	
	sleeping bag [ˈsli:pɪŋ bæg]	Schlafsack	a long thin bag that you sleep in, especially when camping
	awful [ˈɔ:fəl]	furchtbar, schrecklich	terrible
	You can say that again.	Das kann man wohl sagen!	It's really hot today. – *You can say that again!* ⚠ You should stress the word "that" in this phrase.
	lid [lɪd]	Deckel	Don't forget to put the ~ back on the tin.
	torch [tɔ:tʃ]	BE: Taschenlampe	a small light you can carry in your hand
	battery [ˈbætrɪ]	Batterie	My watch has stopped. It probably needs a new ~.
	flat [flæt]	leer *(Batterie)*	My car battery has gone ~ because I didn't switch the lights off.
	down-wind *(adv.)* [ˌdaʊnˈwɪnd]	mit dem Wind, in Windrichtung	in the direction in which the wind is blowing
	(to) sob, -bb- [sɒb]	schluchzen	to cry loudly
	siren [ˈsaɪərən]	Sirene	something that makes a loud noise as a warning, for example on a ship

(p. 67)	glow [gləʊ]	Glühen, Leuchten	You could see the red ~ of Paul's cigarette in the darkness. Ann's face has a healthy ~ from the cold.
	ash [æʃ]	Asche	Be careful with your cigarette. You're dropping ~ on the carpet.
p. 68	(to) **suggest** [sə'dʒest]	nahelegen, andeuten	What do you think *is ~ed* by the first sentence?
	paragraph ['pærəgrɑ:f]	Absatz, Abschnitt	What does the second word in the first line of the third ~ on page 20 mean?
	(to) **comment** (on) ['kɒment]	kommentieren, sich (kritisch) äußern (zu)	Prime Minister, would you like to ~ on the American President's visit?
	beyond *(prep.)* [bɪ'jɒnd]	über . . . hinaus, jenseits	You can't see it from here but there's a pond just ~ the fence. I'm sorry, but it's ~ my power to help you.
	realistic [ˌrɪə'lɪstɪk]	realistisch, wirklichkeitsnah	Tim knows he won't pass his A-levels. He's ~ about his chances.

○Song: Click go the shears

click [klɪk]	klick
shears (pl.) [ʃɪəz]	(große) Schere
(to) shear [ʃɪə]	scheren
shearer ['ʃɪərə]	(Schaf-)Scherer/in
board [bɔ:d]	„Planke" *(Teil der Holzkonstruktion, von der aus die Schafe geschoren werden)*
(to) grasp [grɑ:sp]	festhalten
bony ['bəʊnɪ]	knochig
(to) fix one's gaze on sth. [fɪks, geɪz]	seinen Blick (starr) auf etwas richten
bare-bellied ['beəˌbelɪd]	„barbäuchig"
yoe [jəʊ] (Aust. E, infml.) = *ewe* [ju:]	Mutterschaf
glory ['glɔ:rɪ]	Ruhm, Ehre
the ringer ['rɪŋə] (Aust. E)	*der schnellste Scherer einer Mannschaft*
chorus ['kɔ:rəs]	Refrain
wide	*hier:* weit ausholend
blow [bləʊ] (Aust. E.)	*eine bestimmte Armbewegung bei der Schafschur*
(to) curse [kɜ:s]	verfluchen, fluchen über
snagger ['snægə] (Aust. E)	*alt gewordener und daher langsamer arbeitender Scherer*
cane bottomed chair ['keɪn ˌbɒtəmd]	Stuhl mit Sitzfläche aus Rohr
(to) note [nəʊt]	beachten, bemerken
fleece [fli:s]	Schaffell, Vlies
(to) come to the screen [skri:n]	zur Überprüfung kommen
(to) roll up	auf-, zusammenrollen, schnüren
swag [swæg] (Aust. E)	Bündel *(eines Wanderarbeiters oder Landstreichers)*
and it's off down the track [træk]	und dann weg/und dann los den Pfad hinunter
(to) have a spree [spri:]	einen draufmachen

Unit 6: English: A world language

6 A English around the world

p. 70/71	(to) **complete** [kəm'pli:t]	*(Formular)* ausfüllen	Please ~ the questionnaire in capital letters.
	document ['dɒkjʊmənt]	Dokument, Urkunde	The lawyer asked to see the legal ~*s* to the house.
	form [fɔ:m]	Formular, Vordruck	an official piece of paper which you have to complete, for example, when you need a new passport ⚠ *form* = 1. Form; 2. (BE) Klasse(nstufe); 3. Formular
	fluent ['flu:ənt]	fließend, flüssig *(Sprache, Vortrag)*	Jan can speak French ~*ly* because his mother is French.

70/71) lingua franca [ˌlɪŋɡwə ˈfræŋkə]	Verkehrssprache *(zwischen Menschen verschiedener Landessprachen)*	a language used between people whose own language is different
(to) keep up to date (with)	(sich) auf dem laufenden/ auf dem neuesten Stand halten (über)	It's important to ~ *up* ~ ~ with the latest developments in technology.
up to date [ˌʌp tə ˈdeɪt]	aktuell, modern, auf dem neuesten Stand	modern, based on the latest information Is this map ~ *to* ~? – No, it's at least ten years old.
technique [tekˈni:k]	(Arbeits-)Verfahren, Technik, Methode	How do you learn for exams? Do you have a special ~? ⚠ *technique:* Technik = Verfahren, Methode – *technology:* Technik = Technologie
medical [ˈmedɪkl]	medizinisch, Medizin-; ärztlich	Alison is a ~ student. She's studying medicine at Leeds University.
essential [ɪˈsenʃl]	unerläßlich; wesentlich	A knowledge of English is ~ for my job as a tour guide. Music is an ~ part of my life. I can't live without it.
deal [di:l]	Geschäft, Handel; Abkommen	We've just done a big business ~ with a Dutch firm. I'll do a ~ with you. I'll cook if you clean the flat.
Arab *(n., adj.)* [ˈærəb]	Araber/in; arabisch	~*s* are people who live in ~ countries like Iraq [ɪˈrɑ:k] or Morocco [məˈrɒkəʊ].
Arabic *(n., adj.)* [ˈærəbɪk]	Arabisch; arabisch	the language spoken by Arabs; of the Arabs
°Hindi [ˈhɪndi:]	Hindi *(offizielle Sprache in den nordindischen Bundesstaaten)*	

6 A Why English?

settlement [ˈsetlmənt]	Siedlung; Besiedlung	The first permanent English ~ was founded in Virginia, North America in 1607. The ~ of North America began in the 17th century.
overseas *(adv., adj.)* [ˌəʊvəˈsi:z, ˈəʊvəsi:z]	überseeisch; in/nach/aus Übersee	a place or country across the sea; to or from somewhere across the sea
height [haɪt]	Höhe	What is the ~ of (= how high is) Nelson's Column? At the ~ of the tourist season it's hard to find a hotel room in London. ⚠ *spelling:* high – height
empire [ˈempaɪə]	Reich, Weltreich, Imperium	group of countries or states which are controlled by one ruling power
(to) **spread** [spred] – **spread – spread**	(sich) ausbreiten	The fire quickly ~ to all parts of the building.
°AFN [ˌeɪ‿ef‿ˈen] = American Forces Network	*Rundfunk- und Fernsehanstalt der amerikanischen Streitkräfte außerhalb der USA*	
explosion [ɪkˈspləʊʒn]	Explosion; *hier:* explosionsartige Zunahme	There was a terrible gas ~ in a house in Ship Street last week.
truly [ˈtru:lɪ]	wirklich, wahrhaftig, tatsächlich	Sam is a ~ (= really) talented piano player. ⚠ *spelling:* true – truly
global [ˈɡləʊbl]	Welt-, weltumfassend, global	all over the world, of the whole world
(to) **store** [stɔ:]	speichern; lagern	A computer can ~ large amounts of information. Fresh vegetables should *be* ~*d* in a fridge.
electronics *(sing.)* [ˌɪlekˈtrɒnɪks]	Elektronik, Elektronik-	
advertising [ˈædvətaɪzɪŋ]	Werbung, Reklame	the use of adverts to encourage people to buy certain products

Unit 6

6 A Different "Englishes" ... around the world

p. 72	(to) **vary** (from) ['veərɪ]	abweichen (von), variieren, sich unterscheiden (von); verändern	The rings ~ in price from £5 to £500. American English *~ies* quite a lot from British English. They never ~ the menu here. It's always the same.

... and in the UK

	regional [ˈri:dʒənl]	regional	Simon comes from Manchester. He speaks English with a ~ accent.
	broad [brɔ:d]	breit; weit, ausgedehnt	There are a lot of ~ streets in Berlin. Megan speaks English with a ~ Welsh accent. ⚠ Der Tisch ist 2 m lang und 1 m *breit.* = The table is 2 m long and 1 m *wide.*
	(to) broaden ['brɔ:dn]	(sich) erweitern, verbreitern	to become or make broader
	slang [slæŋ]	Slang; Jargon	very informal words or phrases, used only by a particular group of people or in certain situations "Wheels" is ~ for car or motorbike.

6 A Focus on WORDS

p. 73	(to) **operate** [ˈɒpəreɪt]	(sich) betätigen; bedienen	To ~ the machine, you must first switch on the electricity. Do you know how to ~ this computer?
	(to) **co-operate** [kəʊ'ɒpəreɪt]	zusammenarbeiten, kooperieren	Scientists from the USA and France *~d* on the space programme. If you ~, we'll finish the work more quickly.
	horizon [hə'raɪzn]	Horizont	Can you see the boat on the ~? Travelling around the world may broaden your *~s.*
	(to) acquire [ə'kwaɪə]	erwerben, sich aneignen	a more formal word for "get" How *did* you ~ your knowledge of Arabic?
	skill [skɪl]	Fertigkeit; Kenntnis	Bob didn't have the necessary *~s* so he didn't get the job. He couldn't use a computer, for example. Understanding and speaking a language are two different *~s.*
	(un)familiar [fə'mɪlɪə]	(un)bekannt, (nicht) vertraut, (un)gewohnt	Your face looks *f~*. I'm sure we've met before.
	last but not least	nicht zuletzt, nicht zu vergessen	"Thank you all for coming and, ~ *but* ~ *least*, thanks to class 9c for all their help." ⚠ Don't forget to use the *but: last but not least*
	artificial [ˌɑ:tɪ'fɪʃl]	künstlich, Kunst-	Are those flowers real? – No, they're ~.
	offensive [əˈfensɪv]	beleidigend, anstößig	I know you're angry but you don't have to use ~ language!
	(to) master ['mɑ:stə]	meistern	Andreas still *hasn't ~ed* the passive in English.
	instruction [ɪn'strʌkʃn]	Anleitung; Anweisung, Vorschrift	Read the *~s* carefully before you use the washing-machine. I'll leave you some *~s* so you know what to do.
	novel ['nɒvl]	Roman (⚠ *nicht:* ~~Novelle~~)	a long written story, e.g. "Die Blechtrommel" by Günter Grass
	lab (infml.), laboratory [læb, ləˈbɒrətrɪ]	Labor(atorium)	a place where scientists work Chemistry lessons often take place in a ~.
	(to) **interpret** [ɪnˈtɜ:prɪt]	dolmetschen; interpretieren, auffassen	Could you ~ for me, please? I can't speak French. How would you ~ the first line of the poem?
	besides *(prep.)* [bɪ'saɪdz]	außer, neben	*B~* tennis, Jill also plays squash and basketball. ⚠ Three other people left *besides* Pete. (= Pete left, too.) All of us left *except* Pete. (= Pete didn't leave.)

6 A Focus on GRAMMAR

p. 74	**progress** *(sing.)* ['prəʊgres]	Fortschritt(e)	Since my trip to England I've made a lot of ~ in English.
p. 75	**scissors** *(pl.)* ['sɪzəz]	(eine) Schere	You use (a pair of) ~ to cut paper, material, hair, etc. with.
	binoculars *(pl.)* [bɪ'nɒkjʊləz]	(ein) Fernglas	B~ are useful when you want to look at something that is far away.
	pliers *(pl.)* ['plaɪəz]	(eine) (Kombi-)Zange	a tool used to hold or cut things with
	entry ['entrɪ]	Eintrag, Eintragung *(in Wörter-, Tagebuch)*	There's no ~ in Jane's diary for June 3rd.
	abbreviation (for) [ə,bri:vɪ'eɪʃn]	Abkürzung (von)	"Sb." is the ~ for "somebody".
	(to) mark [mɑ:k]	kennzeichnen, bezeichnen, markieren	Tourist attractions *are ~ed* on the map with a star.
Ex 4	encyclopedia [ɪn,saɪklə'pi:dɪə]	Lexikon, Enzyklopädie	a book or a number of books giving information about many different subjects
6	**various** ['veərɪəs]	verschieden(artig); verschiedene, mehrere	several different There are ~ ways of learning a language. ⚠ *various* ['veərɪəs] – *(to) vary* ['veərɪ] – *variety* [və'raɪətɪ]
	(to) **flow** [fləʊ]	fließen, strömen	Where *does* the River Thames ~ into the sea? ⚠ *(to) flow – flowed – flowed* = fließen, strömen *(to) fly – flew – flown* = fliegen
	reservoir ['rezəvwɑ:]	Stausee, (Speicher-)Becken	an artificial or natural lake where water is stored
	Germanic [dʒə'mænɪk]	germanisch	Dutch, English and German are all ~ languages.
	(to) **split** (up) [splɪt] – **split – split**	(auf)spalten, (auf)teilen; (sich) teilen, (sich) trennen	*S~* up the following verbs into activity and state verbs. If you don't stop talking, I'll have to ~ you up.
	point of view [,pɔɪnt‿əv 'vju:]	Gesichtspunkt, Standpunkt	From my ~ *of* ~ (= in my opinion) there's no problem. I don't share your ~ *of* ~ on space travel.
	°regularity [,regjʊ'lærətɪ]	Regelmäßigkeit	

6 T The language expert

p. 79	(to) **tell**	erkennen, wissen	to know, to realize, to recognize I can ~ that you're lying, Tom.
	conference ['kɒnfrəns]	Konferenz, Besprechung	The Conservative Party held its party ~ in Brighton.
	(to) **take off**	starten, abheben *(Flugzeug)*	We *took* ~ for London at 8 and landed there at 10.30. ⚠ *Never:* the plane ~~started~~
	(to) **point** (to, at)	zeigen (auf), deuten (auf)	The teacher *~ed* with her finger to the most important cities on the map.
	heavy ['hevɪ]	dicht *(Verkehr)*	The traffic was so ~ that I got to work an hour late.
	tank [tæŋk]	Panzer	a large heavy vehicle with guns which is used in war
	(to) blow one's horn – blew – blown	hupen	The driver *blew her* ~ because a dog ran into the road.
	while *(n.)* [waɪl]	Weile, Zeit(spanne)	a certain amount of time I haven't been to the cinema for a ~. I spoke to Juliet a ~ ago and she said she was coming.

Unit 6

(p. 79)	I might (just) as well...	Ich könnte ebensogut...	*I* ~ just *as* ~ come to the party. I've no other plans.
	(to) pass the time (doing sth.)	sich die Zeit vertreiben (mit), die Zeit verbringen (mit)	They *~ed the* ~ playing cards.
p. 80	logical ['lɒdʒɪkl]	logisch	Jill can think very *~ly*. That's why she's good at maths.
	entrance (to) ['entrəns]	Eingang (zu); Eintritts-	How do we get into the museum? – The ~ is just around the corner. The ~ fee is £3 for adults and £1 for children.
	°(to be, stand, leave) ajar [ə'dʒɑː]	angelehnt, halb offen (sein, stehen, lassen)	
	jar [dʒɑː]	(Einmach-)Glas; Topf	 a jam ~  a ~ of jam
	like *(conj.)* [laɪk] (infml.)	wie	an informal word for the conjunction "as" *L~* you said, learning a foreign language is really quite difficult.
	(to) **wave** (to, at sb.) [weɪv]	(jm. zu)winken	Mike *~d* goodbye to his girlfriend from the train.
	Anglo-(Irish, American, etc.) ['æŋgləʊ]	anglo-(irisch, amerikanisch usw.)	Cathy is ~-Irish [,--'--]. Her mother is English and her father Irish.
	(to) **apply** (to) [ə'plaɪ]	anwenden (auf); gelten (für), sich anwenden lassen (auf)	You can ~ many Latin grammar rules to other languages like French or Italian. The school rules ~ to you, too, Paul.

Same form – different word class

(to) **arrest**	verhaften, festnehmen	(to) **question**	befragen, vernehmen (⚠ *nicht:* ~~fragen~~)
arrest	Verhaftung, Festnahme	**question**	Frage
(to) **comment**	kommentieren, sich (kritisch) äußern	(to) **reply**	(be)antworten, erwidern
comment	Kommentar, Bemerkung	**reply**	Antwort, Erwiderung
(to) **concern**	betreffen, angehen	(to) **ruin**	zerstören, ruinieren
concern	Angelegenheit, Belang, Sache	**ruin**	Untergang, Ruin; Ruine
(to) **hate**	hassen	(to) **search**	(durch)suchen, (durch)forschen
hate	Haß	**search**	Suche, Durchsuchung
(to) **heat**	erhitzen; heizen	(to) **stress**	betonen
heat	Hitze	**stress**	Betonung; Streß
(to) **link**	(sich) verbinden	(to) **vote**	(ab)stimmen, wählen
link	Verbindung, Beziehung, Bindeglied	**vote**	Abstimmung; Stimme *(bei Wahlen)*
		(to) **wish**	wünschen
		wish	Wunsch

(to) **empty** *(v.)*	(sich) (ent)leeren	**wrong** *(adj.)*	falsch
empty *(adj.)*	leer	**wrong** *(n.)*	Unrecht

... and different pronunciation

(to) **contrast** [kən'trɑːst]	kontrastieren, gegenüberstellen	(to) **present** [prɪ'zent]	präsentieren, darlegen
contrast ['kɒntrɑːst]	Kontrast, Gegensatz	**present** ['preznt]	Geschenk
(to) **export** [ɪk'spɔːt]	exportieren	(to) **protest** [prə'test]	protestieren
export ['ekspɔːt]	Export, Ausfuhr	**protest** ['prəʊtest]	Protest, Widerspruch
(to) **import** [ɪm'pɔːt]	importieren	(to) **record** [rɪ'kɔːd]	aufzeichnen, aufnehmen *(auf Band)*
import ['ɪmpɔːt]	Import, Einfuhr	**record** ['rekɔːd]	Rekord; Schallplatte
(to) **permit** [pə'mɪt]	erlauben, gestatten	(to) **transport** [træn'spɔːt]	befördern, transportieren
permit ['pɜːmɪt]	Genehmigung(sschein), Erlaubnis	**transport** ['trænspɔːt]	Transport, Verkehrsmittel

Words from the options

Auf den folgenden zwei Seiten sind ausgewählte neue Wörter aus den *Options* zusammengestellt. Sie können entsprechend den Lehrplananforderungen des jeweiligen Bundeslandes dem Lernwortschatz hinzugefügt werden, werden aber in Band 6 nicht vorausgesetzt.

1	exact [ɪg'zækt]	genau	What's the ~ size of West Germany? – 248,574 sq km.
2	chin [tʃɪn]	Kinn	part of the face, below the mouth
	command [kə'mɑ:nd]	Befehl	an order
	(to) disappear [,dɪsə'pɪə]	verschwinden	I can't find my shoes anywhere. They*'ve ~ed.*
3	(to) approach [ə'prəʊtʃ]	sich nähern	We*'ll* ~ Dover at about midday.
	(to) break down	eine Panne haben	The car *broke* ~, so they had to go home by bus.
	step [step]	Stufe	Did you climb the 300 *~s* to the top of the tower?
	(to) recover [rɪ'kʌvə]	sich erholen	Tom still *hasn't ~ed* from the shock.
	(to) resign [rɪ'zaɪn]	kündigen	to leave one's job
5	childhood ['tʃaɪldhʊd]	Kindheit	years as a child
	brain [breɪn]	Gehirn	the part of the head which controls one's thoughts
	(to) spill [spɪl] – spilt [spɪlt] – spilt	verschütten	Who *spilt* their coffee on the carpet?
6	(to) (mis)trust sb. [trʌst, ,mɪs'trʌst]	jm. (miß)trauen	Why did you lend Tom your car? – I thought I could *t~* him.
	brick [brɪk]	Backstein	*B~s* are used to build houses with.
	strength [streŋθ]	Kraft	Ed isn't very strong. He doesn't have much ~.
	(to) kneel [ni:l] – knelt [nelt] – knelt	(nieder)knien	to be on one's knees
7	(to) interfere with [,ɪntə'fɪə]	sich einmischen in	Terry always *~s with* things that don't concern him.
	nephew ['nevju:, 'nefju:]	Neffe	the son of one's brother or sister
	property ['prɒpətɪ]	Eigentum	something that belongs to a person
	(to) elect sb. [ɪ'lekt]	jn. wählen	They *~ed* a new Prime Minister last year.
8	cruelty ['krʊəltɪ]	Grausamkeit	noun from "cruel"
	(to) blame sb. [bleɪm]	jm. die Schuld geben	*Don't* ~ me. It's not my fault.
	responsible [rɪ'spɒnsɪbl]	verantwortungsvoll, verantwortlich	A doctor has a very ~ job.
	signature ['sɪgnɪtʃə]	Unterschrift	the way you sign your name
9	(to) bite [baɪt] – bit [bɪt] – bitten ['bɪtən]	beißen	The dog *bit* the woman in the leg.
	(to) manage ['mænɪdʒ]	zurechtkommen	to succeed in doing something
	(to) approve of [ə'pru:v]	billigen, gutheißen	to like or have a good opinion of somebody or something
	(to) stare at [steə]	anstarren	to look hard at somebody/something for a long time
	What's the matter? ['mætə]	Was ist denn (los)?	= What's wrong?
	(to) be ashamed of [ə'ʃeɪmd]	sich schämen für	Why *are* you so ~ *of* your English? You speak it really well.
	I'd rather not ['rɑ:ðə]	Ich würde lieber nicht	= I'd prefer not to
	furious ['fjʊərɪəs]	wütend	really angry
	(to) be supposed to	sollen	That was a joke. You*'re ~ to* laugh.
	(to) leave sb. alone	jn. in Ruhe lassen	*L~* me *alone.* I'm trying to work.
	apart from [ə'pɑ:t]	außer	John enjoyed the film *~ from* the ending.
	delighted [dɪ'laɪtɪd]	hocherfreut	very happy, very pleased
	actor/actress ['æktə/'æktrɪs]	Schauspieler/in	person who acts in a film or in the theatre
10	judge [dʒʌdʒ]	Richter/in	a person who decides if someone has committed a crime

11	protection [prəˈtekʃn]	Schutz	noun from "to protect"
	grandchild [ˈgræntʃaɪld]	Enkelkind	the child of one's son or daughter
12	former [ˈfɔːmə]	früher	Mrs Bell was my ~ boss.
	(to) represent (sb.) [ˌreprɪˈzent]	(jm.) vertreten	The boss couldn't attend the meeting so her assistant *~ed* her there.
13	(to) replace (with) [rɪˈpleɪs]	ersetzen (durch)	Will you ~ that dirty towel with a clean one, please?
14	(to) sew [səʊ]	nähen	Tina can ~ very well. She makes all her own clothes.
	(to) lay [leɪ] – laid [leɪd] – laid	legen	to put something in a certain place
16	(to) name	benennen	verb from "name"
	type [taɪp]	Typ, Art	It's a ~ (= kind) of cheese.
	slight [slaɪt]	leicht, geringfügig	Is Tom ill? – Not really. He's just got a ~ cold.
	exception [ɪkˈsepʃn]	Ausnahme	Everyone can swim except Mike. He's the only ~.
17	nevertheless [ˌnevəðəˈles]	nichtsdestoweniger, trotzdem	Jill had already seen the film, but she watched it again ~.
	therefore [ˈðeəfɔː]	deshalb, deswegen	for that reason
18	impressed (with) [ɪmˈprest]	beeindruckt (von)	I'm ~ with your French. You speak it very well.
	(to) deal with [diːl] – dealt [delt] – dealt	handeln von	The book *~s with* poverty in developing countries.
	(to) state [steɪt]	feststellen	verb from "statement"
	(to) doubt [daʊt]	be-, anzweifeln	I ~ he'll come. He's got too much work.
	as far as	soweit, soviel	*As ~ as* I know, he'll be back at 6.
	intention [ɪnˈtenʃn]	Absicht	It wasn't my ~ (= I didn't mean) to be rude.
19	valuable [ˈvæljʊəbl]	wertvoll	Is that ring worth a lot? – Yes it's very ~.
	content [ˈkɒntent]	Inhalt	The story is well written, but the ~ is very boring.
	(to) consider [kənˈsɪdə]	überlegen	to think about somebody or something
20	(to) inquire [ɪnˈkwaɪə] (fml.)	sich erkundigen	a formal way of saying "to ask about"
	(to) obtain [əbˈteɪn]	erlangen, erhalten	to get, to receive
22	How do you do. (fml.)	Guten Tag! Grüß Gott!	a formal way of saying "hello" when you meet somebody for the first time
	luggage [ˈlʌgɪdʒ]	Gepäck	what you take on holiday with you, e.g. suitcase, bag, etc.
	(to) greet [griːt]	begrüßen	Carol *~ed* Tim with a kiss.
	(to) ask for/(to) give directions	nach dem Weg fragen/den Weg erklären	We asked the police officer to *give* us ~ to the theatre.
	(to) give sb. a ring	jn. anrufen	= to ring someone up
	(to) do the washing up	abwaschen	= to wash the dishes
	newsagent's [ˈnjuːzˌeɪdʒənts]	Zeitungsladen	shop where you can buy papers, sweets, postcards, etc.
	I feel sick.	Mir ist übel.	Paul is not very well. He *feels* a bit ~.
	appointment [əˈpɔɪntmənt]	Termin	I've got a doctor's ~ at 3 o'clock.
	treatment [ˈtriːtmənt]	Behandlung	Tom is receiving ~ from the doctor for his broken leg.
	dentist [ˈdentɪst]	Zahnarzt/-ärztin	You should go to the *~'s* if you've got toothache.
23	confusion [kənˈfjuːʒn]	Durcheinander	noun from "to confuse"
	application [ˌæplɪˈkeɪʃn]	Bewerbung	noun from "to apply"
25	sense [sens]	Sinn, Bedeutung	The word has several *~s* (= meanings).
26	(to) intend [ɪnˈtend]	beabsichtigen	to plan (to do)
	definitely [ˈdefɪnətlɪ]	eindeutig	It's ~ wrong. I'm sure about that.

Mini-dictionary

Alphabetical list of words (Books 1-5)

Die alphabetische Wortliste enthält den Wortschatz der Bände A1 bis A5. In der Regel wird nur die Schreibweise und Aussprache des britischen Englisch angegeben.
Mit einem ° versehene Wörter sind fakultativ, d.h. sie werden bei erneutem Vorkommen nicht als bekannt vorausgesetzt.
Da alle unbekannten Wörter aus den *Options* am Fuß der jeweiligen Seite erklärt werden und bei erneutem Vorkommen nicht als bekannt vorausgesetzt werden, sind diese Wörter – mit Ausnahme der *Words from the options* (S. 167, 168) – nicht im *Mini-dictionary* enthalten.

sb. = somebody, sth. = something, AE = American English, Aust. E = Australian English, BE = British English, fml. = formal, infml. = informal

A

a [ə] ein, eine; **50p a week** 50 Pence pro Woche
abbey ['æbɪ] Abtei, Kloster
abbreviation (for) [əˌbri:vɪ'eɪʃn] Abkürzung (von)
ability [ə'bɪlətɪ] Fähigkeit
able ['eɪbl]**: be able to** können, fähig sein
abolish [ə'bɒlɪʃ] abschaffen
°**Aboriginal people** [ˌæbə'rɪdʒənl 'pi:pl] australische Ureinwohner/innen; °**Aborigine** [ˌæbə'rɪdʒəni:] australische/r Ureinwohner/in
about [ə'baʊt] **1.** über; **2.** ungefähr, etwa; **3.** wegen; **like sth. about sb.** etwas an jm. mögen; **What about ...?** Wie steht's mit ...?, Wie wär's mit ...?
above [ə'bʌv] **1.** über, oberhalb (von); **2.** oben
abroad [ə'brɔ:d] ins/im Ausland; **from abroad** aus dem Ausland
absent ['æbsənt]**: be absent** fehlen, abwesend sein
abstract ['æbstrækt] abstrakt
academic [ˌækə'demɪk] akademisch, wissenschaftlich
accent ['æksənt] Akzent
accept [ək'sept] annehmen, akzeptieren
access ['ækses] Zugang
accident ['æksɪdənt] **1.** Unfall; **2.** Versehen
according to [ə'kɔ:dɪŋ] entsprechend, gemäß, nach; **accordingly** (dem)entsprechend
ache [eɪk] **1.** Schmerz; **(a) stomach ache** ['stʌmək‿eɪk] Magenschmerzen, Bauchschmerzen;
2. weh tun, schmerzen
achieve [ə'tʃi:v] *(ein Ziel)* erreichen
acquire [ə'kwaɪə] erwerben, sich aneignen
acre ['eɪkə] *Flächenmaß*
across [ə'krɒs] **1.** (quer) über, durch; **2.** hinüber, herüber
act, Act [ækt] **1.** Verordnung, Gesetz; **2. act** spielen, darstellen; **3.** handeln; **action** ['ækʃn] Handlung, Tat
active ['æktɪv] rege, aktiv
activity [æk'tɪvətɪ] Projekt, Beschäftigung
°**actor/actress** ['æktə/'æktrɪs] Schauspieler/in
actually ['æktʃʊəlɪ] tatsächlich; eigentlich
AD [ˌeɪ'di:] n. Chr.
adapted from [ə'dæptɪd] eine Bearbeitung von, frei nach
add [æd] hinzufügen
address [ə'dres] Adresse, Anschrift
admirable ['ædmərəbl] bewundernswert
admire [əd'maɪə] bewundern, verehren
admit [əd'mɪt] **1.** zugeben; **2.** zulassen, (hin)einlassen
adult ['ædʌlt] Erwachsene(r)
advantage [əd'vɑ:ntɪdʒ] Vorteil
adventure [əd'ventʃə] Abenteuer; **adventurer** [əd'ventʃərə] Abenteurer/in
advert ['ædvɜ:t] Anzeige, Reklame; **advertising** ['ædvətaɪzɪŋ] Werbung, Reklame
advice [əd'vaɪs] Rat, Ratschläge
advise [əd'vaɪz] (be)raten
affect [ə'fekt] betreffen, sich auswirken auf; beeinträchtigen
afford [ə'fɔ:d] sich leisten
°**AFN** [ˌeɪ‿ef‿'en] = **American Forces Network** *Rundfunk- und Fernsehanstalt der amerikanischen Streitkräfte außerhalb der USA*
afraid [ə'freɪd]**: be afraid (of)** Angst haben, sich fürchten (vor); **I'm afraid** leider
Africa ['æfrɪkə] Afrika; **African** **1.** Afrikaner/in; **2.** afrikanisch
after ['ɑ:ftə] **1.** nach; **2.** nachdem; **3.** hinter ... her; **after all** schließlich, immerhin; (also) doch; **after that** danach; **look after** sich kümmern um, aufpassen auf
afternoon [ˌɑ:ftə'nu:n] Nachmittag; **Good afternoon.** Guten Tag! **in the afternoon(s)** am Nachmittag; **on that afternoon** an jenem Nachmittag; **this afternoon** heute nachmittag
afterwards ['ɑ:ftəwədz] später, nachher, hinterher
again [ə'gen, ə'geɪn] wieder; noch (ein)mal
against [ə'genst] gegen
age [eɪdʒ] Alter; **aged** [eɪdʒd] im Alter von, -jährig
aggressive (towards) [ə'gresɪv] aggressiv (gegenüber)
ago [ə'gəʊ] vor; **not long ago** vor kurzem
agree (with) [ə'gri:] übereinstimmen (mit); zustimmen, sich einigen, beschließen
aim [eɪm] **1.** Ziel; **2. aim (at)** zielen, *(Waffe usw.)* richten (auf); beabsichtigen; **aimless** ziellos
air [eə] Luft; **air mail** ['eə meɪl] Luftpost
airport ['eəpɔ:t] Flughafen
°**ajar** [ə'dʒɑ:]**: be/stand/leave ajar** angelehnt, halb offen sein/stehen/lassen
alcohol ['ælkəhɒl] Alkohol; **alcoholic** [ˌælkə'hɒlɪk] **1.** Alkoholiker/in; **2.** alkoholisch; **alcoholism** ['ælkəhɒlɪzm] Alkoholismus
A-Level ['eɪ ˌlevl] = **Advanced Level exam** (BE) *etwa:* Abitur
alive [ə'laɪv] am Leben
all [ɔ:l] **1.** alle; alles; **2.** ganz; **all of you** ihr alle; **all over** überall in/auf; **all right** gut, in Ordnung; **I'm all right.** Mir geht's gut. **It's all right for Liz.** Liz ist gut dran. Liz hat's gut. **That's all right.** Schon gut. Nichts zu danken. **Livermore of all places!** Ausgerechnet Livermore!
alley ['ælɪ] Durchgang, schmale Gasse
alligator ['ælɪgeɪtə] Alligator
allow [ə'laʊ] erlauben; **be allowed to** dürfen
almost ['ɔ:lməʊst] fast, beinahe
alone [ə'ləʊn] allein; °**leave sb. alone** jn. in Ruhe lassen
along [ə'lɒŋ] entlang; **bring along** mitbringen; **go along** mitgehen; sich anschließen
aloud [ə'laʊd] laut *(lesen)*
Alps [ælps] Alpen
already [ɔ:l'redɪ] schon, bereits
also ['ɔ:lsəʊ] auch; **not only ... but also** nicht nur ..., sondern auch
alternative [ɔ:l'tɜ:nətɪv] Alternative; **alternatively** andererseits, als Alternative
although [ɔ:l'ðəʊ] obwohl, obgleich
altogether [ˌɔ:ltə'geðə] insgesamt, alles zusammen
always ['ɔ:lweɪz] immer
am [æm] bin
am [ˌeɪ‿'em] ... Uhr morgens/vormittags
amazing [ə'meɪzɪŋ] erstaunlich
ambulance ['æmbjʊləns] Krankenwagen; **ambulance man/woman** Sanitäter/in
America [ə'merɪkə] Amerika; **American** **1.** Amerikaner/in; **2.** amerikanisch
among [ə'mʌŋ] (mitten) unter, zwischen
amount [ə'maʊnt] Menge; Summe; Betrag
amusing [ə'mju:zɪŋ] amüsant, unterhaltsam, komisch
an [æn, ən] ein, eine
analyse ['ænəlaɪz] analysieren
ancestor ['ænsestə] Vorfahre
ancient ['eɪnʃnt] alt, historisch, antik
and [ænd, ən(d)] und
Angles ['æŋglz] Angeln; **Anglo-(Irish, American, ...)** ['æŋgləʊ] anglo-(irisch, amerikanisch, ...); **Anglo-Saxon** [ˌæŋgləʊ'sæksn] **1.** angelsächsisch; **2.** das Angelsächsische
angry (with) ['æŋgrɪ] wütend, böse, zornig (auf)
animal ['ænɪml] Tier
annoy [ə'nɔɪ] ärgern, belästigen; **annoying** ärgerlich, lästig; **be annoyed** verärgert sein, sich ärgern
anorak ['ænəræk] Anorak
another [ə'nʌðə] **1.** ein(e) andere(r, s); **2.** noch ein(e)
answer ['ɑ:nsə] **1.** Antwort; **2.** antworten, beantworten; **answer back** freche Antworten geben; sich *(mit Worten)* verteidigen; **answer the (tele)phone** ans Telefon gehen
anthem: national anthem [ˌnæʃnəl‿'ænθəm] Nationalhymne
anti-(British) ['æntɪ] anti(britisch)
anxiety [æŋ'zaɪətɪ] Angst, Sorge
any ['enɪ] (irgend)welche(r, s); jede(r, s) (beliebige); **not ... any** (gar) kein, keine; keins; **not (...) any more** nicht mehr, kein(e, n); **anybody/anyone** (irgend) jemand; jede/r (beliebige); **not ... anybody** niemand; **anything** (irgend) etwas; irgend etwas (x-beliebiges); **Anything else?** Sonst noch etwas? **not ... anything** nichts; **anyway** außerdem, überhaupt; sowieso; jedenfalls; **anywhere** irgend-

wo(hin); **not ... anywhere** nirgendwo(hin)
apart [ə'pɑ:t] getrennt, auseinander; °**apart from** außer
apartment [ə'pɑ:tmənt] (*meist* AE) Wohnung; **apartment house** (AE) Mietshaus
apologize (to sb.) [ə'pɒlədʒaɪz] sich (bei jm.) entschuldigen; **apology** [ə'pɒlədʒɪ] Entschuldigung
apostrophe [ə'pɒstrəfɪ] Apostroph
appear [ə'pɪə] erscheinen, auftauchen; **appear (to be)** (zu sein) scheinen
apple ['æpl] Apfel
°**application** [,æplɪ'keɪʃn] Bewerbung; **apply (for)** [ə'plaɪ] sich bewerben (um), beantragen; **apply (to)** anwenden (auf); gelten (für), sich anwenden lassen (auf)
°**appointment** [ə'pɔɪntmənt] Termin
appreciate [ə'pri:ʃɪeɪt] schätzen, würdigen, zu schätzen wissen
°**approach** [ə'prəʊtʃ] sich nähern
°**approve of** [ə'pru:v] billigen, gutheißen
April ['eɪprəl] April
Arab ['ærəb] **1.** Araber/in; **2.** arabisch; **Arabic** ['ærəbɪk] **1.** Arabisch; **2.** arabisch
are [ɑ:, ə] bist, sind, seid
area ['eərɪə] **1.** Gebiet, Gegend; **2.** Fläche
argue (about) ['ɑ:gju:] (sich) streiten, zanken (über/wegen); **argument** ['ɑ:gjʊmənt] **1.** Argument, Grund; **2.** Streit
ark [ɑ:k] Arche; **Noah's ark** [,nəʊəz‿'ɑ:k] die Arche Noah
arm [ɑ:m] Arm
armchair [,ɑ:m'tʃeə] Sessel
army ['ɑ:mɪ] Armee, Heer
around [ə'raʊnd] **1.** um ... herum, im Gebiet um; **2.** umher; **around here** hier in der Gegend
arrange [ə'reɪndʒ] **1.** (an)ordnen; **2.** arrangieren, vereinbaren; **arrangement** Vereinbarung Abmachung
arrest [ə'rest] **1.** Verhaftung, Festnahme; **2.** verhaften, festnehmen
arrival [ə'raɪvl] Ankunft; **arrive** [ə'raɪv] ankommen, eintreffen
arrogant ['ærəgənt] arrogant, überheblich
arrow ['ærəʊ] Pfeil
art [ɑ:t] Kunst
article ['ɑ:tɪkl] Artikel
artificial [,ɑ:tɪ'fɪʃl] künstlich, Kunst-
as [æz, əz] **1.** als, während; **2.** da, weil; **3.** wie; **as far as 1.** bis (zu/nach); °**2.** *(conj.)* soweit, soviel; **as from now** ab jetzt, von jetzt an; **as if** als ob; **as late as ...** erst um ...; **as long as** solange, sofern; **(not) as fast as** (nicht) so schnell wie; **the same as** der-/die-/dasselbe wie; **as soon as** *(conj.)* sobald; **as well as** und auch, ebenso wie
ash [æʃ] Asche
°**ashamed** [ə'ʃeɪmd]**: be ashamed of** sich schämen für
Asia ['eɪʃə, 'eɪʒə] Asien; **Asian 1.** Asiat/in; **2.** asiatisch
ask [ɑ:sk] fragen; **ask a question** eine Frage stellen; **ask for** bitten um
asleep [ə'sli:p]: **be asleep** schlafen; **fall asleep** einschlafen
aspect ['æspekt] Aspekt, Gesichtspunkt, Seite
aspirin ['æsprɪn] Aspirin(tablette)
assembly [ə'semblɪ] Versammlung; **assembly line** Fließband(montage), Fertigungsstraße
assistant [ə'sɪstənt] Verkäufer/in; Assistent/in; Gehilfe/-in
astronaut ['æstrənɔ:t] Astronaut/in
asylum [ə'saɪləm] Asyl

at [æt, ət] bei, an; **at Dave's/my house** bei Dave/mir (zu Hause); **at Easter** zu Ostern; **at first** zuerst, anfangs; **at home** zu Hause; **at last** endlich; schließlich; **at least** mindestens; wenigstens, zumindest; **at night** nachts, bei Nacht; **at once** sofort, (so)gleich; **at school** in der Schule; **at the end** am Ende, am Schluß; **at the moment** im Moment, im Augenblick; zur Zeit; **at the weekend** am Wochenende; **at 3 o'clock** um 3 Uhr; **at 22 Albert Road** in der Albertstraße Nr. 22; **at work** bei der Arbeit; **good/bad at** gut/schlecht in; **look at** anschauen; **(not) at all** überhaupt (nicht)
athlete ['æθli:t] (Leicht-)Athlet/in, Sportler/in; **athletic** [æθ'letɪk] athletisch, sportlich; **athletics** Leichtathletik
atmosphere ['ætməsfɪə] Atmosphäre
attack [ə'tæk] **1.** Angriff; **2.** angreifen
attend [ə'tend] besuchen, teilnehmen an *(Kurs, Schule usw.)*
attention [ə'tenʃn] Aufmerksamkeit; **pay attention (to)** aufpassen (auf), beachten
attitude (towards) ['ætɪtju:d] Haltung, Einstellung (gegenüber, zu)
attract [ə'trækt] anziehen, anlocken; **attraction** [ə'trækʃn] Attraktion, Anziehungspunkt; **attractive** [ə'træktɪv] anziehend, attraktiv, reizvoll
au pair [,əʊ 'peə] Au-Pair(-Mädchen, -Junge)
August ['ɔ:gəst] August
aunt [ɑ:nt] Tante; **aunty, auntie** ['ɑ:ntɪ] Tante
Australia [ɒ'streɪlɪə] Australien; **Australian 1.** Australier/in; **2.** australisch
Austria ['ɒstrɪə] Österreich; **Austrian 1.** Österreicher/in; **2.** österreichisch
authentic [ɔ:'θentɪk] authentisch, echt
author ['ɔ:θə] Autor/in
automatic(ally) [,ɔ:tə'mætɪklɪ] automatisch
auto mechanics ['ɔ:təʊ mɪ,kænɪks] (AE) Kfz-Technik; **auto(mobile)** ['ɔ:təʊ, 'ɔ:təməʊbi:l] (AE) Auto, Wagen
autumn ['ɔ:təm] Herbst; **in (the) autumn** im Herbst
avenue ['ævənju:] Allee
average ['ævərɪdʒ] **1.** Durchschnitt; **2.** durchschnittlich, Durchschnitts-
avoid [ə'vɔɪd] (ver)meiden; ausweichen
away [ə'weɪ] **1.** weg, fort; **2.** entfernt; **go away** verreisen; **throw away** wegwerfen
awful ['ɔ:fəl] furchtbar, schrecklich
axe [æks] Axt, Beil

B

baby ['beɪbɪ] Baby
babysitter ['beɪbɪ,sɪtə] Babysitter
back [bæk] **1.** Rückseite, hinterer Teil; Rücken; **2.** hintere(r, s), Hinter-; **3.** zurück, wieder; **back home** daheim
background ['bækgraʊnd] Hintergrund; Herkunft
backwards ['bækwədz] rückwärts
backyard [,bæk'jɑ:d] (AE) Garten hinter dem Haus
bacon ['beɪkn] (Schinken-)Speck
bad [bæd] schlecht; schlimm; **a bad cold** ein starker Schnupfen; **bad at** schlecht in; **(It's) too bad.** (Es ist) schade.
bag [bæg] Tasche, Beutel, Tüte; **mixed bag** bunte Mischung
baker ['beɪkə] Bäcker/in
balcony ['bælkənɪ] Balkon
bald [bɔ:ld] kahl(köpfig); glatzköpfig
ball [bɔ:l] **1.** Ball; **2.** Ball, Tanzfest
banana [bə'nɑ:nə] Banane

band [bænd] Band, (Musik-)Gruppe
bandage ['bændɪdʒ] Verband, Binde
bank [bæŋk] Bank, Sparkasse
barbecue ['bɑ:bɪkju:] Grill; Grillparty
bark [bɑ:k] bellen
barn [bɑ:n] Scheune
baseball ['beɪsbɔ:l] Baseball
based [beɪst]**: be based on** basieren auf
basic ['beɪsɪk] **1.** Grund-; Haupt-; **2.** grundlegend
basket ['bɑ:skɪt] Korb
basketball ['bɑ:skɪtbɔ:l] Basketball
bath [bɑ:θ] Bad; **have a bath** baden, ein Bad nehmen; **bathroom** ['bɑ:θrʊm] Bad(ezimmer)
battery ['bætrɪ] Batterie
battle ['bætl] Schlacht
Bavaria [bə'veərɪə] Bayern
bay [beɪ] Bucht
BC [,bi:'si:] v. Chr.
be [bi:] sein; **be born** geboren sein/werden; **be early** zu früh kommen; **be frightened** Angst haben, sich fürchten; **be fun** Spaß machen; **be hungry** Hunger haben; **be late** zu spät kommen; **be lucky** Glück haben; **be missing** fehlen; **be right** recht haben; **be smelly** stinken; **be thirsty** Durst haben; **be wrong** unrecht haben
beach [bi:tʃ] Strand; **on the beach** am Strand
bean [bi:n] Bohne
bear [beə] Bär
bearable ['beərəbl] erträglich
beard [bɪəd] Bart
beat [bi:t] schlagen, besiegen; **beat sb. up** jn. zusammenschlagen
beautiful ['bju:tɪfəl] (wunder)schön; **beauty** ['bju:tɪ] Schönheit
because [bɪ'kɒz] weil; **because of** wegen
become [bɪ'kʌm] werden
bed [bed] Bett; **bed and breakfast** Übernachtung mit Frühstück; **go to bed** ins Bett gehen; **bedroom** Schlafzimmer
beef [bi:f] Rindfleisch; **roast beef** Rinderbraten, Roastbeef
beer [bɪə] Bier
before [bɪ'fɔ:] **1.** vor; **2.** bevor, ehe; **3.** vorher, schon einmal; **before that** davor, vorher
beggar ['begə] Bettler/in
begin [bɪ'gɪn] beginnen, anfangen; **beginning** Anfang, Beginn
behave [bɪ'heɪv] sich verhalten, sich benehmen; **behaviour (towards)** [bɪ'heɪvjə] Verhalten, Benehmen (gegenüber)
behind [bɪ'haɪnd] hinter
belief (in) [bɪ'li:f] Glaube (an), (religiöse) Überzeugung; **believe (in)** [bɪ'li:v] glauben (an)
bell [bel] Klingel; Glocke
belong to [bɪ'lɒŋ] gehören
below [bɪ'ləʊ] **1.** unten; **2.** unter(halb von)
bend [bend] Kurve, Biegung
besides *(prep.)* [bɪ'saɪdz] außer, neben
best [best] bester, beste, bestes; **best wishes** mit den besten Wünschen; **like best** am liebsten mögen
better ['betə] besser; **like better** lieber mögen; **you had better ...** es wäre besser, wenn du ...; du solltest lieber ...
between [bɪ'twi:n] zwischen
beyond *(prep.)* [bɪ'jɒnd] über ... hinaus, jenseits
BIA = Bureau of Indian Affairs (AE) Behörde für Indianerangelegenheiten
bicycle ['baɪsɪkl] Fahrrad
big [bɪg] groß
bike [baɪk] Fahrrad, Rad; **by bike** mit dem Fahrrad
bill [bɪl] Rechnung; AE *auch:* Geldschein

°**billy(-can)** [ˈbɪlɪkæn] (BE, Aust. E) (Camping-)Kochgeschirr
binoculars *(pl.)* [bɪˈnɒkjʊləz] (ein) Fernglas
biology [baɪˈɒlədʒɪ] Biologie
bird [bɜ:d] Vogel
biro [ˈbaɪrəʊ] (BE) Kugelschreiber, Kuli
birth [bɜ:θ] Geburt
birthday [ˈbɜ:θdeɪ] Geburtstag; **for sb.'s birthday** zum Geburtstag; **Happy birthday (to you)!** Herzlichen Glückwunsch zum Geburtstag! **on your birthday** an deinem Geburtstag; **When's your birthday?** Wann hast du Geburtstag?
biscuit [ˈbɪskɪt] (BE) Keks
bit [bɪt]: **a bit** ein bißchen, etwas
°**bite** [baɪt] beißen
bitter [ˈbɪtə] bitter; verbittert; **bitterness** [ˈbɪtənɪs] Bitterkeit
black [blæk] **1.** schwarz; **2.** Schwarze(r)
°**blame sb.** [bleɪm] jm. die Schuld geben
blanket [ˈblæŋkɪt] (Woll-)Decke
blind [blaɪnd] blind
block: block of flats [ˌblɒk‿əv ˈflæts] (BE) Mietshaus, Wohnblock
blood [blʌd] Blut
°**blossom** [ˈblɒsəm] Blüte *(eines Baumes oder Busches)*
blouse [blaʊz] Bluse
blow [bləʊ] wehen, blasen; **blow one's horn** hupen; **blow up** sprengen, in die Luft jagen
blue [blu:] blau
board [bɔ:d] (Wand-)Tafel; Brett
boarding school [ˈbɔ:dɪŋ sku:l] Internat
boat [bəʊt] Boot; Schiff; **by boat** mit dem Schiff
body [ˈbɒdɪ] Körper; **(dead) body** Leiche
boil [bɔɪl] (ab)kochen, sieden
bomb [bɒm] **1.** Bombe; **2.** bombardieren
book [bʊk] Buch
booklet [ˈbʊklɪt] Broschüre
°**boomerang** [ˈbu:məræŋ] Bumerang
boot [bu:t] Stiefel; BE *auch:* Kofferraum
border [ˈbɔ:də] Grenze, Grenzland
bored [bɔ:d] gelangweilt; **boredom** [ˈbɔ:dəm] Langeweile; **boring** langweilig
born [bɔ:n]: **be born** geboren sein/werden
°**borough** [ˈbʌrə] Stadtbezirk, Stadtteil
borrow [ˈbɒrəʊ] sich (aus)leihen, entleihen
boss [bɒs] Chef/in, Boß
both [bəʊθ] beide, beides; **both ... and** sowohl ... als auch
bottle [ˈbɒtl] Flasche
bottom [ˈbɒtəm] Boden, Fußende, unteres Ende; **from top to bottom** von oben bis/ nach unten
bowl [bəʊl] Schüssel, Schale
box [bɒks] Kiste, Schachtel
Boxing Day [ˈbɒksɪŋ deɪ] (BE) der zweite Weihnachtsfeiertag
boy [bɔɪ] Junge; **boyfriend** [ˈbɔɪfrend] Freund *(eines Mädchens)*
bracket [ˈbrækɪt] Klammer
°**brain** [breɪn] Gehirn
brake [breɪk] **1.** Bremse; **2.** bremsen
branch [brɑ:ntʃ] Ast, Zweig; Zweigstelle
brave [breɪv] tapfer, mutig
bread [bred] Brot
break [breɪk] **1.** Pause; **2.** (zer)brechen; kaputtmachen, kaputtgehen; **break away (from)** sich losreißen (von); °**break down** eine Panne haben; **break into** einbrechen; **break off** abbrechen; **break open** aufbrechen
breakfast [ˈbrekfəst] Frühstück; **for breakfast** zum Frühstück; **have breakfast** frühstücken
breathe (in/out) [bri:ð] (ein-/aus)atmen
°**brick** [brɪk] Backstein, Ziegelstein
bridge [brɪdʒ] Brücke
bright [braɪt] hell, leuchtend
brilliant [ˈbrɪljənt] toll, erstklassig
bring [brɪŋ] (mit-, her)bringen; **bring along** mitbringen
Britain [ˈbrɪtn] Großbritannien; **British** britisch; **the British** die Briten; **Briton** [ˈbrɪtn] Brite/Britin
broad [brɔ:d] breit; weit, ausgedehnt; **broaden** (sich) erweitern, verbreitern
broke [brəʊk] (infml.): **be broke** pleite sein; **go broke** pleite machen/gehen
broken [ˈbrəʊkən] kaputt; zerbrochen, gebrochen
brother [ˈbrʌðə] Bruder; °**brotherhood** [ˈbrʌðəhʊd] Brüderlichkeit
brown [braʊn] braun
brush [brʌʃ] **1.** Bürste; Pinsel; **2.** bürsten
°**brutal** [ˈbru:tl] brutal, gewalttätig
budgie [ˈbʌdʒɪ] (BE) Wellensittich
build [bɪld] (er)bauen; **builder** Baumeister; **building** Gebäude
bulb [bʌlb]: **(light) bulb** Glühbirne, Glühlampe
bull [bʊl] Bulle, Stier
bullet [ˈbʊlɪt] Geschoß, Kugel
bully [ˈbʊlɪ] schikanieren, drangsalieren
bun [bʌn] süßes Brötchen
burn [bɜ:n] (ver)brennen
bus [bʌs] Bus; **bus stop** Bushaltestelle; **by bus** mit dem Bus
bush [bʊʃ] Busch
business [ˈbɪznɪs] Geschäft(e), Unternehmen
busy [ˈbɪzɪ] **1.** beschäftigt; **2.** belebt, mit starkem Verkehr, hektisch
but [bʌt, bət] **1.** aber, sondern; **not only ... but also** nicht nur ..., sondern auch; **2.** *(nichts, nirgends)* als, außer
butcher [ˈbʊtʃə] Fleischer/in, Metzger/in
butter [ˈbʌtə] Butter
buy [baɪ] kaufen
by [baɪ] **1.** von; durch; **2.** (nahe) bei; an, neben; **3.** (spätestens) bis, bis (zu); **by air mail** mit/per Luftpost; **by the time** *(conj.)* wenn, bis; **by the way** übrigens, nebenbei (bemerkt); **go by** vergehen, vorübergehen; **go by bike** mit dem Rad fahren; **two by two** zu zweit, paarweise
Bye. [baɪ] Wiedersehen! Tschüs!

C

c. = circa [ˈsɜ:kə] ca. = circa
cab [kæb] Taxi
cable car [ˈkeɪbl] Seilbahn; *(mit Kabel gezogene)* Straßenbahn
café [ˈkæfeɪ] Café; kleines Restaurant; **cafeteria** [ˌkæfəˈtɪərɪə] Restaurant mit Selbstbedienung, Cafeteria
cage [keɪdʒ] Käfig
cake [keɪk] Kuchen
calculator [ˈkælkjʊleɪtə] Taschenrechner
calendar [ˈkælɪndə] Kalender
call [kɔ:l] **1.** (An-)Ruf, Telefongespräch; **2.** nennen; **What do you call ...?** Wie nennt man ...? **be called** heißen; **3.** (an)rufen
calm [kɑ:m] ruhig, still; **calm down** (sich) beruhigen
camel [ˈkæml] Kamel
camera [ˈkæmrə] Fotoapparat, Kamera
camp [kæmp] **1.** Lager; **2.** zelten, campen; **camp site** Campingplatz, Zeltplatz; **camping** Camping, Zelten; Zelt-
can [kæn] Dose, Büchse
can [kæn, kən] kann, darf; **can't** [kɑ:nt] = **cannot** [ˈkænɒt] kann nicht
Canada [ˈkænədə] Kanada; **Canadian** [kəˈneɪdɪən] **1.** Kanadier/in; **2.** kanadisch
canal [kəˈnæl] Kanal
canister [ˈkænɪstə] Kanister, Blechdose
canoe [kəˈnu:] **1.** Paddelboot; Kanu; **2.** Kanu fahren, paddeln
canteen [kænˈti:n] Kantine, Schulmensa
capital [ˈkæpɪtl] Hauptstadt; **capital (letter)** Großbuchstabe
captain [ˈkæptɪn] Kapitän; Mannschaftskapitän
car [kɑ:] Auto, Wagen; **by car** mit dem Auto; **car park** (BE) (großer) Parkplatz; Parkhaus
caravan [ˈkærəvæn] (BE) Wohnwagen
card [kɑ:d] (Spiel-, Post-)Karte
care [keə] **1.** Sorgfalt; **2. care (about)** sich kümmern (um), wichtig nehmen; **I don't care.** (infml.) Das ist mir egal. **careful** vorsichtig; sorgfältig; **careless** sorglos, nachlässig, unbekümmert
carol [ˈkærəl]: **(Christmas) carol** Weihnachtslied
carpet [ˈkɑ:pɪt] Teppich
carriage [ˈkærɪdʒ] Wagen, Waggon
carrot [ˈkærət] Karotte, Möhre
carry [ˈkærɪ] tragen; befördern; **carry on** weitermachen, fortfahren
case [keɪs] **1.** Fall; **2.** Kiste; Koffer; Behälter
cassette [kəˈset] Cassette; **cassette-recorder** [kəˈset rɪˌkɔ:də] Cassettenrecorder
castle [ˈkɑ:sl] Burg, Schloß
cat [kæt] Katze
catalogue [ˈkætəlɒg] Katalog
catch [kætʃ] fangen, erwischen; **catch a bus** einen Bus erreichen, nehmen
cathedral [kəˈθi:drəl] Kathedrale, Dom
Catholic [ˈkæθlɪk]: **(Roman)Catholic** **1.** Katholik/in; **2.** (römisch-)katholisch
cattle *(pl.)* [ˈkætl] (Rind-)Vieh
cause [kɔ:z] **1.** Ursache; **2.** verursachen
°**causeway** [ˈkɔ:zweɪ] Damm
cave [keɪv] Höhle
ceiling [ˈsi:lɪŋ] Zimmerdecke
celebrate [ˈselɪbreɪt] feiern; **celebration** [ˌselɪˈbreɪʃn] Feier
cellar [ˈselə] Keller
Celtic [ˈkeltɪk] **1.** keltisch; **2.** das Keltische; **the Celts** [kelts] die Kelten
cent [sent] Cent *(US Währung)*
centimetre [ˈsentɪˌmi:tə] Zentimeter
central [ˈsentrəl] Zentral-, Mittel-
centre [ˈsentə] Zentrum, *(Stadt-)*Mitte; **Information Centre** Auskunft, Verkehrsbüro
century [ˈsentʃərɪ] Jahrhundert; **a sixteenth-century house** ein Haus aus dem 16. Jahrhundert
ceremony [ˈserɪmənɪ] Zeremonie; Feier (-lichkeit)
certain [ˈsɜ:tn] sicher, gewiß, bestimmt
chair [tʃeə] Stuhl
chalk [tʃɔ:k] Kreide
chance [tʃɑ:ns] Gelegenheit, Chance; **take a chance** ein Risiko eingehen; es darauf ankommen lassen
change [tʃeɪndʒ] **1.** (Ver-)Änderung, Wechsel, Umstellung; **(small) change** Wechselgeld; Kleingeld; **2.** (sich) verändern, umwandeln; (aus-) wechseln; **3.** umsteigen
Channel [ˈtʃænl] Ärmelkanal
character [ˈkærəktə] Character, Person; **characteristic** [ˌkærəktəˈrɪstɪk] Merkmal
charter flight [ˈtʃɑ:tə flaɪt] Charterflug
cheap [tʃi:p] billig
cheat (sb. of sth.) [tʃi:t] mogeln; (jn. um etwas) betrügen

check [tʃek] 1. Kontrolle, Überprüfung, Nachprüfung; 2. (über)prüfen, kontrollieren
cheer [tʃɪə] anfeuern, Beifall spenden; **Cheer up!** Kopf hoch! Sei nicht traurig! **cheering** Beifall
cheese [tʃi:z] Käse
chemist ['kemɪst] (BE) Apotheker/in; **chemistry** ['kemɪstrɪ] Chemie
cheque [tʃek] (Bank-)Scheck
chess [tʃes] Schach
chewing gum ['tʃu:ɪŋ gʌm] Kaugummi
chicken ['tʃɪkɪn] Huhn; (Brat-)Hähnchen
chief [tʃi:f] Oberhaupt; Häuptling
child, *pl.* **children** [tʃaɪld, 'tʃɪldrən] Kind; °**childhood** ['tʃaɪldhʊd] Kindheit
chimney ['tʃɪmnɪ] Schornstein, Kamin
chimp [tʃɪmp] Schimpanse
°**chin** [tʃɪn] Kinn
chips [tʃɪps] (BE) Pommes frites
chocolate ['tʃɒklət] Schokolade
choice (of) [tʃɔɪs] (Aus-)Wahl (an)
choir ['kwaɪə] Chor
choose [tʃu:z] (aus)wählen, aussuchen
Christ [kraɪst] Christus; **Christian** ['krɪstʃən] 1. Christ/in; 2. christlich; **Christian name** Vor-, Rufname
Christmas ['krɪsməs] Weihnachten, das Weihnachtsfest; **Christmas Day** der erste Weihnachtsfeiertag; **Christmas Eve** Heiligabend
church [tʃɜ:tʃ] Kirche; **go to church** in die Kirche gehen
cigarette [ˌsɪgə'ret] Zigarette
cinema ['sɪnəmə] (BE) Kino
circle ['sɜ:kl] Kreis
citizen ['sɪtɪzn] Staatsbürger/in, Staatsangehörige(r)
city ['sɪtɪ] Stadt, Großstadt
civil rights [ˌsɪvl 'raɪts] Bürgerrechte; **civil war** [ˌsɪvl 'wɔ:] Bürgerkrieg
civilized ['sɪvəlaɪzd] zivilisiert
claim [kleɪm] 1. behaupten; 2. fordern, Anspruch erheben auf; **claim (for, on)** 1. Behauptung; 2. Anspruch (auf), Forderung (nach)
class [klɑ:s] Klasse; **classmate** ['klɑ:smeɪt] Klassenkamerad/in, Mitschüler/in
clean [kli:n] 1. sauber; 2. putzen, reinigen
clear [klɪə] klar, deutlich; **clear (of)** frei (von)
clerk [klɑ:k] Schalterbeamte(r)/-in
clever ['klevə] klug, schlau; **cleverness** ['klevənəs] Klugheit
cliché ['kli:ʃeɪ] Klischee
climate ['klaɪmɪt] Klima
climax ['klaɪmæks] Höhepunkt
climb [klaɪm] klettern, steigen; **climber** ['klaɪmə] Bergsteiger/in
clock [klɒk] *(Wand-, Stand-, Turm-)*Uhr; **o'clock** [ə'klɒk] ... Uhr
close [kləʊz] 1. schließen, zumachen; **close down** *(eine Fabrik usw.)* zumachen, schließen; **closed** geschlossen, zu; 2. **close (to)** [kləʊs] nahe (bei, an); eng; genau, gründlich
cloth [klɒθ] Stoff; Tuch, Lappen
clothes *(pl.)* [kləʊðz] Kleidung(sstücke)
cloud [klaʊd] Wolke; **cloudy** ['klaʊdɪ] bewölkt, wolkig
club [klʌb] Verein, Klub
clue (to) [klu:] Anhaltspunkt (für), Hinweis (auf)
coach [kəʊtʃ] 1. Trainer/in; 2. (BE) Reisebus; **by coach** (BE) mit dem Reisebus
coal [kəʊl] Kohle
coast [kəʊst] Küste; **on the coast** an der Küste; **coastline** ['kəʊstlaɪn] Küstenlinie
coat [kəʊt] Mantel, Jacke
cocoa ['kəʊkəʊ] Kakao
coffee ['kɒfɪ] Kaffee
coin [kɔɪn] Münze
coke [kəʊk] Cola
cold [kəʊld] 1. kalt; 2. Kälte; Unterkühlung; 3. Schnupfen; **a bad cold** ein starker Schnupfen; **have a cold** Schnupfen haben, erkältet sein
colleague ['kɒli:g] Kollege/-in
collect [kə'lekt] 1. (ein)sammeln; 2. abholen
college ['kɒlɪdʒ] Hochschule
collocation [ˌkɒlə'keɪʃn] Kollokation
colon ['kəʊlən] Doppelpunkt
colony ['kɒlənɪ] Kolonie; **colonist** ['kɒlənɪst] Kolonist/in, Siedler/in
colour ['kʌlə] Farbe; **What colour is/are ...?** Welche Farbe hat/haben ...? **coloured** ['kʌləd] farbig; bunt; **colourful** farbenprächtig, bunt
comb [kəʊm] 1. Kamm; 2. kämmen
combination [ˌkɒmbɪ'neɪʃn] Kombination, Zusammenstellung; **combination exercise** Kombinationsübung, Zuordnungsübung; **combine (with)** [kəm'baɪn] (sich) verbinden (mit), kombinieren (mit)
come [kʌm] kommen, mitkommen; **come and see** besuchen kommen; **Come here.** Komm(t) her! **Come on.** Na, komm! Los, komm! **come over** vorbeikommen *(Besucher)*; **come out** herauskommen, hinauskommen
comfortable ['kʌmftəbl] bequem, gemütlich
comic ['kɒmɪk] Comic-Heft
comma ['kɒmə] Komma
°**command** [kə'mɑ:nd] Befehl
comment (about, on) ['kɒment] Kommentar, Bemerkung (über, zu); **comment (on)** kommentieren, sich (kritisch) äußern (zu)
commit [kə'mɪt] *(ein Verbrechen, Selbstmord)* begehen, verüben
common ['kɒmən] gemeinsam, gemeinschaftlich; üblich, normal; **have sth. in common** etwas miteinander gemein haben
communicate (with) [kə'mju:nɪkeɪt] kommunizieren (mit), sich verständigen (mit); **communications** *(pl.)* [kəˌmju:nɪ'keɪʃnz] Nachrichtentechnik, Telekommunikation
community [kə'mju:nətɪ] *(politische)* Gemeinde, Kommune; Gemeinschaft
commute [kə'mju:t] pendeln *(zwischen Wohnung und Arbeitsplatz)*; **commuter** Pendler/in
company ['kʌmpənɪ] Gesellschaft; Firma; Begleitung
compare (with/to) [kəm'peə] vergleichen (mit); **comparison** [kəm'pærɪsn] Vergleich; **make comparisons** Vergleiche machen, vergleichen
compete [kəm'pi:t] konkurrieren, wetteifern, kämpfen; **competition** [ˌkɒmpə'tɪʃn] 1. Wettbewerb, Wettkampf; 2. Konkurrenz
complain [kəm'pleɪn] sich beschweren, sich beklagen
complete [kəm'pli:t] 1. fertigstellen, abschließen; vervollständigen; ergänzen; 2. *(Formular)* ausfüllen; 3. vollständig, völlig
compliment ['kɒmplɪment] ein Kompliment machen, beglückwünschen
compound (word) ['kɒmpaʊnd] Kompositum, zusammengesetztes Wort
comprehensive school [ˌkɒmprɪ'hensɪv sku:l] (BE) Gesamtschule
computer [kəm'pju:tə] Computer; **computer studies** [kəmˌpju:tə 'stʌdɪz] Informatik
concentrate (on) ['kɒnsntreɪt] sich konzentrieren (auf); **concentration** [ˌkɒnsn'treɪʃn] Konzentration
concern [kən'sɜ:n] 1. Angelegenheit, Belang, Sache; 2. betreffen, angehen; **be concerned about** sich Sorgen machen um, sich Gedanken machen über
concert ['kɒnsət] Konzert
conditions [kən'dɪʃnz] Verhältnisse, Umstände; Bedingungen
conference ['kɒnfrəns] Konferenz, Besprechung
confident ['kɒnfɪdənt] (selbst)sicher, selbstbewußt, zuversichtlich
confinement [kən'faɪnmənt] Eingesperrtsein, Gefangenschaft; Arrest, Haft
conflict ['kɒnflɪkt] Konflikt, Auseinandersetzung
confuse [kən'fju:z] verwirren, durcheinanderbringen; °**confusion** [kən'fju:ʒn] Durcheinander
Congratulations. [kənˌgrætʃʊ'leɪʃnz] Herzlichen Glückwunsch! Gratuliere!
connection [kə'nekʃn] Verbindung, Zusammenhang; Anschluß
conquer ['kɒŋkə] erobern, besiegen
conservative, Conservative [kən'sɜ:vətɪv] 1. konservativ; 2. Konservative(r)
°**consider** [kən'sɪdə] überlegen
consist of [kən'sɪst] bestehen aus
consonant ['kɒnsənənt] Konsonant, Mitlaut
construct [kən'strʌkt] bauen, konstruieren
contact ['kɒntækt] Kontakt, Verbindung
container [kən'teɪnə] Behälter; Gefäß
°**content** ['kɒntent] Inhalt
context ['kɒntekst] Zusammenhang, Kontext
continent ['kɒntɪnənt] Kontinent, Erdteil; **the Continent** das europäische Festland
continue [kən'tɪnju:] fortsetzen, fortfahren (mit), weiter(hin) (tun); andauern
contrast 1. ['kɒntrɑ:st] Gegensatz, Kontrast; 2. **contrast sth. (with)** [kən'trɑ:st] etwas kontrastieren (mit), etwas gegenüberstellen
control [kən'trəʊl] 1. Kontrolle; (Selbst-)Beherrschung; Aufsicht; 2. beherrschen; die Kontrolle haben über; steuern
conversation [ˌkɒnvə'seɪʃn] Gespräch, Unterhaltung
convince [kən'vɪns] überzeugen
cook [kʊk] 1. Koch, Köchin; 2. kochen, zubereiten; **cooker** (BE) Herd
cool [ku:l] kühl
co-operate [kəʊ'ɒpəreɪt] zusammenarbeiten, kooperieren
copy ['kɒpɪ] abschreiben; kopieren
corn [kɔ:n] AE: Mais; BE: Korn, Getreide
corner ['kɔ:nə] Ecke
cornflakes ['kɔ:nfleɪks] Cornflakes
Cornish ['kɔ:nɪʃ] 1. kornisch, aus Cornwall; 2. die kornische Sprache; **Cornishman/Cornishwoman** Einwohner/in von Cornwall
correct [kə'rekt] 1. richtig, korrekt; 2. berichtigen, verbessern, korrigieren
correspond (to) [ˌkɒrɪ'spɒnd] entsprechen
cost [kɒst] 1. Kosten; Preis; 2. kosten
costume ['kɒstju:m]: **swimming costume** (BE) Badebekleidung, Badeanzug
cottage ['kɒtɪdʒ] (kleines) Landhaus, Häuschen
cotton ['kɒtn] Baumwolle
cough [kɒf] Husten
could [kʊd] konnte(n); könnte(n)
council ['kaʊnsl]: **(town/city) council** Stadtrat *(Gremium)*
count [kaʊnt] zählen

country [ˈkʌntrɪ] Land, Staat; **in the country** auf dem Land; **countryside** (ländliche) Gegend, Landschaft
county [ˈkaʊntɪ] Grafschaft, Verwaltungsbezirk
couple [ˈkʌpl] Paar; Ehepaar; **a couple of** (infml.) ein paar, einige
course [kɔ:s] Kurs, Lehrgang; **in the course of...** im Lauf...; **of course** natürlich
court [kɔ:t] **1.** (königlicher) Hof; **2.** Spielfeld, Platz; **3.** Gericht(shof), Gerichtssaal; **take sb. to court** jn. verklagen, vor Gericht bringen
cousin [ˈkʌzn] Vetter, Kusine
cover [ˈkʌvə] bedecken, zudecken
cow [kaʊ] Kuh; **cowboy** [ˈkaʊbɔɪ] Cowboy; **cowshed** [ˈkaʊʃed] Kuhstall
crane [kreɪn] Kran
crash [kræʃ] **1.** Zusammenstoß, Absturz; **2. crash (into)** [kræʃ] zusammenstoßen (mit), hineinfahren (in); verunglücken; abstürzen
crazy [ˈkreɪzɪ] verrückt, wahnsinnig; **be crazy about** ganz verrückt sein auf
cream [kri:m] **1.** Creme; **2.** Sahne
create [kri:ˈeɪt] (er)schaffen
cricket [ˈkrɪkɪt] Kricket
crime [kraɪm] Verbrechen; **criminal** [ˈkrɪmɪnl] Verbrecher/in, Kriminelle(r)
crisis, *pl.* **crises** [ˈkraɪsɪs, ˈkraɪsi:z] Krise
crisps [krɪsps] (BE) Kartoffelchips
cross [krɒs] überqueren, kreuzen; **crossing** Überfahrt, Übergang; **(a) crossroads** [ˈkrɒsrəʊdz] (BE) eine Kreuzung; **pedestrian crossing** [pɪˌdestrɪən ˈkrɒsɪŋ] Fußgängerüberweg
crowd [kraʊd] (Menschen-)Menge; **crowded** überfüllt, voll(gestopft)
crown [kraʊn] Krone
cruel [ˈkru:əl] grausam; °**cruelty** [ˈkrʊəltɪ] Grausamkeit
cry [kraɪ] **1.** weinen; **2.** schreien
cultural [ˈkʌltʃərəl] kulturell, Kultur-; **culture** [ˈkʌltʃə] Kultur
cup [kʌp] Tasse
cupboard [ˈkʌbəd] Schrank
curious (about) [ˈkjʊərɪəs] neugierig, gespannt (auf); wißbegierig
currency [ˈkʌrənsɪ] Währung
curtain [ˈkɜ:tn] Vorhang, Gardine
custom [ˈkʌstəm] Brauch, Sitte, Gewohnheit
customer [ˈkʌstəmə] Kunde, Kundin
cut [kʌt] (ab)schneiden
cycle [ˈsaɪkl] radfahren

D

dad(dy) [dæd] Vati, Papa, Papi
daily [ˈdeɪlɪ] täglich
damage [ˈdæmɪdʒ] **1.** Schaden, Beschädigung; **2.** beschädigen
dance [dɑ:ns] **1.** Tanz, Ball; **2.** tanzen
danger [ˈdeɪndʒə] Gefahr; **dangerous** [ˈdeɪndʒərəs] gefährlich
dark [dɑ:k] dunkel, finster; **darkness** [ˈdɑ:knɪs] Dunkelheit
dart [dɑ:t] (Wurf-)Pfeil; **dartboard** [ˈdɑ:tbɔ:d] Dartscheibe, Zielscheibe; **darts** *brit. Pfeilwurfspiel*
dash [dæʃ] Gedankenstrich
date [deɪt] **1.** Datum; **What date is it (today)?** Der Wievielte ist heute? **up to date** aktuell, modern, auf dem neuesten Stand; **keep up to date (with)** (sich) auf dem laufenden/auf dem neuesten Stand halten (über); **2.** Verabredung, Rendezvous
daughter [ˈdɔ:tə] Tochter
day [deɪ] Tag; **the day after tomorrow** übermorgen; **the day before yesterday** vorgestern; **in those days** damals
dead [ded] tot
deaf [def] gehörlos; schwerhörig
deal [di:l] **1.** Geschäft, Handel; Abkommen; °**2. deal with** handeln von
dear [dɪə] liebe, lieber, liebes; **Dear Sir or Madam,** Sehr geehrte Damen und Herren, **Oh dear.** Oh je! Das darf doch nicht wahr sein!
death [deθ] Tod; Todesfall
December [dɪˈsembə] Dezember
decide [dɪˈsaɪd] beschließen, (sich) entscheiden
decision [dɪˈsɪʒn] Entscheidung, Entschluß; **make a decision** eine Entscheidung treffen
deck [dek] Deck; **on deck** auf, an Deck
decoration [ˌdekəˈreɪʃn] Schmuck, Dekoration
deed [di:d] (fml.) Tat
deep [di:p] tief
deer [dɪə] Hirsch, Reh
defeat (of; by) [dɪˈfi:t] **1.** Sieg (über); Niederlage (durch); **2. defeat** besiegen, schlagen
defence [dɪˈfens] Verteidigung
defend [dɪˈfend] verteidigen
°**definitely** [ˈdefɪnətlɪ] eindeutig
degree [dɪˈgri:] Grad
delicious [dɪˈlɪʃəs] köstlich, herrlich
°**delighted** [dɪˈlaɪtɪd] hocherfreut
democracy [dɪˈmɒkrəsɪ] Demokratie
°**dentist** [ˈdentɪst] Zahnarzt/-ärztin
depart (from) [dɪˈpɑ:t] abfahren, abreisen (von); **departure** [dɪˈpɑ:tʃə] Abfahrt, Abreise
department [dɪˈpɑ:tmənt] Dienststelle, Amt; Ministerium; **department store** Kaufhaus, Warenhaus
depend on [dɪˈpend] **1.** abhängig sein von, abhängen von; **2.** sich verlassen auf
descendant [dɪˈsendənt] Nachkomme
describe [dɪˈskraɪb] beschreiben
desert [ˈdezət] Wüste
design [dɪˈzaɪn] **1.** Produktgestaltung, Design, Konstruktion(slehre); Entwurf, Skizze; **2.** entwerfen, konstruieren; **designer** Konstrukteur/in, Gestalter/in, Designer/in
desk [desk] Schreibtisch, Schülertisch
dessert [dɪˈzɜ:t] Nachtisch, Dessert; **for dessert** zum Nachtisch
destroy [dɪˈstrɔɪ] zerstören, vernichten
detached house [dɪˌtætʃt ˈhaʊs] freistehendes Haus
detail [ˈdi:teɪl] Detail, Einzelheit
develop [dɪˈveləp] (sich) entwickeln; **development** [dɪˈveləpmənt] Entwicklung; Erschließung; Verlauf
dial [ˈdaɪəl] wählen *(beim Telefon)*
dialect [ˈdaɪəlekt] Dialekt, Mundart
dialogue [ˈdaɪəlɒg] Dialog
diary [ˈdaɪərɪ] Tagebuch; Taschenkalender, Notizbuch
dictionary [ˈdɪkʃənrɪ] Wörterbuch
die (of) [daɪ] sterben (an); **die out** aussterben; **be dying for sth.** etwas unbedingt haben wollen/brauchen; **be dying to do sth.** etwas unbedingt tun wollen
diesel [ˈdi:zl] Diesel, Dieselöl
difference [ˈdɪfrəns] Unterschied; **different (from)** **1.** verschieden, unterschiedlich; **2.** anders (als)
difficult [ˈdɪfɪkəlt] schwierig, schwer; **difficulty** Schwierigkeit
dig [dɪg] graben
dime [daɪm] (AE) 10¢-Münze
dining-room [ˈdaɪnɪŋ rʊm] Eßzimmer
dinner [ˈdɪnə] (Festtags-, Mittag-, Abend-) Essen
direct [dɪˈrekt, daɪˈrekt] direkt, unmittelbar
direction [dɪˈrekʃn, daɪˈrekʃn] Richtung; °**ask for directions** nach dem Weg fragen; °**give directions** den Weg erklären
dirt [dɜ:t] Schmutz; **dirty** schmutzig, dreckig
disabled [dɪsˈeɪbld] (körper)behindert
disadvantage [ˌdɪsədˈvɑ:ntɪdʒ] Nachteil
disagree (with) [ˌdɪsəˈgri:] nicht übereinstimmen (mit), anderer Meinung sein (als)
°**disappear** [ˌdɪsəˈpɪə] verschwinden
disappointed [ˌdɪsəˈpɔɪntɪd] enttäuscht
disaster [dɪˈzɑ:stə] Katastrophe; Desaster, Fiasko
disc jockey [ˈdɪsk ˌdʒɒkɪ] Diskjockey
discipline [ˈdɪsɪplɪn] Disziplin
disco [ˈdɪskəʊ] Disco
discourage sb. (from doing sth.) [dɪˈskʌrɪdʒ] jn. entmutigen; jn. (davon) abhalten/abbringen (, etwas zu tun)
discover [dɪˈskʌvə] entdecken; feststellen; **discovery** [dɪˈskʌvərɪ] Entdeckung
discriminate against [dɪˈskrɪmɪneɪt] diskriminieren, benachteiligen; **discrimination (against)** [ˌdɪskrɪmɪˈneɪʃn] Diskriminierung (von)
discuss [dɪˈskʌs] besprechen, diskutieren über; **discussion** [dɪˈskʌʃn] Diskussion, Besprechung
dishes *(pl.)* [ˈdɪʃɪz] Geschirr
disk [dɪsk] Diskette, Floppy; **(disk) drive** [ˈdɪsk draɪv] (Disketten-)Laufwerk
dislike [dɪsˈlaɪk] nicht mögen, nicht leiden können
display: wall display [ˈwɔ:l dɪˌspleɪ] Wandzeitung, Schaubild
dissatisfied (with) [dɪˈsætɪsfaɪd] unzufrieden (mit)
distance [ˈdɪstəns] Entfernung; Ferne
distribute (sth. to sb.) [dɪˈstrɪbju:t] verteilen; (etwas) austeilen (an jn.)
district [ˈdɪstrɪkt] Gebiet, Bezirk
disturb [dɪˈstɜ:b] stören
diver [ˈdaɪvə] Taucher/in
divide (into) [dɪˈvaɪd] (auf)teilen (in)
divorced [dɪˈvɔ:st] geschieden
DIY [ˌdi:ˌaɪ ˈwaɪ] = **Do-It-Yourself** Heimwerken
do [du:] tun, machen; **do 50 metres** 50 Meter schaffen; **do well** gut sein *(in einem Fach)*; **do without (sth.)** ohne (etwas) auskommen, verzichten (auf etwas)
doctor [ˈdɒktə] Arzt, Ärztin
document [ˈdɒkjʊmənt] Dokument, Urkunde; **documentary** [ˌdɒkjʊˈmentərɪ] Dokumentarfilm, Filmbericht
dog [dɒg] Hund
dollar [ˈdɒlə] Dollar
dominate [ˈdɒmɪneɪt] beherrschen
°**doodle** [ˈdu:dl] Männchen malen
door [dɔ:] Tür
dot [dɒt] Punkt, Pünktchen
double [ˈdʌbl] doppelt; Doppel-
°**doubt** [daʊt] be-, anzweifeln
down [daʊn] herunter, hinunter; herab, hinab; **down there** dort unten; **down under** *umgangssprachliche Bezeichnung für Australien;* **pull down** ab-, niederreißen; **sit down** sich setzen; **write down** aufschreiben; **downstairs** unten; nach unten; **downtown** (AE) in der/die Innenstadt, im/ins Zentrum; **down-wind** *(adv.)* mit dem Wind, in Windrichtung
Dr = Doctor [ˈdɒktə] Dr. = Doktor
dragon [ˈdrægən] Drache
drama [ˈdrɑ:mə] Drama, Schauspiel

draw [drɔː] 1. zeichnen; 2. ziehen
dream [driːm] 1. Traum; 2. träumen; **dreamer** Träumer/in
dress [dres] Kleid; **dress (as)** sich verkleiden (als); sich anziehen; **get dressed** sich anziehen
drink [drɪŋk] 1. Getränk; 2. trinken
drive [draɪv] 1. (Auto-)Fahrt; 2. (Auto) fahren; 3. (an)treiben; **drive sb. mad** jn. wahnsinnig, verrückt machen; **driver** 1. (Auto-)Fahrer/in; 2. Lokführer/in; **driver's license** (AE)/**driving licence** (BE) ['laɪsəns] Führerschein; **petrol-driven** mit Benzin betrieben
drop [drɒp] fallen lassen; fallen; **drop out (of school)** (die Schule) abbrechen, vorzeitig verlassen
drown [draʊn] ertrinken, ertränken
dry [draɪ] 1. trocken; 2. (ab)trocknen
during ['djʊərɪŋ] während
dust [dʌst] Staub; **dusty** staubig
Dutch [dʌtʃ] holländisch; **the Dutch** die Holländer; **Dutchman/-woman** Holländer/in

E

each [iːtʃ] jeder, jede, jedes (einzelne); **each other** einander, sich (gegenseitig)
ear [ɪə] Ohr
early ['ɜːlɪ] früh, (früh)zeitig; **be early** zu früh kommen
earn [ɜːn] verdienen
earth [ɜːθ] Erde; **(earth)quake** ['ɜːθkweɪk] (Erd-)Beben
east (of) [iːst] 1. östlich (von); 2. Ost-; (nach) Osten
Easter ['iːstə] Ostern, Oster-; **at Easter** zu Ostern
easy ['iːzɪ] leicht, einfach; **easygoing** gelassen, unbeschwert
eat [iːt] essen; **eat out** essen gehen
EC [ˌiː 'siː] = **European Community** Europäische Gemeinschaft
economic(ally) [ˌiːkə'nɒmɪk, -lɪ] (volks)wirtschaftlich; Wirtschafts-; **economy** [ɪ'kɒnəmɪ] Wirtschaft
edge [edʒ] Rand, Kante
edible ['edɪbl] eßbar, genießbar
education [ˌedjʊ'keɪʃn, ˌedʒʊ'keɪʃn] (Aus-)Bildung; Erziehung; **physical education** Turnen, Sport; **religious education** Religion(sunterricht)
effect [ɪ'fekt] (Aus-)Wirkung
e.g. [ˌiː 'dʒiː] z.B. (= zum Beispiel)
egg [eg] Ei
either ... or ['aɪðə, 'iːðə] entweder ... oder; **(not ...) either** auch nicht, auch kein
°**elect sb.** [ɪ'lekt] jn. wählen; **election** [ɪ'lekʃn] *(politische)* Wahl
electric [ɪ'lektrɪk] elektrisch; **electricity** [ˌɪlek'trɪsətɪ] Strom; Elektrizität
electronic [ˌɪlek'trɒnɪk] elektronisch; **electronics** *(sing.)* [ˌɪlek'trɒnɪks] Elektronik; Elektronik-
elephant ['elɪfənt] Elefant
else [els] sonst noch; anderes; **Anything else?** Sonst noch etwas?
emigrate ['emɪgreɪt] auswandern, emigrieren; **emigration** [ˌemɪ'greɪʃn] Auswanderung
emphasize ['emfəsaɪz] betonen, hervorheben
empire ['empaɪə] Reich, Weltreich, Imperium
employ [ɪm'plɔɪ] beschäftigen, anstellen; **employee** [ɪm'plɔiiː, ˌemplɔɪ'iː] Arbeitnehmer/in, Angestellte(r); **employer** Arbeitgeber/in; **employment** Beschäftigung; Arbeit; **self-employed** [ˌselfɪm'plɔɪd, '---] selbständig *(Geschäftsleute)*
empty ['emptɪ] 1. (sich) (ent)leeren; 2. leer; **emptiness** Leere
°**emu** ['iːmjuː] Emu *(straußenähnlicher Laufvogel)*
encourage [ɪn'kʌrɪdʒ] ermutigen, ermuntern; fördern
encyclopedia [ɪnˌsaɪklə'piːdɪə] Lexikon, Enzyklopädie
end [end] 1. Ende, Schluß; **come to an end** zu Ende gehen, ein Ende nehmen; **at the end** am Ende, am Schluß; **in the end** schließlich, am Ende, zum Schluß; 2. **end (in)** enden (auf, mit); beenden; **ending** Ende, (Ab-)Schluß; Endung; **endless** ['endləs] endlos
enemy ['enəmɪ] Feind
energy ['enədʒɪ] Energie
engine ['endʒɪn] Motor, Maschine
engineer [ˌendʒɪ'nɪə] Ingenieur/in, Techniker/in; **engineering** [ˌendʒɪ'nɪərɪŋ] Maschinenbau
England ['ɪŋglənd] England; **English** englisch; **the English** die Engländer; **Englishman/Englishwoman** Engländer/in
enjoy [ɪn'dʒɔɪ] genießen, Spaß haben an, gern haben/tun; **enjoy oneself** viel Spaß haben, sich amüsieren; **enjoyable** [ɪn'dʒɔɪəbl] nett; unterhaltsam
enough [ɪ'nʌf] genug
enter ['entə] betreten, einreisen in
entertainment [ˌentə'teɪnmənt] Unterhaltung, Belustigung
enthusiastic (about) [ɪnˌθjuːzɪ'æstɪk] begeistert (von, über)
entrance (to) ['entrəns] Eingang (zu); Eintritts-; **entrance exam** ['entrəns‿ɪgˌzæm] Aufnahmeprüfung
entry ['entrɪ] 1. Eintrag, Eintragung *(in Wörter-, Tagebuch)*; 2. Einsendung
°**entwine** [ɪn'twaɪn] (sich) ineinanderschlingen, (sich) verflechten
envelope ['envələʊp] Briefumschlag
environment [ɪn'vaɪrənmənt] Umwelt, Umgebung
equal ['iːkwəl] gleich; **equally** gleichmäßig; gleichermaßen; **equality** [ɪ'kwɒlətɪ] Gleichheit
escape [ɪ'skeɪp] 1. Flucht; Entkommen; 2. entkommen, entgehen; fliehen
especially [ɪ'speʃlɪ] besonders; insbesondere
essay ['eseɪ] Aufsatz, Essay
essential [ɪ'senʃl] unerläßlich; wesentlich
estimate ['estɪmeɪt] (ab-, ein)schätzen
etc. [ɪt'setrə] usw. (und so weiter)
ethnic ['eθnɪk] Volks-, zu einem Volk gehörig
Europe ['jʊərəp] Europa; **European** [ˌjʊərə'piːən] 1. Europäer/in; 2. europäisch
eve [iːv] Vorabend, Vortag; **New Year's Eve** Silvester(abend)
even ['iːvn] sogar, selbst; **even if** selbst wenn; **even though** obwohl; **even worse** (sogar) noch schlimmer; **not even** nicht einmal
evening ['iːvnɪŋ] Abend; **in the evening(s)** abends; **on a cold evening** an einem kalten Abend; **this evening** heute abend
event [ɪ'vent] Ereignis; **eventful** [ɪ'ventfəl] ereignisreich
ever ['evə] je(mals), schon mal; **for ever** für immer, ewig; **not ever** nie
every ['evrɪ] jeder, jede, jedes; **everybody/everyone** jeder(mann), alle; **everyday** alltäglich; Alltags-; **everything** alles; **everywhere** überall
evidence (of) *(sing.)* ['evɪdəns] Beweis(e); Beleg(e) (für)
°**exact** [ɪg'zækt] genau
exam(ination) [ɪgˌzæmɪ'neɪʃn] Prüfung, Examen
example [ɪg'zɑːmpl] Beispiel; **for example** zum Beispiel
excellent ['eksələnt] ausgezeichnet, hervorragend
except [ɪk'sept] außer, bis auf; °**exception** [ɪk'sepʃn] Ausnahme
exchange [ɪks'tʃeɪndʒ] 1. (Aus-, Um-)Tausch; (Geld-)Wechsel; 2. austauschen, umtauschen, *(Geld)* wechseln
excited (about) [ɪk'saɪtɪd] aufgeregt, freudig erregt (wegen, über); **exciting** aufregend, spannend
exclamation mark [ˌekskla'meɪʃn mɑːk] Ausrufezeichen
exclusive [ɪk'skluːsɪv] vornehm, exklusiv
excuse [ɪk'skjuːs] Entschuldigung; **Excuse me** [ɪk'skjuːz ˌmiː] Entschuldigen Sie
execute ['eksɪkjuːt] hinrichten; **execution** [ˌeksɪ'kjuːʃn] Hinrichtung, Exekution
exercise ['eksəsaɪz] Übung(saufgabe); **exercise book** Heft, Schulheft
exist [ɪg'zɪst] existieren, vorhanden sein
expect [ɪk'spekt] erwarten; annehmen, vermuten; **expectation** [ˌekspek'teɪʃn] Erwartung
expensive [ɪk'spensɪv] teuer
experience [ɪk'spɪərɪəns] 1. Erfahrung, Erlebnis; 2. erfahren, erleben
expert (at/in) ['ekspɜːt] 1. Fachmann/-frau; Experte, Expertin (für); 2. erfahren, geschickt
explain [ɪk'spleɪn] erklären, erläutern; **explanation** [ˌeksplə'neɪʃn] Erklärung
explore [ɪk'splɔː] erforschen; **explorer** Forscher/in, Forschungsreisende(r)
explosion [ɪk'spləʊʒn] Explosion
export 1. ['ekspɔːt] Ausfuhr, Export; 2. [ɪk'spɔːt] exportieren
express [ɪk'spres] äußern, ausdrücken; **expression** [ɪk'spreʃn] Ausdruck, Äußerung
extra ['ekstrə] zusätzlich, Extra-; **extra-curricular activities** [ˌekstrəkə'rɪkjʊlə] außerunterrichtliche Aktivitäten, Arbeitsgemeinschaften
extract (from) ['ekstrækt] Auszug (aus)
extreme [ɪk'striːm] äußerst, extrem; **extremist** [ɪk'striːmɪst] 1. Extremist/in; 2. extremistisch
eye [aɪ] Auge; °**an eye for an eye** Auge um Auge

F

face [feɪs] 1. Gesicht; 2. **face sb./sth.** sich jm./einer Sache gegenübersehen; jm./einer Sache ins Auge sehen; **face (east)** (nach Osten) gehen, liegen *(Zimmer usw.)*
fact [fækt] Tatsache, Information; **in fact** eigentlich, genau gesagt, tatsächlich
factor ['fæktə] Faktor
factory ['fæktərɪ] Fabrik
fail [feɪl] versagen, scheitern; **fail (an exam)** (bei einer Prüfung) durchfallen, nicht bestehen
fair [feə] 1. fair, gerecht; 2. ganz ordentlich, genügend *(Note, Leistung)*
faithfully ['feɪθfəlɪ]: **Yours faithfully** Mit freundlichen Grüßen; Hochachtungsvoll
fall [fɔːl] 1. (AE) Herbst; 2. fallen; **fall asleep** einschlafen; **fall in love (with)** sich verlieben (in); **fall off** herunterfallen; **fall over** hinfallen, umfallen
false [fɔːls] falsch, unecht
familiar [fə'mɪlɪə] bekannt, vertraut, gewohnt

family ['fæmɪlɪ] Familie
famous ['feɪməs] berühmt
fan [fæn] Fan
fancy ['fænsɪ] (BE, infml.) gern haben
fantastic [fæn'tæstɪk] phantastisch, toll
far [fɑ:] weit (entfernt); **so far** bis jetzt, bisher
fare [feə] Fahrpreis, Fahrgeld
farewell [feə'wel] Abschieds-
farm [fɑ:m] **1.** Bauernhof, Farm; **2.** *(Land)* bebauen; **farmer** Bauer, Bäuerin; Farmer/in; **farmhouse** Bauernhaus; **farming** Landwirtschaft, Ackerbau
farther ['fɑ:ðə] weiter (entfernt); **farthest** ['fɑ:ðɪst] am weitesten (entfernt)
fascinate ['fæsəneɪt] faszinieren, begeistern
fashion ['fæʃn] Mode
fast [fɑ:st] schnell; **fast food place** Schnellimbiß, Schnellrestaurant
fat [fæt] dick
°**fatal (to)** ['feɪtl] tödlich (für); verhängnisvoll, fatal (für)
father ['fɑ:ðə] Vater; **Father Christmas** [ˌfɑ:ðə 'krɪsməs] (BE) der Weihnachtsmann
fault [fɔ:lt] Schuld, Fehler
favour ['feɪvə] Gefallen; **do sb. a favour** jm. einen Gefallen tun
favourite ['feɪvrɪt] Lieblings-
fear (of) [fɪə] Furcht, Angst (vor)
feather ['feðə] Feder
February ['februərɪ] Februar
fed: be fed up (with) [ˌfed‿'ʌp] satt haben, die Nase voll haben (von)
federal ['fedrəl] Bundes-; **federal holiday** (AE) Feiertag *(, an dem alle Bundesbehörden geschlossen sind)*; **Federal Republic of Germany** Bundesrepublik Deutschland
fee [fi:] Gebühr, Beitrag; Schulgeld; Honorar
feed [fi:d] füttern; ernähren; **feeding-time** Fütterungszeit
feel [fi:l] (sich) fühlen; **feel for** tasten nach; **feel sorry (for)** bedauern, bereuen; °**I feel sick.** Mir ist übel. **I feel cold/hot.** Mir ist kalt/heiß. **feeling** Gefühl
fellow (pupil etc.) ['feləʊ] Mit-(schüler/in usw.)
felt-tip ['felt tɪp] Filzstift
female ['fi:meɪl] **1.** weibliche Person; Weibchen; **2.** weiblich
fence [fens] Zaun
ferry (boat) ['ferɪ] Fähre
fertile ['fɜ:taɪl] fruchtbar
festival ['festəvl] Festspiele, Festival; Fest (-tag)
fetch [fetʃ] **1.** holen; **2.** abholen
few [fju:] wenige; **a few** ein paar, einige (wenige)
fiction ['fɪkʃn] Dichtung; Prosaliteratur; Fiktion
field [fi:ld] **1.** Feld, Wiese, Weide; **2.** (Sport-)Platz; **in the field(s)** auf dem Feld; **playing field** Sportplatz
fifth [fɪfθ] Fünftel
fight [faɪt] **1.** Kampf; **2.** (be)kämpfen
figure ['fɪgə] **1.** Figur, Gestalt; **2.** Zahl, Ziffer
fill [fɪl] füllen, voll machen; **fill in** einsetzen
film [fɪlm] Film
final ['faɪnl] letzte(r, s), Abschluß-; endgültige(r, s); **finally** schließlich, endlich
financial [faɪ'nænʃl] finanziell
find [faɪnd] finden; **find out** herausfinden, erfahren
fine [faɪn] **1.** Bußgeld, Geldstrafe; **2.** gut, fein, schön
finger ['fɪŋgə] Finger
finish ['fɪnɪʃ] (be)enden, aufhören (mit); aufessen; **I've finished.** Ich bin fertig. **finish line** Ziellinie
fire ['faɪə] **1.** Feuer, Brand; **2.** feuern, rausschmeißen; **3.** *(Schußwaffe)* abfeuern; **fire brigade** ['faɪə brɪˌgeɪd] (BE)/**fire department** ['faɪə dɪˌpɑ:tmənt] (AE) Feuerwehr; **fireworks** *(pl.)* ['faɪəwɜ:ks] Feuerwerk(skörper)
firm [fɜ:m] Firma
first [fɜ:st] (zu)erst, zunächst; **at first** zuerst, anfangs; **be first** der erste sein, als erster (an)kommen; **firstly** erstens
fish [fɪʃ] Fisch, Fische; **fishing 1.** Fischen, Fischerei; **2.** Fischer-; **go fishing** fischen, angeln (gehen)
fit [fɪt] **1.** fit, gut in Form; **2.** passen; **fitness** ['fɪtnəs] Fitness, Kondition
flag [flæg] Fahne, Flagge
flame [fleɪm] Flamme
flat [flæt] **1.** (BE) Wohnung; **2.** flach, eben; **3.** leer *(Batterie)*
fleet [fli:t] Flotte
flight [flaɪt] Flug
flood [flʌd] **1.** Flut, Überflutung; **2.** überfluten, überschwemmen
floor [flɔ:] **1.** Fußboden; **2.** Stockwerk; **first floor** (BE) erster Stock; (AE) Erdgeschoß; **ground floor** (BE) Erdgeschoß
floppy disk ['flɒpɪ dɪsk] Diskette, Floppy
flow [fləʊ] fließen, strömen
flower ['flaʊə] Blume, Blüte
flu [flu:] Grippe
fluent ['flu:ənt] fließend, flüssig *(Sprache, Vortrag)*
fly [flaɪ] fliegen
focus ['fəʊkəs] Blick-, Brennpunkt
fog [fɒg] (dicker) Nebel; **foggy** neblig
folk song ['fəʊk sɒŋ] Volkslied, Folksong
follow ['fɒləʊ] **1.** folgen; **2.** verfolgen, nachfolgen; **following** folgend
fond [fɒnd]: **be fond of** gern haben; mögen
food [fu:d] Essen, Lebensmittel, Nahrung; Futter
fool [fu:l] Dummkopf, Narr; **make a fool of oneself/sb.** sich/jn. blamieren, sich/jn. lächerlich machen; **foolish** dumm, töricht
foot, *pl.* **feet** [fʊt, fi:t] **1.** Fuß; **2.** *Längenmaß (= 30,5 cm)*; **on foot** zu Fuß; **football** ['fʊtbɔ:l] Fußball
for [fɔ:, fə] **1.** für; **2.** seit; **for a long time** lange Zeit; **for breakfast, etc.** zum Frühstück usw.; **for ever** für immer, ewig; **for example** zum Beispiel; **for four weeks** seit vier Wochen; vier Wochen (lang); **for hours** stundenlang; **for sale** zu verkaufen; **for sb.'s birthday** zum Geburtstag; **for seven miles** sieben Meilen weit; **for this reason** aus diesem Grund, deshalb; **for the first time** zum ersten Mal; **good for** gut gegen; **leave for** abfahren nach
force [fɔ:s] **1.** Kraft; Zwang; **2.** zwingen
foreign ['fɒrən] ausländisch, fremd; **foreigner** Ausländer/in, Fremde(r)
forest ['fɒrɪst] Wald, Forst
forget [fə'get] vergessen
forgive [fə'gɪv] vergeben, verzeihen
fork [fɔ:k] Gabel
form [fɔ:m] **1.** (BE) Klasse, Jahrgangsstufe; **2.** Form; **be in form** in Form sein; **3.** Formular, Vordruck; **4.** bilden, sich formen, gründen
formal ['fɔ:ml] formal; formell
°**former** ['fɔ:mə] frühere(r, s)
fortunately ['fɔ:tʃnətlɪ] glücklicherweise
forward(s) ['fɔ:wəd, 'fɔ:wədz] vorwärts
found [faʊnd] gründen, errichten
fountain ['faʊntɪn] Springbrunnen
fox [fɒks] Fuchs
France [frɑ:ns] Frankreich; **French** [frentʃ] französisch; **the French** die Franzosen; **Frenchman/Frenchwoman** Franzose/Französin
free [fri:] **1.** frei; **2.** kostenlos; **3.** freilassen; befreien; **free time** Freizeit; **freedom** Freiheit
freeze [fri:z] (ge)frieren; erstarren
frequency ['fri:kwənsɪ] Häufigkeit
fresh [freʃ] frisch
FRG [ˌef‿ɑ:'dʒi:] = **Federal Republic of Germany** Bundesrepublik Deutschland
Friday ['fraɪdɪ, -deɪ] Freitag
fridge [frɪdʒ] Kühlschrank
friend [frend] Freund/in; **friendliness** Freundlichkeit; **friendly** freundlich
frighten ['fraɪtn] ängstigen, erschrecken; **be frightened (of)** Angst haben (vor), sich fürchten (vor)
frog [frɒg] Frosch
from [frɒm, frəm] aus; von; **from now on** von jetzt an, ab jetzt; **I'm from ...** Ich bin/komme aus ...; **Where are you from?** Wo kommst du her?
front [frʌnt] Vorderseite; **front door** Haustür; **in front of** vor
frontier ['frʌntɪə] Grenze; AE *auch: Grenzgebiet zwischen dem Land, das den Indianern gehörte, und dem der Weißen*
frozen food [ˌfrəʊzn 'fu:d] Tiefkühlkost
fruit [fru:t] Obst, Früchte
frustrated [frʌ'streɪtɪd] frustriert, enttäuscht
full (of) [fʊl] voll (mit/von); **be full** satt sein; **full stop** (BE) Punkt *(am Satzende)*; **full-time** Vollzeit-, Ganztags-; ganztags
fun [fʌn] Spaß; **be fun** Spaß machen; **funny** ['fʌnɪ] lustig, komisch; seltsam
°**furious** ['fjʊərɪəs] wütend
furniture ['fɜ:nɪtʃə] Möbel; **furniture van** (BE) Möbelwagen
further ['fɜ:ðə] **1.** weiter; **2.** weitere(r, s), zusätzlich, noch; **furthermore** [ˌfɜ:ðə'mɔ:] außerdem, überdies
future ['fju:tʃə] **1.** Zukunft; **2.** (zu)künftig; **in future** künftig, ab jetzt

G

game [geɪm] Spiel; **games** Sport
gang [gæŋ] Bande, Gang
garage ['gærɑ:dʒ] **1.** Garage; **2.** Tankstelle mit Reparaturwerkstatt
garden ['gɑ:dn] Garten
gas [gæs] Gas; AE *auch:* Benzin; **gas station** ['gæs ˌsteɪʃn] (AE) Tankstelle
gate [geɪt] Tor
gay [geɪ] **1.** froh; **2.** homosexuell, schwul
°**GCSE** [ˌdʒi: si:‿es‿'i:] **(= General Certificate of Secondary Education)** (BE) *eine Art Mittlere Reife oder Hauptschulabschluß*
general ['dʒenrəl] allgemein, generell; **generally** im allgemeinen, im großen und ganzen
generous ['dʒenərəs] großzügig
gentle ['dʒentl] zart; sanft
gentleman ['dʒentlmən] Mann, Herr; netter Mann; (feiner) Herr
geography [dʒɪ'ɒgrəfɪ] Geographie, Erdkunde
Germanic [dʒə'mænɪk] germanisch
Germany ['dʒɜ:mənɪ] Deutschland; **German 1.** Deutsche(r); **2.** deutsch

get [get] **1.** bekommen, kriegen; **2.** werden; **3.** holen, besorgen; **4.** gelangen, (hin-) kommen; **get along** zurechtkommen, sich zurechtfinden; **get along (with)** auskommen (mit), sich verstehen (mit); **get divorced** sich scheiden lassen; **get dressed** sich anziehen; **get in (the train)** (in den Zug) einsteigen; **get into trouble** in Schwierigkeiten geraten; **get married** (sich ver)heiraten; **get off** aussteigen (aus), absteigen (von); **get off (sb's land)** weggehen, verschwinden; **get on** einsteigen (in), aufsteigen (auf); **get out (of the train)** (aus dem Zug) aussteigen; **get sth. out of the way** etwas aus dem Weg/zur Seite schaffen; **get ready** sich fertigmachen, bereitmachen; **get to know** kennenlernen; **get up** aufstehen
ghost [gəʊst] Geist, Gespenst
giant ['dʒaɪənt] **1.** Riese; **2.** riesig
giraffe [dʒɪ'rɑːf] Giraffe
girl [gɜːl] Mädchen; **girlfriend** ['gɜːlfrend] Freundin *(eines Jungen)*; **Girl Scout** [ˌgɜːl 'skaʊt] (AE) Pfadfinderin
give [gɪv] **1.** geben; **2.** schenken; **give up** aufgeben
glad [glæd]**: be glad** froh sein, sich freuen
glass [glɑːs] Glas; **glasses** *(pl.)* (eine) Brille
global ['gləʊbl] Welt-, weltumfassend, global
glow [gləʊ] Glühen, Leuchten; °**glow worm** ['gləʊ wɜːm] Glühwürmchen
go [gəʊ] **1.** gehen; **2.** fahren; **Go!** Los! **go along** mitgehen; sich anschließen; **go away** verreisen; **go back to** zurückgehen auf, zurückreichen bis; **go by** vergehen, vorübergehen; **go fishing, etc.** fischen usw. gehen; **go home** nach Hause gehen; **go in** hineingehen; **go on 1.** weitermachen, weitergehen; **2.** im Gange sein, vorgehen; **Go on.** Na, komm schon. Na, mach schon. **go on a bus tour** eine Bus-(rund)fahrt machen; **go on a guided tour** eine Führung (mit)machen; **go on a trip** eine Reise/Fahrt machen; **go on holiday** (BE) in Urlaub fahren, Ferien machen; **go out (with)** ausgehen (mit); **go to bed** ins Bett gehen; **go to school** zur Schule gehen; **I'm going to** Ich werde/will, Ich habe vor/habe die Absicht, zu
God, god [gɒd] Gott
gold [gəʊld] **1.** Gold; **gold rush** ['gəʊld rʌʃ] Goldrausch, Goldfieber; **2.** gold(en)
golf [gɒlf] Golf; **golf club** ['gɒlf klʌb] Golfschläger; **golf course** ['gɒlf kɔːs] Golfplatz
good [gʊd] gut; brav, artig; **good at** gut in, geschickt in; **good for** gut gegen; **Good afternoon.** Guten Tag! **Good morning.** Guten Morgen!/Tag! **Goodbye.** [gʊd'baɪ] Auf Wiedersehen! **Goodnight.** [gʊd'naɪt] Gute Nacht! **for good** für immer, endgültig
gorilla [gə'rɪlə] Gorilla
gotten ['gɒtn] (AE) *Partizip Perfekt von „to get"*
government ['gʌvnmənt] Regierung
grade [greɪd] (Zeugnis-)Note, Zensur; AE *auch:* Klasse, Jahrgangsstufe
graffiti [grə'fiːtiː] Graffiti; Wandkritzeleien
gram [græm] Gramm
grammar ['græmə] Grammatik; **grammar school** (BE) Gymnasium
°**grandchild** ['græntʃaɪld] Enkelkind; **grandfather** ['grænˌfɑːðə] Großvater; **grandmother** ['grænˌmʌðə] Großmutter; **grandpa** ['grænpɑː] Opa, Großvater; **grandparents** Großeltern
grapefruit ['greɪpfruːt] Grapefruit, Pampelmuse
grass [grɑːs] **1.** Gras; °**2.** (BE, slang) Spitzel, Informant/in; °**3. grass on sb.** (BE, slang) jn. verpfeifen
grave [greɪv] Grab
gravy ['greɪvɪ] (Braten-)Soße
great [greɪt] **1.** großartig, prima, toll; **2.** groß, beträchtlich; **3.** bedeutend, berühmt; **great-grandparents** [ˌgreɪt 'grænˌpeərənts] Urgroßeltern
Greece [griːs] Griechenland; **Greek** [griːk] **1.** Grieche/Griechin; **2.** griechisch
green [griːn] grün
°**greet** [griːt] begrüßen
grey [greɪ] grau
greyhound ['greɪhaʊnd] Windhund
grocery store ['grəʊsərɪ stɔː] Lebensmittelgeschäft
ground [graʊnd] (Erd-)Boden; **ground floor** (BE) Erdgeschoß
group [gruːp] Gruppe
grow [grəʊ] **1.** wachsen; **grow up** aufwachsen, groß werden; **grown-up** ['grəʊnʌp] Erwachsene(r); **2.** anbauen, anpflanzen
guard [gɑːd] Wächter/in, Wachmann/-frau
guess [ges] (er)raten; **I guess** (*meist* AE) ich nehme an, ich denke
guest [gest] Gast; **guest house** Pension, Gästehaus
guidance counselor ['gaɪdns ˌkaʊnsələ] (AE) *Beratungslehrer/in an einer amerik. High School, berät Schüler/innen über Schullaufbahn und Beruf*
guide [gaɪd] (Fremden-)Führer/in; **go on a guided tour** eine Führung (mit-) machen
guitar [gɪ'tɑː] Gitarre; **play the guitar** Gitarre spielen
gun [gʌn] (Schuß-)Waffe
guy [gaɪ] (infml.) Kerl, Typ; **you guys** (AE, infml.) ihr Leute *(schließt auch Mädchen/Frauen ein)*
gym [dʒɪm] **1.** Turnen, Turnunterricht; **2.** Turnhalle, Sporthalle; **gymnastics** [dʒɪm'næstɪks] Turnen, Gymnastik

H

habit ['hæbɪt] (An-)Gewohnheit
hair [heə] Haar, Haare; **hairstyle** ['heəstaɪl] Frisur
half [hɑːf] Hälfte; halb; **half a mile** eine halbe Meile; **half past ten** halb elf (= 10.30)
hall [hɔːl] Flur, Diele; Halle, Saal
Hallo. [hə'ləʊ] = **Hello.**
ham [hæm] Schinken; **ham salad** Schinken mit Salat
hamburger ['hæmbɜːgə] Hamburger
hammer ['hæmə] Hammer
hamster ['hæmstə] Hamster
hand [hænd] **1.** Hand; **on the one hand** einerseits; **on the other hand** andererseits; **handball** ['hændbɔːl] Handball; **handbook** ['hændbʊk] Handbuch; **handbrake** ['hændbreɪk] Handbremse; **handlebars** *(pl.)* ['hændlbɑːz] Lenkstange; **2. hand out** austeilen
hang [hæŋ] hängen, aufhängen; **hang around** sich herumtreiben, herumlungern
happen (to) ['hæpən] passieren, geschehen (mit); **happen to do** zufällig(erweise) tun
happiness ['hæpɪnəs] Glück
happy ['hæpɪ] glücklich, froh; **Happy birthday (to you)!** Herzlichen Glückwunsch zum Geburtstag!
harbour ['hɑːbə] Hafen
hard [hɑːd] **1.** schwer; hart; **2.** heftig, mit aller Kraft; **hard-working** fleißig, hart arbeitend
hardly ['hɑːdlɪ] kaum
harm [hɑːm]**: do sb. harm** jm. Schaden zufügen; jm. eine Verletzung zufügen; **harmless** ['hɑːmləs] harmlos; unschädlich
harvest ['hɑːvɪst] Ernte
hat [hæt] Hut
hate [heɪt] **1.** Haß; **2.** hassen, gar nicht mögen; **hatred (of, for)** ['heɪtrɪd] Haß (auf)
have [hæv] **1.** haben; **2.** essen, trinken; **have a bath** baden, ein Bad nehmen; **have a child** ein Kind bekommen; **have a disco** eine Fete feiern/veranstalten; **Have a good time!** Viel Spaß! Viel Vergnügen! **have a nice time** eine schöne Zeit/viel Spaß haben; **have a picnic** ein Picknick machen; **have a race** ein Rennen veranstalten; **have a shower** (sich) duschen; **have a wash** sich waschen; **have breakfast** frühstücken; **have lunch** (zu) Mittag essen; **have tea** Abendbrot essen, zu Abend essen; **have got** haben, besitzen; **have got to** (tun) müssen; **have to** (tun) müssen; **have sth. done** etwas *(von jm.)* tun/machen lassen
he [hiː] er
head [hed] Kopf; **headache** ['hedeɪk] Kopfschmerzen, Kopfweh; **head of state** [ˌhed‿əv 'steɪt] Staatsoberhaupt; **headmaster/headmistress** [ˌhed'mɑːstə, ˌhed'mɪstrəs] (BE) Schulleiter/in, Direktor/in; **headset** ['hedset] Kopfhörer
heal [hiːl] heilen
health [helθ] Gesundheit; **healthy** gesund
hear [hɪə] hören
heart [hɑːt] Herz
heat [hiːt] **1.** Hitze; **2.** erhitzen; heizen; **heater** (Heiz-)Ofen; Campingkocher; **heating** Heizung
heavy ['hevɪ] **1.** schwer; heftig; **2.** dicht *(Verkehr)*
hectic ['hektɪk] hektisch
height [haɪt] Höhe
helicopter ['helɪkɒptə] Hubschrauber
Hello. [hə'ləʊ] Hallo! (Guten) Tag! **say hello (to)** grüßen
helmet ['helmɪt] Helm
help [help] **1.** Hilfe; **with the help of** mit Hilfe (von); **2.** helfen; **help oneself** zugreifen, sich bedienen; **helpful** hilfreich, nützlich; **helpless** hilflos
her [hɜː] **1.** ihr, ihre; **2.** ihr, sie
herb [hɜːb] (Heil-, Küchen-)Kraut
herd [hɜːd] Herde
here [hɪə] hier; **Come here.** Komm(t) her! **Here you are.** Hier bitte. Bitte sehr.
hero, *pl.* **heroes** ['hɪərəʊ] Held; **heroine** ['herəʊɪn] Heldin
hers [hɜːz] ihre(r, s); **herself** [hɜː'self] sich (selbst)
Hey! [heɪ] He! Hör mal!
Hi. [haɪ] (infml.) Hallo!
hide [haɪd] (sich) verstecken
high [haɪ] hoch; **high school** ['haɪ skuːl] (AE) Oberschule *(in den USA)*; **high tech(nology)** Hochtechnologie; **Highlander** ['haɪləndə] *Bewohner/in des schottischen Hochlands*; **Highlands** *(pl.)* ['haɪləndz] das *(schottische)* Hochland; **highway** ['haɪweɪ] (AE) Fernstraße
hill [hɪl] Hügel, (kleiner) Berg
him [hɪm] ihm, ihn; **himself** [hɪm'self] sich (selbst)
°**Hindi** ['hɪndiː] Hindi *(offizielle Sprache in den nordindischen Bundesstaaten)*

hippo ['hɪpəʊ] Flußpferd, Nilpferd

hire ['haɪə] *(Boot, Auto, Saal)* mieten, leihen; *(Arbeitnehmer/innen)* einstellen

his [hɪz] sein, seine(r, s)

historical [hɪ'stɒrɪkl] historisch, alt; **history** ['hɪstrɪ] Geschichte

hit [hɪt] schlagen, treffen

hobby ['hɒbɪ] Hobby

hockey ['hɒkɪ] Hockey

hold [həʊld] halten; **hold up** hochhalten, hochheben

hole [həʊl] Loch

holiday(s) ['hɒlɪdeɪ] **1.** Feiertag, freier Tag; **2.** (BE) Ferien, Urlaub; **go/be on holiday** (BE) in Urlaub fahren/sein, Ferien machen/haben

Holland ['hɒlənd] Holland

holy ['həʊlɪ] heilig, geweiht

home [həʊm] Heim, Zuhause; **at home** zu Hause, daheim; **go home** nach Hause gehen; **homeless** obdachlos; **be homesick (for)** Heimweh haben (nach); **homework** Hausaufgabe(n); **do one's homework** seine Hausaufgabe(n) machen

honest ['ɒnɪst] ehrlich

hoof [hu:f], *pl.* **hooves** [hu:vz] *or* **hoofs** Huf

hooligan ['hu:lɪgən] Rowdy, Schläger

hope [həʊp] **1.** Hoffnung; **2.** hoffen; **hopeful** hoffnungsvoll, voller Hoffnung; **hopeless** hoffnungslos

horizon [hə'raɪzn] Horizont

horn [hɔ:n] Hupe

horror ['hɒrə] Horror, Entsetzen; Horror-

horse [hɔ:s] Pferd; **horse power** ['hɔ:s ˌpaʊə] Pferdestärke

hospital ['hɒspɪtl] Krankenhaus, Klinik; **in/to hospital** (BE) im/ins Krankenhaus

hostel ['hɒstl]**: youth hostel** Jugendherberge

hostile (to) ['hɒstaɪl] feindselig, feindlich (gegenüber)

hot [hɒt] heiß, warm

hotel [həʊ'tel] Hotel

hour ['aʊə] Stunde; **for hours** stundenlang

house [haʊs] Haus; **at Dave's/my house** bei Dave/mir zu Hause; **housework** Haus(halts)arbeit; **do the housework** die Haus(halts)arbeit machen

hovercraft ['hɒvəkrɑ:ft] Luftkissenfahrzeug(e)

how [haʊ] wie; **How are you?** Wie geht es dir? °**How do you do.** (fml.) Guten Tag! Grüß Gott! **How many?** Wie viele? **How much?** Wieviel? **How much is ...?** Was kostet ...? **How old are you?** Wie alt bist du? **however** [haʊ'evə] jedoch, aber; wie (auch) immer

huge [hju:dʒ] sehr groß, riesig

human being [ˌhju:mən 'bi:ɪŋ] Mensch

hunger ['hʌŋgə] Hunger; **hungry** ['hʌŋgrɪ] hungrig; **be hungry** Hunger haben

hunt [hʌnt] jagen; **hunter** Jäger/in

hurrah! [hʊ'rɑ:] hurra!

hurry ['hʌrɪ]**: be in a hurry** in Eile sein, es eilig haben; **hurry up** sich beeilen

hurt [hɜ:t] weh tun, verletzen

husband ['hʌzbənd] (Ehe-)Mann

hut [hʌt] Hütte

hyphen ['haɪfn] Bindestrich

I

I [aɪ] ich

ice [aɪs] Eis; **ice-cream** [ˌaɪs'kri:m] (Speise-)Eis; **ice-cream parlor** ['pɑ:lə] (AE) Eisdiele; **ice-skating** ['aɪsˌskeɪtɪŋ] Schlittschuhlaufen; **icy** eisig

idea [aɪ'dɪə] Idee, Einfall; Begriff, Vorstellung; Meinung; **No idea.** Keine Ahnung.

identify (with) [aɪ'dentɪfaɪ] (sich) identifizieren (mit)

identity [aɪ'dentɪtɪ] Identität

i.e. [ˌaɪ‿'i:] **(= that is)** d.h. (= das heißt)

if [ɪf] **1.** wenn, falls; **2.** ob; **if I were you** (ich) an deiner Stelle

ignore [ɪg'nɔ:] ignorieren; **ignorance** ['ɪgnərəns] Unwissenheit, Unkenntnis, Ignoranz; **ignorant** ['ɪgnərənt] unwissend, ungebildet, ignorant

ill [ɪl] krank; **illness** ['ɪlnəs] Krankheit

illegal [ɪ'li:gl] ungesetzlich, illegal

illustrate ['ɪləstreɪt] veranschaulichen, illustrieren

image ['ɪmɪdʒ] Image, Ruf

imagine [ɪ'mædʒɪn] sich vorstellen; sich einbilden; **Just imagine.** Denk dir nur! Stell dir mal vor! **imaginary** [ɪ'mædʒɪnərɪ] erfunden; eingebildet; **imagination** [ɪˌmædʒɪ'neɪʃn] Phantasie, Einbildung

immigrant ['ɪmɪgrənt] Einwanderer/-in

immigrate ['ɪmɪgreɪt] einwandern, immigrieren; **immigration** [ˌɪmɪ'greɪʃn] Einwanderung, Immigration

impatience [ɪm'peɪʃns] Ungeduld; **impatient** [ɪm'peɪʃənt] ungeduldig

impolite [ˌɪmpə'laɪt] unhöflich; **impoliteness** [ˌɪmpə'laɪtnəs] Unhöflichkeit

import **1.** ['ɪmpɔ:t] Einfuhr, Import; **2.** [ɪm'pɔ:t] einführen, importieren; **importer** [ɪm'pɔ:tə] Importeur/in

importance [ɪm'pɔ:təns] Wichtigkeit; **important** wichtig, bedeutend

impossible [ɪm'pɒsəbl] unmöglich

°**impressed (with)** [ɪm'prest] beeindruckt (von); **impression** [ɪm'preʃn] Eindruck

improve [ɪm'pru:v] (sich) (ver)bessern; besser machen/werden

in [ɪn] in; hinein; **go in** hineingehen; **in a hurry** in Eile; **in a minute** gleich, sofort; **in bed** im Bett; **in doing sth.** indem; beim; **in English** auf englisch; **in front of** vor; **in future** künftig, ab jetzt; **in January** im Januar; **in my opinion** meiner Meinung nach; **in 1980** (im Jahre) 1980; **in ruins** zerstört; **in spite of** trotz; **in the country** auf dem Land; **in the field(s)** auf dem Feld; **in the morning(s)** am Morgen, morgens; **in the picture/photo** auf dem Bild/Foto; **in (the) spring** im Frühling/ Frühjahr; **in the street** auf der Straße; **in those days** damals; **in town** in der (Innen-)Stadt; **interested in** interessiert an; **one in four** jede(r) vierte, eine(r) von/unter vieren

inch [ɪntʃ] Zoll (= 2,54 cm)

include [ɪn'klu:d] (mit) einschließen, enthalten, beinhalten

income ['ɪŋkʌm] Einkommen

indeed [ɪn'di:d] in der Tat, tatsächlich

independence (from) [ˌɪndɪ'pendəns] Unabhängigkeit (von); **independent (of)** [ˌɪndɪ'pendənt] unabhängig (von)

India ['ɪndɪə] Indien; **Indian** **1.** Inder/in; indisch; **2.** Indianer/in; indianisch

indirect [ˌɪndɪ'rekt, ˌɪndaɪ'rekt] indirekt, mittelbar

individual [ˌɪndɪ'vɪdʒʊəl] **1.** Einzelperson, Individuum; **2.** individuell, Einzel-

indoor ['ɪndɔ:] im Haus; **indoors** [ˌɪn'dɔ:z] (nach) drinnen, im Haus

industrial [ɪn'dʌstrɪəl] Industrie-; industriell; **industry** ['ɪndəstrɪ] Industrie(zweig)

inedible [ɪn'edɪbl] nicht eßbar, ungenießbar

infertile [ɪn'fɜ:taɪl] unfruchtbar

influence ['ɪnflʊəns] **1.** Einfluß; **2.** beeinflussen

inform [ɪn'fɔ:m] informieren, benachrichtigen; **informer** Informant/in, Spitzel; **information** [ˌɪnfə'meɪʃn] Information(en), Auskunft; **Information Centre** Auskunft, Verkehrsbüro

informal [ɪn'fɔ:ml] informell, nicht förmlich

injured ['ɪndʒəd] verletzt

inland ['ɪnlənd] Binnen-, inländisch

inner city [ˌɪnə 'sɪtɪ] problematisches Wohngebiet im Stadtkern

innocent ['ɪnəsənt] unschuldig

°**inquire** [ɪn'kwaɪə] (fml.) sich erkundigen

insect ['ɪnsekt] Insekt

inside [ɪn'saɪd] **1.** innen/drinnen; nach drinnen; **2.** innerhalb (von)

insist (on) [ɪn'sɪst] bestehen (auf), verlangen

install [ɪn'stɔ:l] einrichten, einbauen, installieren

instead [ɪn'sted] statt dessen, dafür; **instead of** (an)statt, an Stelle von

instruction [ɪn'strʌkʃn] Anleitung; Anweisung, Vorschrift; **instructor** [ɪn'strʌktə] Betreuer/in, Lehrer/in

instrument ['ɪnstrəmənt] Instrument

intelligent [ɪn'telɪdʒənt] klug, intelligent

°**intend** [ɪn'tend] beabsichtigen; °**intention** [ɪn'tenʃn] Absicht

interest ['ɪntrɪst] interessieren; **interest (in)** Interesse (an); **interested (in)** interessiert (an); **interesting** interessant

°**interfere with** [ˌɪntə'fɪə] sich einmischen in

interior [ɪn'tɪərɪə] (das) Innere; Innen-

international [ˌɪntə'næʃnl] international

interpret [ɪn'tɜ:prɪt] **1.** dolmetschen; **2.** interpretieren, auffassen

interrupt [ˌɪntə'rʌpt] unterbrechen

intersection ['ɪntəˌsekʃn] (AE) (Straßen-)Kreuzung

interview ['ɪntəvju:] **1.** Interview; **2.** befragen, interviewen; **interviewer** ['ɪntəvju:ə] Interviewer/in

into ['ɪntʊ, 'ɪntə] in ... (hinein)

intolerance (towards) [ɪn'tɒlərəns] Intoleranz (gegenüber); **intolerant (towards)** [ɪn'tɒlərənt] intolerant (gegenüber)

introduce (to) [ˌɪntrə'dju:s] **1.** vorstellen, bekanntmachen (mit); **2.** einführen; **introduction** [ˌɪntrə'dʌkʃn] Einführung

invade [ɪn'veɪd] einmarschieren in, einfallen in; **invader** Invasor/in, Eindringling; **invasion (of)** [ɪn'veɪʒn] Einmarsch (in), Einfall (in), Invasion

invent [ɪn'vent] erfinden; **invention** [ɪn'venʃn] Erfindung; **inventor** [ɪn'ventə] Erfinder/in

invisible [ɪn'vɪzəbl] unsichtbar

invitation [ˌɪnvɪ'teɪʃn] Einladung; **invite** [ɪn'vaɪt] einladen

°**IRA** [ˌaɪ‿ɑ:r‿'eɪ] **= Irish Republican Army** Irisch-Republikanische Armee

Ireland ['aɪələnd] Irland; **Irish** ['aɪrɪʃ] irisch; **the Irish** die Iren; **Irishman/ Irishwoman** Ire/Irin

iron ['aɪən] **1.** Eisen; Bügeleisen; **2.** bügeln

is [ɪz] ist

island ['aɪlənd] Insel; **isle** [aɪl] Insel

it [ɪt] es (er, sie; ihn, sie)

Italy ['ɪtəlɪ] Italien; **Italian** [ɪ'tælɪən] **1.** Italiener/in; **2.** italienisch

its [ɪts] sein, seine; ihr, ihre; **itself** [ɪt'self] sich (selbst)

J

jacket ['dʒækɪt] Jacke, Jackett

jam [dʒæm] Marmelade

January ['dʒænjʊərɪ] Januar

jar [dʒɑ:] (Einmach-)Glas; Topf

jazz [dʒæz] Jazz(musik)

jealous (of) [ˈdʒeləs] eifersüchtig (auf); neidisch (auf)

jeans *(pl.)* [dʒi:nz] Jeans

Jew [dʒu:] Jude, Jüdin; **Jewish** [ˈdʒu:ɪʃ] jüdisch

jewel(s) [ˈdʒu:əl(z)] Juwel(en)

job [dʒɒb] Beruf, Arbeit, Job; Aufgabe

jog [dʒɒg] joggen

join [dʒɔɪn] sich anschließen, mitmachen; eintreten *(in einen Klub usw.)*

joke [dʒəʊk] Scherz, Spaß; Witz; **You must be joking.** Das ist ja wohl nicht dein Ernst. Du machst wohl Witze.

journey [ˈdʒɜ:nɪ] Reise, Fahrt

°**judge** [dʒʌdʒ] Richter/in

judo [ˈdʒu:dəʊ] Judo

juice [dʒu:s] Saft; **juicy** saftig

July [dʒu:ˈlaɪ] Juli

jump [dʒʌmp] springen

June [dʒu:n] Juni

junior [ˈdʒu:nɪə] Junioren-, Jugend-

just [dʒʌst] **1.** nur, bloß (mal); **2.** gerade (eben); **3.** einfach, wirklich; **4.** gerecht; **just about** so ungefähr, etwa, fast; **just (like, as)** genau (wie); **just (to the south of)** gleich (südlich von)

K

kangaroo [ˌkæŋgəˈru:] Känguruh

karate [kəˈrɑ:tɪ] Karate

keep [ki:p] **1.** behalten; aufbewahren; **2.** *(Gesetz, Vorschrift)* einhalten, befolgen; **keep a promise** ein Versprechen halten; **keep away from** sich fernhalten von; **keep cattle** (sich) Rinder halten; **keep ... ing** etwas weiter tun, weiter-; **keep (out)** (draußen) halten; **keep the peace** den Frieden bewahren; **keep to** sich halten an; **keep up to date (with)** (sich) auf dem laufenden/auf dem neuesten Stand halten (über); **keeper** Wärter/in, Wächter/in

ketchup [ˈketʃəp] Ketchup

key [ki:] Schlüssel

keyboard [ˈki:bɔ:d] Tastatur, Keyboard

kick [kɪk] **1.** Tritt; **2.** treten

kid [kɪd] (infml.) Kind; Jugendliche(r)

kill [kɪl] töten, umbringen; **killing** Töten, Tötung; Mord

kilo [ˈki:ləʊ] Kilo

kilometre [ˈkɪləˌmi:tə] Kilometer

kilt [kɪlt] Schottenrock

kind (of) [kaɪnd] Art; **kind (of you)** nett, freundlich (von dir)

king [kɪŋ] König; **kingdom** [ˈkɪŋdəm] Königreich

kit [kɪt]: **repair kit** Flickzeug

kitchen [ˈkɪtʃɪn] Küche

knee [ni:] Knie; °**kneel** [ni:l] (nieder)knien

knife, *pl.* **knives** [naɪf, naɪvz] Messer

knock [nɒk] **1.** (an)klopfen; **2.** schlagen, stoßen

know [nəʊ] **1.** kennen; **2.** wissen; **3.** erkennen; **get to know** kennenlernen; **you know** weißt du, nämlich; **known** bekannt; **be known to do sth.** etwas bekanntlich tun; **unknown** unbekannt; **well-known** (wohl)bekannt

knowledge [ˈnɒlɪdʒ] Wissen; Kenntnis(se)

°**koala (bear)** [kəʊˈɑ:lə ˌbeə] Koala(bär)

L

lab (infml.), **laboratory** [læb, ləˈbɒrətrɪ] Labor(atorium)

ladder [ˈlædə] Leiter

lady [ˈleɪdɪ] Dame

lake [leɪk] (ein) See

lamp [læmp] Lampe

land [lænd] **1.** (festes) Land, Boden; **landlord/landlady** [ˈlændlɔ:d, ˈlændleɪdɪ] Hauswirt/in, Hauseigentümer/in; Gastwirt/in; **landowner** [ˈlændˌəʊnə] Grundbesitzer/in; **landscape** [ˈlænskeɪp] Landschaft, Landschaftsbild; **2.** landen *(Flugzeug)*; **3.** anlegen *(Schiff)*

language [ˈlæŋgwɪdʒ] Sprache

large [lɑ:dʒ] groß, umfangreich

last [lɑ:st] **1.** letzte(r, s); **at last** endlich, schließlich; **be last** der letzte sein, als letzter (an)kommen; **last but not least** nicht zuletzt, nicht zu vergessen; **last night** gestern abend; letzte Nacht; **last Saturday** (am) letzten Samstag; **2.** (an-, fort)dauern; **3.** ausreichen

late [leɪt] spät; **be late** zu spät kommen; **latest** [ˈleɪtɪst] neueste(r, s); **at the latest** spätestens

Latin [ˈlætɪn] Latein, lateinisch

laugh [lɑ:f] lachen; **laugh at** lachen über; auslachen; **laughter** Lachen, Gelächter

launching pad [ˈlɔ:ntʃɪŋ pæd] Abschußrampe

law [lɔ:] Gesetz; **law firm** [ˈlɔ: fɜ:m] Anwaltskanzlei; **lawless** gesetzlos; gesetzwidrig; **lawyer** [ˈlɔ:jə] Rechtsanwalt/Rechtsanwältin; Jurist/in

lawn [lɔ:n] Rasen

°**lay** [leɪ] legen

laziness [ˈleɪzɪnəs] Faulheit; **lazy** faul, träge

lead [li:d] führen, leiten; **leader** [ˈli:də] (An-)Führer/in

leaf, *pl.* **leaves** [li:f, li:vz] Blatt *(einer Pflanze)*

learn [lɜ:n] lernen; **learn (about)** herausfinden (über), erfahren (über); **learner** [ˈlɜ:nə] Lernende(r), Anfänger/in

least [li:st] (der/die/das) wenigste, am wenigsten; **at least** mindestens; wenigstens, zumindest; **last but not least** nicht zuletzt, nicht zu vergessen

leather [ˈleðə] Leder

leave [li:v] **1.** (ver-, zurück)lassen; **2.** stehen-/liegenlassen; **3.** weggehen, abfahren; °**leave sb. alone** jn. in Ruhe lassen; **leave school** von der Schule abgehen; **be left** übrig sein

left [left] linke(r, s), nach links; **on the left** links, auf der linken Seite

leg [leg] Bein

legal [ˈli:gl] gesetzlich, legal

legend [ˈledʒənd] Legende, Sage; **legendary** [ˈledʒəndrɪ] berühmt; legendär

lemonade [ˌleməˈneɪd] Limonade

lend [lend] (ver)leihen

less [les] weniger

lesson [ˈlesn] Unterrichtsstunde

let [let] **1.** (zu)lassen; **Let me see.** Warte mal! Laß mich mal überlegen! **let's = let us** laß(t) uns; **Let's see.** Wollen mal sehen. **2. let down** im Stich lassen; enttäuschen

letter [ˈletə] **1.** Brief; **2.** Buchstabe; **letter box** [ˈletə bɒks] *(meist* BE) Briefkasten

liberty [ˈlɪbətɪ] Freiheit

library [ˈlaɪbrərɪ] Bibliothek, Bücherei

licence [ˈlaɪsəns] Genehmigung, Lizenz

lid [lɪd] Deckel

lie [laɪ] **1.** Lüge; **2. lie (to sb.)** (jn. an-, be-)lügen; **3.** liegen

life, *pl.* **lives** [laɪf, laɪvz] Leben; **lifeboat** [ˈlaɪfbəʊt] Rettungsboot; **lifeline** [ˈlaɪflaɪn] Rettungsleine

lift [lɪft] heben, hochheben

light [laɪt] **1.** Licht, Lampe; **traffic lights** *(pl.)* [ˈtræfɪk laɪts] (Verkehrs-)Ampel; **2.** leicht *(von Gewicht)*; **3.** hell; **light (blue)** hell(blau)

like [laɪk] **1.** wie; **like this** so, auf diese Weise; folgendermaßen; **like that** so; **things like that** so etwas, solche Sachen; **What's it like?** Wie ist es? Wie sieht es aus? **2.** *(conj.)* (infml.) wie; **3.** mögen, gern haben/tun; **How do you like ...?** Wie gefällt dir ...? Wie findest du ...? **I'd like** ich möchte; **like better/best** lieber/am liebsten mögen

likely [ˈlaɪklɪ]: **be likely to do sth.** etwas wahrscheinlich tun

limit [ˈlɪmɪt] (oberste) Grenze, Beschränkung

line [laɪn] **1.** Zeile; Linie; **2.** (Telefon-)Leitung; **3.** (*meist* AE) Schlange *(wartender Menschen)*, Reihe

lingua franca [ˌlɪŋgwə ˈfræŋkə] Verkehrssprache *(zwischen Menschen verschiedener Landessprachen)*

link [lɪŋk] **1.** Verbindung, Beziehung, Bindeglied; **2.** (sich) verbinden; **be linked (by/with)** verbunden, verknüpft sein (durch/mit)

lion [ˈlaɪən] Löwe

lip [lɪp] Lippe

list [lɪst] Liste

listen (to) [ˈlɪsn] zu-, anhören; **listener** Zuhörer/in; **listening comprehension** [ˈlɪsnɪŋ ˌkɒmprɪˌhenʃn] Hörverstehen

litter [ˈlɪtə] Abfall, herumliegendes Papier

little [ˈlɪtl] klein, jung; **a little** ein wenig, ein bißchen

live [lɪv] wohnen, leben; **live on sth.** von etwas leben, sich von etwas ernähren; **living-room** Wohnzimmer

live [laɪv] live, direkt; **liveliness** Lebendigkeit; **lively** lebhaft

Liverpudlian [ˌlɪvəˈpʌdlɪən] Liverpooler/in

load [ləʊd] (auf)laden, (be)laden

loaf, *pl.* **loaves** [ləʊf, ləʊvz] Laib (Brot)

local [ˈləʊkl] Orts-, Lokal-, örtlich

lock [lɒk] ab-, zuschließen; **lock (in)** einschließen, einsperren (in)

logical [ˈlɒdʒɪkl] logisch

loneliness [ˈləʊnlɪnəs] Einsamkeit; **lonely** einsam, verlassen

long [lɒŋ] lang; **no longer** nicht mehr, nicht länger; **not long ago** vor kurzem

look [lʊk] **1.** Blick; **2.** sehen, schauen; **3.** aussehen; **look after** sich kümmern um, aufpassen auf; **look at** anschauen; **look for** suchen; **look forward to (doing) sth.** sich auf etwas freuen; sich darauf freuen, etwas zu tun; **look round** sich umsehen; **look up** *(ein Wort usw.)* nachschlagen

lord [lɔ:d] Herr, Adliger; Lord; **Lord** Herr(gott)

lorry [ˈlɒrɪ] (BE) Lastwagen

lose [lu:z] verlieren; **loser** [ˈlu:zə] Verlierer/in

lots [lɒts]/**a lot (of)** viele, viel, eine Menge

loud [laʊd] laut

love [lʌv] **1.** Liebe; **fall in love (with)** sich verlieben (in); **Love** Viele liebe Grüße von; **send/give one's love to sb.** jn. grüßen (lassen); **2.** lieben, sehr mögen, sehr gern haben/tun; **I'd love** ich hätte (liebend) gern; **I'd love to** ich würde sehr gern; **lovely** schön, herrlich, hübsch

low [ləʊ] niedrig, tief

°**Loyalist** [ˈlɔɪəlɪst] Loyalist/in

LP [ˌel ˈpi:] **(long-playing record)** LP (Langspielplatte)

luckily [ˈlʌkɪlɪ] glücklicherweise

lucky [ˈlʌkɪ]: **be lucky** Glück haben

°**luggage** ['lʌgɪdʒ] Gepäck
lump [lʌmp]: **(sugar) lump** (Zucker-)Stück
lunch [lʌntʃ] Mittagessen; **for lunch** zum Mittagessen; **have lunch** (zu) Mittag essen; **What's for lunch?** Was gibt's zum Mittagessen?

M

machine [mə'ʃi:n] Maschine
mad (at) [mæd] (*meist* AE, infml.) böse, sauer, wütend (auf)
madam ['mædəm] meine Dame *(höfliche Anrede)*; **Dear Sir or Madam,** Sehr geehrte Damen und Herren,
made of (wax) ['meɪd‿əv] aus (Wachs)
magazine [,mægə'zi:n] Zeitschrift, Illustrierte
magic ['mædʒɪk] Zauberkunst, Magie; **do magic** zaubern; **magician** [mə'dʒɪʃn] Zauberer, Zauberin
mail [meɪl] **1.** (*meist* AE) Post(sendungen); **air mail** Luftpost;
2. (*meist* AE) *(Brief)* abschicken, einwerfen; *(Paket)* aufgeben
main [meɪn] Haupt-; **mainly** hauptsächlich
maintain [meɪn'teɪn] *(finanziell)* unterhalten; aufrechterhalten
major ['meɪdʒə] gewichtig, bedeutsam
majority [mə'dʒɒrətɪ] Mehrheit
make [meɪk] machen, bauen; **make friends** Freunde finden; sich anfreunden; **make into** machen zu, umwandeln in; **make sb. do sth.** jn. veranlassen/zwingen, etwas zu tun; jn. etwas tun lassen; **make sb. sth.** jn. zu etwas machen; **make tea** Tee kochen; **make up** sich ausdenken; erfinden
male [meɪl] **1.** männliche Person; Männchen; **2.** männlich
°**malign** [mə'laɪn] böswillig, boshaft
man, *pl.* **men** [mæn, men] Mann, Männer; **mankind** [,mæn'kaɪnd] (die) Menschheit; **man-made** künstlich
°**manage** ['mænɪdʒ] zurechtkommen; **manager** ['mænɪdʒə] Geschäftsführer/in, Filialleiter/in, Manager/in; Führungskraft
many ['menɪ] viele
map [mæp] Landkarte, Stadtplan
marathon ['mærəθən] Marathon
march [mɑ:tʃ] marschieren
March [mɑ:tʃ] März
mark [mɑ:k] **1.** (BE) Note, Zensur;
2. kennzeichnen, bezeichnen, markieren
market ['mɑ:kɪt] Markt
marriage (to) ['mærɪdʒ] Ehe (mit); Heirat; **marry** ['mærɪ] heiraten; **get married** (sich ver)heiraten; **married (to)** verheiratet (mit)
master ['mɑ:stə] meistern
match [mætʃ] **1.** Spiel, Wettkampf;
2. Streichholz; **3.** passend zusammenfügen; zusammenpassen
material [mə'tɪərɪəl] Material, Stoff
math (AE)/**maths** (BE) [mæθ, mæθs] Mathe(matik)
matter ['mætə]: **It doesn't matter.** Das macht doch nichts. **no matter (how/what/...)** egal, (wie/was/...); °**What's the matter?** Was ist denn (los)?
may [meɪ] darf, kann; (kann) vielleicht
May [meɪ] Mai
maybe ['meɪbi:] vielleicht
mayor [meə] Bürgermeister/in
me [mi:] mir, mich; **(It wasn't) me.** Ich (war's nicht). **older than me** älter als ich
meal [mi:l] Mahlzeit, Essen
mean [mi:n] **1.** bedeuten; **meaning** Bedeutung;
2. meinen; **mean by** verstehen unter, meinen mit; **mean to do sth.** etwas absichtlich tun, etwas tun wollen; **meant as** [ment] gedacht als, gemeint als;
3. geizig; gemein
measurement ['meʒəmənt] Maß; (Ver-) Messung
meat [mi:t] Fleisch
mechanic [mɪ'kænɪk] Mechaniker/in
medical ['medɪkl] medizinisch, Medizin-; ärztlich; **medicine** ['medsn] Medizin, Arznei
meet [mi:t] **1.** (sich) treffen, kennenlernen;
2. abholen; **meeting** ['mi:tɪŋ] Treffen, Versammlung; Veranstaltung
melt [melt] schmelzen
member (of) ['membə] Mitglied (in, von); **MP** [,em 'pi:] = **Member of Parliament** (BE) Mitglied des Unterhauses; **membership card** ['membəʃɪp ,kɑ:d] Mitgliedsausweis
memory ['memərɪ] Gedächtnis
mention ['menʃn] erwähnen
menu ['menju:] Speisekarte
°**mercy** ['mɜ:sɪ] Gnade, Erbarmen
merry ['merɪ] froh, fröhlich
message ['mesɪdʒ] Nachricht, Botschaft; **(bike) messenger** ['mesɪndʒə] (Fahrrad-) Bote/-in
metal ['metl] Metall
metre ['mi:tə] Meter
microphone ['maɪkrəfəʊn] Mikrophon
midday [,mɪd'deɪ] Mittag
middle ['mɪdl] Mitte; **Middle Ages** [,mɪdl‿'eɪdʒɪz] Mittelalter
midnight ['mɪdnaɪt] Mitternacht
the Midwest [,mɪd'west] der mittlere Westen *(der USA)*
might [maɪt] könnte(n) vielleicht; **I might (just) as well ...** Ich könnte ebensogut ...
mile [maɪl] Meile; **miles per hour = mph** [,maɪlz pər‿'aʊə] Meilen pro Stunde; **mil(e)ometer** [maɪ'lɒmɪtə] (BE) Tacho, Meilenzähler; **milestone** ['maɪlstəʊn] Meilenstein
milk [mɪlk] **1.** Milch; **2.** melken
millimetre ['mɪlɪ,mi:tə] Millimeter
million ['mɪljən] Million
mind [maɪnd] **1.** Meinung; **change one's mind** seine Meinung ändern; **come to mind** einfallen; **have sth. in mind** etwas im Sinn haben, an etwas denken;
2. etwas (einzuwenden) haben gegen; **Never mind.** Das macht doch nichts.
mine [maɪn] meine(r, s)
mine [maɪn] Bergwerk; **miner** Bergarbeiter, Bergmann; **mining** Bergbau; Bergbau-, Bergwerks-
minerals ['mɪnərəlz] Mineralien, Bodenschätze
minister ['mɪnɪstə] Minister/in; **prime minister** (infml.: **PM**) [,praɪm 'mɪnɪstə] Premierminister/in, Ministerpräsident/in
minority [maɪ'nɒrətɪ] Minderheit
°**minster** ['mɪnstə] Münster
minus ['maɪnəs] minus
minute ['mɪnɪt] Minute; **in a minute** gleich, sofort; **Wait a minute.** Einen Augenblick! Moment mal!
mirror ['mɪrə] Spiegel
miserable ['mɪzrəbl] unglücklich, traurig; elend
Miss [mɪs] Fräulein/Frau; **miss** *häufige Anrede für eine Lehrerin in Großbritannien*
miss [mɪs] verpassen, verfehlen; vermissen; **missing** fehlend; **be missing** fehlen
mistake [mɪ'steɪk] Fehler, Irrtum
°**mistrust sb.** [,mɪs'trʌst] jm. mißtrauen
misunderstand [,mɪsʌndə'stænd] mißverstehen; **misunderstanding** Mißverständnis
mix (with) [mɪks] (sich) mischen (mit); (miteinander) verkehren; **mix up** verwechseln, durcheinanderbringen; **mixed** ge-, vermischt; **mixed bag** bunte Mischung; **mixture** ['mɪkstʃə] Mischung
mobility ['məʊbɪlətɪ] Mobilität
model ['mɒdl] Modell, Modell-
modern ['mɒdn] modern
mom [mɒm] (AE) Mutti, Mama, Mami
moment ['məʊmənt] Moment, Augenblick; **at the moment** im Moment, im Augenblick; zur Zeit
Monday ['mʌndɪ, -deɪ] Montag; **on Monday(s)** montags, am Montag
money ['mʌnɪ] Geld
monitor ['mɒnɪtə] Monitor
monkey ['mʌŋkɪ] Affe
monster ['mɒnstə] Ungeheuer
month [mʌnθ] Monat
moon [mu:n] Mond
moped ['məʊped] Moped
more [mɔ:] mehr; **more and more** immer (mehr); **more exciting** aufregender; **more than** mehr als; **not (...) any more, no more** nicht mehr, kein(e, n) mehr; **some more** noch einige/etwas
morning ['mɔ:nɪŋ] Morgen, Vormittag; **Good morning.** Guten Morgen!/Tag! **in the morning(s)** am Morgen, morgens; **on Monday morning(s)** am Montag morgen; **this morning** heute morgen; **tomorrow morning** morgen früh
most [məʊst] **1.** (der/die/das) meiste; **2.** am meisten; **(the) most exciting** (der/die/das) aufregendste; am aufregendsten; **mostly** meistens, hauptsächlich
motel [məʊ'tel] Motel
mother ['mʌðə] Mutter
motorbike ['məʊtəbaɪk] BE: Motorrad; AE: Moped, Mofa; **motorhome** (AE) Wohnmobil, Campingbus; **motorway** (BE) Autobahn
mountain(s) ['maʊntən] Berg; Gebirge
mouse, *pl.* **mice** [maʊs, maɪs] Maus
mouth [maʊθ] Mund
move [mu:v] **1.** Umzug; **moving van** (AE) Möbelwagen;
2. (um)ziehen; **3.** (sich) bewegen; **be on the move** unterwegs sein, in Bewegung sein
movie ['mu:vɪ] (*meist* AE) Film; **go to the movies** (AE) ins Kino gehen; **movie theater** (AE) Kino(gebäude)
mph = miles per hour [,maɪlz pər‿'aʊə] Meilen pro Stunde
Mr ['mɪstə] Herr; **Mrs** ['mɪsɪz] Frau; **Ms** [məz] Frau *(familienstandneutrale Anrede)*
much [mʌtʃ] viel; **(like) very much** sehr (gern mögen); **Thank you very much.** Vielen Dank.
mud [mʌd] Schlamm, Matsch; **muddy** schlammig, schmutzig
mug [mʌg] überfallen und berauben
multi- ['mʌltɪ] mehr-, multi-
mum(my) [mʌm] (BE) Mutti, Mama, Mami
murder ['mɜ:də] **1.** Mord; **2.** (er)morden; **murderer** Mörder/in
museum [mju:'zɪəm] Museum
music ['mju:zɪk] Musik; **musician** [mju:'zɪʃn] Musiker/in
Muslim ['mʊzlɪm, 'mʌzlɪm] **1.** Moslem;
2. moslemisch
must [mʌst, məst] muß; **mustn't** ['mʌsnt] darf nicht
my [maɪ] mein, meine; **myself** [maɪ'self] mir/mich (selbst)
mystery ['mɪstrɪ] Geheimnis, Rätsel

N

nail [neɪl] Nagel
name [neɪm] 1. Name; **What's your name?** Wie ist dein Name? Wie heißt du? °2. benennen
narrow ['nærəʊ] eng, schmal
nation ['neɪʃn] Nation, Volk; Stamm; **national** ['næʃnəl] national, National-; **nationality** [ˌnæʃə'nælətɪ] Staatsangehörigkeit, Nationalität
native ['neɪtɪv] 1. Eingeborene(r), Einheimische(r); 2. einheimisch, gebürtig, Heimat*(land)*, Mutter*(sprache)*; **Native American** Indianer/in, amerikanische(r) Ureinwohner/in
natural ['nætʃrəl] natürlich, Natur-; **natural resources** [rɪ'sɔ:sɪz] Bodenschätze; **nature** ['neɪtʃə] Natur; **close to nature** naturverbunden
NB, nb [ˌen 'bi:] = **nota bene** (Latin) bitte beachten
near [nɪə] in der Nähe von, nahe; **nearly** ['nɪəlɪ] fast, beinahe
necessary ['nesəsərɪ] notwendig, nötig; **necessity** [nɪ'sesɪtɪ] Notwendigkeit
neck [nek] Hals
need [ni:d] 1. Bedürfnis, Not; 2. brauchen, benötigen; **needn't** ['ni:dnt] braucht nicht, muß nicht; **Need we ...?** Müssen wir ...?; **That's all I needed.** Das hat mir gerade noch gefehlt!
negative ['negətɪv] negativ; verneinend
neighbour ['neɪbə] Nachbar/in; **neighbourhood** ['neɪbəhʊd] Nachbarschaft; (Wohn-)Gegend
neither (of) ['naɪðə, 'ni:ðə] keine(r, s) (von beiden); **neither ... nor** weder ... noch
°**nephew** ['nefju:, 'nevju:] Neffe
nerves [nɜ:vz]: **get on sb.'s nerves** jm. auf die Nerven gehen; **nervous** ['nɜ:vəs] ängstlich, aufgeregt, nervös; **nervousness** ['nɜ:vəsnəs] Nervosität
net [net] Netz; **netball** ['netbɔ:l] Korbball; **network** ['netwɜ:k] Netz(werk); Vernetzung
never ['nevə] nie, niemals
°**nevertheless** [ˌnevəðə'les] nichtsdestoweniger, trotzdem
new [nju:] neu; **news** [nju:z] Nachricht(en), Neuigkeit(en); °**newsagent's** ['nju:zˌeɪdʒənts] Zeitungsladen; **newspaper** Zeitung
New Zealand [ˌnju: 'zi:lənd] 1. Neuseeland; 2. neuseeländisch; **New Zealander** Neuseeländer/in
next [nekst] nächste(r, s); **next Monday** (am) nächsten Montag; **next to** direkt neben
nice [naɪs] nett, schön, hübsch
nickel ['nɪkl] (AE) 5¢-Münze
night [naɪt] Nacht, (später) Abend; **at night** nachts, bei Nacht; **last night** gestern abend; letzte Nacht; **on the first night** in der ersten Nacht
no [nəʊ] 1. nein; 2. kein, keine; **no longer** nicht mehr, nicht länger; **no more** kein(e, n) mehr; **nobody/no one** niemand; **nowhere** nirgendwo, nirgends
no = **number** ['nʌmbə] Nr = Nummer
Noah's ark [ˌnəʊəz‿'ɑ:k] die Arche Noah
noble ['nəʊbl] adlig, edel, erhaben
nod [nɒd] 1. Kopfnicken; 2. nicken (mit)
noise [nɔɪz] Lärm, Geräusch; **noisy** ['nɔɪzɪ] laut, lärmend
non- [nɒn] nicht-; Nicht-
none (of) [nʌn] keine(r, s) (von)
noon [nu:n] Mittag
normal ['nɔ:ml] normal; **normality** [nɔ:'mælətɪ] Normalität
Norman ['nɔ:mən] normannisch; Normanne/-in
north (of) [nɔ:θ] 1. nördlich (von); 2. Nord-; (nach) Norden; **northern** ['nɔ:ðən] Nord-, nördlich
nose [nəʊz] Nase
not [nɒt] nicht; **not ... any** (gar) kein, keine; keins; **not ... any more** nicht mehr; **not ... anybody** niemand; **not ... anything** nichts; **not ... anywhere** nirgends, nirgendwohin; **not at all** überhaupt nicht, ganz und gar nicht; **not (...) either** auch nicht, auch kein; **not ever** nie; **not yet** noch nicht
note [nəʊt] 1. (BE) (Geld-)Schein; 2. Notiz; 3. Entschuldigung(sschreiben); 4. **note sth. down** (sich) etwas notieren, aufschreiben
nothing ['nʌθɪŋ] nichts
notice ['nəʊtɪs] 1. (be)merken, beachten; 2. Anschlag; Mitteilung, Hinweis (-schild); **give (sb.) notice** 1. (jm.) kündigen; 2. (bei jm.) kündigen
nought [nɔ:t] (BE) Null
novel ['nɒvl] Roman
November [nəʊ'vembə] November
now [naʊ] jetzt, nun; **now and again** hin und wieder; **nowadays** ['naʊədeɪz] heutzutage
nuclear power station [ˌnju:klɪə 'paʊə ˌsteɪʃn] Atomkraftwerk
number ['nʌmbə] 1. Zahl, Nummer; 2. Ausgabe, Nummer *(einer Zeitschrift)*; 3. Anzahl; **a number of** mehrere
nurse [nɜ:s] Krankenschwester/-pfleger

O

object ['ɒbdʒɪkt] Gegenstand
obligation [ˌɒblɪ'geɪʃn] Verpflichtung, Pflicht
°**obtain** [əb'teɪn] erlangen, erhalten
obvious ['ɒbvɪəs] offensichtlich
ocean ['əʊʃn] Ozean
o'clock [ə'klɒk] ... Uhr
October [ɒk'təʊbə] Oktober
Odd one out! [ˌɒd wʌn‿'aʊt] Welches Wort paßt hier nicht?
of [ɒv, əv] von; **bottle of lemonade** Flasche Limonade; **both of them** sie beide, alle beide; **nice of you** nett von dir; **of course** [əv 'kɔ:s] natürlich; **the name of the street** der Name (von) der Straße; **the island of ...** die Insel ...
off [ɒf] von ... herunter
offend [ə'fend] kränken, beleidigen; **offensive** [ə'fensɪv] beleidigend, anstößig
offer ['ɒfə] 1. Angebot; 2. anbieten
office ['ɒfɪs] Büro; **officer** ['ɒfɪsə] Polizist/-in; Beamte(r)/-in; Offizier/in; **official** [ə'fɪʃl] offiziell, amtlich
often ['ɒfn, 'ɒftən] oft
oil [ɔɪl] Öl; **oil rig** ['ɔɪl rɪg] (Öl-)Bohrinsel
OK = **okay** [əʊ'keɪ] gut, in Ordnung; **I'm OK.** Mir geht's gut.
old [əʊld] alt
omelette ['ɒmlɪt] Omelett
on [ɒn] auf; an; **be on** an sein, laufen; **(drive/go/...) on** weiter(-fahren/-gehen/...); **from now on** von jetzt an, ab jetzt; **on a visit to ...** bei einem Besuch in ...; **on holiday** (BE) auf Urlaub, in den Ferien; **on Monday(s)** montags, am Montag; **on Monday morning(s)** am Montag morgen; **on my way to** auf dem Weg/unterwegs nach; **on October 12th** am 12. Oktober; **on the first night** in der ersten Nacht; **on the left/right** links/rechts; **on the phone** am Telefon; **on the radio/on TV** im Radio/Fernsehen; **on the River Thames** an der Themse; **on the team** (AE) = **in the team** (BE) im Team; **on the train/bus/plane** im Zug/Bus/Flugzeug; **on the weekend(s)** (AE) = **at the weekend(s)** (BE) am Wochenende; **on your birthday** an deinem Geburtstag; **questions on the text** Fragen zum Text, Textfragen
once [wʌns] 1. einmal; 2. (früher) einmal, einst; **at once** sofort, (so)gleich; **once more, once again** noch einmal
one/one's [wʌn, wʌnz] man/sein; **the blue one, the blue ones** der/die/das blaue, die blauen; **oneself** [wʌn'self] sich (selbst)
only ['əʊnlɪ] nur; **not only ... but also** nicht nur ..., sondern auch; **only one week old** erst eine Woche alt; **the only** der/die/das einzige, die einzigen
onto ['ɒntʊ, 'ɒntə] auf ... (hinauf)
open ['əʊpən] 1. offen, geöffnet, auf; 2. öffnen, aufmachen; **opening times** Öffnungszeiten
opera ['ɒprə] Oper; Opern-
operate ['ɒpəreɪt] (sich) betätigen; bedienen; **co-operate** [kəʊ'ɒpəreɪt] zusammenarbeiten, kooperieren; **operation** [ˌɒpə'reɪʃn] Operation, Unternehmen, Untersuchung
opinion [ə'pɪnjən] Meinung; **in my opinion** meiner Meinung nach
opposite ['ɒpəzɪt] 1. Gegenteil; 2. gegenüberliegend; 3. entgegengesetzt; gegenüber (von)
or [ɔ:] oder
oral ['ɔ:rəl] mündlich
orange ['ɒrɪndʒ] 1. orange(farben); 2. Apfelsine, Orange
orchestra ['ɔ:kɪstrə] Orchester
order ['ɔ:də] 1. Reihenfolge, (An-)Ordnung; 2. Befehl; 3. bestellen; 4. **order sb. to do sth.** jm. befehlen, etwas zu tun; jn. damit beauftragen, etwas zu tun; **in order to** um ... zu
ordinary ['ɔdənrɪ] einfach, gewöhnlich, normal
organization [ˌɔ:gənaɪ'zeɪʃn] Organisation; **organize** ['ɔ:gənaɪz] organisieren, veranstalten
origin ['ɒrɪdʒɪn] Ursprung; Entstehung; Herkunft; **original** [ə'rɪdʒənl] ursprünglich; Original-
orphan ['ɔ:fn] Waise, Waisenkind
other ['ʌðə] andere(r, s); **otherwise** ['ʌðəwaɪz] sonst, andernfalls
ought to ['ɔ:tə] sollte eigentlich, müßte eigentlich
our ['aʊə] unser(e); **ours** ['aʊəz] unsere(r, s); **ourselves** [ˌaʊə'selvz] uns (selbst)
out [aʊt] 1. hinaus, heraus; 2. draußen; **come out** herauskommen, hinauskommen; **die out** aussterben; **find out** herausfinden, erfahren; **get out (of the train)** (aus dem Zug) aussteigen; **go out (with)** ausgehen (mit); **out of** aus (... heraus/hinaus); von
°**outback** *(sing.)* ['aʊtbæk] Busch, Hinterland (Australiens)
outdoor ['aʊtdɔ:] im Freien; **outdoors** [ˌaʊt'dɔ:z] (nach) draußen, im Freien
outgoing [ˌaʊt'gəʊɪŋ] gesellig, kontaktfreudig
outside [aʊt'saɪd] 1. draußen; nach draußen; 2. außerhalb (von)
outskirts *(pl.)* ['aʊtskɜ:ts] Stadtrand, Außenbezirke
over ['əʊvə] über; vorüber; **be over** vorüber sein, zu Ende sein; **over there** dort drüben, da drüben; **over the years** im Laufe der Jahre

overcrowded [ˌəʊvəˈkraʊdɪd] überfüllt; übervölkert
overhead projector [ˌəʊvəhed prəˈdʒektə] Tageslichtprojektor, Overheadprojektor
overnight [ˌəʊvəˈnaɪt] über Nacht
overpower [ˌəʊvəˈpaʊə] überwältigen
overseas [ˌəʊvəˈsiːz] 1. überseeisch; 2. in/nach/aus Übersee
overtake [ˌəʊvəˈteɪk] überholen
own [əʊn] 1. eigene(r, s); **I pay for my own clothes.** Ich bezahle meine Kleidung selbst. **on my/your own** allein, ohne Hilfe;
2. besitzen; **owner** Besitzer/in
Oxfam [ˈɒksfæm] *brit. Hilfsorganisation zur Bekämpfung der Hungersnot*

P

p [piː] = **pence** Pence
Pacific [pəˈsɪfɪk] Pazifik; pazifisch
pack [pæk] (ein)packen
packet [ˈpækɪt] Paket, Päckchen; Packung
page [peɪdʒ] Seite *(im Buch)*
pain [peɪn] Schmerz
paint [peɪnt] 1. Farbe *(zum Malen)*; 2. streichen, anstreichen; 3. malen; **painter** Maler/in; Anstreicher/in
pair [peə] Paar; **au pair** [ˌəʊ ˈpeə] Au-Pair (-Mädchen, -Junge)
°**Paki** [ˈpækɪ] (BE, slang) *(Schimpfwort für)* Pakistaner/in
palace [ˈpælɪs] Palast, Schloß
panic [ˈpænɪk] in Panik geraten
paper [ˈpeɪpə] Papier; **paper = newspaper** Zeitung; **do a paper round** (BE) Zeitungen austragen
parade [pəˈreɪd] Umzug, Parade
paragraph [ˈpærəgrɑːf] Absatz, Abschnitt
parenthesis, *pl.* **parentheses** [pəˈrenθɪsɪs, pəˈrenθɪsiːz] Klammer
parents [ˈpeərənts] Eltern
park [pɑːk] 1. Park; 2. parken; **parking lot** (AE) großer Parkplatz; Parkhaus; **parking space** [ˈpɑːkɪŋ speɪs] Parklücke, Parkplatz
parliament [ˈpɑːləmənt] Parlament
parrot [ˈpærət] Papagei
part [pɑːt] 1. Teil; 2. Gegend; 3. Rolle *(eines Schauspielers)*; **part-time** Teilzeit-, halbtags; **take part (in)** teilnehmen (an), mitmachen (bei); **partly** zum Teil, teilweise
particular [pəˈtɪkjʊlə] bestimmte(r, s), spezielle(r, s)
partner [ˈpɑːtnə] Partner/in
party [ˈpɑːtɪ] 1. Party, Fest, Fete; 2. Partei
pass [pɑːs] 1. vorbeigehen (an); vorbeifahren (an); **pass through** gehen/fahren durch, passieren;
2. vergehen, vorübergehen *(Zeit)*; **pass the time (doing sth.)** sich die Zeit vertreiben (mit), die Zeit verbringen (mit);
3. *(eine Prüfung)* bestehen; 4. (herüber-)reichen; *(Ball)* abgeben, abspielen;
5. *(ein Gesetz)* verabschieden
passage [ˈpæsɪdʒ] Gang
passenger [ˈpæsɪndʒə] Fahrgast, Passagier
passport [ˈpɑːspɔːt] (Reise-)Paß
past [pɑːst] 1. Vergangenheit; 2. vergangen; 3. vorbei, vorüber (an); **half past ten** halb elf (= 10.30)
path [pɑːθ] Pfad, Fußweg
patience [ˈpeɪʃns] Geduld; **patient** [ˈpeɪʃnt] geduldig
pavement [ˈpeɪvmənt] (BE) Gehweg
pay [peɪ] 1. Bezahlung, Entgelt; 2. **pay (for)** (be)zahlen
pea [piː] Erbse
peace [piːs] Friede(n); **peaceful** [ˈpiːsfəl] friedlich, friedfertig
pedal [ˈpedl] Pedal
pedestrian [pɪˈdestrɪən] Fußgänger/in; **pedestrian crossing** [pɪˌdestrɪən ˈkrɒsɪŋ] Fußgängerüberweg; **pedestrian precinct** [pɪˌdestrɪən ˈpriːsɪŋkt] (BE) Fußgängerzone
pen [pen] Füller; Stift; **pen-friend** Brieffreund/in
pence [pens] Pence
pencil [ˈpensl] Bleistift; **pencil-case** [ˈpenslkeɪs] Federtasche, Federmäppchen
penguin [ˈpeŋgwɪn] Pinguin
penny [ˈpenɪ] 1. *kleinste britische Münze*; 2. (AE) 1¢-Münze
pension [ˈpenʃn] Altersrente, Pension
people [ˈpiːpl] Leute, Menschen
per cent [pəˈsent] Prozent
perfect [ˈpɜːfɪkt] vollkommen, perfekt
perhaps [pəˈhæps] vielleicht
period [ˈpɪərɪəd] Unterrichtsstunde; Zeitspanne, Zeitraum; AE *auch:* Punkt *(am Satzende)*
permanent [ˈpɜːmənənt] dauerhaft, (be)ständig
permission [pəˈmɪʃn] Erlaubnis, Genehmigung
permit 1. [ˈpɜːmɪt] Genehmigung(sschein), Erlaubnis; 2. [pəˈmɪt] erlauben, gestatten
persecute [ˈpɜːsɪkjuːt] verfolgen *(aus politischen oder religiösen Gründen)*
person [ˈpɜːsn] Person, Mensch; **personal** [ˈpɜːsnl] persönlich, Personal-
pet [pet] Haustier, Tier; **pet shop** Tierhandlung
petrol [ˈpetrəl] (BE) Benzin; **petrol station** [ˈpetrəl ˌsteɪʃn] (BE) Tankstelle
phone = telephone [fəʊn] 1. Telefon; 2. anrufen
photo [ˈfəʊtəʊ] Foto, Bild; **in the photo** auf dem Foto; **take photos** fotografieren; **photograph** [ˈfəʊtəgrɑːf] Fotografie, Bild; **photographer** [fəˈtɒgrəfə] Fotograf/in
phrase [freɪz] 1. Redewendung; 2. Wortgruppe; **phrasal verb** [ˌfreɪzl ˈvɜːb] feste Verb-Adverb-Verbindung
physical education (P.E.) [ˌfɪzɪkl‿edʒʊˈkeɪʃn] Leibesübungen, Turnen, Sport
physics [ˈfɪzɪks] Physik
piano [pɪˈænəʊ] Klavier
pick [pɪk] pflücken; **pick up** aufheben; abholen, mitnehmen
picnic [ˈpɪknɪk] Picknick; **have a picnic** ein Picknick machen
picture [ˈpɪktʃə] Bild; Aufnahme, Foto; **in the picture** auf dem Bild; **picture postcard** Ansichtskarte; **take pictures** fotografieren, Fotos/Bilder machen
pie [paɪ] (Fleisch-)Pastete; Obstkuchen
piece [piːs] Stück
pier [pɪə] Landungssteg
pig [pɪg] Schwein
pink [pɪŋk] pink, rosa
pipe [paɪp] Pfeife
°**pirate** [ˈpaɪərət] Seeräuber/in, Pirat/in
pitch a tent [pɪtʃ] ein Zelt aufschlagen
pity [ˈpɪtɪ]: **It's a pity.** Das ist schade.
pizza [ˈpiːtsə] Pizza
place [pleɪs] Ort, Platz, Stelle
plan [plæn] 1. Plan, Vorhaben; 2. planen; 3. beabsichtigen; **planner** Planer/in
plane [pleɪn] Flugzeug; **by plane** mit dem Flugzeug
plant [plɑːnt] 1. Pflanze; 2. (ein)pflanzen, setzen
plastic [ˈplæstɪk] Kunststoff, Plastik; Plastik-
plate [pleɪt] Teller
platform [ˈplætfɔːm] Bahnsteig
play [pleɪ] 1. (Theater-)Stück; 2. spielen; **play a team** gegen ein Team spielen; **play a trick (on)** einen Streich spielen; **player** Spieler/in
please [pliːz] bitte; **be pleased (with)** sich freuen (über); zufrieden sein (mit)
pleasure [ˈpleʒə] Vergnügen, Freude; Vergnügungs-
plenty (of...) [ˈplentɪ] eine Menge (...); viel(e)...
pliers *(pl.)* [ˈplaɪəz] (eine) (Kombi-)Zange
pm [ˌpiː‿ˈem] Uhr nachmittags/abends
pocket [ˈpɒkɪt] Tasche; **pocket-money** Taschengeld
poem [ˈpəʊɪm] Gedicht
poetry [ˈpəʊɪtrɪ] Dichtung, Dichtkunst
point [pɔɪnt] 1. Punkt; 2. Sinn, Zweck; 3. **point out** hinweisen auf; **point sth. at sb.** etwas auf jn. richten *(Waffe usw.)*; **point (to, at)** zeigen (auf), deuten (auf)
poisonous [ˈpɔɪznəs] giftig
polar bear [ˈpəʊlə beə] Eisbär
police [pəˈliːs] Polizei; **police station** Polizeiwache, Polizeirevier; **policeman** Polizist; **policewoman** Polizistin
policy [ˈpɒləsɪ] Politik
polio [ˈpəʊlɪəʊ] Kinderlähmung, Polio
polite [pəˈlaɪt] höflich; **politeness** [pəˈlaɪtnəs] Höflichkeit
political [pəˈlɪtɪkl] politisch
politician [ˌpɒləˈtɪʃn] Politiker/in
politics *(sing.)* [ˈpɒlɪtɪks] Politik
pollute [pəˈluːt] verschmutzen; **pollution** [pəˈluːʃn] (Umwelt-)Verschmutzung
pond [pɒnd] Teich
pony [ˈpəʊnɪ] Pony
poor [pʊə, pɔː] 1. arm; 2. mangelhaft, schlecht *(Note, Leistung)*
pop music [ˈpɒp ˌmjuːzɪk] Popmusik; **pop song** Popsong
popcorn [ˈpɒpkɔːn] Popcorn
popular (with) [ˈpɒpjʊlə] beliebt (bei)
population [ˌpɒpjʊˈleɪʃn] Bevölkerung, Einwohner(zahl)
port [pɔːt] Hafen; Hafenstadt
portion (of) [ˈpɔːʃn] Portion
position [pəˈzɪʃn] Lage; Position
positive [ˈpɒzətɪv] positiv
possess [pəˈzes] besitzen; **take possession of** [pəˈzeʃn] Besitz ergreifen von, in Besitz nehmen
possibility [ˌpɒsəˈbɪlətɪ] Möglichkeit; **possible** [ˈpɒsəbl] möglich; **possibly** möglicherweise, vielleicht; **We can't possibly do it.** Wir können es beim besten Willen nicht/unmöglich tun.
post [pəʊst] (BE) 1. Post; 2. *(Brief)* abschicken, einwerfen; *(Paket)* aufgeben; **post office** Post(amt); **postcard** Postkarte; **postcode** [ˈpəʊstkəʊd] *britische Postleitzahl*
poster [ˈpəʊstə] Poster, Plakat
potato [pəˈteɪtəʊ], *pl.* **potatoes** Kartoffel
pound [paʊnd] 1. Pfund *(britische Währung)*; 2. *engl./amerik.* Pfund (= 454 g)
poverty [ˈpɒvətɪ] Armut
power [ˈpaʊə] 1. Macht, Kraft, Gewalt; 2. Befugnis; **power station** Kraftwerk; **powerful** [ˈpaʊəfəl] mächtig, stark; **powerless** [ˈpaʊələs] machtlos, kraftlos
practical [ˈpræktɪkl] praktisch
practice [ˈpræktɪs] 1. Übung; Praxis; 2. (AE) üben, trainieren
practise [ˈpræktɪs] (BE) üben, trainieren
prayer [preə] Gebet
precinct: pedestrian precinct [pɪˌdestrɪən ˈpriːsɪŋkt] (BE) Fußgängerzone; **shopping precinct** (BE) Geschäfts-, Einkaufsviertel
predict [prɪˈdɪkt] vorhersagen

prefer (to) [prɪ'fɜ:] vorziehen, lieber haben (als)
prefix ['pri:fɪks] Vorsilbe, Präfix
prejudice (against) ['predʒʊdɪs] Vorurteil, Voreingenommenheit (gegen, gegenüber); **prejudiced (against)** voreingenommen (gegenüber)
preparation [,prepə'reɪʃn] Vorbereitung, Zubereitung; **prepare** [prɪ'peə] vorbereiten, zubereiten; **be prepared (to do sth.)** bereit sein, willens sein (, etwas zu tun)
prescription [prɪ'skrɪpʃn] (ärztliches) Rezept
present 1. ['preznt] Geschenk; 2. Gegenwart; 3. gegenwärtig, heutig; 4. [prɪ'zent] präsentieren, darlegen
president ['prezɪdənt] Präsident/in
pressure ['preʃə] Druck, Zwang
prestige [pre'sti:ʒ] Ansehen, Prestige
pretend [prɪ'tend] so tun, als ob; vortäuschen
pretty ['prɪtɪ] (infml.) ziemlich
price [praɪs] (Kauf-)Preis
priest [pri:st] Priester
primary school ['praɪmərɪ sku:l] (BE) Grundschule
prime minister (infml.: **PM**) [,praɪm 'mɪnɪstə] Premierminister/in, Ministerpräsident/in
prince [prɪns] Prinz, Fürst; **princess** [prɪn'ses] Prinzessin, Fürstin
principal ['prɪnsɪpl] (AE) Schulleiter/in, Direktor/in
printer ['prɪntə] Drucker
prison ['prɪzn] Gefängnis; **prisoner** ['prɪznə] Gefangene(r)
private ['praɪvɪt] 1. privat, Privat-; 2. persönlich
privilege ['prɪvɪlɪdʒ] Privileg, Bevorzugung; **privileged** privilegiert, bevorzugt
prize [praɪz] Preis, Gewinn
pro-(British) [prəʊ] pro(britisch)
probably ['prɒbəblɪ] wahrscheinlich
problem ['prɒbləm] Problem
produce [prə'dju:s] produzieren, herstellen, erzeugen; **producer** [prə'dju:sə] Produzent/in, Produktionsleiter/in; **product** ['prɒdʌkt] Produkt, Erzeugnis
profession [prə'feʃn] (freier, akademischer) Beruf; **professional** [prə'feʃnl] Berufs-, professionell, Fach-; Berufssportler/in, Profi
professor [prə'fesə] Professor/in
profile ['prəʊfaɪl] Kurzbiografie, -portrait; Profil
program ['prəʊgræm] (Computer-)Programm; AE *auch:* Sendung, Programm
programme ['prəʊgræm] (BE) Sendung, Programm
progress *(sing.)* ['prəʊgres] Fortschritt(e); **in progress** im Gange
project ['prɒdʒekt] Projekt; Aufgabe
projector: overhead projector [,əʊvəhed prə'dʒektə] Tageslichtprojektor, Overheadprojektor
promise ['prɒmɪs] 1. Versprechen; 2. versprechen
prompt [prɒmpt] Stichwort (= Hilfe, Hinweis)
pronounce [prə'naʊns] aussprechen; **pronunciation** [prə,nʌnsɪ'eɪʃn] Aussprache
proof [pru:f] Beweis(e), Nachweis(e)
propaganda [,prɒpə'gændə] Propaganda
proper ['prɒpə] richtig, passend, geeignet
°**property** ['prɒpətɪ] Eigentum
protect [prə'tekt] (be)schützen; °**protection** [prə'tekʃn] Schutz
protest 1. ['prəʊtest] Protest, Widerspruch; 2. **protest (against, about)** [prə'test] protestieren (gegen)
Protestant ['prɒtɪstnt] 1. Protestant/in; 2. protestantisch, evangelisch
proud (of) [praʊd] stolz (auf)
proverb ['prɒvɜ:b] Sprichwort
province ['prɒvɪns] Provinz
pub [pʌb] (BE) Kneipe, Lokal
public ['pʌblɪk] öffentlich; **public school** (BE) (teure) Privatschule *(meist mit Internat)*
pull [pʊl] ziehen; **pull down** abreißen, niederreißen
pullover ['pʊl,əʊvə] Pullover
punctual ['pʌŋktʃʊəl] pünktlich
puncture ['pʌŋktʃə] (BE) Reifenpanne
punish ['pʌnɪʃ] bestrafen; **punishment** ['pʌnɪʃmənt] Strafe, Bestrafung
°**punt** [pʊnt] Pfund *(irische Währung)*
pupil ['pju:pl] Schüler/in
push [pʊʃ] stoßen, schieben; drängeln
put [pʊt] stellen, legen, setzen, *(an einen Platz)* tun; **put down** 1. hinlegen, abstellen; 2. aufschreiben, eintragen; **put in** einsetzen; **put on** *(Kleidung)* anziehen; **put out** *(Feuer, Licht)* (aus)löschen, ausmachen; **put up** aufbauen, aufstellen; aufhängen, anbringen; **Put yourself in my place.** Versetze dich in meine Lage.
puzzle ['pʌzl] Rätsel; **puzzled** verwirrt
pyjamas *(pl.)* [pə'dʒɑ:məz] Schlafanzug, Pyjama

Q

quality ['kwɒlətɪ] Qualität; Qualitäts-
quarter ['kwɔ:tə] 1. Viertel; 2. viertel; **quarter past/to ten** viertel nach/vor zehn; 3. (AE) 25¢-Münze
queen [kwi:n] Königin
question ['kwestʃən] 1. Frage; **ask a question** eine Frage stellen; **question mark** Fragezeichen; 2. befragen, vernehmen
questionnaire [,kwestʃə'neə] Fragebogen
queue [kju:] (BE) Schlange *(wartender Menschen)*, Reihe
quick [kwɪk] schnell
quiet ['kwaɪət] still, ruhig, leise
quit [kwɪt] aufhören; *(eine Stelle)* aufgeben
quite [kwaɪt] 1. ziemlich; 2. ganz; **quite a** ein(e) ziemlich(er, e, es)
quiz [kwɪz] Quiz
quotation mark [kwəʊ'teɪʃn mɑ:k] Anführungszeichen

R

rabbit ['ræbɪt] Kaninchen
°**rabble** ['ræbl] Pöbel, Mob
race [reɪs] 1. Rasse; 2. Rennen, (Wett-)Lauf; **have a race** ein Rennen veranstalten; **racing driver** Rennfahrer/in; 3. rennen; rasen
racism ['reɪsɪzm] Rassismus
radical ['rædɪkl] radikal
radio ['reɪdɪəʊ] Radio, Rundfunk; **on the radio** im Radio
raid [reɪd] 1. eine Razzia durchführen (in, bei); überfallen; 2. **raid (on)** Razzia (in); Überfall
railway ['reɪlweɪ] Eisenbahn(strecke)
rain [reɪn] 1. Regen; 2. regnen; **rainy** regnerisch, verregnet
raise [reɪz] (hoch)heben; erhöhen
°**rape** [reɪp] Vergewaltigung
rat [ræt] Ratte
rate [reɪt] *(Geburten-, Inflations- usw.)* Rate
°**rather** ['rɑ:ðə]: **I'd rather not** ich würde lieber nicht
raw [rɔ:] roh; Roh-
reach (for) [ri:tʃ] erreichen; greifen (nach)
react (to) [ri:'ækt]] reagieren auf; **reaction (to)** [ri:'ækʃn] Reaktion (auf)
read [ri:d] (vor)lesen; **read out** vorlesen; **readable** ['ri:dəbl] lesbar; **reader** Leser/in
ready ['redɪ] bereit, fertig
real [rɪəl] echt, wirklich; **realistic** [,rɪə'lɪstɪk] realistisch, wirklichkeitsnah; **really** wirklich, tatsächlich
realize ['rɪəlaɪz] erkennen; sich klar machen; einsehen; merken
reason ['ri:zn] Grund, Begründung; **for this reason** aus diesem Grund, deshalb; **reasonable** ['ri:znəbl] vernünftig
rebellion [rɪ'beljən] Rebellion; Aufstand
receive [rɪ'si:v] 1. erhalten, bekommen; 2. empfangen
recent ['ri:snt] letzte(r, s), neueste(r, s); vor kurzem *(geschehen, entstanden usw.)*
recognize ['rekəgnaɪz] 1. erkennen; 2. anerkennen
reconstruct [,ri:kən'strʌkt] rekonstruieren, (wiederauf)bauen
record 1. ['rekɔ:d] Rekord; 2. Schallplatte; **record-player** Plattenspieler; 3. [rɪ'kɔ:d] aufzeichnen, aufnehmen *(auf Band)*
°**recover** [rɪ'kʌvə] sich erholen
recreation [,rekrɪ'eɪʃn] Erholung, Freizeitaktivität
red [red] rot
°**re-enact** [,ri:ɪ'nækt] nachspielen, nachstellen, neu inszenieren
refer to [rɪ'fɜ:] sich beziehen auf
refuse [rɪ'fju:z] sich weigern; verweigern, ablehnen
region ['ri:dʒn] Gegend, Gebiet, Region; **regional** ['ri:dʒənl] regional
register ['redʒɪstə] (BE) Klassenbuch, Namensliste
regular ['regjʊlə] regelmäßig; **a regular job** eine feste Anstellung; °**regularity** [,regjʊ'lærətɪ] Regelmäßigkeit
reject [rɪ'dʒekt] ablehnen, zurückweisen
related [rɪ'leɪtɪd]: **be related (to)** 1. verwandt sein (mit); 2. sich beziehen (auf)
relations (with) *(pl.)* [rɪ'leɪʃnz] Beziehungen (mit)
relative ['relətɪv] Verwandte(r)
relax [rɪ'læks] (sich) entspannen, sich ausruhen
release [rɪ'li:s] los-, freilassen; **release the brake** die Bremse lösen
reliable [rɪ'laɪəbl] zuverlässig
religion [rɪ'lɪdʒn] Religion
religious [rɪ'lɪdʒəs] religiös; **religious education (R.E.)** [rɪ,lɪdʒəs‿edʒʊ'keɪʃn] Religion(sunterricht)
remain [rɪ'meɪn] bleiben; übrigbleiben
remember [rɪ'membə] 1. sich erinnern (an); daran denken; 2. sich merken
remind (of) [rɪ'maɪnd] erinnern (an)
renew [rɪ'nju:] erneuern; verlängern
rent [rent] mieten, leihen
repair [rɪ'peə] 1. Reparatur; 2. reparieren; **repair kit** [rɪ'peə kɪt] Flickzeug
repeat [rɪ'pi:t] wiederholen
°**replace (with)** [rɪ'pleɪs] ersetzen (durch)
reply (to) [rɪ'plaɪ] 1. Antwort, Erwiderung (auf); **in reply (to)** als Antwort (auf); 2. antworten (auf), beantworten; erwidern
report [rɪ'pɔ:t] 1. Bericht; 2. Zeugnis; 3. berichten; melden; *(bei der Polizei)* anzeigen; **reporter** Reporter/in
°**represent (sb.)** [,reprɪ'zent] (jn.) vertreten
republic [rɪ'pʌblɪk] Republik; **Republican** [rɪ'pʌblɪkən] 1. Republikaner/in; 2. republikanisch

reputation [ˌrepjʊˈteɪʃn] Ansehen, Ruf
request [rɪˈkwest] Bitte
reservation [ˌrezəˈveɪʃn] **1.** Reservation, Reservat; **2.** Reservierung; **reserve** [rɪˈzɜːv] reservieren (lassen), buchen
reservoir [ˈrezəvwɑː] Stausee, (Speicher-)Becken
°**resign** [rɪˈzaɪn] kündigen
resort [rɪˈzɔːt] Ferienort, Urlaubsort
resources *(pl.)* [rɪˈsɔːsɪz]: **natural resources** Bodenschätze
respect [rɪˈspekt] Achtung, Respekt; **in this/that respect** in dieser/jener Hinsicht, Beziehung; **respectful** [rɪˈspektfəl] respektvoll
°**responsible** [rɪˈspɒnsɪbl] verantwortlich, verantwortungsvoll
rest [rest] Rest
restaurant [ˈrestrɒnt] Restaurant, Gaststätte
restless [ˈrestləs] rastlos, ruhelos; unruhig
restore [rɪˈstɔː] wiederherstellen; restaurieren; neu aufbauen
result [rɪˈzʌlt] Ergebnis, Resultat
retell [ˌriːˈtel] nacherzählen
retire [rɪˈtaɪə] in den Ruhestand treten, in Rente/Pension gehen; **retired** im Ruhestand; pensioniert
return [rɪˈtɜːn] **1.** Rückkehr, Wiederkehr; **2.** zurückkommen, -gehen; **3.** Rück-; **return (ticket)** (BE) Rückfahrkarte
revise [rɪˈvaɪz] (BE) *(Lernstoff)* wiederholen
revolution [ˌrevəˈluːʃn] Revolution
reward [rɪˈwɔːd] Belohnung; Finderlohn
rewrite [ˌriːˈraɪt] neu schreiben, noch mal schreiben
rhyme [raɪm] Reim, Vers
rich [rɪtʃ] **1.** kräftig *(Geruch, Farbton)*; schwer, nahrhaft *(Speise)*; **2. rich (in)** reich (an)
rid: get rid of [ˌget ˈrɪd‿əv] loswerden
ride [raɪd] **1.** *(auf einem Pferd)* reiten; **2.** (rad)fahren; **a one-minute ride by bus/car** eine Minute mit dem Bus/Auto; **go for a ride** herumfahren, eine Spritztour machen; **rider** [ˈraɪdə] (Rad-)Fahrer/in; Reiter/in
rifle [ˈraɪfl] Gewehr, Büchse
right [raɪt] **1.** richtig; **all right** gut, in Ordnung; **be right** recht haben; **My watch is right.** Meine Uhr geht richtig. **That's right.** Richtig! Stimmt! **2.** rechte(r, s), nach rechts; **on the right** rechts, auf der rechten Seite; **3.** direkt, genau; **4. rights** *(pl.)* Rechte
ring [rɪŋ] **1.** Ring; **2.** klingeln, läuten; **3.** anrufen; °**give sb. a ring** jn. anrufen; **ring up** anrufen
riot [ˈraɪət] Krawall, Aufruhr
ripe [raɪp] reif
rise [raɪz] aufgehen *(Sonne, Mond)*; (an-, auf)steigen
risk [rɪsk] **1.** Risiko; **2.** riskieren, wagen
rival [ˈraɪvl] Rivale/-in, Konkurrent/in
river [ˈrɪvə] Fluß; **on the (River) Thames** an der Themse
road [rəʊd] (Land-)Straße; **road sign** Verkehrszeichen
roast beef [ˌrəʊst ˈbiːf] Rinderbraten, Roastbeef
rob [rɒb] be-, ausrauben; **robber** Räuber/-in; **robbery** [ˈrɒbərɪ] Raub(überfall)
rock [rɒk] Fels(en); **rock-climbing** [ˈrɒk ˌklaɪmɪŋ] Klettern (im Fels); **rocky** felsig
rocket [ˈrɒkɪt] Rakete
role-play [ˈrəʊl pleɪ] Rollenspiel
roll [rəʊl] **1.** Brötchen, Semmel; **2.** rollen
Roman [ˈrəʊmən] römisch; Römer/in
roof [ruːf] Dach
room [ruːm, rʊm] Zimmer, Raum; Platz
root [ruːt] Wurzel
rope [rəʊp] Seil
rose [rəʊz] Rose
rough [rʌf] rauh, stürmisch; grob; **rough looking kids** gewalttätig aussehende Jugendliche
round [raʊnd] **1.** um (...herum); **2.** rund; **3.** Kanon
route [ruːt] Route, Strecke
row [rəʊ] Reihe
royal [ˈrɔɪəl] königlich
rub [rʌb] (ein)reiben
rubber [ˈrʌbə] **1.** (BE) Radiergummi; **2.** Gummi
rude [ruːd] unhöflich, grob; unanständig
rugby [ˈrʌgbɪ] Rugby
ruin [ˈruːɪn] **1.** zerstören, ruinieren; **2.** Untergang, Ruin; **3.** Ruine; **in ruins** zerstört
rule [ruːl] **1.** Regel, Vorschrift; **2.** (be)herrschen, regieren
ruler [ˈruːlə] Lineal
run [rʌn] **1.** rennen, laufen; **2.** verkehren, fahren *(Zug, Bus)*; **3.** *(eine Schule, Farm)* leiten, betreiben; **runner** Läufer/in
rush [rʌʃ] **1.** Ansturm, Andrang; Eile, Hetze(rei); **2.** eilen, hetzen; **rush hour** Hauptverkehrszeit
Russia [ˈrʌʃə] Rußland; **Russian 1.** Russe/Russin; **2.** russisch

S

sad [sæd] traurig; **sadness** Traurigkeit
saddle [ˈsædl] Sattel
safari park [səˈfɑːrɪ pɑːk] Safaripark
safe [seɪf] sicher, gefahrlos
sail [seɪl] **1.** Segel; **2.** segeln, fahren; **sailor** Seemann, Matrose
salad [ˈsæləd] (angemachter) Salat; **ham salad** Schinken mit Salat
salary [ˈsælərɪ] Gehalt
sale [seɪl] Verkauf; **for sale** zu verkaufen
salt [sɔːlt] Salz; **salty** salzig; versalzen
same [seɪm]: **the same** der-, die-, dasselbe
sand [sænd] Sand; **sandy** sandig
sandwich [ˈsænwɪdʒ] belegtes Butterbrot
Santa Claus [ˈsæntə klɔːz] Weihnachtsmann
sari [ˈsɑːrɪ] Sari
satellite [ˈsætəlaɪt] Satellit
satisfaction [ˌsætɪsˈfækʃn] Zufriedenheit; Befriedigung
satisfactory [ˌsætɪsˈfæktrɪ] befriedigend *(Note, Leistung)*
satisfied (with) [ˈsætɪsfaɪd] zufrieden (mit)
Saturday [ˈsætədɪ, -deɪ] Samstag, Sonnabend
sauce [sɔːs] Soße
saucer [ˈsɔːsə] Untertasse
sausage [ˈsɒsɪdʒ] Wurst, Würstchen
save [seɪv] **1.** sparen; **2.** retten
saw [sɔː] Säge
Saxon [ˈsæksn] Sachse, Sächsin
say [seɪ] sagen; **say hello (to)** grüßen; **The text says ...** Im Text steht/heißt es ...; **What do you say?** Was meinst du dazu? Was hältst du davon? **You can say that again.** Das kann man wohl sagen! **saying** Redensart, Sprichwort, Spruch
scarce [skeəs] knapp, rar
scatter [ˈskætə] verstreuen, (sich) zerstreuen
scene [siːn] Schauplatz, Ort; Szene
scenery [ˈsiːnərɪ] (schöne) Landschaft
schedule [ˈʃedjuːl] Zeitplan; AE *auch:* Stundenplan
scholarship [ˈskɒləʃɪp] Stipendium
school [skuːl] Schule; **at school** in der Schule; **go to school** zur Schule gehen; **schoolchildren** Schüler und Schülerinnen, Schulkinder; **school leaver** [ˈskuːl ˌliːvə] Schulabgänger/in
science [ˈsaɪəns] (Natur-)Wissenschaft; **scientist** [ˈsaɪəntɪst] (Natur-)Wissenschaftler/in
scissors *(pl.)* [ˈsɪzəz] (eine) Schere
score [skɔː] **1.** Spielstand; Ergebnis; **2.** *(einen Punkt/Treffer)* erzielen, *(ein Tor)* schießen
Scotland [ˈskɒtlənd] Schottland; **Scot** Schotte/Schottin; **the Scots** die Schotten; **Scotsman/Scotswoman** Schotte/Schottin; **Scottish** schottisch
scout [skaʊt]: **Girl Scout** (AE) Pfadfinderin
scream [skriːm] **1.** Schrei; Aufschrei; **2.** schreien, kreischen
screen [skriːn] Bildschirm; Leinwand
screw [skruː] Schraube; **screwdriver** [ˈskruːˌdraɪvə] Schraubenzieher
sea [siː] Meer; **sea lion** [ˈsiː ˌlaɪən] Seelöwe; **seasick** [ˈsiːsɪk] seekrank; **seaside** [ˈsiːsaɪd] See-, Küsten-; Küste
search [sɜːtʃ] **1.** Suche, Durchsuchung; **2. search (for)** (durch)suchen (nach), (durch)forschen (nach)
season [ˈsiːzn] Jahreszeit; Saison
seat [siːt] Sitzplatz; **seatbelt** [ˈsiːtbelt] Sicherheitsgurt
second [ˈsekənd] Sekunde
secondary modern school [ˌsekəndrɪ ˈmɒdn skuːl] (BE) *Mischung aus Haupt- und Realschule*; **secondary school** Oberschule
secret [ˈsiːkrət] Geheimnis
secretary [ˈsekrətrɪ] Sekretär/in; **Secretary of State 1.** (BE) Minister/in; Staatssekretär/in; **2.** (AE) Außenminister/in
security [sɪˈkjʊərɪtɪ] Sicherheit; Sicherheitsvorkehrungen
see [siː] sehen; besuchen; **I see.** Ich verstehe. Ach so! **Let me see, ...** Warte mal! Laß mich mal überlegen! **Let's see.** Wollen mal sehen. **See you soon.** Tschüs. Bis bald. **you see** weißt du, nämlich
seem [siːm] scheinen
selfish [ˈselfɪʃ] egoistisch
sell [sel] verkaufen
semi-colon [ˌsemɪˈkəʊlən] Semikolon
semi-detached house [ˌsemɪ dɪˌtætʃt ˈhaʊs] (BE) Doppelhaushälfte
send [send] schicken, senden; **send for** holen, kommen lassen; **send sb. to sleep** jn. einschläfern, zum Schlafen bringen
senior citizen [ˌsiːnɪə ˈsɪtɪzn] Senior/in, ältere(r) Mitbürger/in
°**sense** [sens] Sinn, Bedeutung
sentence [ˈsentəns] Satz
separate [ˈseprət] getrennt, selbständig
September [sepˈtembə] September
series [ˈsɪəriːz] (Sende-)Reihe, Serie
serious [ˈsɪərɪəs] **1.** ernst(haft); **2.** schlimm
serve [sɜːv] (be)dienen, servieren; **servant** [ˈsɜːvnt] Diener/in, Dienstmädchen
service [ˈsɜːvɪs] *(Zug-, Bus- usw.)* Verbindung; Dienst(leistung)
set [set] **1.** Satz *(im Tennis)*; **2.** Kurs(gruppe); **3.** setzen, stellen, legen; **4.** untergehen *(Sonne, Mond)*
setting [ˈsetɪŋ] Schauplatz
settle [ˈsetl] sich niederlassen, ansiedeln; **settlement** Siedlung; Besiedlung; **settler** Siedler/in
several [ˈsevrəl] mehrere; verschiedene
°**sew** [səʊ] nähen
sewage [ˈsuːɪdʒ] Abwasser
sex [seks] **1.** Geschlecht; **2.** Sex
shabby [ˈʃæbɪ] schäbig
shade [ʃeɪd] (Farb-)Ton, Schattierung, Nuance
shake [ʃeɪk] schütteln; zittern; **(milk) shake** (Milch-)Shake, Mixgetränk

Shall I/we ...? [ʃæl, ʃəl] Soll ich/Sollen wir ...? **I shall (= I will)** ich werde/will
°**shame** [ʃeɪm] beschämen
shampoo [ʃæm'pu:] Shampoo, Haarwaschmittel
shan't [ʃɑ:nt]: **I shan't = I shall not**
shape [ʃeɪp] Gestalt, Form; **...-shaped** ...förmig
share (with) [ʃeə] (sich) teilen (mit), gemeinsam benutzen
she [ʃi:] sie
sheep [ʃi:p] Schaf, Schafe
shelf, *pl.* **shelves** [ʃelf, ʃelvz] Bord, Brett; Regal
shell [ʃel] Muschel(schale)
shine [ʃaɪn] scheinen *(Sonne)*; glänzen
ship [ʃɪp] Schiff
shirt [ʃɜ:t] (Ober-)Hemd
shock [ʃɒk] **1.** Schreck, Schock; Schlag, Stoß; **2.** schockieren; **shocked** schockiert, bestürzt
shoe [ʃu:] Schuh
shoot [ʃu:t] (er)schießen; **shot** [ʃɒt] Schuß
shop [ʃɒp] Laden, Geschäft; **pet shop** Tierhandlung; **shop assistant** ['ʃɒp‿əˌsɪstənt] (BE) Verkäufer/in; **shopping** Einkauf(en); BE *auch:* eingekaufte Sachen; **do the shopping** einkaufen, Einkäufe machen/erledigen; **go shopping** einkaufen gehen
short [ʃɔ:t] **1.** kurz; **short-sighted** [ˌʃɔ:t'saɪtɪd] kurzsichtig; **2.** klein *(von Gestalt)*; **3. be short of** zu wenig haben von, knapp sein mit; **shortage** ['ʃɔ:tɪdʒ] Knappheit; Mangel; **shorts** *(pl.)* Shorts, kurze Hose(n)
should [ʃʊd, ʃəd] sollte(n), müßte(n)
shoulder ['ʃəʊldə] Schulter
shout [ʃaʊt] **1.** (laut) rufen, schreien; **2.** (lauter) Schrei, Ruf
show [ʃəʊ] **1.** Schau; Show; **2.** zeigen
shower ['ʃaʊə] Dusche, Brause; (Regen-)Schauer; **have a shower** (sich) duschen
shut [ʃʌt] schließen, zumachen
shy [ʃaɪ] scheu, zurückhaltend
sick [sɪk] krank; **be sick** (BE) sich übergeben (müssen); **be sick of** (etwas) satt haben; °**I feel sick.** Mir ist übel. **sickness** ['sɪknəs] Krankheit
side [saɪd] Seite; Straßenrand
sidewalk ['saɪdwɔ:k] (AE) Gehweg
sigh (with) [saɪ] seufzen (vor)
sight [saɪt] Sehenswürdigkeit; Anblick; **see the sights** sich die Sehenswürdigkeiten ansehen
sign [saɪn] **1.** Zeichen; (Hinweis-)Schild; **road sign** Verkehrszeichen; **2.** unterschreiben; **sign out/in** sich schriftlich abmelden/(wieder)anmelden, sich aus-/eintragen
signal ['sɪgnl] Signal, Zeichen
°**signature** ['sɪgnɪtʃə] Unterschrift
silly ['sɪlɪ] albern, dumm, doof, blöd; **silliness** ['sɪlɪnəs] Dummheit
silver ['sɪlvə] **1.** silbern; **2.** Silber
similar ['sɪmɪlə] ähnlich
simple ['sɪmpl] einfach; einfältig, naiv; **simply** einfach, bloß
since [sɪns] seit
sincerely [sɪn'sɪəlɪ]: **Sincerely (yours)** (AE) Mit freundlichen/herzlichen Grüßen; **Yours sincerely** (BE) Mit freundlichen/herzlichen Grüßen
sing [sɪŋ] singen; **singer** ['sɪŋə] Sänger/in
single ['sɪŋgl] einzig; einzeln, Einzel-; ledig, unverheiratet; **single (ticket)** (BE) einfache Fahrkarte
sink [sɪŋk] **1.** sinken, untergehen; **2.** versenken
sir [sɜ:] *höfliche Anrede für einen Mann*; **Dear Sir or Madam** Sehr geehrte Damen und Herren
siren ['saɪərən] Sirene
sister ['sɪstə] Schwester
sit [sɪt] sitzen; **sit down** sich setzen
site [saɪt] Stätte, Stelle; **camp site** Campingplatz, Zeltplatz
situation [ˌsɪtjʊ'eɪʃn] Situation
sixth form ['sɪksθ fɔ:m] (BE) Oberstufe, Sekundarstufe II; **sixth former** (BE) Schüler/in der Oberstufe; **lower sixth (form)/upper sixth (form)** (BE) vorletzte/letzte Klasse der Oberstufe
size [saɪz] Größe; **What size do you take?** Welche Größe hast du/haben Sie?
ski [ski:] **1.** Ski; **2.** Ski laufen, fahren
skill [skɪl] **1.** Geschick, Geschicklichkeit; **2.** Fertigkeit; Kenntnis
skin [skɪn] Haut
skirt [skɜ:t] Rock
sky [skaɪ] Himmel; **skyscraper** ['skaɪˌskreɪpə] Wolkenkratzer
slang [slæŋ] Slang; Jargon
slave [sleɪv] Sklave/-in; **slavery** ['sleɪvərɪ] Sklaverei
sleep [sli:p] **1.** Schlaf; **2.** schlafen; **sleeping bag** ['sli:pɪŋ bæg] Schlafsack; **sleepless** ['sli:pləs] schlaflos; **sleepy** ['sli:pɪ] schläfrig; verschlafen
°**slight** [slaɪt] leicht, geringfügig
slow [sləʊ] langsam
small [smɔ:l] klein
smell [smel] **1.** Geruch; **2.** riechen; **smelly** stinkend; **They're smelly.** Sie stinken.
smile (at) [smaɪl] **1.** (an)lächeln; **2.** Lächeln
smoke [sməʊk] **1.** Rauch, Dampf, Dunst; **2.** rauchen
smuggler ['smʌglə] Schmuggler/in
snack bar ['snæk bɑ:] Snackbar, Imbißstube
snake [sneɪk] Schlange
snow [snəʊ] **1.** Schnee; **2.** schneien; **snowy** verschneit
so [səʊ] **1.** darum, deshalb; **2.** also; **3.** so; **4.** so daß, damit; **I don't think so.** Das glaube/finde ich nicht. **I think so.** Ich glaube (ja). **so-called** sogenannte(r, s); **so that** damit, so daß; **So what?** Na und?
soap [səʊp] Seife
sob [sɒb] **1.** Schluchzer; **2.** schluchzen
social ['səʊʃl] gesellschaftlich; sozial; Sozial-; gesellig
society [sə'saɪətɪ] Gesellschaft; Verein, Arbeitsgemeinschaft
sock [sɒk] Socke, Strumpf
sofa ['səʊfə] Sofa
soft [sɒft] **1.** weich; **2.** leise
soldier ['səʊldʒə] Soldat/in
solution (to) [sə'lu:ʃn] (Auf-)Lösung (für)
solve [sɒlv] *(Aufgabe, Problem)* lösen
some [sʌm, səm] **1.** einige, ein paar; **2.** etwas; **some more** noch einige/etwas; **somebody/someone** jemand; **somehow** irgendwie; **something** etwas; **sometimes** manchmal; **somewhere** irgendwo(hin)
son [sʌn] Sohn
song [sɒŋ] Lied
soon [su:n] bald; **as soon as** *(conj.)* sobald
sore [sɔ:] wund, rauh, entzündet; **sore throat** Halsschmerzen, Halsweh
°**sorrow** ['sɒrəʊ] Kummer, Sorge; Trauer
sorry ['sɒrɪ]: **(I'm) sorry.** Entschuldigung! Tut mir leid! **Sorry?** Wie bitte? **Sorry I'm late.** Entschuldigen Sie, daß ich zu spät komme.
soul [səʊl] Seele
sound [saʊnd] **1.** Laut, Ton; Klang; **2.** klingen, sich anhören
soup [su:p] Suppe
sour ['saʊə] sauer; °**The magic of the day had gone sour on them.** Der Zauber des Tages war verflogen/war ihnen verdorben.
south (of) [saʊθ] **1.** südlich (von); **2.** Süd-; (nach) Süden; **southern** ['sʌðən] südlich, Süd-; **southernmost** ['sʌðənməʊst] südlichste(r, s)
souvenir [ˌsu:və'nɪə] (Reise-)Andenken, Souvenir
space [speɪs] **1.** (Welt-)Raum; **2.** Platz
spaghetti [spə'getɪ] Spaghetti
Spain [speɪn] Spanien; **Spaniard** ['spænjəd] Spanier/in; **Spanish** spanisch; **the Spanish** die Spanier
speak (to) [spi:k] sprechen (mit); **speaker** Sprecher/in; **Amy Connor speaking.** (Hier) Amy Connor. *(am Telefon)*
°**spear** [spɪə] Speer
special ['speʃl] **1.** besondere(r, s); **2.** Sonder-
spectator [spek'teɪtə] Zuschauer/in
speech [spi:tʃ] Rede, Vortrag; Sprache, Sprechweise; **give a speech** eine Rede halten
speed [spi:d] Geschwindigkeit
spell [spel] buchstabieren, schreiben
spend [spend] **1.** *(Geld)* ausgeben; **2.** *(Zeit)* verbringen
spider ['spaɪdə] Spinne
°**spill** [spɪl] verschütten
°**spirits: methylated spirits** [ˌmeθɪleɪtɪd 'spɪrɪts], (Aust. E infml.:) **metho** ['meθəʊ] Brennspiritus
spite: in spite of [ɪn 'spaɪt‿əv] trotz
split (up) [splɪt] (auf)spalten, (auf)teilen; (sich) teilen, (sich) trennen
spoil [spɔɪl] verderben, verschandeln; *(Kinder)* verwöhnen, verziehen
spoon [spu:n] Löffel
sport [spɔ:t] Sport, Sportart; **do sport(s)** Sport treiben; **sporting activity** sportliche Aktivität
spotlight ['spɒtlaɪt] Scheinwerfer(licht), Rampenlicht
spread [spred] (sich) ausbreiten
spring [sprɪŋ] Frühling, Frühjahr; **in (the) spring** im Frühling/Frühjahr
square [skweə] **1.** Platz *(in einer Stadt)*; **2.** Quadrat; **3.** quadratisch, viereckig
squash [skwɒʃ] Squash
stadium ['steɪdɪəm] Stadion
stairs *(pl.)* [steəz] Treppe(nstufen)
stamp [stæmp] (Brief-)Marke
stand [stænd] stehen; **stand up 1.** aufstehen; **2.** aufrecht stehen
standard ['stændəd] Niveau; Standard
star [stɑ:] Stern; **the Stars and Stripes** *(sing.)* [ˌstɑ:z‿n 'straɪps] das Sternenbanner *(Nationalflagge der USA)*
°**stare at** [steə] anstarren
start [stɑ:t] **1.** Anfang, Beginn, Start; **2.** anfangen, beginnen (mit); **3.** starten; **4.** gründen; **start school** eingeschult werden; **starter** ['stɑ:tə] Starter/in
starve [stɑ:v] aushungern; (ver)hungern
state [steɪt] **1.** Staat; **head of state** Staatsoberhaupt; **state school** (BE) staatliche Schule; °**2.** feststellen
statement ['steɪtmənt] Aussage, Feststellung; Erklärung
station ['steɪʃn] Bahnhof; **police station** Polizeiwache, Polizeirevier; **(sheep/cattle) station** *australische Bezeichnung für* (Schafszucht-/Rinderzucht-)Farm
statue ['stætʃu:] Statue
stay [steɪ] **1.** bleiben; **2.** übernachten, wohnen; **stay up** aufbleiben
steak [steɪk] Steak
steal [sti:l] stehlen
steel [sti:l] Stahl
steering wheel ['stɪərɪŋ wi:l] Steuer(rad), Lenkrad
stem [stem] *(Wort-)*Stamm
°**step** [step] Stufe

stereo ['sterɪəʊ] **1.** Stereoanlage; **2.** Stereo, Stereo-
stick [stɪk] Stock; (trockener, abgebrochener) Zweig
still [stɪl] **1.** (immer) noch; **2.** trotzdem, dennoch; **stand still** stillstehen
stomach ache ['stʌmək‿eɪk] Magenschmerzen, Bauchschmerzen
stone [stəʊn] Stein
stop [stɒp] **1.** Station, Haltestelle; **bus stop** Bushaltestelle; **2.** aufhören; anhalten, stoppen; **stopwatch** ['stɒp wɒtʃ] Stoppuhr
store [stɔ:] **1.** Kaufhaus, Warenhaus; **grocery store** ['grəʊsərɪ stɔ:] Lebensmittelgeschäft; **2.** speichern; lagern
storm [stɔ:m] **1.** Sturm; Gewitter; **2. storm (into)** (hinein)stürmen; **stormy** ['stɔ:mɪ] stürmisch
story ['stɔ:rɪ] Geschichte, Erzählung; **storyteller** ['stɔ:rɪ,telə] (Geschichten-)Erzähler/in
stove [stəʊv] (Koch-)Herd; Ofen
straight [streɪt] gerade(wegs), direkt
strange [streɪndʒ] seltsam, sonderbar; fremd; **stranger** ['streɪndʒə] Fremde(r)
street [stri:t] Straße; **in Sandfield Street** in der Sandfieldstraße; **in the street/on the street** auf der Straße
°**strength** [streŋθ] Kraft
stress [stres] **1.** Streß; **2.** Betonung; **3.** betonen
strict [strɪkt] streng; **strictness** ['strɪktnəs] Strenge
strike [straɪk] Streik; **be on strike** streiken, im Ausstand sein; **go on strike** in den Streik treten, streiken
stripe [straɪp] Streifen
strong [strɒŋ] **1.** stark; **2.** kräftig
structure ['strʌktʃə] Struktur, Konstruktion
student ['stju:dənt] Student/in; AE *auch*: Schüler/in
study (for an exam) ['stʌdɪ] (für eine Prüfung) lernen, sich vorbereiten; studieren
stuff [stʌf] (infml.) Zeug, Kram
stupid ['stju:pɪd] dumm, blöd
style [staɪl] **1.** Stil, Mode; **2.** Art, Weise
subject ['sʌbdʒɪkt] (Schul-)Fach
suburb ['sʌbɜ:b] Vorstadt, Vorort, Randbezirk
subway ['sʌbweɪ] (AE) U-Bahn
succeed (in) [sək'si:d] Erfolg haben (in, bei)
success [sək'ses] Erfolg; **successful** [sək'sesfəl] erfolgreich
such [sʌtʃ] solch, so (ein/e), so; **such as** (wie) zum Beispiel
suddenly ['sʌdnlɪ] plötzlich
suffer (from) ['sʌfə] ertragen; leiden (unter, an)
suffix ['sʌfɪks] Suffix, Nachsilbe
sugar ['ʃʊgə] Zucker
suggest [sə'dʒest] **1.** vorschlagen; **2.** nahelegen, andeuten; **suggestion** [sə'dʒestʃn] Vorschlag, Anregung
suicide ['su:ɪsaɪd] Selbstmord
suit [su:t] *(jm.)* stehen *(Kleidung)*
suitcase ['su:tkeɪs] Koffer
summarize ['sʌməraɪz] zusammenfassen; **summary** ['sʌmərɪ] Zusammenfassung
summer ['sʌmə] Sommer; **in (the) summer** im Sommer
sun [sʌn] Sonne; **sunburn** ['sʌnbɜ:n] Sonnenbrand; **sunshine** Sonne(nschein); **suntan** ['sʌntæn] Sonnenbräune; **sunny** sonnig
Sunday ['sʌndɪ, -deɪ] Sonntag
super ['su:pə] phantastisch, toll; Super-; **supermarket** ['su:pə,mɑ:kɪt] Supermarkt
superstitious [,su:pə'stɪʃəs] abergläubisch
supper ['sʌpə] Abendessen
supply [sə'plaɪ] (be)liefern; versorgen; **supplier** [sə'plaɪə] Lieferant/in
support [sə'pɔ:t] **1.** Unterstützung, Beistand; **2.** unterstützen, befürworten; **supporter** Anhänger/in; Befürworter/in
suppose [sə'pəʊz] annehmen, vermuten; °**be supposed to** sollen
sure [ʃʊə, ʃɔ:] **1.** sicher, gewiß; **be sure of oneself** selbstsicher sein; **be sure to do sth.** etwas bestimmt/sicher(lich) tun; **make sure** sich vergewissern; darauf achten, dafür sorgen (, daß); **Sure!** Sicher! Klar! Natürlich! **2.** (*meist* AE, infml.) wirklich, „echt"
surprised [sə'praɪzd] überrascht; **surprising** erstaunlich, überraschend
surrender [sə'rendə] sich ergeben, kapitulieren
surrounded by [sə'raʊndɪd] umgeben von
survey (of, on) ['sɜ:veɪ] Umfrage, Untersuchung (über)
survive [sə'vaɪv] überleben
sweet [swi:t] süß; **sweets** (BE) Süßigkeiten, Bonbons
swim [swɪm] schwimmen; **swimming-pool** ['swɪmɪŋ pu:l] Schwimmbad; Schwimmbecken; **swimming costume** ['kɒstju:m] (BE) Badebekleidung, Badeanzug; **swimming trunks** *(pl.)* [trʌŋks] Badehose
switch [swɪtʃ] **1.** Schalter; **2.** (um)schalten; **switch on/off** ein-/ausschalten
Switzerland ['swɪtsələnd] die Schweiz; **Swiss** [swɪs] **1.** Schweizer/in; **2.** schweizerisch, Schweizer
sword [sɔ:d] Schwert
syllable ['sɪləbl] Silbe
symbol (of, for) ['sɪmbl] Symbol, Zeichen (für)
system ['sɪstəm] System; Plan, Ordnung

T

table ['teɪbl] **1.** Tisch; **2.** Tabelle; **table-tennis** Tischtennis
tablet ['tæblɪt] Tablette
tailor ['teɪlə] Schneider/in
take [teɪk] **1.** (mit)nehmen; (hin)bringen; **2.** dauern; **it takes** es dauert; man braucht; **it takes me (an hour)** ich brauche (eine Stunde); **take an exam** eine Prüfung ablegen, machen; **take sth. off** etwas ausziehen *(Kleidung)*; **take off** starten, abheben *(Flugzeug)*; **take part (in)** teilnehmen (an), mitmachen (bei) **take photos/ pictures** fotografieren, Fotos/ Bilder machen; **take place** stattfinden; **take the dog for a walk** mit dem Hund rausgehen; **What size do you take?** Welche Größe hast du/haben Sie?
talk [tɔ:k] **1.** Gerede, Gespräch; **2.** Vortrag, Referat; **give a talk (on)** einen Vortrag/ ein Referat halten (über); **3.** sprechen, reden; sich unterhalten
tall [tɔ:l] groß; hoch
tank [tæŋk] Panzer
task [tɑ:sk] Aufgabe
taste [teɪst] **1.** Geschmack; **2. taste (of)** schmecken (nach); kosten; **tasteless** geschmacklos
tax [tæks] Steuer; **put a tax on** besteuern
taxi ['tæksɪ] Taxi
tea [ti:] Tee; **have tea** (BE) Abendbrot essen, zu Abend essen; **make tea** Tee kochen
teach [ti:tʃ] unterrichten, lehren, beibringen; **teacher** ['ti:tʃə] Lehrer/in
team [ti:m] Team, Mannschaft, Gruppe
tear [tɪə] Träne
technique [tek'ni:k] (Arbeits-)Verfahren, Technik, Methode
technology [tek'nɒlədʒɪ] Technologie, Technik
teenage ['ti:neɪdʒ] Teenager-; im Teenageralter; **teenager** ['ti:neɪdʒə] Teenager, Jugendliche(r)
(tele)phone ['telɪfəʊn] **1.** Telefon; **answer the telephone** ans Telefon gehen; **be on the telephone** am Telefon sein, gerade telefonieren; **telephone call** Anruf, Telefongespräch; **2.** anrufen
television ['telɪ,vɪʒn, ,telɪ'vɪʒn] Fernsehen, Fernseher; **on television** im Fernsehen; **watch television** fernsehen
tell [tel] **1.** sagen, nennen; **2.** erzählen, berichten; **3.** erkennen, wissen; **tell the way** den Weg beschreiben
temperature ['temprətʃə] Temperatur; Fieber
temporary ['tempərərɪ] vorläufig, vorübergehend, (zeitlich) begrenzt
tennis ['tenɪs] Tennis
tense [tens] (an)gespannt, nervös; **tension** ['tenʃn] Spannung(en)
tent [tent] Zelt
terraced house [,terəst 'haʊs] (BE) Reihenhaus
terrible ['terəbl] schrecklich, furchtbar
terrified ['terɪfaɪd]**: be terrified (of)** entsetzt sein, schreckliche Angst haben (vor)
terror ['terə] Terror; Entsetzen
test [test] **1.** Test, Prüfung, Klassenarbeit; **do a test** eine Arbeit schreiben, eine Prüfung machen; **2.** prüfen, testen
text [tekst] Text
than [ðæn, ðən] als *(nach Komparativ)*
thank [θæŋk] danken, sich bedanken (bei); **Thank you.** Danke (schön). **Thank you very much.** Vielen Dank. **Thanks.** Danke (schön). **Thanks a lot.** Vielen Dank.
that [ðæt, ðət] **1.** der/die/das (da), jene(r, s) (dort); **2.** daß; **3.** der/die/das *(Relativpronomen)*; **(not) that bad** (nicht) so schlimm; **so that** damit, so daß; **that is (i.e.)** das heißt (d.h.); **that is why** deshalb, darum
the [ðə, ðɪ] der, die, das; die *(Plural)*; **the …, the …** je …, um so/desto …
theatre ['θɪətə] Theater
their [ðeə] ihr, ihre; **theirs** [ðeəz] ihre(r, s)
them [ðem, ðəm] ihnen, sie; **themselves** [ðəm'selvz] sich (selbst)
then [ðen] **1.** dann; **2.** zu der Zeit, damals
there [ðeə] **1.** da, dort; **2.** dahin, dorthin; **over there** dort drüben, da drüben; **there is/are** da ist/sind, es gibt
°**therefore** ['ðeəfɔ:] deshalb, deswegen
these [ði:z] diese, die (hier)
they [ðeɪ] **1.** sie; **2.** man
thick [θɪk] dick
thief, *pl.* **thieves** [θi:f, θi:vz] Dieb/in
thin [θɪn] dünn
thing [θɪŋ] Ding, Sache; **He could not see a thing.** Er konnte absolut nichts sehen.
think [θɪŋk] meinen, finden, glauben, denken; **I don't think so.** Das finde/ glaube ich nicht. **I think so.** Ich glaube (ja). **think of** denken an; halten von; sich ausdenken; **think up** ausdenken; **What do you think about …?** Was hältst du von …? Wie findest du …?
third [θɜ:d] Drittel
thirst [θɜ:st] Durst; **thirsty** ['θɜ:stɪ] durstig; **be thirsty** Durst haben
this [ðɪs] diese(r, s), der/die/das (hier); **This is how you do it.** So/Auf diese

Weise macht man es. **this morning** heute morgen
those [ðəʊz] die/diese (da), jene (dort)
though [ðəʊ] jedoch, (aber) doch; **(even) though** obwohl
thought [θɔ:t] Gedanke; Einfall
threaten [ˈθretn] (be)drohen
throat [θrəʊt] Hals, Kehle; **a sore throat** Halsschmerzen, Halsweh
through [θru:] durch, hindurch; **throughout** [θru:ˈaʊt] überall in; während des/der ganzen
throw [θrəʊ] werfen
thumb [θʌm] Daumen
Thursday [ˈθɜ:zdɪ, -deɪ] Donnerstag
ticket [ˈtɪkɪt] **1.** Eintrittskarte; Fahrkarte, Fahrschein; **2.** Strafmandat, -zettel; **ticket inspector** [ɪnˈspektə] Kontrolleur/in
tidy [ˈtaɪdɪ] ordentlich, aufgeräumt; **tidy up** aufräumen
tie [taɪ] **1.** Krawatte, Schlips; **2. tie (to)** binden (an)
tiger [ˈtaɪgə] Tiger
tight [taɪt] eng(anliegend), stramm
till [tɪl] bis; **not till six** erst um sechs, nicht vor sechs
time [taɪm] **1.** Zeit; **have a nice time** eine schöne Zeit/viel Spaß haben; **Have a good time.** Viel Spaß! Viel Vergnügen! **What time is it?** Wie spät ist es? **timeless** [ˈtaɪmləs] zeitlos; **timetable** (BE) Fahrplan; Stundenplan;
2. time(s) Mal; -mal; **for the first time** zum ersten Mal
tin [tɪn] (BE) Dose, Büchse
tin mine [ˈtɪn maɪn] Zinnmine, Zinnbergwerk
tiny [ˈtaɪnɪ] winzig
tired [ˈtaɪəd] müde; **be tired of** (etwas) satt haben, genug haben von
title [ˈtaɪtl] Titel
to [tu:, tʊ, tə] **1.** zu, nach, in; **2.** um zu; **give to sb.** jm. geben; **happen to** passieren, geschehen mit; **I've been to ...** Ich bin in ... gewesen. **listen to** (sich) anhören; **next to** neben; **quarter to ten** viertel vor zehn; **speak to** sprechen mit; **talk to** sprechen mit; **Try to come.** Versuche zu kommen. **write to** schreiben an
toast [təʊst] Toast
tobacco [təˈbækəʊ] Tabak
today [təˈdeɪ] heute; **today's paper** die heutige Zeitung, die Zeitung von heute
together [təˈgeðə] zusammen
toilet [ˈtɔɪlɪt] Toilette; **toilet article** [ˈtɔɪlɪt‿ɑ:tɪkl] Toilettenartikel
tolerance (towards) [ˈtɒlərəns] Toleranz (gegenüber); **tolerant (towards)** [ˈtɒlərənt] tolerant (gegenüber)
tomato, *pl.* **tomatoes** [təˈmɑ:təʊ] Tomate
tomorrow [təˈmɒrəʊ] morgen; **tomorrow morning** morgen früh; **tomorrow's paper** die morgige Zeitung, die Zeitung von morgen; **the day after tomorrow** übermorgen
ton [tʌn] *engl.* Tonne *(Gewicht)*
tonight [təˈnaɪt] heute abend, heute nacht
too [tu:] auch; **too small** zu klein
tool [tu:l] Werkzeug
tooth, *pl.* **teeth** [tu:θ, ti:θ] Zahn; **toothbrush** [ˈtu:θbrʌʃ] Zahnbürste; **toothpaste** [ˈtu:θpeɪst] Zahnpasta, Zahncreme
top [tɒp] **1.** Spitze; **2.** Kopfende, oberes Ende; **from top to bottom** von oben bis/nach unten; **on top (of)** oben, zuoberst (auf); **top speed** [ˌtɒp ˈspi:d] Höchstgeschwindigkeit
topic [ˈtɒpɪk] Thema
torch [tɔ:tʃ] BE: Taschenlampe
torture [ˈtɔ:tʃə] Folter
total [ˈtəʊtl] gesamt; völlig, total
touch [tʌtʃ] berühren, anfassen
tough [tʌf] zäh; stark; robust
tour [tʊə] (Rund-)Reise, (Rund-)Fahrt, Tour; **go on a bus tour** eine Bus(rund)-fahrt machen; **go on a guided tour** eine Führung (mit)machen;
tourist [ˈtʊərɪst] Tourist/in
towards [təˈwɔ:dz] auf ... zu, in Richtung auf; gegen *(zeitlich)*; **towards sb.** *(sich verhalten)* zu jm., gegenüber jm.
towel [ˈtaʊəl] Handtuch
tower [ˈtaʊə] Turm
town [taʊn] Stadt; **in town** in der (Innen-) Stadt; **town hall** Rathaus
toy [tɔɪ] Spielzeug; **toymaker** Spielwarenhersteller/in
trace [treɪs] Spur
track [træk] (Renn-)Bahn, Rennstrecke, Piste
tractor [ˈtræktə] Traktor
trade [treɪd] **1.** Handel; **2. trade (with)** Geschäfte machen, handeln (mit)
tradition [trəˈdɪʃn] Tradition; **traditional** [trəˈdɪʃənl] traditionell, volkstümlich
traffic [ˈtræfɪk] Verkehr; **traffic jam** [ˈtræfɪk dʒæm] (Verkehrs-)Stau; **traffic lights** *(pl.)* (Verkehrs-)Ampel
tragedy [ˈtrædʒədɪ] Tragödie, (großes) Unglück
trail [treɪl] **1.** Pfad; Spur, Weg; **2.** Wanderweg
trailer [ˈtreɪlə] (AE) Wohnwagen
train [treɪn] (Eisenbahn-)Zug; **by train** mit dem Zug
train [treɪn] trainieren, ausbilden; **training** Ausbildung, Schulung; Training
trait (of character) [treɪt] Charakterzug
tram [træm] Straßenbahn
transfer (to) [trænsˈfɜ:] versetzen, verlegen (nach, in)
translate [trænzˈleɪt] übersetzen; **translation** [trænzˈleɪʃn] Übersetzung
transplant [trænsˈplɑ:nt] verpflanzen, transplantieren
transport **1.** [ˈtrænspɔ:t] (BE) Transport, Verkehrsmittel; **2.** [trænˈspɔ:t] befördern, transportieren
travel [ˈtrævl] **1.** (das) Reisen; **2.** reisen, fahren; **space travel** [ˈspeɪs ˌtrævl] Raumfahrt; **traveller** Reisende(r)
treat [tri:t] behandeln; °**treatment** [ˈtri:tmənt] Behandlung
tree [tri:] Baum
trend [trend] Tendenz, Trend
tribal [ˈtraɪbl] Stammes-; **tribe** [traɪb] (Volks-)Stamm
trick [trɪk] **1.** Kunststück; **2.** Trick; **play a trick** einen Streich spielen; **tricky** verzwickt, schwierig; heikel
trip [trɪp] Reise, Ausflug; **go on a trip** eine Reise/Fahrt machen, einen Ausflug machen
trouble [ˈtrʌbl] Schwierigkeiten; **get into trouble** in Schwierigkeiten geraten, Probleme bekommen; °**the troubles, the Troubles** die Unruhen *(Bezeichnung für den Konflikt in Nordirland)*; **trouble spot** [ˈtrʌbl ˌspɒt] „Achtung Falle!" **troubled** beunruhigt, bekümmert
trousers *(pl.)* [ˈtraʊzəz] (lange) Hose(n)
truck [trʌk] LKW
true [tru:] wahr
truly [ˈtru:lɪ] wirklich, wahrhaftig, tatsächlich
trunk [trʌŋk] (Baum-)Stamm; AE *auch:* Kofferraum
trunks *(pl.)* [trʌŋks]: **swimming trunks** Badehose
°**trust sb.** [trʌst] jm. trauen
truth [tru:θ] Wahrheit
try [traɪ] versuchen, probieren; **try and do sth.** versuchen, etwas zu tun; **try on** anprobieren
T-shirt [ˈti:ʃɜ:t] T-shirt
tube [tju:b] **1.** Rohr, Röhre; **2.** (BE) *(Londoner)* U-Bahn
Tuesday [ˈtju:zdɪ, -deɪ] Dienstag
tunnel [ˈtʌnl] **1.** Tunnel; **2.** Bergwerksstollen
turkey [ˈtɜ:kɪ] Truthahn
turn [tɜ:n] abbiegen, einbiegen; **It's your turn.** Du bist an der Reihe. **turn into** (sich) verwandeln in, sich entwickeln zu; **turn round** (sich) (um)drehen; **turn to** sich wenden an, sich zuwenden
TV [ˌti:ˈvi:] = **television** Fernsehen, Fernseher; **on TV** im Fernsehen; **watch TV** fernsehen
twice [twaɪs] zweimal
twin [twɪn] **1.** Zwilling; **2.** Partner-, Zwillings-; **3.** (BE) (sich) verschwistern *(Städte)*, eine (Städte-)Partnerschaft eingehen
°**type** [taɪp] Typ, Art
typewriter Schreibmaschine; **typing** Maschineschreiben
typical (of) [ˈtɪpɪkl] typisch (für)
tyre [ˈtaɪə] Reifen

U

°**UDA** [ˌju: di:‿ˈeɪ] = **Ulster Defence Association** [əˌsəʊsɪˈeɪʃn] Ulster Verteidigungsverband
ugliness [ˈʌglɪnəs] Häßlichkeit; **ugly** [ˈʌglɪ] häßlich
unable [ʌnˈeɪbl] unfähig, untalentiert
unanswerable [ʌnˈɑ:nsərəbl] unbeantwortbar
unbearable [ʌnˈbeərəbl] unerträglich
unbelievable [ˌʌnbɪˈli:vəbl] unglaublich
unbreakable [ʌnˈbreɪkəbl] unzerbrechlich
uncle [ˈʌŋkl] Onkel
under [ˈʌndə] unter; **Underground** [ˈʌndəgraʊnd] (BE) Untergrundbahn, U-Bahn; **by Underground** (BE) mit der U-Bahn
underline [ˌʌndəˈlaɪn] unterstreichen
understand [ˌʌndəˈstænd] verstehen, begreifen; **understandable** [ˌʌndəˈstændəbl] verständlich; **understanding** verständnisvoll
underwater [ˌʌndəˈwɔ:tə] **1.** Unterwasser-; **2.** unter Wasser
unemployable [ˌʌnɪmˈplɔɪəbl] nicht vermittelbar (für Arbeitsstellen); **unemployed** arbeitslos; **unemployment** Arbeitslosigkeit
unexpected [ˌʌnɪkˈspektɪd] unerwartet
unfairness [ʌnˈfeənəs] Ungerechtigkeit
unfamiliar [ˌʌnfəˈmɪlɪə] unbekannt, nicht vertraut, ungewohnt
unforgettable [ˌʌnfəˈgetəbl] unvergeßlich
unfortunately [ʌnˈfɔ:tʃnətlɪ] unglücklicherweise, leider
unfriendliness [ʌnˈfrendlɪnəs] Unfreundlichkeit
unhappy [ʌnˈhæpɪ] unglücklich, traurig
uniform [ˈju:nɪfɔ:m] Uniform
unimaginable [ˌʌnɪˈmædʒɪnəbl] unvorstellbar
unit [ˈju:nɪt] **1.** Lektion; **2.** Einheit
united [ju:ˈnaɪtɪd] vereinigt; **the United Kingdom (UK)** das Vereinigte Königreich; **the United Nations** die Vereinten Nationen (UNO); **the United States of America (USA)** die Vereinigten Staaten von Amerika (USA)

university [ˌju:nɪ'vɜ:sətɪ] Universität, Hochschule
unjust [ˌʌn'dʒʌst] ungerecht
unless [ʌn'les, ən'les] wenn nicht, außer wenn, es sei denn (, daß)
unlike [ˌʌn'laɪk] anders als, im Gegensatz zu; **be unlikely to do sth.** etwas wahrscheinlich nicht tun
unload [ʌn'ləʊd] ausladen, abladen
unlucky day [ʌn'lʌkɪ] Unglückstag
unpack [ʌn'pæk] auspacken
unpronounceable [ˌʌnprə'naʊnsəbl] nicht aussprechbar
unsatisfactory [ˌʌnsætɪs'fæktrɪ] unbefriedigend, ungenügend *(Note, Leistung)*
unsingable [ʌn'sɪŋəbl] unsingbar, nicht singbar
unsinkable [ʌn'sɪŋkəbl] unsinkbar
unthinkable [ʌn'θɪŋkəbl] undenkbar
untidy [ʌn'taɪdɪ] unordentlich, unaufgeräumt
until [ʌn'tɪl, ən'tɪl] bis; **not until (six)** erst um (sechs), nicht vor (sechs)
unusual [ʌn'ju:ʒʊəl] un-, außergewöhnlich
up [ʌp] herauf, hinauf; **get up** aufstehen; **go up** steigen, in die Höhe gehen; **put up** aufbauen, aufstellen; aufhängen, anbringen; **stand up** aufstehen; aufrecht stehen; **up there** dort oben; **up to** bis (zu); **(walk) up to sb.** auf jn. zu(gehen); **up to date** aktuell, modern, auf dem neuesten Stand
upset (about) [ʌp'set] **1.** durcheinander, aufgeregt, betrübt (wegen); **upset stomach** [ˌʌpset 'stʌmək] Magenverstimmung;
2. upset aus der Fassung bringen, ärgern, beunruhigen
upstairs [ˌʌp'steəz] oben; nach oben
us [ʌs] uns
use 1. [ju:s] Benutzung, Gebrauch;
2. [ju:z] benutzen, verwenden; **be/get used to sth./doing sth.** ['ju:stə] an etwas gewöhnt sein/sich an etwas gewöhnen; **I used to do** ['ju:stə] Früher habe/bin ich immer . . . ; **useful** ['ju:sfəl] nützlich, brauchbar; **useless** ['ju:sləs] nutzlos, unnütz
usual ['ju:ʒʊəl] üblich, gewöhnlich; **usually** ['ju:ʒʊəlɪ] normalerweise, gewöhnlich

V

vacation [və'keɪʃn] (AE) Ferien, Urlaub
vacuum ['vækjʊəm] luftleerer Raum, Vakuum; **vacuum cleaner** ['vækjʊəm ˌkli:nə] Staubsauger
valley ['vælɪ] Tal
value ['vælju:] Wert; °**valuable** ['væljʊəbl] wertvoll
van [væn] Lieferwagen, Kleinlastwagen, Transporter
variety [və'raɪətɪ] Abwechslung; Vielfalt; Sorte
various ['veərɪəs] verschieden(artig); verschiedene, mehrere
vary ['veərɪ] **1.** verändern; **2. vary (from)** abweichen (von), variieren, sich unterscheiden (von)
vegetables ['vedʒtəblz] Gemüse
vehicle ['vi:ɪkl] Fahrzeug
°**velvet** ['velvɪt] Samt
verbal ['vɜ:bl] verbal, mit einem Verb gebildet
very ['verɪ] sehr; **(like) very much** sehr (gern mögen)
via ['vaɪə] über, per, via
vice (president) [ˌvaɪs 'prezɪdənt] Vize-(präsident/in)
vicious circle [ˌvɪʃəs 'sɜ:kl] Teufelskreis
victim ['vɪktɪm] Opfer
video ['vɪdɪəʊ] Video
view [vju:] **1.** Aussicht, Blick; **2.** Ansicht; **point of view** Gesichtspunkt, Standpunkt
village ['vɪlɪdʒ] Dorf
violence ['vaɪələns] Gewalt, Gewalttätigkeit; **violent** gewaltsam, gewalttätig; heftig
virus ['vaɪərəs] Virus, Krankheitserreger
visa ['vi:zə] Visum
visibility [ˌvɪzə'bɪlətɪ] Sicht(weite); **visible** ['vɪzəbl] sichtbar
visit ['vɪzɪt] **1.** Besuch; **on a visit** bei einem Besuch;
2. besuchen, besichtigen;
visitor ['vɪzɪtə] Besucher/in, Gast
vocabulary [vəʊ'kæbjʊlərɪ] Vokabular, Wortschatz
voice [vɔɪs] Stimme
volleyball ['vɒlɪbɔ:l] Volleyball
voluntary ['vɒləntrɪ] freiwillige(r, s)
vote [vəʊt] **1.** Abstimmung; Stimme *(bei Wahlen)*; **2. vote for** (ab)stimmen für, wählen
vowel ['vaʊəl] Vokal, Selbstlaut

W

waffle ['wɒfl] Waffel
wages *(pl.)* ['weɪdʒɪz] (Arbeits-)Lohn
waggon ['wægən] Pferdewagen, Planwagen
wait (for) [weɪt] warten (auf); **I can't wait** Ich kann es kaum erwarten; **Wait a minute.** Einen Augenblick! Moment mal!
waiter ['weɪtə] Kellner, Ober; **waitress** Kellnerin, Serviererin
wake (up) [weɪk] **1.** aufwachen; **2.** (auf-) wecken
Wales [weɪlz] Wales; **Welsh** [welʃ] walisisch; **the Welsh** die Waliser; **Welshman/Welshwoman** Waliser/in
walk [wɔ:k] **1.** Spaziergang, Wanderung; **a one-minute walk** eine Minute zu Fuß; **go for a walk** spazierengehen, einen Spaziergang machen; **take the dog for a walk** mit dem Hund rausgehen, mit dem Hund spazierengehen;
2. (zu Fuß) gehen, laufen; **go walking** wandern
wall [wɔ:l] Wand; Mauer
°**wander** ['wɒndə] schlendern (durch), umherwandern (in)
want (to) [wɒnt] wollen, mögen; **wanted** ['wɒntɪd] gesucht
war [wɔ:] Krieg
warden ['wɔ:dn] (BE) Herbergsvater/-mutter
wardrobe ['wɔ:drəʊb] Kleiderschrank
warm [wɔ:m] warm; **warmth** [wɔ:mθ] Wärme
warn [wɔ:n] warnen; **warning** Warnung
wash [wɒʃ] (sich) waschen; **have a wash** sich waschen; **wash the dishes** (das Geschirr) spülen, abwaschen;
washable ['wɒʃəbl] waschbar; **washing machine** ['wɒʃɪŋ məˌʃi:n] Waschmaschine; °**do the washing up** abwaschen; **washroom** Waschraum
waste (of) [weɪst] **1.** Verschwendung (von);
2. waste verschwenden; **wasteground** ['weɪstgraʊnd] Ödland
watch [wɒtʃ] **1.** (Armband-)Uhr; **My watch is wrong.** Meine Uhr geht falsch. **watchmaker** ['wɒtʃˌmeɪkə] Uhrmacher/in;
2. ansehen, beobachten; **3.** zuschauen; **watch TV** fernsehen
water ['wɔ:tə] **1.** Wasser; **2.** bewässern, gießen; tränken; **water colour** Wasserfarbe; Aquarell; **waterfall** Wasserfall; **watering can** ['wɔ:tərɪŋ kæn] Gießkanne; **waterpower** Wasserkraft; **waterway** Wasserstraße; **watery** wässerig
wave [weɪv] **1.** Welle, Woge; **2. wave (to, at sb.)** (jm. zu)winken
wax [wæks] Wachs
way [weɪ] Weg; Art und Weise; **a long way** ein weiter Weg; weit (entfernt); **by the way** übrigens, nebenbei (bemerkt); **find the way back** zurückfinden (nach, zu); **in different ways** auf verschiedene Weise(n); **in a way** in gewisser Hinsicht; **in the way** im Weg; **on my way (to)** unterwegs (nach); **tell the way** den Weg beschreiben; **This is the way you do it.** So/Auf diese Weise macht man es. **way of life** [ˌweɪ‿əv 'laɪf] Lebensart, -weise
we [wi:] wir
weak [wi:k] schwach; **weakness** Schwäche
wealth [welθ] Reichtum, Wohlstand; **wealthy** ['welθɪ] wohlhabend, reich
weapon ['wepən] Waffe
wear [weə] tragen, anhaben
weather ['weðə] Wetter
wedding ['wedɪŋ] Hochzeit
Wednesday ['wenzdɪ, -deɪ] Mittwoch
week [wi:k] Woche; **weekday** ['wi:kdeɪ] Wochentag, Werktag; **weekend** [ˌwi:k'end, 'wi:kend] Wochenende; **at the weekend** am Wochenende
weigh [weɪ] wiegen; **weight** [weɪt] Gewicht; **weightlifting** Gewichtheben
welcome ['welkəm] **1.** begrüßen, willkommen heißen; **2. welcome (to)** willkommen (in); **You're welcome.** Bitte (sehr). Nichts zu danken.
well [wel] **1.** gut; **2.** wohlauf, gesund; **3.** nun; also; **do well** gut sein (in einem Fach); **Well!** Na so was! Du meine Güte! Wirklich? **well-known** (wohl-) bekannt; **well-off** wohlhabend, reich
west (of) [west] **1.** westlich (von);
2. West-; (nach) Westen; **western** ['westən] westlich, West-
wet [wet] naß; feucht
what [wɒt] was; was für ein(e); welche(r, s); **What a question!** Was für eine Frage! **What about . . . ?** Wie steht's mit . . . ? Wie wär's mit . . . ? **What colour is . . . ?** Welche Farbe hat . . . ? **What date is it (today)?** Der Wievielte ist heute? **What do you call . . . ?** Wie nennt man . . . ? **What is it?** Was ist denn (los)? **What's it like?** Wie ist es? Wie sieht es aus? **What's wrong with Kevin?** Was fehlt Kevin? Was hat Kevin? **What time is it?** Wie spät ist es? **whatever** [wɒt'evə] was (auch) immer
wheat [wi:t] Weizen
wheel [wi:l] Rad; **steering wheel** Steuer (-rad), Lenkrad; **wheelchair** Rollstuhl; °**wheels** (slang) fahrbarer Untersatz
when [wen] **1.** wann; **2.** wenn; **3.** als; **whenever** [wen'evə] immer wenn, wann (auch) immer
where [weə] wo, wohin; **Where are you from?** Wo kommst du her? **wherever** [ˌweər'evə] wo(hin) (auch) immer
whether ['weðə] ob
which [wɪtʃ] **1.** welche(r, s); **Which of you?** Wer von euch?
2. der, die, das *(Relativpronomen)*; **whichever** [wɪtʃ'evə] welche(r, s) (auch) immer
while [waɪl] **1.** Weile, Zeit(spanne);
2. während
whisky, whiskey ['wɪskɪ] Whisky

whisper ['wɪspə] flüstern
white [waɪt] **1.** weiß; **2.** Weiße(r)
who [hu:] **1.** wer; wem, wen; **2.** der, die; dem, den *(Relativpronomen)*; **whoever** [hu:'evə] wer/wen (auch) immer
whole [həʊl] ganz, gesamt; **the whole of** ganz
whom [hu:m] (fml.) **1.** den, die, das; dem, der *(Relativpronomen)*; **2.** wen, wem
whose [hu:z] **1.** wessen; **Whose is it?** Wem gehört es?
2. dessen, deren *(Relativpronomen)*
why [waɪ] warum, weshalb; **Why not ...?** Warum nicht ...? Könnten wir nicht ...?
wide [waɪd] breit
widow/er ['wɪdəʊ, 'wɪdəʊə] Witwe/r
width [wɪdθ] Breite
wife, *pl.* **wives** [waɪf, waɪvz] (Ehe-)Frau
wild [waɪld] wild; ausgelassen; stürmisch
will [wɪl] wird (tun)
willing ['wɪlɪŋ] bereit(willig), gewillt
win [wɪn] gewinnen; **winner** Gewinner/in, Sieger/in
wind [wɪnd] Wind; **windsurfing** ['wɪnd,sɜ:fɪŋ] Windsurfen; **windy** windig
window ['wɪndəʊ] Fenster, Schaufenster
wine [waɪn] Wein
winter ['wɪntə] Winter; **in (the) winter** im Winter
wish [wɪʃ] **1.** Wunsch; **2.** wünschen
with [wɪð] **1.** mit; **2.** bei; **within** [wɪ'ðɪn] innerhalb, in; **without** [wɪ'ðaʊt] ohne; **do without** ohne (etwas) auskommen, verzichten (auf etwas)
wolf, *pl.* **wolves** [wʊlf, wʊlvz] Wolf
woman, *pl.* **women** ['wʊmən, 'wɪmɪn] Frau
wonder ['wʌndə] **1.** Wunder, Verwunderung; **2.** sich fragen, gern wissen wollen; **wonderful** ['wʌndəfəl] wunderbar
won't [wəʊnt] = **will not** wird/will nicht
wood [wʊd] **1.** Holz; **2.** Wald; **wooden** hölzern; Holz-
wool [wʊl] Wolle
word [wɜ:d] Wort
work [wɜ:k] **1.** Arbeit; **at work** bei der Arbeit; **go to work** zur Arbeit gehen; **out of work** arbeitslos;
2. arbeiten; in Betrieb sein, funktionieren; **work out** (her)ausarbeiten, herausbekommen; ausrechnen; **worker** Arbeiter/in
world [wɜ:ld] Welt; **(be) out of this world** phantastisch (sein); **in the world** auf der Welt
worry ['wʌrɪ] **1.** Kummer; Sorge; Unruhe; **2.** sich Sorgen machen; **Don't worry.** Mach dir keine Sorgen! Ist schon gut! **worried (about)** besorgt (um), beunruhigt (wegen)
worse (than) [wɜ:s] schlechter (als); schlimmer als; **(the) worst** [wɜ:st] **1.** (der/die/das) schlechteste, schlimmste; **2.** am schlechtesten, schlimmsten
worth [wɜ:θ] **1.** Wert; **2.** wert; **worthless** wertlos
would [wʊd, wəd] würde(n) (tun); **I'd like = I would like** ich möchte; **I'd love (to)** ich hätte (liebend) gern; ich würde sehr gern
wound [wu:nd] verwunden; verletzen
Wow! [waʊ] (infml.) Toll!
wreck [rek] Wrack; **wrecker** ['rekə] Strandräuber
write (to) [raɪt] schreiben (an); **write down** aufschreiben; **writer** Schriftsteller/in, Verfasser/in
wrong [rɒŋ] **1.** Unrecht; **2.** falsch; **be wrong** unrecht haben; **My watch is wrong.** Meine Uhr geht falsch. **What's wrong with Kevin?** Was fehlt Kevin? Was hat Kevin?

Y

yard [jɑ:d] Yard *(= ca. 90 cm)*
year [jɪə] Jahr; **... – year-old** ...jährig, ... Jahre alt
yellow ['jeləʊ] gelb
yes [jes] ja
yesterday ['jestədɪ] gestern; **the day before yesterday** vorgestern; **yesterday's lesson** die gestrige Stunde, die Stunde gestern
yet [jet] **1.** schon; **2.** doch, dennoch; **not ... yet** noch nicht
YHA [,waɪ_eɪtʃ_'eɪ] = **Youth Hostels Association**
°**yob** [jɒb] (BE, slang) Rowdy
yoghurt ['jɒgət] Joghurt
you [ju:, jʊ, jə] **1.** du, ihr, Sie; **2.** man; **you know** weißt du, nämlich; **you see** weißt du, nämlich
young [jʌŋ] jung
your [jɔ:] dein(e); Ihr(e); euer, eure; **yours** [jɔ:z] deine(r, s); Ihre(r, s); eure(r, s); **Yours** Dein(e); Ihr(e); Euer/Eure *(am Briefende)*; **yourself** [jɔ:'self] dir/dich (selbst); **yourselves** [jɔ:'selvz] euch (selbst)
youth [ju:θ] Jugend(liche); junger Mann/Kerl; **youth club** ['ju:θ klʌb] Jugendclub, Jugendzentrum; **youth hostel** ['ju:θ ,hɒstl] Jugendherberge

Z

zebra ['zebrə] Zebra
zero ['zɪərəʊ] Null
zone [zəʊn] Zone
zoo [zu:] Zoo

Bildquellen: Anthony Verlag, Starnberg (S. 56 unten; S. 71 oben, Mitte); Archiv für Kunst und Geschichte, Berlin (S. 84 oben, Mitte); Australian Tourist Commission, Frankfurt (S. 57; S. 60 oben); Kirsten Bleck, Berlin (S. 29 oben); Bavaria-Verlag, Gauting (S. 58; S. 60 unten); BBC Enterprises, London (S. 17 oben; S. 21; S. 48; S. 53); BBC Hulton Picture Library, London (S. 84 unten; S. 85 oben; S. 102 oben; S. 103); Bildarchiv Preußischer Kulturbesitz, Berlin (S. 13); BP Oil, Herts (S. 82); British Tourist Authority, London (S. 92); Camera Press, London (S. 110); Allan Cash, London (S. 17 unten; S. 71 unten); Central Office of Information, London (S. 94 Mitte, unten); David Dore, Guildford (S. 19; S. 94 oben); Bildarchiv Engelmeier, München (S. 105); Mary Evans, London (S. 102 unten); Folkestone Herald, Folkestone (S. 56 oben rechts); Hewett Street Studios, London (S. 9; S. 30; S. 42; S. 44; S. 46; S. 49; S. 72); Martin Kearns, Southport (S. 20 oben); Werner Lüning, Lübeck (S. 136); The Mansell Collection, London (S. 101); National Portrait Gallery, London (S. 104); Northern Ireland Tourist Board, Belfast (S. 34); Pacemaker International, Belfast (S. 85 unten); Rugby School, Rugby (S. 26); Sefton Photo Library, Manchester (S. 70 oben); Uwe Seidel, Berlin (S. 68); Silvestris Fotoservice, Kastl (S. 70 unten); Sonja Stabl, Moers (S. 20 unten, unten rechts); Tierheim Lankwitz, Berlin (S. 93); Transglobe Agency, Hamburg (S. 87); Ullstein Bilderdienst, Berlin (S. 29 unten); Romina Wontka, Moers (S. 20 Mitte)

Seiten 6 und 7: BTA, London; Allan Cash, London; Hewett Street Studios, London; Wales Tourist Board, Cardiff

Karte vordere Umschlag-Innenseite: © Cornelsen & Schroedel Geographische Verlagsgesellschaft, Berlin
Karte S. 57: COUP (Gabriele Heinisch)

Einband: Hewett Street Studios, London (David Graham)

Textquellen: *A different kind of exchange* and *Changing places* based on the BBC television programme *Changing Places,* produced by Chris Curling and broadcast on 11. 2. 1988, © BBC Enterprises; *You can't keep asking ...* adapted from *The Independent,* 21. 3. 1988, © 1988 Newspaper Publishing PLC; *A survey of young people's opinions in Northern Ireland* adapted from *Viewing 'the Other Side' in Northern Ireland* by John Greer, from *Journal for the Scientific Study of Religion,* 1985; *An eye for an eye* based on the BBC television programme *The Diary of Rita Patel,* produced by Carole Boyer and broadcast on 14. 9. 1988, © Carole Boyer; *Bush Fire* and *They who run away* adapted from *Ash Road* by Ivan Southall, published by Angus & Robertson, New South Wales, © Ivan Southall, 1965; *Why not use a dictionary?* – extracts from the *Oxford Student's Dictionary of Current English,* © Oxford University Press, 1988; *Class Four-D's trip to the British Museum* slightly adapted from *The Secret Diary of Adrian Mole Aged 13¾* by Sue Townsend, © Methuen, London; *The lost years* by Fionnuala Bogues from *The Scrake of Dawn,* © The Blackstaff Press, Belfast; *The winds are singing freedom* by Tommy Makem, © Aktive Musik Verlagsgesellschaft mbH; *IRA Victim* by Siobhan Aiton from *Observer Magazine* of 20th December 1987; *The Fight* adapted from *The Twelfth Day of July* by Joan Lingard, © Hamish Hamilton, London; *Neighbours with Long Teeth* is printed by kind permission of Peter Griffith. *The Archers* based on *The Archers – The New Official Handbook* by William Smethurst, published by George Weidenfeld & Nicolson Limited; *Christopher Nolan* adapted from the introduction by Marjorie Wallace to *Dam Burst of Dreams* by Christopher Nolan, © George Weidenfeld & Nicolson Limited; *Magazines advertising computers ...* based on the *Hutchinson Encyclopedia of Modern Technology,* © Century Hutchinson; *Return to Kilmakilloge* from *Round Ireland in Low Gear* by Eric Newby, © Collins Publishers.

Names

Family names

Carlin [ˈkɑ:lɪn]
Curtis [ˈkɜ:tɪs]
Dunlop [ˈdʌnlɒp]
Hastings [ˈheɪstɪŋz]
Hoskins [ˈhɒskɪns]
Matthews [ˈmæθju:z]
McCall [məˈkɔ:l]
McKay [məˈkaɪ, məˈkeɪ]
McLeod [məˈklaʊd]
Mehta [ˈmeɪtə]
Nolan [ˈnəʊlən]
O'Brian [əʊˈbraɪən]
O'Hare [əʊˈheə]
Parekh [ˈpærek]
Patel [pəˈtel]
Pattinson [ˈpætɪnsn]
Tanner [ˈtænə]
Weaver [ˈwi:və]

Girls/women

Carrie [ˈkærɪ]
Cathy [ˈkæθɪ]
Gillian [ˈdʒɪlɪən]
Gwyneth [ˈgwɪnəθ]
Jennifer [ˈdʒenɪfə]
Kirsty [ˈkɜ:stɪ]
Leela [ˈli:lə]
Melanie [ˈmelənɪ]
Olivia [ɒˈlɪvɪə]
Sudhamani [ˌsʊdˈhɑ:mənɪ]
Suki [ˈsu:kɪ]

Boys/men

Jolyon [ˈdʒɒljən]
Lyle [laɪl]
Melvin [ˈmelvɪn]
Oliver [ˈɒlɪvə]
Sean [ʃɔ:n]
Sumit [ˈsʊmɪt]
Vance [væns]
Wallace [ˈwɒlɪs]

Place names

Accra [əˈkrɑ:]
Adelaide [ˈædəleɪd]
Alice Springs [ˌælɪs ˈsprɪŋz]
Alton Towers [ˌɔ:ltən ˈtaʊəz]
Amsterdam [ˌæmstəˈdæm]
Andersonstown [ˈændəsənzˌtaʊn]
Antrim [ˈæntrɪm]
Armagh [ɑ:ˈmɑ:]
Ayers Rock [ˌeəz ˈrɒk]
Ballycastle [ˌbælɪˈkɑ:sl]
Bangladesh [ˌbæŋgləˈdeʃ]
Bangor [ˈbæŋgə]
Barkley [ˈbɑ:klɪ]
Belfast [ˌbelˈfɑ:st]
Bradford [ˈbrædfəd]
Brazil [brəˈzɪl]
Brisbane [ˈbrɪzbən]
Burma [ˈbɜ:mə]
Cairns [keənz]
Canberra [ˈkænbərə]
Cloncurry [klɒnˈkʌrɪ]
Conwy [ˈkɒnwɪ]
Cork [kɔ:k]
Coventry [ˈkɒvəntrɪ]
Crumlin Road [ˌkrʌmlɪn ˈrəʊd]
Darwin [ˈdɑ:wɪn]
Delhi [ˈdelɪ]
Derry [ˈderɪ]
Eilean Donan [ˌi:lən ˈdəʊnən]
Eire [ˈeərə]
Eton [ˈi:tn]
Federal Republic of Germany [ˌfedrəl rɪˌpʌblɪk‿əv ˈdʒɜ:mənɪ]
Fermanagh [fəˈmænə]
Ghana [ˈgɑ:nə]
Great Barrier Reef [ˌgreɪt ˌbærɪə ˈri:f]
Grosvenor Road [ˌgrəʊvnə ˈrəʊd]
Kalgoorlie [kælˈgʊəlɪ]
Karachi [kəˈrɑ:tʃɪ]
Kirkby [ˈkɜ:bɪ]
Knowsley [ˈnəʊzlɪ]
Leicester [ˈlestə]
Limerick [ˈlɪmərɪk]
Londonderry [ˌlʌndənˈderɪ]
Melbourne [ˈmelbən]
Netherlands [ˈneðələndz]
New Zealand [ˌnju: ˈzi:lənd]
North Rhine-Westphalia [ˌnɔ:θ ˌraɪnwestˈfeɪlɪə]
Perth [pɜ:θ]
Polperro [ˌpɒlˈperəʊ]
Rangoon [ræŋˈgu:n]
Rhyl [rɪl]
Rio de Janeiro [ˌri:əʊ də dʒəˈnɪərəʊ]
Roedean [ˈrəʊdi:n]
Rugby [ˈrʌgbɪ]
Shannon [ˈʃænən]
Stonehenge [ˌstəʊnˈhendʒ]
Switzerland [ˈswɪtsələnd]
Sydney [ˈsɪdnɪ]
Tasmania [tæzˈmeɪnjə]
Tokyo [ˈtəʊkjəʊ]
Townsville [ˈtaʊnzvɪl]
Tyrone [tɪˈrəʊn]
Ulster [ˈʌlstə]
Uluru [jʊˈlu:rʊ]
Vatican [ˈvætɪkən]
Warwickshire [ˈwɒrɪkʃə]
Wigan [ˈwɪgən]

Other names

Amy Johnson [ˌeɪmɪ ˈdʒɒnsn]
Armada [ɑ:ˈmɑ:də]
Basil Boothroyd [ˌbæzɪl ˈbu:θrɔɪd]
Burnum Burnum [ˈbɜ:nəm ˈbɜ:nəm]
Carole Boyer [ˌkærəl ˈbɔɪə]
Chris Curling [ˌkrɪs ˈkɜ:lɪŋ]
Dexter [ˈdekstə]
Einstein [ˈaɪnstaɪn]
Esperanto [ˌespəˈræntəʊ]
Father Alec Reid [ˌælɪk ˈri:d]
George Bernard Shaw [ˌdʒɔ:dʒ ˌbɜ:nəd ˈʃɔ:]
Ivan Southall [ˌaɪvən ˈsaʊθɔ:l]
Kath Walker [ˌkæθ ˈwɔ:kə]
Lagan College [ˈlægən]
Margaret Thatcher [ˌmɑ:grɪt ˈθætʃə]
Mary Shelley [ˈʃelɪ]
Percy B. Shelly [ˌpɜ:sɪ ˌbi: ˈʃelɪ]
Perry Mason [ˌperɪ ˈmeɪsn]
Roby [ˈrəʊbɪ]
Ruffwood [ˈrʌfwʊd]
Sir Francis Drake [sɜ: ˌfrɑ:nsɪs ˈdreɪk]
Titanic [taɪˈtænɪk]
Victor Frankenstein [ˌvɪktə ˈfræŋkənstaɪn]
Yirara College [jɪˈrɑ:rə]

Grammatical terms (Books 1-5)

abstract noun [ˈæbstrækt]	abstraktes Nomen, Abstraktum
active [ˈæktɪv]	Aktiv
activity verb [ækˈtɪvətɪ]	Tätigkeits- oder Vorgangsverb
adjective [ˈædʒɪktɪv]	Adjektiv
adverb [ˈædvɜ:b] (of frequency [ˈfri:kwənsɪ]/of manner [ˈmænə])	Adverb (der Häufigkeit/der Art und Weise)
adverbial (of place/of time) [ədˈvɜ:bɪəl]	adverbiale Bestimmung (des Ortes/der Zeit)
article [ˈɑ:tɪkl]	Artikel
auxiliary (verb) [ɔ:gˈzɪljərɪ]	Hilfsverb
backshift of tenses [ˌbækʃɪft‿əv ˈtensɪz]	Verschiebung der Tempora *(in der indirekten Rede)*
clause [klɔ:z]	Gliedsatz, Teilsatz
clause of concession [kənˈseʃn]/of reason/of time	Nebensatz der Einräumung/des Grundes/der Zeit
common noun [ˈkɒmən]	Gattungsname
comparative [kəmˈpærətɪv]	Komparativ, erste Steigerungsform
comparison (of adjectives/of adverbs) [kəmˈpærɪsn]	Steigerung (der Adjektive/Adverbien)
compound (word) [ˈkɒmpaʊnd]	Kompositum, zusammengesetztes Wort
conditional sentence [kənˈdɪʃnəl]	Bedingungssatz
conjunction [kənˈdʒʌŋkʃn]	Konjunktion
contact clause [ˈkɒntækt klɔ:z]	Relativsatz ohne Relativpronomen
countable noun [ˈkaʊntəbl]	zählbares Nomen
defining relative clause [dɪˈfaɪnɪŋ ˌrelətɪv ˌklɔ:z]	bestimmender Relativsatz
definite article [ˈdefɪnɪt]	bestimmter Artikel
direct object [ˌdaɪrekt‿ˈɒbdʒɪkt]	direktes Objekt
direct speech [ˌdaɪrekt ˈspi:tʃ]	direkte Rede
dynamic verb [daɪˈnæmɪk]	Tätigkeits- oder Vorgangsverb

emphasizing pronoun ['emfəsaɪzɪŋ]	verstärkendes Pronomen
gerund ['dʒerənd]	Gerundium
going to-future ['fju:tʃə]	Futur mit *going to*
if-clause	Nebensatz mit *if*, *if*-Satz
imperative [ɪm'perətɪv]	Imperativ
indefinite article [ɪn'defɪnɪt]	unbestimmter Artikel
indirect object [,ɪndɪrekt‿'ɒbdʒɪkt]	indirektes Objekt
indirect/reported speech [,ɪndɪrekt/rɪ,pɔ:tɪd 'spi:tʃ]	indirekte Rede
infinitive [ɪn'fɪnɪtɪv]	Infinitiv
-ing form	*-ing*-Form
irregular verb [ɪ'regjʊlə]	unregelmäßiges Verb
main clause ['meɪn klɔ:z]	Hauptsatz
main verb ['meɪn vɜ:b]	Vollverb
modal (auxiliary) [,məʊdl‿ɔ:g'zɪljərɪ]	modales Hilfsverb
negative statement ['negətɪv]	verneinter Aussagesatz
non-defining relative clause ['nɒndɪ,faɪnɪŋ ,relətɪv ,klɔ:z]	nicht-bestimmender Relativsatz
noun [naʊn]	Nomen
object ['ɒbdʒɪkt]	Objekt
pair noun [peə]	„Paarwort“
participle construction ['pɑ:tɪsɪpl kən,strʌkʃn]	Partizipialkonstruktion
passive ['pæsɪv]	Passiv
past participle [,pɑ:st 'pɑ:tɪsɪpl]	Partizip Perfekt
past perfect [,pɑ:st 'pɜ:fɪkt]	Plusquamperfekt
past progressive [,pɑ:st prə'gresɪv]	Verlaufsform der Vergangenheit
personal pronoun [,pɜ:sənl 'prəʊnaʊn]	Personalpronomen
phrasal verb [,freɪzl 'vɜ:b]	feste Verb-Adverb-Verbindung
plural ['plʊərəl]	Plural
plural noun	Nomen, das nur im Plural steht
positive statement ['pɒzɪtɪv]	bejahter Aussagesatz
possessive adjective [pə,zesɪv‿'ædʒɪktɪv]	adjektivisch gebrauchtes Possessivpronomen
possessive pronoun [pə,zesɪv 'prəʊnaʊn]	nominal gebrauchtes Possessivpronomen
prefix ['pri:fɪks]	Vorsilbe, Präfix
preposition [,prepə'zɪʃn]	Präposition
prepositional verb [,prepə,zɪʃənl 'vɜ:b]	Verbindung aus Verb + Präposition
present participle [,preznt 'pɑ:tɪsɪpl]	Partizip Präsens
present perfect [,preznt 'pɜ:fɪkt]	*present perfect* (Perfekt)
present perfect progressive [,preznt ,pɜ:fɪkt prə'gresɪv]	Verlaufsform des *present perfect*
present progressive [,preznt prə'gresɪv]	Verlaufsform des Präsens
pronoun ['prəʊnaʊn]	Pronomen
proper name/proper noun ['prɒpə]	Eigenname
prop-word ['prɒpwɜ:d]	Stützwort
question tag [tæg]	Frageanhängsel
question word	Fragewort, Interrogativpronomen
reflexive pronoun [rɪ,fleksɪv 'prəʊnaʊn]	Reflexivpronomen
regular verb ['regjʊlə]	regelmäßiges Verb
relative clause ['relətɪv]	Relativsatz
relative pronoun [,relətɪv 'prəʊnaʊn]	Relativpronomen
reported/indirect speech [rɪ,pɔ:tɪd/,ɪndɪrekt 'spi:tʃ]	indirekte Rede
sentence ['sentəns]	Satz, Satzgefüge
simple past [,sɪmpl 'pɑ:st]	einfache Form der Vergangenheit
simple present [,sɪmpl 'preznt]	einfache Form des Präsens
singular ['sɪŋgjʊlə]	Singular
state verb/stative verb [steɪt/'steɪtɪv]	Zustandsverb
stem [stem]	(Wort-)Stamm
subject ['sʌbdʒɪkt]	Subjekt
subordinate clause [sə'bɔ:dnət]	Nebensatz
suffix ['sʌfɪks]	Nachsilbe, Suffix
superlative [su:'pɜ:lətɪv]	Superlativ, zweite Steigerungsform
tense [tens]	Tempus, Zeitform
transitive verb ['trænsətɪv]	transitives Verb, Verb mit direktem Objekt
uncountable noun [ʌn'kaʊntəbl]	nicht-zählbares Nomen
verb [vɜ:b]	Prädikat, Satzaussage
verb (of perception [pə'sepʃn]/of rest/movement ['mu:vmənt])	Verb (der Sinneswahrnehmung/der Ruhe/der Bewegung)
will-future ['fju:tʃə]	Futur mit *will*
will-future progressive	Verlaufsform des Futurs mit *will*
word order ['wɜ:d‿,ɔ:də]	Wortstellung
word stress ['wɜ:d stres]	Wortbetonung
yes/no question ['kwestʃən]	Entscheidungsfrage

Irregular verbs

Infinitive	Simple past	Past participle	
(to) be	(I) was, (you) were	(I've/she has) been	sein
beat	beat	beaten	schlagen, besiegen
become	became	become	werden
begin	began	begun	beginnen, anfangen
blow	blew [uː]	blown [əʊ]	blasen, wehen
break [eɪ]	broke [əʊ]	broken [əʊ]	(zer)brechen; kaputtmachen
bring	brought [ɔː]	brought [ɔː]	(mit)bringen, (her)bringen
build	built	built	(er)bauen
burn	burned, burnt	burned, burnt	(ver)brennen
buy	bought [ɔː]	bought [ɔː]	kaufen
catch	caught [ɔː]	caught [ɔː]	fangen, erwischen; erreichen
choose [uː]	chose [əʊ]	chosen [əʊ]	(aus)wählen, aussuchen
come	came	come	kommen
cost [ɒ]	cost [ɒ]	cost [ɒ]	kosten
cut	cut	cut	schneiden
dig	dug	dug	graben
do	did	done [ʌ]	tun, machen
draw	drew [uː]	drawn	zeichnen; ziehen
dream	dreamt [e], dreamed	dreamt [e], dreamed	träumen
drink	drank	drunk	trinken
drive	drove	driven [ɪ]	(Auto) fahren; (an)treiben
eat	ate [eɪ, BE *also:* e]	eaten	essen
fall	fell	fallen	fallen
feed	fed	fed	füttern
feel	felt	felt	(sich) fühlen
fight	fought [ɔː]	fought [ɔː]	(be)kämpfen
find	found [aʊ]	found [aʊ]	finden
fly	flew [uː]	flown [əʊ]	fliegen
forget	forgot	forgotten	vergessen
forgive	forgave	forgiven	vergeben, verzeihen
freeze	froze	frozen	(ge)frieren; erstarren
get	got	BE: got, AE: gotten	bekommen; gelangen, (hin)kommen; holen, besorgen; werden
give	gave	given	geben; schenken
go	went	gone [ɒ]	gehen; fahren
grow	grew [uː]	grown [əʊ]	wachsen; anbauen, anpflanzen
hang	hung	hung	(auf)hängen
have (got)	had	had	haben
hear [ɪə]	heard [ɜː]	heard [ɜː]	hören
hide [aɪ]	hid [ɪ]	hidden [ɪ]	(sich) verstecken
hit	hit	hit	schlagen, treffen
hold	held	held	halten
hurt [ɜː]	hurt	hurt	verletzen, weh tun
keep	kept	kept	(be)halten, aufbewahren; einhalten
know [əʊ]	knew [juː]	known [əʊ]	kennen; wissen; erkennen
lead [iː]	led [e]	led [e]	führen, leiten
learn [ɜː]	learned, learnt	learned, learnt	lernen
leave	left	left	weggehen, verlassen; (zurück)lassen
lend	lent	lent	(ver-, aus)leihen
let	let	let	(zu)lassen
lie [aɪ]	lay [eɪ]	lain [eɪ]	liegen

Infinitive	Simple past	Past participle	
lose [u:]	lost [ɒ]	lost [ɒ]	verlieren
make	made	made	machen; (veran)lassen
mean [i:]	meant [e]	meant [e]	bedeuten; meinen
meet	met	met	(sich) treffen, kennenlernen
misunderstand	misunderstood	misunderstood	mißverstehen, nicht verstehen
overtake	overtook [ʊ]	overtaken	überholen
pay [eɪ]	paid [eɪ]	paid [eɪ]	(be)zahlen
put [ʊ]	put [ʊ]	put [ʊ]	stellen, legen, setzen
quit	quit	quit	aufhören, aufgeben
read [i:]	read [e]	read [e]	(vor)lesen
ride [aɪ]	rode	ridden [ɪ]	reiten; (rad)fahren
ring	rang	rung	klingeln, läuten; anrufen
rise [aɪ]	rose	risen [ɪ]	steigen; aufgehen *(Sonne, Mond)*
run	ran	run	rennen, laufen; fahren *(Zug, Bus)*
say	said [e]	said [e]	sagen
see	saw	seen	sehen
sell	sold	sold	verkaufen
send	sent	sent	schicken, senden
set	set	set	setzen, stellen, legen; untergehen *(Sonne, Mond)*
shake	shook [ʊ]	shaken	schütteln; zittern
shine	shone [BE: ɒ, AE: əʊ]	shone [BE: ɒ, AE: əʊ]	scheinen *(Sonne)*; glänzen
shoot [u:]	shot [ɒ]	shot [ɒ]	(er)schießen
show [əʊ]	showed [əʊ]	shown [əʊ]	zeigen
shut [ʌ]	shut [ʌ]	shut [ʌ]	schließen, zumachen
sing	sang	sung	singen
sink	sank	sunk	sinken; versenken
sit	sat	sat	sitzen
sleep	slept [e]	slept [e]	schlafen
smell	smelt, smelled	smelt, smelled	riechen
speak	spoke	spoken	sprechen
spell	spelt, spelled	spelt, spelled	buchstabieren, schreiben
spend	spent	spent	*(Geld)* ausgeben; *(Zeit)* verbringen
split	split	split	(auf)spalten; (sich) teilen
spoil	spoilt, spoiled	spoilt, spoiled	verderben, verschandeln; verwöhnen, verziehen
spread [e]	spread [e]	spread [e]	(sich) ausbreiten
stand	stood [ʊ]	stood [ʊ]	stehen
steal	stole	stolen	stehlen
swim	swam	swum	schwimmen
take	took [ʊ]	taken	(mit)nehmen; (hin-, weg)bringen
teach	taught [ɔ:]	taught [ɔ:]	unterrichten, lehren
tell	told	told	sagen, nennen; erzählen; erkennen
think	thought [ɔ:]	thought [ɔ:]	meinen, denken
throw [əʊ]	threw [u:]	thrown [əʊ]	werfen
understand	understood [ʊ]	understood [ʊ]	verstehen, begreifen
upset	upset	upset	verärgern
wake up	woke up	woken up	aufwachen; (auf)wecken
wear [eə]	wore [ɔ:]	worn [ɔ:]	*(Kleidung)* tragen, anhaben
win	won [ʌ]	won [ʌ]	gewinnen
write	wrote	written	schreiben